THE POET and THE PUBLISHER

THE POET *and the* PUBLISHER

THE CASE of
ALEXANDER POPE, Esq.,
of TWICKENHAM
VERSUS
EDMUND CURLL,
Bookseller *in* GRUB STREET

PAT ROGERS

REAKTION BOOKS

for
Christine Rees

Published by
REAKTION BOOKS LTD
Unit 32, Waterside
44–48 Wharf Road
London N1 7UX, UK
www.reaktionbooks.co.uk

First published 2021
Copyright © Pat Rogers 2021

Printed and bound in Great Britain
by TJ Books Ltd, Padstow, Cornwall

A catalogue record for this book is available from the British Library

ISBN 978 1 78914 416 1

Contents

Preface

Literary feuds have gone on since antiquity. In Britain alone, there were enough of them by 1814 to provide abundant materials for the writer Isaac D'Israeli, whose son would become the Victorian prime minister. These he used for a book called *Quarrels of Authors*. Since then, celebrated spats have continued right up to the present, among them those of Mary McCarthy with Lillian Hellman, Salman Rushdie with John le Carré, and Gore Vidal with Truman Capote (and with practically everyone). Niggling disputes between writers and publishers are also quite common, over matters such as financial terms, cover designs or advertising budgets, but few such slanging matches acquire legendary status. Most of the serious altercations in this area belong to what Adrian Johns calls 'the intellectual property wars'.[1] However, the clash that emerged in the early eighteenth century went beyond a struggle over copyright.

The episode we are exploring here remains the most famous of its kind, but it is not representative in every way. It brought into collision two individuals with very different historical reputations. One is acknowledged as a major writer, Alexander Pope, beloved by much of the nation's ruling class; the other is Edmund Curll, seen as a rascally publisher who had spent his career dodging prosecution for various scandalous breaches of the law. Pope enjoyed immense prestige as the greatest European poet of the age. Indeed, his works were known on the banks of the Susquehanna,

7

and would be translated into Russian not long after his death. By contrast, Curll was a London bookseller churning out mostly ephemeral publications, and hardly anybody outside Britain would have heard of him. Many of his methods were downright illegal, and he did not belong to the respected Company of Stationers, charged with keeping up the good name of the trade. Late in the course of their quarrel, Curll visited Pope's Thames-side home without permission, and brought out an illustrated description of the house and garden: it was called *The Honour of Parnassus*. Pope had reached the pinnacle of literary renown; Curll had merely been elevated to the pillory for offences including sedition and obscene publications.

D'Israeli covered 22 feuds, and installed Pope at the centre of the first eight.[2] The chapters in question relate to his dealings with Joseph Addison, Colley Cibber and other luminaries of what used to be called the Augustan age. D'Israeli gave his last section a slightly odd title, 'Literary Quarrels from Personal Motives' – aren't they all, in one way or another, however noble their professed justification? The bloodiest of these contests, and the one that has resonated most strongly down the last three centuries, figures in *Quarrels of Authors* as 'Pope and Curll: Or a Narrative of the Extraordinary Transactions Respecting the Publication of Pope's Letters'. The strange thing is that D'Israeli says nothing at all in his book about the earlier stages of the feud, which involve an episode when Pope was suspected of poisoning Curll, along with threats of retribution by the assorted hacks who worked for the bookseller. This tension mounted after the appearance of *The Dunciad*, a mock epic in which Grub Street stands in for Parnassus. Curll got one of the lead roles there.

The story takes us into a world where, according to one view, there was an absence of political correctness; and, according to another, a dearth of sensitivity towards the unprivileged. Pope belonged to two persecuted minorities, as a Catholic and a disabled man, but he certainly was not given any sort of pass by his critics on that account. Moreover, some of his closest friends were impeached, exiled, locked up in the Tower of London or stripped of their estates, titles and honours, all for political or religious reasons. The poet himself was allied to a party whose members were denied any chance of power for more than forty years. At the same time, Curll lived constantly on the brink of ruin, facing prosecution for three modes of libel – the most serious being sedition, which was increasingly used in his lifetime, as Thomas Keymer has recently shown.[3] It is hardly a surprise that he ended up on several occasions in the courtroom, to be dispatched to gaol or the pillory; one of his colleagues in the book trade was actually dispatched in another sense, that is, drawn on a cart to Tyburn and hanged there. To the possible disappointment of spectators, a last-minute remission of the full sentence meant that his body was not disembowelled on the spot. Some thought that Curll's publications should have earned him a similar fate. It was not a cosy environment in which to work as a writer or a publisher.

In spite of their disparate positions in society, no other conflict between an author and a publisher holds such importance in the history of the book. This owes a lot to the prominence of each combatant in the life of the time. An aim of this book is to expose the underlying issues that surface during the war of words. As we shall see, it could not have happened at any other time, and it could not have been conducted as it was by anyone other than these two men, startlingly different as they were.

Two famous scenes occur at almost opposite ends of the struggle. The first took place in 1716 at a Fleet Street tavern when Pope spiked Curll's drink, half a pint of Canary wine, with a substance 'antimonially prepared'. Almost twenty years later, in 1735, a mysterious stranger turned up at Curll's establishment one night, dressed in a parson's gown and lawyer's bands (the extended collar worn by barristers). He was there to make a clandestine offer of Pope's letters. As it happened, he was neither a clergyman nor a man of law, but probably an actor and painter, hired by Pope himself. These are exceptional occurrences, but they illustrate parts of the curious course of events, instigated by either man.

The story of the quarrel is treated here as objectively as possible. It may help that I belong to neither the Whig nor the Tory party, in eighteenth-century terms, although if I had been allowed a vote I might have supported Walpole against the opposition. Neither Ancients nor Moderns command my unqualified support in the great *querelle* that rocked the age. Equally, I am without any allegiance to the Protestant or Catholic faith, or to the Hanoverian or Jacobite cause. Having no local connections with Covent Garden or Twickenham – or other roots in the city, for that matter – I view metropolitan squabbles from the safe distance of a provincial outsider. As neither a lawyer nor a politician, I am free from any vested interest regarding the outcome of contests waged in the courtroom and Parliament. I can't even claim the title of poet or publisher. This should mean that it is open for readers to make up their own mind about the respective cases mounted on behalf of the two men.

A DEATHBED LEGEND has it that Queen Mary I said that when her body was cut open, they would find, together with the name of her husband, Philip, the word 'Calais' inscribed on her heart. This was, of course, a reminder that England had lost its only remaining possession in France during her reign. Much the same thing may happen in my case, except that the fatal name will be Curll. Since I began in the early 1960s to collect material relating to the quarrel between the two men, many thousands of hours have been eaten up in the hopeless quest to find out everything about the reasons for their enmity, to untangle the bibliographical course of their disputes, and to establish a full record of each transaction between them. Contemplating the results, like Queen Mary, I am pervaded by a sense of heroic failure. All I can hope for is that the story, incomplete and baffling as it may be in places, will prompt a similar fascination among readers.

Samuel Scott, *A View of Alexander Pope's Villa, Twickenham, on the Banks of the Thames*, *c*. 1759, oil on canvas. The poet's sanctuary, which Curll invaded so that he could publish a description of the property.

Introduction

A great deal has been written about Alexander Pope, and rather a lot in disparate places about his quarrel with Edmund Curll. However, no one has ever compiled an account devoted solely to this battle, covering every phase of their lengthy engagements. They were perhaps natural enemies, doomed to clash sooner or later: a poet renowned for his supreme skill in the most highly esteemed branches of writing, and a rogue bookseller known for his dirty tricks and indecorous publications. Their confrontation dramatizes a number of struggles surrounding English literary life as the Hanoverian era began, when social tendencies visible today first became apparent. These include the dependence of authors on the marketplace, rather than private patrons, a process in which the emergence of modern copyright played its part. Just as relevant is the rise of the periodical press, supported by the new dark skills of advertising, which would produce in its turn a previously unimagined celebrity culture. Many of the things Pope and Curll fought over are still issues that divide us as consumers of the printed word.

To explain the rationale for the chapters that follow, it may be helpful to set out an answer to three simple questions about this book. First, why the formula *Pope* v. *Curll*? Second, which materials are used? Third, what are the overall aims and method of this work?

POPE V. CURLL

No other form of words makes such good sense. There was an actual Chancery suit described in this very way, which helped to define copyright in personal letters for a quarter of a millennium. Some years earlier a case had gone before the House of Lords in which the two men were effectively the principals whose arguments were under review by the members. On another occasion, Curll was hauled up before the Lords by Black Rod, after which he was forced to kneel at the feet of the Lord Chancellor and apologize for issuing the writings of deceased peers without permission from their family and heirs. The outcome was a standing order of the House, and it did not fall into desuetude for more than a century. As we shall see, Pope almost got into hot water for a similar publication a year later.

The jousts brought with them other judicial manoeuvres, either carried out or threatened, sometimes involving proxy figures such as Pope's own tame booksellers. More than once, Curll's name made it into the standard sources used by lawyers and legal historians, such as *State Trials*. He has been described as the progenitor of obscenity acts; this is not altogether accurate, but his arrest by the authorities on a charge of issuing pornographic works, styled in the arraignment 'Lewd & Infamous Books', certainly made headlines at the time. Contrary to what is often stated, it was not the publisher's dirty books that landed him in the pillory, but another conviction for seditious libel, a topic of equal (if not more) interest to advocates of free speech. No wonder that Jonathan Swift, a victim of fraud even before it happened to Pope, told his friend, 'I had a long design upon the ears of that Curl.'[1] We might expect that the traditional punishment for libel and other crimes of cropping one or both ears would have gone for good by this date. But no; in 1731 a forger with the apt name of Crook was placed in the pillory at Charing Cross to have his ears slashed off before his nostrils were sliced and seared with a red-hot iron. Augustan satire often re-enacts the savagery of Hanoverian penal methods.

Curll has his own distinctive niche in legal history. At one stage he was the subject of leading suits that entrenched case law in both sedition and obscenity, and while in custody he even got himself arraigned for the uncommon offence of blasphemous libel, an ancient crime that survived on the statute book in England and Wales until 2007. As we shall see, Pope was well aware of these legal troubles, and left damaging reminders in the notes to *The Dunciad*.

Another circumstance links Curll to our concerns here. He had carved out a specialism in reprinting notorious trials. In this category of his list, we encounter collections of proceedings relating to divorce, impotence, seduction, polygamy, rape, virginity, murder and sodomy – Pope referred scathingly to the last of these in his *Full and True Account* of Curll's misfortunes. These titles come from Curll's own advertisements; he also had room for a work about 'debauching young virgins'. This connection adds one more layer of humour when we see the bookseller cast by Pope as Curll *agonistes*, since the gloss for the Greek term in the standard Liddell and Scott dictionary is 'a combatant, a rival, esp. at the games'. Secondary senses are 'a pleader, debater' and 'a champion'. In the section of *The Dunciad* that parodies Homeric games, the most competitive among all the contestants in this degraded ἀγών is Curll, instantly ready to 'accept the glorious strife'. He emerges as an easy winner of the pissing contest, confident of victory since 'happy Impudence obtains the prize'.

Among the occasions when Curll found himself shrouded in the mists of Chancery, the most noteworthy involved turf wars over literary property between bookseller and bookseller, with no author directly implicated.[2] A good example is found in the proceedings lodged in 1721 by Robert Knaplock and Jacob Tonson junior (nephew and heir of the great publisher who issued major editions of Shakespeare, Milton, Dryden and Pope). They claimed that Curll had breached their rights under the Copyright Act. Curll defended himself vigorously in his rejoinder, contriving to blur the issues raised by the provisions of the new act. The court's decision has not been traced, but Curll quietly dropped the offending item from his list. At another time, he was the hunter in Chancery, while the prey was a certain Charles Davis, who ran a business in Paternoster Row, close to the site of Curll's shop for a brief period. The plaintiff claimed that the defendant had reneged on a deal by which he would sell Curll's antiquarian stock. Neither the rejoinder nor the adjudication has come to light. That was often the way, since most such disputes did not go to trial. We might wonder whether the judges could keep a straight face when they saw that Curll was making accusations of cheating against another member of the trade.

As for Pope, he was no stranger to the courtroom, mounting various suits to safeguard his literary property. He took care to assign the copyright of his nakedly provocative *Dunciad Variorum* in 1729 to three of the most conspicuously great and good aristocrats in the land. One of his most trusted advisers was the Catholic barrister Nathaniel Pigott, who lived in the next village to Twickenham, and had looked after some legal affairs for the poet's father. Pigott gave the son help in connection with a case in the ecclesiastical courts. Among other lawyers who moved into the orbit of Pope, an especially noteworthy figure was the future Lord Mansfield.

However, the most significant in this group was William Fortescue, one of Pope's closest friends in the 1730s. Fortescue, a barrister with excellent political connections, held a number of important offices on the bench before he became Master of the Rolls. It is not just that Pope turned to Fortescue for help with ticklish issues regarding his publications, especially when he heard that a new affront from Curll was scheduled to hit the bookstands.[3] Pope even used the first of his brilliant imitations of Horace (modernizing a late satiric dialogue of the poet, addressed to a great jurist in Rome) to dramatize a consultation with Fortescue, in which the interlocutor spouts back to his client some amusing law-school jargon. The title follows a familiar pattern, referring to 'a Dialogue between Alex. Pope of Twickenham in the County of Middlesex, esq; and his Learned Council'. Like its original, the English version debates what is permissible for a contemporary satirist under a repressive regime. It starts with the idea that people think the poet's work may have gone beyond acceptable limits (*ultra legem* in Horace, modified by Pope as 'my Satire seems too bold'). Naturally Curll got in on the act. In one of the cleverest ripostes in his raggle-taggle edition of Pope's letters, he imitated his enemy's imitation – that is, produced a version that plays around Pope as the poet had played around Horace. Word has now got around, the opening couplet tells us, that there may be 'Wretches as bad as me, and full as *bold*' – a shrewd transposition from the satires to their author.

In any event, it was common at this period for writers to couch their works in the form of a mock trial. Within the satiric genre, rights and wrongs were argued out along the antagonistic lines endemic to the English legal tradition. Here we can draw on relevant observations by one of the most distinguished present-day commentators on eighteenth-century law. In his book *The Origins of Adversary Criminal Trial*, John H. Langbein notes that it was during this precise period that the development of a new mode of procedure occurred, based on the mediation of evidence between competing advocates for the prosecution and the defence. To some extent, he argues, this 'can be depicted as the absorption into criminal procedure of a model already operating in the civil trial'. It was from this date that 'the English legal system came to exhibit a broadly similar adversary system for both civil and criminal cases.'[4] Langbein makes a further point, that whereas criminal cases normally went to trial, the civil courts on the common-law side strove to settle the matter on the basis of written pleadings, so that the case need not go before a jury. This helps to explain the form taken by most satiric versions of a legal action in the age of Pope and Curll. They are often couched as adversarial documents, but usually they resemble the text of pleadings set down by scribes, rather than the cut and thrust of the courtroom.

We might also look at the quarrel as carried out in a series of alternating suits and counter-suits, a form of civil litigation common then as now. This enables us to view first one party to the dispute as the plaintiff, then the other. Certainly, either man was prepared to take the offensive when he felt he held the advantage.

The Materials

This book seeks to augment, rather than replace, the biographies of Pope (their numbers run into dozens) and of Curll, who has two full-length lives of his own. It carries the story of the quarrel from its inception around 1714 to the death of Curll in 1747 – Pope had died in 1744, but the shouts and murmurs prompted by his work lingered. Although chronological in outline, the book consists at its heart of a dossier of relevant documents, showing how the clashes between Pope and Curll evolved. It is hard to understand the nature of their quarrel unless we have a full record of their exchanges before our eyes, which has not been possible until now. Sometimes a complete document is presented; where the materials are long, as with *The Dunciad*, for instance, extracts are printed that supply the most essential elements of the text. At the end of this process, advocates on either side are allowed to make their closing statements on behalf of the parties in contention. A brief epilogue opens up the issues for readers to make their own verdict.

With the exception of the first two chapters, the central material of the book largely matches the description given by the supposed 'editor' of *The Documents in the Case*, a novel by Dorothy L. Sayers: 'I thought it best to send the originals, complete and untouched, exactly as they stand. Many of the incidental details, though unimportant in themselves, throw useful sidelights on the situation, and will, I think, help a stranger . . . to understand exactly what took place.'[5] The items in the dossier assembled here are indeed all original, taken from books, collections, pamphlets, private letters, newspapers, advertising and publicity materials, with no substantive changes to their content. Many of them have never been edited, and a good proportion of the promotional copy – especially on Curll's side – has very seldom if ever been reprinted. No single volume exists that collects all these disparate materials, some of which need to be extracted from the unlikely places where their creator left them. There weren't many books on any topic where Curll could not find room for a quotation from Pope, sometimes misleadingly splashed on the title page, quite out of context.

The documents are not in every case complete. In the interests of economizing on space, I have had to omit some piquant details in throwaway comments by both participants. Much of the battle that Curll waged was conducted in brief prefaces, glosses on Pope's text and flippant asides, in verse or prose. He spent a lot of time quibbling over small details, mostly to show that what Pope had written was unoriginal, inaccurate, irrelevant or inconsistent.

As for Pope, the direct commentary he makes about his opponent is often found in passing references, especially in personal correspondence with his allies: writers such as Swift, private individuals such as his Catholic friends Martha Blount and John Caryll, and aristocratic patrons such as Lord Bathurst and the Earl of Orrery. There are a few addressed to booksellers, such as Benjamin Motte, the publisher of *Gulliver's Travels*. A more earnest tone pervades messages to Fortescue, which indicates that legal action may be in the offing. There is no room to reproduce every stray comment here, but I have tried to include the most revelatory instances.

The Method

In his agreeable and amusing biography of Curll, published in 1927, the novelist and critic Ralph Straus allotted three chapters to the quarrel.[6] He called each of them 'Rounds', and wrote of the contest in the terms of a boxing match. The first round concerned the rival pamphlets and advertisements of 1716, which first brought the affair to a wide public. The second dealt with *The Dunciad* and its contentious aftermath in 1728–9. The third centred on the publication of Pope's letters in rival editions by both antagonists, starting in 1735. Each man had a combative side to his nature, although Curll displayed more obvious pugnacious qualities.[7] His foe could respond in kind, using not only his celebrated sleek, insinuating style but the frontal aggression of his prose pamphlets, which flayed the bookseller with a joyous and rambunctious energy. Nevertheless, I have preferred to tell this story in the form of a case fought out between two men who were in sober reality quite litigious. A courtroom can be just as dramatic a setting as a boxing ring. In addition, the exchange of documents mirrors the course of a legal contest more precisely than the flurry of blows in a prizefight.

In order to make the big flashpoints fully intelligible, we obviously need to know something about the age of the two combatants. The first chapter seeks to bring to life the time and place in which the quarrel occurred. It describes the venue of the fisticuffs between Pope and Curll, physically and in the virtual world of print, around what came to be known as the West End of London. The second chapter outlines a number of the similarities and dissimilarities between Pope and Curll, in terms of family background, professional career, political and religious leanings, economic circumstances, social relationships, outlook on literature and preferred locale. Succeeding chapters trace the course of their disputes, with a particular focus on the three junctures that Straus identified as rounds of the bout. Then follow the concluding arguments from both sides.

Major documents created by either party in the protracted cause are set off as 'exhibits', to distinguish them from the editorial commentary. The original spelling has been retained, since it supplies much of the flavour of the age and presents few obstacles to a modern reader. However, outside the documents adduced as exhibits, I have brought some conventions of capitalization and italicization into line with contemporary usage, and in a few places punctuation has been altered to ensure that the sense is clear. Contractions are expanded and superscript letters brought down. Blanks such as 'E—d C—l', originally employed for legal reasons, are often filled in – but not where the gap makes a telling point. Any omissions are clearly indicated. The text is normally that of the earliest version known; in the case of works and letters by Pope, I follow standard editions published in recent years, where they exist.

But first, some words are required on the background to the whole affair. Despite a number of obvious parallels, there is a temporal gap to our own age that must be bridged. More surprisingly, although the events are set mostly in London, neither a modern resident nor a visitor to the city would recognize many of the topographic features that underlie the action. Before going any further, we need to familiarize ourselves with the world in which these two formidable combatants moved and had their being.

I

THE TIME
and THE PLACE

I t wasn't just a tiff. While the contest involved a large dose of
personal dislike, which culminated in some unedifying physical threats, there was more to it than a mere collision of competing
egos. As with many historic rivalries, commonplace feelings such as
malice and jealousy were overlaid by the wider cultural disparities
between Alexander Pope and Edmund Curll. The events could not
have played out exactly as they did in a location other than London
or a period other than the early eighteenth century.

1688 AND ALL THAT

The dispute brought under review major issues of literature, both
elite and popular. At times it involved political or religious subjects
that arose in the fraught climate after the Revolution of 1688. These
years brought the end of the Stuart regime, the first Jacobite Rising,
the South Sea Bubble and the dominance of Robert Walpole, still
the nation's longest-serving prime minister.

Particularly important for the quarrel was the deposition of
the Catholic monarch James II, which brought in the aggressively
Protestant reign of William and Mary. The supporters of James
Stuart (the 'Old Pretender') continued to plot against the new
regime throughout the 1690s. Even when Queen Anne came to
the throne in 1702 and the Hanoverian line was confirmed as her
successors, they did not give up. In one abortive attempt halfway
through her reign, a fleet bearing the Old Pretender was dispatched

from Dunkirk up the North Sea with the intention of landing in the Firth of Forth. The plan had never been one of the best laid, and when the small convoy overshot its target, bad weather forced the Pretender to abandon Plan B, a landing near Inverness. He had to scuttle back with his retinue, licking his wounds.

But the cause refused to go away. The Jacobites were back in 1715, then again briefly in 1719, and they plotted an invasion again in 1722. Their last hurrah came with the invasion led by the Young Pretender, 'Bonnie Prince Charlie', in 1745 – but by that time Pope had gone to his grave, Curll was on his last legs, and the great feud had run its course.

A second issue festered under the surface of national life, largely although not wholly independent of the question of who should succeed Anne. This concerned the Union of the English and Scottish parliaments in 1707. The measure was supported by most, but not all, of the ruling class in Scotland. They tended to be based in Edinburgh and the Lowlands, and to be Presbyterians, Whigs – and, of course, prosperous. Many had links with commercial operations that stood to gain by greater access to markets at home and abroad. By contrast, opposition to the Union was strongest among the Highland clans, Episcopalians and elements of the common people who valued national independence above most things.

A deeper fissure that penetrated nearly all public life was that separating Whigs from Tories. Under Anne the former had attained a growing ascendancy, based in large measure on their support for the War of the Spanish Succession, a costly struggle marked by the military triumphs of the Duke of Marlborough. In 1710 their dominance would evaporate after a number of missteps, notably the decision to prosecute the High Anglican preacher Dr Henry Sacheverell – an event that prompted a huge groundswell of commentary, in which Edmund Curll cut some of his publishing teeth. A Tory government took over, led by Robert Harley, later Earl of Oxford, and Henry St John, Viscount Bolingbroke, both of whom would play a significant role in Pope's career. It was during the period of this administration that the poet acquired some lifetime alliances among the literary fraternity, especially with Jonathan Swift, Harley's *chef de la propagande*. Much of Pope's later work was written in support, direct or indirect, of these three men, and some of his onslaughts against Curll bear on this matter.

In 1714 the partnership between Oxford and Bolingbroke, always fragile, burst apart. The need, as Tories such as Swift saw it, to 'bring this long and expensive war to an honourable and happy conclusion' caused further ruptures.[1] Although most people yearned for peace, the Whigs argued that Britain's allies such as the Dutch had been sold out in the Treaty of Utrecht, an accord Pope had lauded in his poem *Windsor Forest* (1713). As the United States found out after Vietnam, ending an unpopular war does not heal all the wounds in civil society. Oxford was forced from office, and the whole Tory edifice collapsed just as the queen died.

This prompted the arrival of the first monarch in a new line, the former Elector of Hanover, George I. Rapidly a new regime set about supplanting the previous order. The Whigs won an election by a landslide in early 1715. They impeached leaders of the outgoing administration, and Oxford was dispatched to the Tower to await trial for treason. Bolingbroke fled to France to join the Pretender. Very soon afterwards came the first great Jacobite Rising, which was launched by the Earl of Mar in the autumn of the year with high hopes for a multi-pronged invasion. Its collapse within months signalled the beginning of a decades-long supremacy for the Whigs. Beyond that, it brought show trials of Jacobite leaders, as well as the introduction of severe measures by the government against Catholics, held to be the instigators of the Rising. As we shall see, this fraught juncture starting in 1714 and reaching a climax in 1716 provided the backdrop for the first exchanges in the quarrel between Pope and Curll. Mainly for political and religious reasons, the poet was at his most vulnerable as he endeavoured to get off the ground his massive new undertaking, a translation into English verse of Homer's *Iliad*. By contrast, Curll was entering one of his most cocky phases, having prudently taken the winning side in the recent tumults.

Historians have identified the growth of party conflict in England between 1694 and 1716 as marking 'the divided society'.[2] The clashes on the national stage had their echoes in the pamphleteering sideshows and journalistic brawls of the day. This is where our principal actors make their entrance.

Crucially for the quarrel, this short span of time marked the precise moment when a vibrant press emerged, with newspapers and journals an unprecedented force. This was partly because the old system of official censorship had lapsed in 1695, and had not been replaced. It is true that governments found alternative ways to cow and control the press, but these did not always succeed.[3] In addition, the ancient stranglehold on the London book trade held by the Stationers' Company had begun to weaken. At the same time avenues began to open up for a new generation of entrepreneurs with the passage of the first Copyright Act in 1710, a measure that in practice helped publishers more than authors. (Pope was among the few writers to see ways of exploiting the new commercial possibilities.) There was a huge surge in print culture more generally, and a spike in controversial pamphlets on every topic. This was the moment when what is commonly recognized as 'the rise of the novel' occurred, with the arrival of work by Daniel Defoe and Eliza Haywood, and the indeterminate status of this new genre between high and low culture symbolized a current aspect of the literary scene acted out in the quarrels of Pope and Curll.

THE KILLING FIELDS

The scene of virtually all the crimes we shall trace, committed or alleged, is London. It was the largest city in Europe, as its population went past the more stagnant figures for Paris, and the biggest in England by a factor of at least fifteen, contributing around 600,000 people to a national total of about 5,500,000. Only Norwich and Bristol had reached 30,000, and the former had slowed in its growth.

We must imagine ourselves in a very different city. The first impression that a time traveller would get might be a kind of sensory overload, affecting not just phenomena perceived through the eyes but also those taken in by the ears and the nose. One of the best evocations of the odours that would assail a visitor comes in a book by the French historian Alain Corbin in 1982, translated into English as *The Foul and the Fragrant* (1986). It describes the impact of various urban pollutants, such as slaughterhouses, rotting human corpses, primitive sewers, stagnant pools – all found in London as well as Paris. Corbin writes of 'the phantasm of the excremental swamp, the horror aroused by the mishaps that befell cesspool cleaners or individual stories of lost travellers swallowed up at Montfaucon. The stench and corruption from the accumulation of excrement challenged the city's very existence.'[4] Small wonder that writers surrounded by this miasma had a lot to say about it. *The Dunciad* is just a more extensive and more sophisticated treatment of the theme that lesser writers attempted in fifty other places. In a letter, moreover, Pope once referred to Curll as a 'Tom Turdman', that is, someone employed to empty cesspools.[5] As Sophie Gee has shown in her book *Making Waste* (2010), Pope forges a Miltonic idiom for his epic, which is filled with 'the literal filth of London's streets and the intellectual and cultural dross of its literary world'.[6]

It was not only smells that would batter the senses. Emily Cockayne demonstrates in *Hubbub: Filth, Noise and Stench in England, 1600–1770* (2007) that one of the main public nuisances in the era derived from the clatter that enveloped people's lives. Whether it was clanking machinery, the rattle of coaches and the clip-clop of horses' hooves, the jingle of harnesses, the ringing of almost endless church bells, the cries of street vendors, the piteous moans of animals brought in for slaughter, the savage barking of dogs, the drunken brawls in or outside taverns, or the surprising range of travelling musicians who scraped their fiddles or blasted their trumpets – these and much more contributed to a ceaseless pandemonium against which anything that resembled polite living had to compete for attention.[7] Hogarth depicted this in his print *The Enraged Musician* (1741), and its contents have been vividly detailed by Jenny Uglow. 'Music was everywhere,' she observes, picking out the wandering oboe player and the woman holding her baby as she croons a sad ballad:

> But how could these compete with the bashing of the pavior in his Irish cap, the clattering of the dustman heaving his basket to his head, the tinny beating of the pewterer at his shop in the background, the knifegrinder sharpening his screeching blades, the pealing bells ringing from the steeple . . . Small boys join in, beating a drum and trapping squawking birds. The little girl holds a rattle, and even the city wildlife adds its chorus, from the screeching parrot to the rooftop cats howling at the emerging chimney-sweep.[8]

Uglow suggests that the scene may be St Martin's Lane or Drury Lane. She doesn't even need to mention the snarling dog, the sow-gelder blowing his horn or the milkmaid in the centre of the picture crying her wares. In the face of all this, the distracted performer who has put his hands over his ears as he tries to rehearse in his upstairs room has no chance 'of making sweet music'.[9]

Of course, there was a world of grace and civility, too – but it had little immunity from these ever-present clamours. The cacophony percolated almost everywhere, just as the smells from the back-stairs crept into the drawing room. Let no one assume that it was only the Industrial Revolution that produced deafening noise. In the London of Pope and Curll, there was no soundproofing.

What of the scale of the place? In terms of its extent, the city was one that modern residents or visitors would struggle to find worthy of the name. In every direction fields surrounded areas that are now regarded as the inmost suburbs, and a green belt ran out as far as outlying villages such as Chelsea and Islington. Eastwards the bounds stretched no further than Stepney. To the south, there was nothing beyond Southwark. The western perimeter was marked by Hyde Park Corner and the road to Tyburn (now Park Lane). In the northern quadrant, many of the streets and squares in Marylebone and Bloomsbury had only just been developed, thanks partly to the efforts of landowners such as Lord Oxford and the Duke of Chandos, as well as architects such as James Gibbs – all friends of Pope. From there it was a short stroll into Lamb's Conduit Field, and in the absence of really tall buildings (except for church spires), Londoners could sometimes get glimpses of Hampstead and Highgate from quite close to the centre of town. You would spend most of your life within the limits defined on today's public transport as Fare Zone 1.

Yet this is misleading. London had long since become a teeming social mix, showing signs of what we might regard as modern urbanism. It enjoyed many advantages from an economic point of view. We may forget that it possessed a large manufacturing capacity; the largest share of domestic and overseas shipping; the youngest, most diverse and most mobile labour force; virtually all the major financial establishments; the main legal and political institutions; a greater presence than now of quasi-democratic bodies allowing middle-class citizens in particular more say in how society was regulated; and an unparalleled abundance of well-heeled consumers. On the negative side, it had more disease, more organized crime and more civic disturbance, the last of which feeds into much of the satire written in this age. Relevant to the quarrel is the fact that London dominated the production of books and journals, far surpassing its nearest competitors at Edinburgh and Dublin in the scale of its enterprise and the number of its print workers. By

1700 there were perhaps eighty printing presses in the capital, and a comparable but slightly smaller number of booksellers. We ought to add ancillary trades such as paper-makers and type-founders.

The venue of the lengthy battle of the books between Curll and Pope vacillated between the literal and virtual space of Grub Street, in printed works and newspaper ads, migrating to the law court, where major copyright issues were raised and settled, and the taverns of Fleet Street, where the clash took on an upfront personal character. The publisher started out in the environs of the booksellers' historic quarter around Paternoster Row, near St Paul's Cathedral. Later he moved from the stiff and starchy City, governed by the prim mercantile elders of the ancient corporation, who imposed heavy regulation on tradespeople. We have only to glance at a map of the main book-trade districts in 1750, provided by James Raven in his study *The Business of Books*, to see how the axis had inexorably crept out of the City of London into Westminster.[10] By the time Curll came to the end of his career, the fulcrum of activity was plainly situated around Temple Bar.

Over time, Curll had shifted his business down Ludgate Hill, westwards along Fleet Street and the Strand, chasing the more free and easy milieu populated by theatregoers, pleasure-seekers and aspirant lawyers, notoriously one of the groups keenest on partying. The only places in the country where you could gain a serious legal qualification were the Inns of Court. The four surviving Inns that continue to provide training for barristers were the most important centres of education, but there were other establishments that have disappeared, such as Serjeant's Inn and Clement's Inn. All lay within a short distance of the axis of Fleet Street and the Strand, some on Chancery Lane as it wound its way up to Holborn. Another north–south artery was Drury Lane, famous for its playhouse and its prostitutes alike. The newly popular coffee houses first acquired a heavy concentration in the City around Exchange Alley, the epicentre of the South Sea imbroglio, but they had also pullulated in

Balthazar Nebot, *Covent Garden Market*, 1737, oil on canvas.

the vicinity of the theatre district. In January 1724 Curll conducted a book auction over seven days at Dick's coffee house in the Little Piazza, Covent Garden, with catalogues available from three other similar establishments. At one time he sent out his own catalogue from 'next the Temple Coffee-house in Fleet Street', a good address if you wanted to target young customers with an income of which they were only too eager to dispose.

MR CURLL'S WINDOWS

Within this relatively small area of London was played out much of the satiric action of the day. This is where authors, journalists and booksellers mounted their campaigns to slay their opponents in a public battle of wits.

In *The Dunciad*, the authors and booksellers embark on their unruly escapades in several locales, none very far from Curll's own haunts. Most conspicuously, the Queen of Dulness chooses as the main stadium for the games dunces play a site meticulously apt to the satirist's purposes: 'Amid that Area wide she took her stand, / Where the tall May-pole once o'erlook'd the Strand; / But now

ANNE and Piety ordain the saints of Drury-lane.'[11] Any edition of the poem will tell you that this refers to a maypole that was removed and a statue of the queen that was installed there when one of the piously ordained so-called Queen Anne churches, St Mary le Strand, went up (it had been designed by Gibbs, a Catholic and possibly a Jacobite). The diligent editor may well add that the 'saints' were the ladies of the night famously busy about their trade there. Pope had first mentioned them in one of his earliest verse letters, explaining to his friend the man about town Henry Cromwell why he called them 'Nymphs of Drury':

> Far be it, Sirs, from my more civill Muse,
> Those loving Ladies to traduce,
> Alleys and Lanes are Terms too vile and base,
> And give Idea's of a narrow Pass;
> But the well-worn Paths of the Nymphs of Drury
> Are large and wide.[12]

The hundred of Drury, as the district was often styled, certainly experienced a heavy footfall in Augustan satire and drama.

As part of his vivid description of London nightlife in *Trivia* (1716), John Gay had hit on exactly the same crossroads:

> O! may thy Virtue guide thee through the Roads
> Of *Drury*'s mazy Courts, and dark Abodes,
> The Harlot's guileful Paths, who nightly stand
> Where *Katherine-street* descends not the *Strand*.

He does not attempt to disguise the nature of the commerce that was conducted there:

> Soft, at low Doors, old Letchers tap their Cane,
> For fair Recluse, that travels *Drury-lane*.[13]

John Rocque, Covent Garden and Strand area, from *A Plan of the Cities of London and Westminster, and Borough of Southwark* (1746). Westminster Bridge was not completed until 1750, after the death of both Pope and Curll.

By association with this district, Curll himself has often been supposed to have lived a profligate life, but there is no real evidence to show it.

What usually gets left out is the fact that Curll's outlet for almost the whole of the 1720s stood just yards from this spot. The imprint of several items that offended Pope would read, 'Printed for E. Curll over against Catherine-street in the Strand.' Pope, a native Londoner, was too clever to miss the potential of these environmental clues. To have the lowlife activities depicted in *The Dunciad* begin on Curll's doorstep was a typical barb of his antagonist.

That was not the only time Curll's shop entered the public prints. Just twelve months before Pope's lines appeared in print, an unfortunate man convicted of sodomy was 'erected' on the pillory at this very junction in the Strand. The crime was one that the mob regarded as among the most flagitious. Despite the miscreant's efforts to don protective armour and a shield formed by a ring of carts, the crowd were able to evade the sheriff's officers and strip off his breeches and shirt while pelting him with missiles. According to a newspaper report, 'a Battery in Catherine-street, conducted by a great Number of Drury-lane Ladies[,] play'd with good Success for Half an Hour, Mr. Curll's Windows suffer'd pretty much by it.'[14] The hapless man had to be taken down in a terrible condition and returned to prison before his allotted span was completed. Some probably thought the broken windows a fit punishment for Curll.

In addition, when Pope tricked the unlucky bookseller into imbibing his adulterated wine in 1716 – one of the first semi-farcical episodes that dot the story of their quarrel – it was at the Swan Tavern in Fleet Street. This stood at the east end of the thoroughfare, near the point where it descended to a bridge spanning the malodorous Fleet Ditch – also a precise location on the itinerary of the dunces. But the poet did not always have things his own way. His enemies knew that when he had first arrived in London he had been an habitué of the coffee houses near Covent Garden, such as Will's, where John Dryden had once held court, and Button's, where Joseph Addison presided over his 'little senate' of minor *littérateurs*. As Pope later told his young friend Joseph Spence, the two establishments were opposite each other in Russell Street. But both were favoured by the Whigs, and in time Button's became identified with the more rabid political views of Richard Steele, Ambrose Philips, Thomas Burnet and Eustace Budgell. Another habitué was the plump dramatist Charles Johnson, of whom we are told in a note to *The Dunciad* that he was 'famous for writing a Play every season, and for being at *Button*'s every day'.[15] Pope began to distance himself from the place as his relations with Addison became frostier. Allegedly Philips hung up a rod at the bar in Button's, and Pope was able to evade chastisement only 'by his usual Practice after every Lampoon, of remaining a close Prisoner at Home'.[16] Still, it is evident that he did not skulk in his tent by the banks of the Thames all the time.

Curll's last address, in Rose Street, lay in the parish of St Paul's, Covent Garden, as the famous suit *Pope* v. *Curll* will disclose in our last chapter. All of his later career was spent close to the area around the adjoining parish of St Giles in the Fields, where criminals frequented the thieves' lairs, brothels, gin shops and night cellars. The piazza of Covent Garden gave on to what has been called 'the square of Venus', notable as much for its market in human flesh as for fruit or vegetables.

And Pope? The best-known attempt to link him with the louche side of the West End of London did not appear for another quarter of a century. It came in the course of an encounter late in the poet's life, when the actor-manager (and, unbelievably, Poet Laureate) Colley Cibber launched the first in a series of attacks. In it he describes a supposed sexual humiliation for the young man, probably set around 1715. The anecdote begins by reminding Pope of a time 'when *Button's* Coffee-house was in vogue, and so long ago, as when he had not translated above two or three Books of *Homer*'. It

35

relates a skittish tale of how a young nobleman who fancied himself a wag 'one Evening slily seduc'd the celebrated Mr. Pope as a Wit, and myself as a Laugher, to a certain House of Carnal Recreation, near the *Hay-Market*'. Is any of this true? We cannot be sure.

The story goes on to say that the peer slipped 'his little *Homer*, as he call'd him, at a Girl of the Game', to see how the celebrated man of rhymes would perform. As it turned out, a 'smirking Damsel' serving tea had 'Charms sufficient to tempt the little-tiny Manhood of Mr. *Pope* into the next Room with her'. The outcome is predictable. Cibber follows the pair and finds 'this little Hasty Hero, like a terrible *Tom Tit*, perching upon the Mount of Love!' He snatches Pope by the heels and pulls him 'safe and sound from his Danger'. The lord is angry to have his fun spoilt, but Cibber defends his actions as having rescued the version of Homer by ensuring that its author did not contract a malady 'which his thin Body might never have been cured of'.[17] Like so much of the satiric material directed at Pope, the narrative lays a strong emphasis on his misshapen physique. What a great pity for Curll that he seemingly did not hear of this story! It would have provided fodder for a ballad or two, half a dozen pamphlets, and at least a score of notices in the press.

ALL ACTION ON THE WESTERN FRONT

From Pope's *Further Account*, which we shall examine later, it is possible to gauge something of his intimate knowledge of the capital.[18] Of course, he would have had well-situated informants. Some could dish the dirt from the seamier parts of London, such as those inhabited by the hack writers who figure in the *Further Account*. Others might provide dispatches from the more fashionable districts around what is now called the West End – a name for the area that had still to be invented. A pervasive strain in writing about London is the contrast between two disparate sides of the capital.

One is the businesslike City, symbolized by bleak offices and dedicated to the quest for money, exhibiting qualities of the hard-faced Teutonic races. The other is the softer West End, addicted to the pursuit of pleasure, with an almost Mediterranean use of space in its open vistas, culinary opportunities and places of entertainment. This dialectic, whether soundly based or not, lies behind the plot of *The Dunciad*.

Among the observers on whom Pope was able to rely, one stands out. This is Dr John Arbuthnot, polymath, physician, mathematician, numismatist, whose studies also extended to classical literature, religion, history, grammar and gambling – not to mention his activities as musician, book collector and author of some of the most brilliant satires in the language. After the Hanoverians arrived, the doctor was ejected from his grace-and-favour apartment in the royal palace, but he could still keep an eye on the doings in the locality. He regularly worshipped at St James's, Piccadilly, where both he and his wife would ultimately be buried. It had a fashionable congregation, much less diverse than that of the straggling parish of St Martin-in-the-Fields, whose church had lately been rebuilt just up the road, also to a design by James Gibbs. It was less than two hundred yards from the doctor's house to the home in Bolton Street of Martha Blount, a woman close to both Pope and the doctor.

From Arbuthnot's home, first in Dover Street off Piccadilly and then in nearby Cork Street, he had a perfect vantage point to follow the *va et vient* of place-seekers at court and (only a little further away) in Parliament at Westminster. He was able to attend the grand new opera house in the Haymarket, where he served for a time on the board of the Royal Academy of Music, and where the fashionable masquerades that turn up in every second Augustan satire took place. In 1724 Curll, predictably, brought out a pamphlet guying the chief promoter of Haymarket entertainments, John James Heidegger, who was also given a walk-on part in *The Dunciad*. Almost equally predictable was the reaction of the authorities, who took up Curll along with two distributors and a printer. They were all bailed to appear at the King's Bench court, a place that Curll came to know well; but the case seems to have fizzled out in the end.

On top of this, Arbuthnot could visit the gentlemen's clubs of St James's to satisfy his taste for gambling. If he strolled a short distance in the opposite direction, he would quickly reach St Martin's Lane, where a diverse collection of painters, sculptors, engravers, cabinetmakers, architects and craftspeople had assembled. This was the site of popular coffee houses, where actors and musicians met prominent émigrés such as Arbuthnot's friend the Huguenot mathematician Abraham de Moivre. It was a comfortable ten-minute walk to Covent Garden, and from there a short saunter to Drury Lane, which as we have seen gave access to a couple of theatres and more coffee houses, as well as taverns and bookshops, not to mention Curll's premises.

Another local speciality was several bagnios, in effect massage parlours. Even if Arbuthnot had no occasion to visit any of these, he was summoned in 1726 to just such an establishment in Long Acre. His mission was to examine Mary Toft, the young woman who had excited all the people of London and further afield with her claim to have been delivered of seventeen rabbits. The experienced physician was of course a serious student of obstetrics, as of so much else, but he does not seem to have been sure at first whether to believe Toft or not.

Westwards, if Arbuthnot wanted to get a flavour of the diversions of fashionable Londoners at the Ring at Hyde Park, mentioned in Pope's *The Rape of the Lock*, he had only to take a short step to get to the park. It was bordered by a tree-lined lane that formed the road to Tyburn, where villains such as Jack Sheppard and Jonathan Wild breathed their last. Closer at hand, right in front of Arbuthnot's house in Cork Street, stood the newly built Burlington House, on the site of the present-day Royal Academy. Its owner was a celebrated patron of the arts, to whom Pope addressed a famous verse epistle (Curll had a lot to say about *that*). Burlington also gave a home from home to Handel, John Gay and Pope's friend the architect William Kent. Another resident of Cork Street was the Welsh civil servant Erasmus Lewis, who worked for the first Lord Oxford over a period of several years. He was a particular friend of Arbuthnot and Swift, and his place on the fringe of the Scriblerus club entitles him to recognition as a fifth Beatle; it was from his residence, for example, that he took part in the clandestine measures that surrounded the publication of *Gulliver's Travels*. Pope sometimes stayed at his house on short trips to London.

Heidegger, on whom we touched earlier, managed two sorts of entertainment at the King's theatre, indicated by the title of Hogarth's print *Masquerades and Operas* (1724), which shows the impresario peering out of an upstairs room. Just below is a poster advertising the 'dexterity' of the conjuror and sleight-of-hand artist Isaac Fawkes. 'Dextrous' was a word then applied to pickpockets and corrupt South Sea projectors alike. On the other side of the scene stands the impressive gate of Burlington House, a symbol for Hogarth (although not for Pope or Arbuthnot) of false aristocratic taste. On the right we see the facade of Lincoln's Inn theatre, home of harlequinades (shows with spectacular stage effects, then called 'pantomimes'). One featuring Dr Faustus is shown on a billboard across the fascia. At the same time, in the middle of the street, copies of Shakespeare, Ben Jonson and William Congreve are being loaded on to carts as so much waste paper. The frontage of each building here has two things in common with the others: they hosted activities that Pope would write about, making some of them central to *The Dunciad*; and they were locations intimately known to Arbuthnot, who would pass most of them as he went about his daily business.

It can be no accident that the introduction of the *Memoirs of Martinus Scriblerus*, in which Arbuthnot had a large hand, begins with a chance sight of their supposed author in the precincts of

St James's Palace. He is then seen in the Mall (where the manuscript drops from his hands), and our last glimpse is of him standing 'under the Piazza by the Dancing-room in *St. James's*.'[19] This was a spot to which access was restricted, that would have been known only to an insider. But Pope was no stranger to the district either. When he first came up regularly to London from Berkshire, he normally stayed with his friend the painter Charles Jervas, who lived right across from the palace. A suggestive address is the one Nicholas Rowe used for a letter in August 1713: 'To Mr. Pope att Mr Jervas's in Cleaveland: Court by St James's house or att Button's Coffee house in Coventgarden.'[20] Those alternative directions show how the poet got about the West End, both geographically and socially.

GRUB STREET

Where was Grub Street? Physically it was a road in the parish of St Giles, Cripplegate, that stretched about a quarter of a mile north from the site of the old City walls. In the nineteenth century it acquired the more dignified name of Milton Street – aptly, since the great poet had lived close by. The area was badly damaged in the Second World War and the road mostly disappeared under the huge Barbican arts centre, which opened in 1982.

Mythically, the place has special connotations, as explained in a famous *Dictionary* definition by Samuel Johnson: 'Originally the name of a street in Moorfields in London, much inhabited by writers of small histories, dictionaries, and temporary poems; whence any mean production is called grubstreet.' This usage evolved in the later seventeenth century, but it was in the early decades of the following century that the phrase gained wider traction. For the Scriblerians, above all, it came to symbolize low-grade commercial literature, manufactured to order. An early draft of *The Dunciad* begins, 'Books and the Man I sing, who first from Grubstreet brings / The Smithfield muses to the Courts of kings.'[21] The allusion was dropped in printed versions, but it is clear that the nerve centre of Dulness, an oppressive anti-cultural movement, lies not too far away from Grub Street – in the revised text of 1743 it is located close to Bedlam hospital for the insane, a mere hop, skip and a jump down London Wall. In 1730 a group of supporters founded the *Grub Street Journal*, supposedly based at the Flying Horse Tavern, halfway up the road. Within its pages Curll came in for persistent ridicule. Both Arbuthnot and Pope himself are thought to have contributed material to the paper, but which bits cannot now be identified.

Many but not all of the hacks who were pilloried in *The Dunciad* had written for Curll; most of the targets came from the ranks of publishers, professional writers and journalists, but the poem also attacks politicians, courtiers, theatre managers, operatic impresarios, classical scholars and many other groups. They are united by adherence to a reductive modernism that threatens to destroy the high culture of the West. Pope presents this as a form of anarchy, much as in the nineteenth century Matthew Arnold feared that the

John Thomas Smith, *Old Houses in Sweedon's Passage, Grub Street*, 1791, engraving. Also known as Sweating Alley, Sweedon's Passage ran close to where Daniel Defoe died in 1731.

Philistines of his day would drive out the civic virtues of sweetness and light they had not learned to appreciate.

The relevance of this topographic background should soon become clear. Book production, buying and selling made up a largely face-to-face activity, in an age that had not heard of online commerce or Far Eastern printing. Many volumes were printed and warehoused on the same site from which they were sold. You could buy the unbound sheets almost before the ink had dried. Moreover, it was an easy matter to walk from Grub Street to St James's in a few minutes. Although the adversaries hardly ever met in person, and Pope spent much of his time a few hours away by land or water in Twickenham, they moved in social circles that were, if not exactly similar, by no means mutually exclusive. The publisher managed to detect an underlying parallel:

> Thus easy 'tis, in *Parody* to shine,
> *Pope* shares the *Dunciad*, and the *Curliad*'s Mine;
> Alike too, next the Road, our Houses lye,
> Backward he views the Thames, and so do I.[22]

Later, Curll would report that he went on a trip to survey the poet's home in June 1735, just as controversy over the publication of the letters was hotting up. He took with him an artist to make sketches of the property. The outcome was 'An Exact Draught and View of Mr. Pope's House at Twickenham'. Until then, Curll had restricted himself to purloining letters and scraps of verse. Now he invaded Pope's private space, even penetrating his famous grotto and passage leading to the river. To the poet, it must have seemed a violation of his inner being. We could view it as celebrity stalking, one of several modern practices that this expert publicist has some claim to have invented.

If you drew a Venn diagram to represent pictorially how the relationships of the two men overlapped, there would be several points where their fields of activity crossed one another. The key fact is the small scale of these intersections. A literary feud today would very probably be conducted over long distances, by electronic means. The participants might not be on the same continent now, even if they came from the same country. They might have no friends in common, because they wouldn't need personal contacts to keep up hostilities. Self-evidently, the world was a different place when the great quarrel took place and its two gladiators trod the streets of London. It would not be true to say that everyone knew everyone, but we can reasonably claim that almost everyone knew *about* everyone. Supposing the Internet had existed in their day, nobody would have had to Google the names of Pope and Curll.

2

The
ANTAGONISTS

They seem an unlikely pairing, these parties in the case. There is spindle-shanked Edmund Curll, muckraking publisher, widely reviled in his own time and since described as 'a disgrace and a nuisance to mankind . . . as dangerous a villain as ever breathed'.[1] Loud, aggressive and self-publicizing, he stands for all that the 'refined' eighteenth century was supposed to deplore. Opposite him, we can easily make out the misshapen figure of Alexander Pope, a pygmy in stature, but universally recognized as a literary giant. Not only the greatest English poet of his day, he became a revered figure among thinkers of the Enlightenment across Europe and North America. Yet these two near contemporaries, so unalike in their public profile, waged a vicious battle that went on for a full thirty years. Some observers are reluctant to see either man as a conclusive victor.

Contrary Combatants

While the key figures were very different in character, background and attainments, both loved a good fight. On one side of the courtroom stood Alexander Pope (1688–1744), the most financially successful author of the age and the one who had most reaped the benefits of a newly liberalized publishing regime. This was despite a severely restricted background, as a boy from comparatively humble beginnings, plus a member of the proscribed Catholic faith, who suffered numerous setbacks during his lifetime, and who was condemned to a permanent state of invalidism. He achieved fame early, and by the time he clashed with Curll he had already made his mark as a poet. In the process he had acquired notable patrons and mentors from the ruling elite, including the government leaders Robert Harley, later Earl of Oxford, and Henry St John, later Viscount Bolingbroke. Even more important to his career and his standing were the friendships he made in 1710–14 with other writers, most significantly Jonathan Swift, John Gay, Dr John Arbuthnot, Nicholas Rowe and Matthew Prior.

Each of these five men had his own gripe with respect to Curll (1683–1747), whom we may imagine settling himself in the court-room as he looks forward to the battle in prospect. Most of these spats concerned his alleged piracy of their work. Arbuthnot came up with the most quoted jibe at the bookseller's methods when he called the instant biographies produced after the demise of a famous individual 'a new terror of death'. Curll attained considerable notoriety during his career as a bookseller, auctioneer and publisher. But it was his skill as polemical writer and publicist that allowed him to challenge the greatly admired (and by now well-connected) Pope on his own ground. One of the earliest masters of advertising, Curll turned books into news and sometimes humdrum works into objects of controversy, bringing a culture of celebrity to the literary marketplace. Ever present in the prints of the day, he devised a list in which works of piety, scholarship and authority lay cheek by jowl with nakedly populist items. If most readers today know anything about him, it is that Curll stood in the pillory (an event duly reported in Pope's *Dunciad*), and that he was prosecuted for obscene libels, including books on sexual taboos such as lesbianism and sadomasochism; he also had a special line in accounts of salacious divorce trials.

Unfortunately, there is no portrait of Curll, and we have only a vague idea of how he looked. His appearance, according to the Irish writer Laetitia Pilkington, was that of 'an ugly squinting old

Fellow'.[2] A later novelist described him in fairly similar terms as 'in person very tall and thin, an ungainly, aukward, white-faced man. His eyes were a light-grey, large, projecting, gog[g]le, and pur-blind. He was splay-footed, and baker-kneed.'[3] But this may be invention, worked up to fit Curll's supposed character. The strange expression 'baker-kneed' derives from an idea that there were 'deformities of the lower extremities incident to bakers', in the quaint formulation of the *OED*.

Some backing for this depiction emerges in a poem by Elijah Fenton, Pope's later colleague on the *Odyssey* translation. Advertised by the publisher Bernard Lintot in 1716 under the title *A Letter to the Knight of the Sable Shield*, it was an attack on the writer and physician Sir Richard Blackmore. As will shortly emerge, Blackmore often faced a tongue-lashing from the Scriblerians. Despite its mock-antique language, one passage points unmistakably at Curll:

> Oft' in the wizard's cell I've seen
> A sorrel man, of awkward mien,
> Prying with busy leer about,
> As if he were the devil's scout.
> I ne'er was vers'd in modish vice,
> But sure those whoreson gloating eyes
> Have travell'd much on love-affairs,
> Between the key-hole and the stairs.[4]

'Sorrel' here means a light reddish brown colour, and 'whoreson' is something less than a euphemism for bastard. Lots of people, it is clear, found something diabolic about Curll.

By contrast, Pope's features are very familiar. He was depicted in portraits and sculptures more often than almost any previous English writer, by eminent artists such as Godfrey Kneller, Charles Jervas, Michael Dahl, John Michael Rysbrack and Louis-François Roubiliac. It was the last of these who observed with a sculptor's

Alexander Pope, by Charles Jervas, *c.* 1714, oil on canvas. The lady
in the background possibly represents Martha Blount.

eye certain lines of tension in the poet's face that indicated he was 'much afflicted with headache'. Along with fine, large eyes and a long, handsome nose, Joshua Reynolds also noticed prominent muscles on the poet's cheeks that looked like small cords – a result of his painful and constricting tubercular condition.[5]

Pope's physical problems affected his everyday life, never mind the image created in the satires of his enemies. The underlying cause was Pott's disease, contracted in infancy probably as a result of infected milk. This results in uneven lateral curvature of the spine, a medical condition known as kyphoscoliosis. It can cause restriction of the lungs, leading to respiratory problems. In Pope's case it may have been the root of asthmatic symptoms that emerged in later life and hastened his death. As a boy he was able to walk and ride, but over time he needed help to perform ordinary daily functions. Another side effect was migraine, which may explain the tension in his face that Roubiliac observed. To most people who encountered him, the obvious features of his appearance were his extremely short stature (no more than 1.4 m/4 ft 6 in.) and his hunchback. These made him an easy target for caricature, both graphic and verbal.

We know almost nothing of Curll's origins.[6] There are signs that his father may have been a London tradesman, and he just possibly grew up around Maidenhead – which would have made him almost a neighbour of the Pope family in the 1690s, since they lived across the county of Berkshire, barely ten miles away. A mercantile background would also be a shared attribute, since Pope's father was a retired linen merchant in the City of London, and had run his business just yards from the great financial artery of Lombard Street. Young Edmund was probably immersed in the book business by the time he was sixteen, a standard age for such an initiation. Although he acquired some facility in Latin, this must have been at school, because he certainly did not attend either of the two universities that made up the grand tally for the whole of England. But then,

Pope didn't go to college or have very much formal schooling. His precarious health and his religion saw to that. What he did achieve was a considerable feat of self-education, leading to a wide mastery of languages if not a scholar's grasp of ancient Greek.

STARTING UP

As it happened, the two men got started on their professional careers at almost the same juncture. The precocious Pope, five years junior to Curll, published his first collection of verse in 1709, including *Pastorals*, his hugely accomplished refurbishment of the classical eclogue. The lines on 'Summer' are where Handel got his memorable words for the aria 'Where-e'er you walk', via William Congreve's opera *Semele*. But the young author was already known to the cognoscenti for his learning, technical skill and imagination, and he had attracted the patronage of a group of elderly politicians and men of letters who lived near his home in Windsor Forest.

The Popes had retired from the City to a small village near Wokingham a few years after the Revolution. Their modest home was surrounded by fourteen acres of land. The place was suitably bucolic; once as a little boy the future poet was gored by a cow, which tore off his hat and trampled on him. For the most part, though, it was a very quiet life. His parents were well into middle age, and as early retirees they seem to have kept up few contacts with the busy world of the City, where their home and workplace had stood. The child's nurse Mary Beach belonged to the same generation; she had looked after her charge since his birth, and helped him with some of the routine tasks that he found difficult, such as dressing himself. Pope was always conscious of 'an ugly Body' that stood 'much in the way of any Friendship, when it is between different Sexes'.[7] He remained deeply attached to Beach until her death in 1725, and set up a monument in Twickenham church paying tribute to her constant service over nearly forty years.

Young Alexander grew up in a happy family, even though the Popes' religion subjected them to myriad petty restrictions, and he enjoyed the presence of a wise mentor nearby in the former diplomat Sir William Trumbull, who helped to guide his reading – which was naturally voracious, given his circumstances. Just across the forest lay the home of his older half-sister Magdalen, who lived with her husband and troublesome progeny near Bagshot. Still, the boy must have passed much of his time in solitude, some of it spent exploring the woods and fields in the vicinity of present-day Bracknell – a town that now houses 80,000 people and several international companies, but was then little more than a lone straggling street, bypassed until the turnpike arrived long after Pope was gone.[8]

Within a few years the youthful prodigy had shown himself to be the most distinguished English poet since the death of John Dryden in 1700. A succession of brilliant works brought him to general attention: the wittily iconoclastic *Essay on Criticism* (1711), the vividly coloured *Messiah* (1712) and the noble tribute to his boyhood locale and his homeland, *Windsor Forest* (1713). Above all, he had produced two versions of one of his greatest masterpieces, *The Rape of the Lock* (1712, 1714), a mock-heroic work that remains supreme of its kind. Thanks to its extraordinary imaginative power, it still delights readers brought up in a wholly different climate as regards matters such as gender politics.

Around the same date, the earliest translations Pope made of Ovid and other Latin writers marked the inception of a prominent aspect of his life's work. He was on the verge of committing himself to the immense task of rendering the *Iliad* in English verse; the contract with the bookseller Bernard Lintot was signed in March 1714. Along with these substantial works, he had started to write shorter pieces for the influential journals of Joseph Addison and Richard Steele. The first of his wildly comic satires in prose, *The Narrative of Dr. Robert Norris*, appeared in 1713 and heralded his use of this form to mock Curll. All in all, by the time Queen Anne died, on 1 August 1714, Pope had established himself as a prime figure in the national landscape. If he had himself gone to his grave, he would already have left a lasting mark in the annals of English literature – at just twenty-six.

It is not the same at all with Curll. He had begun to publish in his own name in 1706, having previously emerged in the trade when he held book auctions. Oddly, there is no record of a formal apprenticeship, although he undoubtedly served his time in some capacity with an older member of the industry, one Richard Smith. Nor did he go through the next rite of passage that apprentices normally experienced: admission to the Stationers' Company, a hallowed professional guild in the City that had wielded great (although now declining) monopoly power since its incorporation in the sixteenth century. For some reason we do not understand, Curll refused to 'take the cloth' of the Stationers in 1710, and instead joined a rival livery company, the Cordwainers, or shoemakers. There seems to have been no family connection with this group, since he obtained his membership by paying a fee, rather than through the right of patrimony.[9] From this distance it seems a strange decision for an aspirant in the book trade, rather as though today a young footballer should sign forms with the academy of a Championship club rather than one connected with a Premier League team. But Curll was ever a contrarian, and he spent his whole career as a liveryman and citizen of London (a status he liked to blazon on all occasions), often taking perverse and unpopular positions.

Both men had joined a wider circle of colleagues and fellow practitioners during the time of the Tory administration (1710–14). As his business evolved, Curll had become associated with the trade publishers (that is, distributors) Anne Baldwin and John Baker, as well as copyright-holding booksellers such as Egbert Sanger and John Pemberton. In later years he tended to go it alone, engaging with others in a few expensive projects only on rare occasions, and often keeping his most desirable literary properties to himself.[10]

Meanwhile Pope got to know many of the best-established writers in London. At first these included Whigs such as Addison, Steele, Samuel Garth and Nicholas Rowe. But relations with the first two would soon sour, mainly on account of political differences. Swift had already realized that his own friendship with Addison could not survive long in the fraught climate of 1710, soon after the Tory ministry took over, because it was threatened by 'this damned business of Party'.[11] More and more, the young poet found himself drawn into the orbit of the Tory wits.

The most significant event for Pope came with his recruitment as a founder member of the 'Scriblerus' club. This was a small and highly select group who met in 1713–14 to discuss their latest satiric projects, until the death of the queen and subsequent events led to their break-up. Its other members were Swift, John Gay, the Irish poet Thomas Parnell and – along with Pope the most active participant – Dr Arbuthnot. Significantly, the Lord Treasurer, Lord Oxford, was allowed to sit in from time to time and contribute his own amateurish offerings. The clique takes its name from the pedant Martin Scriblerus, putative author of many of the club's works satirizing pretenders to learning, which made up a kind of eighteenth-century Pseuds Corner. Although the friends rarely managed to raise a quorum in the years to come, they continued to share ideas and frequently to come together in literary collaborations. Some traces of their schemes can be found in *Gulliver's Travels* and *The Dunciad*, as well as the farce *Three Hours after Marriage*, the handbook of bad writing entitled *The Art of Sinking in Poetry*, and the professed *Memoirs* of Scriblerus himself.

One major difference between the two adversaries emerged over time. Curll's politics were not wholly consistent – little about him was. But after seeming to align himself with the Tory opposition at the time of the major political storm in 1709 over Henry Sacheverell (author of a fire-and-brimstone High Church sermon), he generally followed the ruling Whigs when later controversies divided the nation. The pattern is not so clear during the time of the Tory administration, when his associates in the trade were often Whigs in opposition to the government. With the change in ministry in 1714 came a full-blown change in heart from his earlier sympathies, so that Curll would endorse the Hanoverian dynasty with enthusiasm at the time of the Jacobite Rising. When the South Sea Bubble embarrassed complicit members of the royal family and government in 1720, he studiously avoided joining the clamour raised by disaffected voices. Soon afterwards Robert Walpole began his twenty-year reign as prime minister. Curll invariably proclaimed his loyalty to the great man, and sought his patronage – but characteristically he blurred the lines of allegiance by voting for opposition candidates in municipal elections.

We have no evidence that Pope ever became a fully paid-up Jacobite, but, as the next chapter will show, his Catholic faith made him an automatic suspect in 1715. Some of his closest personal contacts and literary allies had been caught up in the Rising. His most intimate female friend, Martha Blount, was (as it would then be defined, through a series of linked marriages) the sister-in-law of the principal victim of the affair. This was the handsome young Earl of Derwentwater, virtually canonized by his co-religionists as a martyr slaughtered at the altar of evil. After a rapid show trial, the earl was convicted of high treason and beheaded in February 1716 on Tower Hill, where he accepted his fate with exceptional courage. Not even the legal skill of Nathaniel Pigott, the ablest Catholic advocate of his day (and, as we have seen, a good friend of Pope), could save the earl. This episode took place amid a welter of sentimental ballads and tendentious pamphleteering, creating an atmosphere that resembled in some ways the mood surrounding the funeral of the Princess of Wales in 1997.

Then, seven years after the Rising fizzled out, Pope became embroiled against his will in the fate of Bishop Francis Atterbury, tried before his peers in the House of Lords for helping to organize a fresh invasion by the Pretender. Years later Curll would find it still worth his while to advertise *The Pleadings at Large before the House of Lords, 1723, by Sir Constantine Phipps and Mr. Sergeant Wynne, upon the Trial . . . of Dr Atterbury.* When the Lords came to sit in judgment, the defence called on Pope as a character witness. By all accounts he made a poor fist of it, ending up a bag of nerves and fluffing the lines he was supposed to say in mitigation of the bishop's guilt. However, in the years that followed he played a much more effective role as a sort of literary consultant to the growing opposition to Walpole's government. This first emerges clearly in *The Dunciad*, a poem that concerns us through its treatment of Curll, but which holds wider significance as an attack on the king and the government by means of a satirical code not too difficult to break. Throughout the 1730s Pope brought out a stream of eloquent denunciations of Walpole's regime, notably in his *Imitations of Horace*. This put him in the opposite camp to the one where Curll – most of the time – found his home.

By 1728, when *The Dunciad* made its strident entrance, both combatants were already famous. Pope, as we have seen, had earned his renown through a series of major works in several genres, but Curll too had become a byword for his daring and innovative publishing methods. A pamphlet in this year refers to 'a Bookseller in the *Strand, tota notus in Urbe*'.[12] That was taken from an epigram by Martial, 'known in the whole city'. Now, it must be acknowledged that the works listed as his productions in this source were dirty books; that the pamphlet is about a loose woman; and that Curll was behind the publicity scheme. But it was a true comment.

DIVERGENCE – OR CONVERGENCE?

Two features make the battle especially noteworthy, in addition to its importance in the history of the book. The first is that, despite its serious content, the quarrel frequently takes on elements of high and low farce. Like Sir John Falstaff, Curll was not only witty in himself, but the cause of wit in other men – such as those in the club of 'Scriblerian' satirists, Swift, Gay and Arbuthnot, and above all the most egregiously witty of them all, Pope. Indeed, it was the quarrel with the bookseller that prompted him to compose his masterpieces of comic prose, three pamphlets about Curll, two of which (from 1716) deal with the affair of a supposed poisoning. These go along with an exceedingly amusing passage in *The Dunciad*, mentioned in the Introduction. Then came an 'elaborate charade' in 1735, by which Pope tricked Curll into issuing his letters in a sequence of events appropriate to the theatre of the absurd.

Second, the two men lived in different social circles, but moved within the same broad environment centred on the capital. They had a number of acquaintances in common (again, mostly in the world of books). Thus Daniel Defoe enters Pope's satiric drama of duncehood almost in the same breath as Curll. Perhaps once, and once only, the publisher issued a production by Defoe. But they fell out, and in 1718 Defoe launched a coruscating attack on 'Curlicism', labelling his victim's output 'printed Bestiality' and describing its sponsor as 'odious in his Person, scandalous in his Fame', with 'a bawdy Countenance, and a debauch'd Mien'.[13] Not even the minor writers who produced savage caricatures of Pope's character and appearance generally went quite as far as that. While these events were going on, both antagonists in the main quarrel kept close tabs on each other. As already noted, Pope had his informants in Grub Street, including Richard Savage (a *poète maudit* and friend of Samuel Johnson); his own notes to *The Dunciad* make it evident just how closely he followed his opponent's career. Meanwhile Curll scoured the litter bins of everyone who might possibly have dropped into them a scribbled verse of Pope's composition. Then he would tantalize the reading public with any snippets he had unearthed.

Pope is remembered partly for his enmities. As well as Curll, these involved among others Walpole, John Dennis, Lady Mary

Wortley Montagu, Addison, Lord Hervey, Colley Cibber and Lewis Theobald (the last two appointed king of the dunces in successive versions of *The Dunciad*). Few of his adversaries, with the exception of Lady Mary and Hervey, had the talent or inclination to get back at him. But Pope was also notable for long and loyal friendships, and in some cases his satiric bark was worse than his personal bite. It is possible that a measure of grudging respect on each side underlay the verbal melees. Yet we should not be deceived by the casual air with which Pope sometimes dismissed the exchanges into which he had been drawn. Nor should we take Curll's bluff and even genial affect as representing his real attitude. A sizeable amount of money was at stake, and that was something both men had to take seriously – Curll in order to stay in business, Pope to keep up a gentlemanly way of life without large private means. And of course their brushes with the law had important personal consequences. For Curll, his liberty if not his life was often in peril. For Pope, the threats were less dire, especially because he took care to have influential figures in the state as his minders. Yet he had much more of a reputation to preserve, and there were occasions during the prolonged battle when he risked losing face at the bar of public opinion.

What about their human qualities? Curll generally comes across as brash and extroverted, someone who enjoyed the limelight and thrived when facing a hostile audience. Later chapters will show that he survived the physical and psychological strain of the pillory with some equanimity. Pope could never have done as much. His bodily delicacy went with a nervous disposition, a liking for retirement, a gentle manner in company and a fondness for animals, especially dogs. In print he could be as aggressive as his opposite number; but in private he cultivated a gracious and agreeable affect. Where Curll carried his argument and won the case in the House of Lords, Pope, as we have seen, stumbled when defending his friend Bishop Atterbury before the peers. His filial piety came out in his respect for his father and his devoted care for his elderly mother. It must be said that the only thing we know about Curll and his servants is that he gave evidence against a fifteen-year-old maid who had taken antiquarian books from the shop and sold them for 12*s*. 6*d*. The jury knocked down the value of the stolen items to a ridiculous tenpence. As a result, the girl was spared the gallows, and she got away with being transported to the colonies. Small thanks to her employer, some might add. 'God forbid that I should be guilty of the blood of anyone,' said Curll in evidence.[14] Apart from Pope's, of course.

Pope never married, like Swift and Gay. His deformities made it unlikely that he would ever have physical relations with a woman, and some of the pamphlet attacks scorn his capacity for virile activity. But, as usual with people from the past, we have no proper record of his sexual activity. The same is true of Curll. His critics suggested that he led a dissolute life, and Pope hints in *The Dunciad* that he suffered from a venereal condition. We know that he was twice married, and at one time he had a shadowy woman named Susanna Gray living with him as a companion. His son Henry seems to have predeceased him, but even before that he drifted mysteriously in and out of his father's business affairs.

One way in which the present book differs from earlier treatments lies in the broader context it provides. Ralph Straus's entertaining biography has one major flaw: it suppresses the large ideological struggles of the age, within which the lesser battle of author and publisher took place. Similarly, historians of the book who discuss Curll's career seldom turn their gaze very far from the operations of the trade. Straus and others confine the motives for the dispute almost entirely to spite, malice, jealousy, revenge and mere personal irritation. Feelings of this kind assuredly came into play at times, but they do not explain everything that went on. One would hardly know from these sources that Pope's religion lay behind so many of the hostile broadsides he faced, including those of Curll, or that his supposed Jacobitism underlies the campaign to vilify his

Homer. We can confirm these facts by going to a list of pamphlets belabouring Pope, where the very first item, an assault on the *Essay on Criticism* in 1711 by the ever bellicose critic John Dennis, concludes that 'he who Libels our Confederates [the Dutch] must be by Politicks a *Jacobite*,' aiming 'to introduce and to establish Popery'.[15] These charges are repeated by a good proportion of the authors of the pamphlets, and they supply a running joke in one of the earliest and funniest attacks, John Oldmixon's ballad *The Catholick Poet*, which we shall consider in more detail later.

In their opinions the two men straddled some of the great dividing lines drawn in the period. One was a Catholic, albeit a moderate one; the other a Protestant, if not a very devout one. One was drawn, however reluctantly, into the orbit of the Jacobite movement, simply through the accident of allegiances shared by friends, neighbours, comrades in literary arms, and patrons. The other may have flirted very briefly with Jacobitism, but soon came to think that his bread was more amply buttered on the Hanoverian side. One was aligned with the proscribed Tory party, where most of his influential allies found their home. The other identified with the Whigs, even when he did not gain the rewards he was seeking from the leaders whom he courted.

One was by instinct an Ancient, whose literary development meant drawing on a noble inheritance; it involved 'finding his relation to the poetry of the European past and to the mind of Europe'. These are the words of Reuben Arthur Brower, in one of the best books ever written about Pope. Brower goes on to argue that 'In following Dryden and surpassing him, Pope became after Chaucer, Shakespeare, and Milton the most European of English poets.'[16] By comparison Curll was a modern, scavenging the marketplace for novelty, sensation and topical scandal. It would have been apt if he, rather than his sometime collaborator William Taylor, had published *The Life and Strange Surprizing Adventures of Robinson Crusoe*.

A wider disparity can be detected in social and economic terms. Pope looked back fondly on the rural idyll of his childhood, cultivating a genteel way of life in a pleasant village safely removed from the city; Curll set up business in a noisy quarter of town and made it noisier than ever with a range of publicity stunts. There was undoubtedly an element of class distinction: where Pope clung to some of the traditional pieties and unashamedly relished the company of members of great ancestral families, Curll made his career in a raffish milieu. The bookseller was the subject of official prosecutions, more than once served time in gaol, and endured a number of conspicuous punishments. As a note to *The Dunciad* has it, 'he was taken notice of by the *State*, the *Church*, and the *Law*, and received marks of particular Distinction from each.'[17] Pope escaped such indignity, although his enemies thought he deserved no better.

It is misleading to think of Pope as belonging to the rentier class, since his father was a self-made man who took early retirement from his business in the City, and did so at least in part because of religious persecution. This precluded advancement in the civic and municipal life of London. Curll, on the other hand, was entitled to give himself the proud style of 'Bookseller and Citizen of London', as a liveryman who could take part in parliamentary elections. Pope, of course, had no vote. It is true that he inherited money and investments (many in France) from his father. Some of this he lost in the South Sea Bubble, when he proved no smarter in managing his portfolio than most of the people around him. But his financial independence was gained chiefly on the back of his writing, thanks to the shrewd deals he made for his translations of Homer and, to a lesser extent, his edition of Shakespeare. We do not know how well-off Curll became. In his will he left everything to his second wife, his son and heir apparent having died in unknown circumstances. Some of the literary property he owned may have been valuable, but there's nothing to indicate that he ever acquired great wealth. While there was an undeniable gap between Alexander Pope, Esquire, and Mr Edmund Curll, this was primarily not because of their respective incomes.

A Class War?

Those who have spoken up for Curll in recent years tend to emphasize a supposed class division. They portray the contest as one fought by a posh poet against a feisty businessman, an elitist insider tangling with an uppity outsider, a self-appointed Goliath of the old literary world confronted by a forward-looking pioneer of the book trade. One has his corner in a *locus amoenus*, literally a 'pleasant place', one of idealized refuge and agreeableness. For Pope, this was the villa he built at Twickenham, complete with a secret grotto and classical inscriptions scattered around the garden furniture. The other has his corner in the centre of the biggest city in Europe, surrounded by the clash and din of urban life in a neighbourhood populated by market traders, raucous street vendors, habitués of the playhouses, prostitutes and dissolute young men about town. This was the site of almost all Curll's activity, as publisher, retailer, auctioneer and self-publicist.

This reading of the story has some truth. It might be defended by appealing to the view expressed by some historians, who would depict the battle as a skirmish in the class war between traditional aristocratic values, represented by the Tory satirists, and the upstart world of commerce, innovation and bourgeois projecting.[18] However, Pope did not generally attempt to disguise the fact that he grew up in a modest household. It is undeniable that he pursued the company of many individuals of noble birth, but they were all people with marked cultural interests who valued his input on matters relating to literature, landscape gardening and other shared concerns. On the other hand, his work is littered with hostile commentary on the richest and most powerful in the land. He never regarded the aristocracy as inherently superior to everyone else, and he was fully alive to the absurdity of trying to ape its members, as in his version on a tiny scale of a stately home at Twickenham. Nor, of course, is his commentary on the world made up wholly of gloom, satire or misanthropy, any more than that of his friends Swift, Gay and Arbuthnot. All left joyous accounts of the things they found funny in the life of their times. To the point here, Pope depicts Curll in a ridiculous light, but the tone is one of mock-dismay rather than genuine hatred, since it derives from a gleeful recognition of absurdity and preposterous blunders on the part of the other man – who, to be fair, usually responds in much the same vein.

Nor does the model fit Curll. True, he sought to ingratiate himself with Walpole and his brother-in-law Lord Townshend, who led the ministry in the 1720s. He sent the prime minister begging letters, nominated himself for a government job as a press censor, and blew the whistle on the subversive activities of authors and printers. Once he alerted Walpole to the doings of Bolingbroke and a group 'who intend to overturn you'.[19] In 1731 he published an effusive biography with a grandiloquent title that began, *The Life of the Right Honourable Sir Robert Walpole, first Lord Commissioner of his Majesty's Treasury; Chancellor of the Exchequer; and Knight of the Most Noble Order of the Garter. Part 1. Containing, 1. The Reasons for Writing this Great Man's Life.* But he did not receive much encouragement from this quarter, nor from any other high-up among the Whigs. As a liveryman and citizen, he voted in City of London elections, but he held no office there. Unlike the publisher with whom he was so closely associated, James Roberts, he failed to rise to a position in the trade such as Master of the Stationers' Company. And unlike Jacob Tonson senior, he was not given an appointment remotely close in prestige to that of secretary to the Kit-Cat Club, the circle of Whigs eminent in politics and literature.

In fact, neither Curll nor Pope fully represented the forces mounted on either side of the class struggle. Their quarrel had its roots in other issues. On Pope's side these included his religion, which made him vulnerable to attack. But there were personal factors, too. One was his malformed shape, which attracted so much savage mockery from Curll and his cohorts. Further reasons were his abiding loyalty to Robert Harley and his son, the second Earl of Oxford; his distaste of the bloodthirsty and avaricious Duke of Marlborough, a hero of some Curllian panegyrics; his worsening relations with the cold and formal Addison, whose works Curll published in and out of season; his desire to promote his own professional career, without undue reliance on members of the book trade; his cosmopolitan outlook, drawing not just on classical antiquity but also on the Renaissance humanist tradition; and his delight in philosophic study, something the hurly-burly of his encounters within the literary marketplace often impeded. These considerations are enough to explain why Curll opposed him so often. There were indeed two worlds brought into collision by the great quarrel, but Twickenham and Grub Street were separated by more than a narrow class divide.

The Catholic Poet

We must look elsewhere for the most important *casus belli*. One candidate lies in the sphere of religion. Nothing else explains the frantic efforts of half of literary London, abetted by Curll, to portray the *Iliad* as motivated by 'downright *Popery*', with the prime support of '*Rome* and *St Omers*'.[20] This last was the Jesuit college in Flanders attended by the expatriate community, which had been producing men destined to be saints and martyrs from among its British alumni since the start of the seventeenth century. Pope was known to have personal links with papist families who sent their sons to study abroad. Because of the Rising, he belonged to the faith at a moment when it was at its most unpopular since the Elizabethan age. He was a Catholic and 'a Professor of the worst Religion', according to the logic of Dennis and other pamphleteers, ergo he was a Jacobite.[21] On the other hand, Curll, as we have seen, was a convinced Protestant with an interest in church history – he published and probably wrote the life of a seventeenth-century Bishop of Winchester, Walter Curll, a namesake but not a relative as far as can be traced.

Today it is hard to realize the degree of bigotry in religious matters, or the harsh penalties imposed on those who did not adhere to the established faith. The historian Jeremy Black provides a trenchant summary:

> Anti-Catholicism was the prime ideological stance in eighteenth-century Britain. The methods, practices and aspirations of the Catholic Church appear to have appalled many. Newspapers, sermons, parliamentary speeches and much correspondence reflected a reiterated theme: that Catholicism was equated with autocracy, drew on credulity and superstition, and led to misery, poverty, clerical rule and oppression.[22]

To these effects we could add disloyalty, deception and an addiction to corrupt practices allied to sexual abnormality. As it happened, Pope did not wish to promote autocracy, superstition, poverty, clerical rule or oppression. But it was enough that he belonged to the recusant community, along with members of families to whom he was strongly attached – those of Caryll, Englefield, Blount, Stonor, Swinburne and Dancastle, among many. The fact that he had an impressive array of friends, patrons and admirers among the Protestants did nothing to appease the enmity of his critics. Curll, as we shall see, was ready to pour out vitriol on popery whenever the occasion presented itself.

We can find the anti-Catholicism on which the bookseller traded as it loomed over the poet's entire life. A year after Pope was born, a massive series of demonstrations were laid on as part of the Lord Mayor's Show: 'the theme of each pageant presented a variation on the theme of the country's deliverance from popery and slavery.'[23] If we fast-forward 22 years, we find Swift sending a report to his women friends in Dublin about some action planned in the London streets to mark the anniversary of Queen Elizabeth's accession:

> The Whigs designed a mighty procession by midnight, and had laid out a thousand pounds to dress up the Pope, Devil, Cardinals, Sacheverell, &c., and carry them with torches about, and burn them . . . But they were seized last night, by order from the Secretary: you will have an account of it, for they bawl it about the streets already. They had some very foolish and mischievous designs; and it was thought they would have put the rabble upon assaulting my lord treasurer's house and the secretary's, and other violences. The Militia was raised to prevent it, and now, I suppose, all will be quiet. The figures are now at the secretary's office at White-hall. I design to see them if I can.[24]

Sure enough, two days later Swift went to see the waxwork figures, and was told that 'the figure of the Devil is made as like the lord treasurer as they could.'[25] What he may not have known is that the guards seized these implements in Drury Lane, the archetypal home of showy histrionic display. After the Rising was put down, demonstrations increasingly featured the Pretender alongside the pontiff, sometimes riding on a donkey, sometimes carrying papist trinkets. Pope-burnings in this vein had gone on in the capital and elsewhere for years. No doubt the poet got used to them. But he may sometimes have wished he had a surname that was less easily traduced.

THE ENTIRE CASE of *Pope* v. *Curll*, then, must be seen in the round. It goes beyond local differences, commercial squabbles and personal pique. Many of the Augustan pieties were interrogated along the way. Pope wrote *The Dunciad* to lament the dissolution of high culture, in the form of an epic that denies the existence of epic values in the world of his day. Curll replied in the breezy journalistic style of his day, to demonstrate the futility of moribund jeremiads composed by a disappointed author.

In the chapters that follow, I serve as counsel neither for the prosecution nor for the defence, still less as judge. An editor's role is more akin to that of a humble court stenographer, leaving the verdict to a jury of readers. The book does not attempt to white-wash the participants, or to blackguard them. Pope and Curll are both inherently funny, so I do not try to outdo them, letting the documents speak for themselves wherever possible.

The court will shortly be in session.

3

⬥

TRUE *and* FALSE

REPORTS, 1714–15

For many British people, the summer and autumn of 1714 marked a significant watershed. As the ministry fell precipitously into a dysfunctional slide, and Queen Anne's health declined further, all eyes were on the heirs presumptive in Hanover. Perhaps seeing what was to come, Jonathan Swift retreated to a secluded village on the chalk downs of Berkshire, 'weary to death of Courts and Ministers'.[1] Pope went out to stay with him briefly, while friends including John Arbuthnot kept him abreast of London news; but he did not return until events had already reached crisis point. John Gay went on a diplomatic mission to the electorate, hoping for patronage that never arrived. In a smart move, Susanna Centlivre dedicated one of her best plays, *The Wonder: A Woman Keeps a Secret*, to the young Duke of Cambridge, later Prince of Wales and then George II. Curll published this work in May, and may have sold a few extra copies when a command performance of the comedy was mounted by the prince towards the end of the year.

Neither the bookseller nor the poet felt such strong immediate effects as some of their colleagues and friends, but they could not shelter themselves entirely from the winds of political change. Like the rest of the nation, Pope and Curll were forced to watch from the sidelines as momentous events passed before them. On 27 July Queen Anne dismissed the Earl of Oxford from the position of Lord Treasurer, meaning the end of the so-called Harley administration that he had led since 1710 with Henry St John, Viscount Bolingbroke. Five days later the ailing queen finally succumbed to a variety of complications. A superannuated courtier, the Duke of Shrewsbury, was hastily lined up to fill the vacancy in government, but everyone knew this could be only a stopgap measure. According to the Act of Settlement passed in 1701, the crown now passed to the Elector of Hanover, as George I. According to one reckoning, the new king came no higher than number 57 in the true order of succession – but those in front of him had the fatal blemish of being Roman Catholics. He had some priceless advantages, though: he was a Protestant, he was not a member of the widely reviled Stuart family, and he had no close connection with the lately ousted ministry. It was seven weeks before he came over to England, and in the meantime almost everything was up for grabs. 'The Earl of Oxford was removed on Tuesday, the Queen died on Sunday,' Bolingbroke wrote to Swift on 3 August as the first shock began to dissipate. 'What a world is this! And how does fortune banter us?'[2]

As it turned out, the transition was managed more smoothly than might have been expected. The privy council acted quickly, with measures to forestall any opposition to the new regime. Orders went out to senior figures in the law and the armed forces. Steps were taken to revictual fortresses, while garrisons were put on a sturdier footing and overseas troops called home. Ports were sealed off, and the London militia were mustered for action. The de facto government sent James Craggs, a close friend of Pope in years to come, to Hanover to alert the king in waiting. Steps were even introduced to disarm Roman Catholics. Historians have sometimes represented these measures as a Whig *coup d'état*, but it wasn't really that – the Tories had lost the capacity to govern. However, it is a striking reminder of Pope's vulnerability that all Catholics became suspected persons, and that his horse (which he had) and his arms (which he didn't) were now open to seizure.

The Whigs, chafing to exercise their new-found power after four years in the wilderness, strengthened their hold on key government bodies. A list of the lord justices to run the country until the king arrived was approved by the new monarch, and it banished almost all the leading Tories. A story often repeated would have it that Francis Atterbury, Bishop of Rochester, the standard-bearer of the High Church, planned to stand at Charing Cross to proclaim the accession of James III, but it has no basis in fact. Atterbury, who would soon become one of Pope's closest friends and advisers, could be rash, but he was not a fool. He knew the moment was not right for open rebellion, and he took no active role in the Rising that took place a year later. Unfortunately, he would show less judgement in helping to lead the projected invasion almost a decade later. That episode, as will become clear, furnished an abundance of welcome copy to the book trade, not least to Curll.

The transfer of power meant that a number of Pope's most trusted colleagues found themselves out of a job. Everyone linked with the old ministry, from the top down, was suspect. As we have seen, Lord Oxford had been an honorary member of the Scriblerus group, welcome to attend meetings and even to make his own efforts at light verse. Bolingbroke had forged a close alliance with Swift at one stage, although as the ministry started to unravel the distance between the two men grew when Swift left for his deanery in Dublin. Both leaders of the administration underwent impeachment within a year of the new king's arrival; Bolingbroke fled to France to join the Pretender, while Oxford was incarcerated in the Tower for two years. He festered there until he was finally brought to trial for treason before his peers in the summer of 1717, when a split inside the Whig ranks assured his acquittal. One of Curll's hacks, under the thin disguise of 'Mr. Joseph Gay', produced a crudely written 'Westminster Ballad' to celebrate the occasion.

Others were imprisoned without trial for varying spells. One was Matthew Prior, Pope's only rival at this date as the nation's finest poet, who had been heavily involved in the negotiations for the Peace of Utrecht; while the ministry accorded less stringent terms to Sir William Wyndham, an agreeable West Country magnate who was implausibly cast by Stuart sympathizers as the leader of a Jacobite administration. He helped to organize the English side of the Rising, with Lord Lansdowne; but both men found themselves under arrest before the insurrection had properly started. Lansdowne was held prisoner in the Tower for eighteen months. He had served as secretary at war during the Harley administration. Most relevantly here, he was a minor poet and dramatist, celebrated by Pope as 'Granville the polite', and in 1713 he had been the dedicatee of *Windsor Forest*, the most directly political work the poet had yet written.

A little lower down the scale, Arbuthnot lost his position as physician to the monarch, and had to quit his apartment in St James's Palace. The new power elite also kicked him off the board in charge of the construction of the new Queen Anne churches. But he was in good company there; the Hanoverians thought fit to remove James Gibbs from his role as surveyor and to dispense with the services of board members including Christopher Wren, Edmond Halley, Atterbury and of course Bolingbroke. Isaac Newton would probably have gone too, but he was a Whig and could not be spared.

POLITICS AND THE POET

It was at this fraught moment, in a highly divided society, that the light opening skirmishes took place between Pope and Curll. Naturally we may wonder what got the quarrel started. The publisher had already antagonized some of the prominent writers whom Pope had met during the previous few years. At the head of this list comes Jonathan Swift, a recent acquaintance but a figure who had achieved considerable fame as a satirist and political polemicist. Curll had purloined some unpublished manuscripts, which he issued to the world in 1710 together with a key explaining the occasion and meaning of Swift's great *Tale of a Tub*, which had first come out in 1704. This was the start of a decades-long campaign to unearth items by Swift (genuine or spurious), and bring them before the public whether or not the writer had given permission. This task would be made easier as time went on by the absence of a proper copyright agreement between London and Dublin, the city where most of Swift's new works appeared after he was made Dean of St Patrick's Cathedral in 1713. Small wonder that Swift complained in May 1711 to his Dublin friends, 'That villain Curl has scraped up some trash, and calls it Dr Swift's miscellanies, with the name at large, and I can get no [legal] satisfaction of him.'[3] Over the course of five years more than one hundred separate publications by Whig writers appeared, attacking Swift for his journalism and pamphleteering on behalf of the Harley government.[4] Maybe as many as twenty of these came from the pen of John Oldmixon, who started to write more for Curll and subsequently became a thorn in Pope's side.

Nor was Swift the only member of the Scriblerus group to suffer the unwanted ministrations of the bookseller. Curll brought out another meddlesome key not long afterwards, designed to whip up scandal and spread mischief. This time he offered to unlock Dr Arbuthnot's *succès fou*, a satire known from its hero as *John Bull*, whose name would come to represent the archetypal Brit. The purpose of this work was to make fun of the participants in the seemingly endless War of the Spanish Succession, which had dragged on the conflict with France until it reached a duration of almost twenty years. Other literary acquaintances of Pope suffered similarly at the hands of Curll, notably in the case of works by Matthew Prior, a poet and diplomat who had been a lead negotiator on behalf of the Harley ministry. It would not be the last time the bookseller got away with such piracy.

Pope himself had just burned his boats. This happened on 23 March 1714, when he contracted with Bernard Lintot to translate the *Iliad*.[5] This remarkable agreement provided the author with privileges never enjoyed before by an English writer. Among other things, the publisher consented to Pope's choosing the font and the printer's ornaments. He let the poet have 750 copies for subscribers, and withheld from the market the trade copies for his own benefit until these had been disposed of. Most startling of all, Lintot assented to a financial deal of great generosity: he would pay 200 guineas for each volume as copyright money. Half of this would be paid in advance, and the remainder on delivery of the copy. It is estimated that the author would clear a total of £1,290 copyright money, and £4,837 from the sale of 'his' 750 copies of each volume. These are sums that would have made Midas blush. Small wonder that the dunces hated Pope ever after, and never forgave Lintot for allowing their enemy such munificent terms.

The project became generally known because proposals were issued to attract subscribers, taking this form:

EXHIBIT 3.1

Proposals for printing, by Subscription, a Translation of Homer's Iliad into Verse and Rhime. By Mr. Pope. To which will be added, explanatory and critical Notes; wherein the most curious and useful Observations, either of the Ancients or Moderns, in relation to this Author in general, or to any Passages in particular, shall be collected and placed under their proper Heads.

This Work shall be printed in six Volumes in Quarto, on the finest Paper, and on a letter new Cast on purpose; with Ornaments and initial Letters engraven on Copper. Each Volume containing four Books of the Iliad; with Notes to each Book.

It is proposed at the rate of one Guinea for each Volume; The first Volume to be deliver'd in Quires within the space of a Year from the Date of this Proposal, and the rest in like manner annually; Only the Subscribers are to pay two Guineas in hand, advancing one in regard of the Expence the Undertaker must be at in collecting the several Editions, Cricks and Commentators, which are very numerous upon this Author.

A third guinea was payable to Lintot by subscribers on the delivery of each volume. By the end of the year the venture had proceeded so far that Pope could advance the date for publishing the first volume to March 1715. Long before that, however, the cavils had started to come in. In the previous April, almost before the ink on the contract was dry, a writer named Charles Gildon added 'a word or two upon Mr. Pope's *Rape of the Lock*' to his critique of the plays of Nicholas Rowe, entitled *A New Rehearsal*.[6] Not long before, Gildon had produced an unauthorized life of the famous writer of allegorical romances Delarivier Manley. He had also been involved in Curll's edition of the poems of Shakespeare in 1709, and a year later had produced a life of the actor Thomas Betterton (one of Pope's early mentors), of which Curll was co-publisher. He went on writing for the bookseller over a number of years, most significantly with a collection of *Memoirs of William Wycherley* (1718), devoted to a writer who played a key role in Pope's literary evolution as a young man. As will emerge, Pope complained that Gildon had abused him 'very scandalously' in this work.[7] This is our first meeting with a man who was one of a small army of professional authors, such as Oldmixon, who slaved away for Curll. As with most of this group, Gildon scarcely has a name to conjure with today. But in any survey of the quarrel with Pope, these writers will become increasingly familiar, since they figure among the heroes (often ironic) and villains of the satiric exchanges.

The *New Rehearsal* carries in its imprint only one name, that of James Roberts. He was a wholesale distributor who generally did not own copyrights, and he is found on the title page of numerous books where we know that Curll was the true agent of publication – in some cases, Curll placed newspaper advertisements in his own name for a 'Roberts' title. A second edition appeared in May 1715, under the same flag of convenience. Undoubtedly Pope believed Curll was the responsible party, since in *A Full and True Account* (1716) he has his adversary state, 'Mr. *Gildon*'s *Rehearsal*

... did more harm to me than to Mr. *Rowe*; though upon the Faith of an honest Man, I paid him double for abusing both him and Mr. *Pope*.'[8] Confirmation soon arrived, when the title was included in Curll's catalogue.

It is understandable that the sensitive Pope took umbrage at what he found in the *New Rehearsal*. The dialogue is set in a Covent Garden tavern, with an easily identifiable young poet named Sawney Dapper characterized as 'one of the most Empty and most Conceited of the whole Tribe'. The criticism soon deflects from *The Rape of the Lock* to Pope's recently announced plans for the *Iliad* version. Sawney boasts that he has the Greek poets lying on his hands 'for a Translation'. This provokes a comment by the bland raisonneur, Sir Indolent Easie, possibly representing the universal patron Lord Halifax. Sawney replies, 'Why, ... if I did not understand *Greek*, what of that; I hope a Man may translate a *Greek* Author without understanding *Greek* ... Ah! Sir *Indolent*, you don't know half the Arts of getting a Reputation in this Town for *Learning* and *Poetry*.'[9] Here is a criticism that will be heard again and again, belittling Pope's claims to competence in Greek and accusing him of defrauding the public.

In the same month came an episode that has been seen as an 'offence against Pope', which stands near the beginning of Curll's 'life-long quarrel' with the poet. It relates to a volume entitled *Poems and Translations. By Several Hands*, edited by Oldmixon and published by John Pemberton. The offensive material consists of the inclusion under Pope's name of a rather childish though clever item of seven lines, 'A Receipt [recipe] to make a Cuckold'. This had come out in the previous year, but the author then suppressed it, or tried to. Pope told his friend John Caryll that the lines had been 'stolen' from him; but some degree of complicity is possible. In his preface Oldmixon described the poem as 'a very little One', which could easily have been lost among the other manuscripts 'that seem intended for the Press, which certainly that [the 'Receipt'] never was'.

EXHIBIT 3.2

A Receipt to make a Cuckold.
By Mr. POPE.

Two or three Visits, and two or three Bows,
Two or three Civil Things, and two or three Vows;
Two or three Kisses, and two or three Sighs,
Two or three Jesu's and Let me Dye's;
Two or three Squeezes, and two or three Towzes,
Two or three Hundred Pounds lost at their Houses,
Can ne're fail Cuckolding two or three Spouses.[10]

'Towzes' here means affectionately rough horseplay. Bearing in mind the brevity of the text, the author's name could hardly be blazoned much more conspicuously. For some reason, Curll did not make a point of recycling this item, as he did most of the scraps he managed to pick up from Pope's litter bin.

Later in the volume we encounter lines addressed 'To Mr. Pope, on his Intended Translation of Homer's Iliads'. By the standards of the attacks to come, this was not a wholly unfriendly allusion to the money that the translator, unlike his source in the ancient world, would be making from his project. The author was Handel's poet and librettist John Hughes, with whom Pope generally got on well. This was one of the first unsolicited admonitions the poet would receive:

EXHIBIT 3.3

Advice to Mr. Pope,
On his Intended Translation of Homer's Iliads

O Thou, who with a Happy Genius born,
Can'st tuneful Verse in flowing Numbers turn,

Crown'd on thy *Windsor*'s Plains with Early Bays,

Be early wise, nor trust to barren Praise.

Blind was the Bard that sung *Achilles*' Rage,

He sung and begg'd, and curs'd th' ungiving Age;

If *Britain* his translated Song wou'd hear,

First take the Gold – then charm the list'ning Ear,

So shall thy Father *Homer* smile to see

His Pension pay'd, tho' late, and pay'd to Thee."

Pope had good reason to believe that Curll was responsible for this affront. The bookseller regularly worked in tandem with Pemberton, his neighbour in Fleet Street close to Temple Bar. The two men would be linked in the forthcoming satires *A Full Account* and *A Further Account*, which we shall reach shortly. Oldmixon, a vehement Whig historian and miscellaneous writer, had come to the fore with brutal assaults on the Harley ministry, as well as its defenders Swift and Daniel Defoe. Moreover, a few weeks earlier Curll had actually issued his own volume, *A Collection of Original Poems, Translations, and Imitations, by Mr. Prior, Mr. Rowe, Dr. Swift, and other Eminent Hands*. The three authors named in it were all friends of Pope. But Curll had made things worse when he brought out what *A Full and True Account* called 'an incorrect Edition of [Rowe's] Poems without his Leave'.[12]

One offence would have passed by most observers, though not Pope. In his unauthorized collection of the poems of Nicholas Rowe, Curll inserted a risqué little item entitled 'On a Lady who P---st at the Tragedy of *Cato*'. It concerns the reactions of a Tory lady named Celia who sat dry-eyed at the big stage hit of the year, Joseph Addison's *Cato*, a high-minded (and, to most modern tastes, highly uninteresting) tragedy that had been claimed by the Whigs as a defence of English liberty.

EXHIBIT 3.4

On a Lady who P---st at the tragedy of Cato

While maudlin Whigs deplor'd their Cato's Fate,
Still with dry Eyes the Tory Celia sate,
But while her Pride forbids her Tears to flow,
The gushing Waters find a Vent below:
Tho' secret, yet with copious Grief she mourns,
Like twenty River-Gods with all their Urns.
Let others screw their Hypocritick Face,
She shews her Grief in a sincerer Place;
There Nature reigns, and Passion void of Art,
For that Road leads directly to the Heart.[13]

The piece was not assigned an author, and it remains unclear what share Rowe and Pope took respectively in its composition. More than a decade later Pope allowed it to appear in the *Miscellanies* compiled by his friends and himself. But by that time Curll had reprinted it four times, most recently with the title bowdlerized for polite ears as 'a Lady who shed her Water'. Another version substituted 'a Tory Lady who happen'd to open her Floodgates'. One scribe making a copy for the Harley family was less squeamish about the significant verb.

From this time Curll adopted a plan with regard to Pope's works. If he could not claim the ownership of a major poem, he would find a way to profit from its success by concocting some kind of spin-off volume. This happened in early 1714. On 2 March Lintot published *The Rape of the Lock* in five cantos, an expansion of the much briefer version issued two years earlier. It took very little discernment to see immediately that this was an extraordinary achievement, likely to echo down the ages as one of the greatest satires in the language. In less than a fortnight the author could report to Caryll that the *Rape* had sold 3,000 copies within four days, a phenomenal total for any book, let alone a sophisticated mock-heroic text whose concerns went well beyond the real-life scandal that had prompted its invention.[14]

Curll saw his chance in a flash. One of the additions to the poem was a subplot involving sylphs, gnomes and other fairy-like creatures who act as diminished equivalents of the gods in traditional epic, directing the actions of the heroine, Belinda. Pope's source for this fanciful sideshow to the main amatory business was a largely flippant exposition of Rosicrucian ideas called *Le Comte de Gabalis* (1670) by a French priest, Nicolas de Montfaucon de Villars. He was long dead, found murdered on a roadside near Lyon (Voltaire suggested he was killed by the sylphs). His work consists of dialogues on hermetic philosophy cast in a light-hearted tone. One of Curll's regular hacks, John Ozell – always a speedy man for such a task – had a translation ready by 8 April, when it was jointly published by Lintot and Curll, billed as 'a diverting History'.[15] To enhance its otherwise limited sales potential, the volume was issued in a format 'to bind up with the Rape of the Lock'. Today its interest lies purely in showing how a great poet can conjure something miraculously delicate, refined and subtle out of a tissue of silly nonsense that might have bored the heroine herself.

All in all, relations between poet and bookseller had started to go downhill in 1714. It would take only a slight provocation for open warfare to break out. Events in the upcoming year would split the entire nation, providing ample incentives to extend the feud.

Triumphant Whigs and Desponding Tories

On 6 September 1715 the Earl of Mar raised the Jacobite standard in his home county of Braemar, northeastern Scotland. Within six months the Rising had been crushed, the Pretender had been forced to retreat to France after a stay in Scotland that lasted barely six weeks, and some of the leaders had been convicted of high treason.

Mar had proved an ineffectual commander, so much so that he even had trouble getting his own clansmen to support the campaign as it fizzled out into oblivion. On the brink of triumph at the Battle of Sheriffmuir, not far from Stirling, he allowed the Hanoverian army to escape with an honourable draw, in effect a strategic victory. The section of the rebel army made up of Lowland Scots and Catholic recusants from northeastern England got no nearer London than Preston in Lancashire.

Safely ensconced in and around the capital – as they were, to all appearances – neither Pope nor Curll had too much obvious need to get involved in this distant affair. But, as we know, appearances can deceive. In order to understand the opening skirmishes of their battle, which on the surface was just about Pope's translation of Homer, we must realize that this was a proxy war that regularly shadowed larger conflicts in society. It is significant, too, that Curll's own first serious clash with the authorities occurred when he tried to get in on the lucrative market for accounts of the trials of captured Jacobite peers – a prerogative jealously guarded by the Whig establishment. The poet was born in the year of the Glorious Revolution, the bookseller five years before it. They died respectively one year before and two years after the Young Pretender, Bonnie Prince Charlie, launched his invasion a generation further on. The biggest national trauma during the interval came when they were in midlife, with the inglorious rebellion of the Old Pretender. It was at this exact moment that their own literary contest entered a mode of full hostility.

In the summer of 1715, following a sweeping Whig victory in the general election, apprehension grew among the Tories about the course that events would take. Pope affected a light tone in writing to his friends the Blount sisters at their riverside home in Berkshire, but his anxiety is obvious just below the surface: 'You will say you knew . . . that the Pretender is coming (which is more than I, & my Brother Newsmongers know). You may soon have your

Wish to enjoy the Gallant Sights of Armies, Campagnes, Standards waving over your Brother's Cornfields, & the pretty windings of the Thames about Mapledurham, staind with the blood of Men.' After giving them the preposterous assurance, 'God forgive me – in this martial Age – if I could – I would buy a Regiment for your sake,' he attempted some awkward gallantry about the reaction of women to the military precautions the government was taking:

> Those Eyes that care not how much Mischief is done, or how great Slaughter committed, so they have but a fine show; those Very-female Eyes will be infinitely delighted with the Camp which is speedily to be form'd in Hyde park. The Tents are carried thither this morning, New Regiments ready rais'd, with new Clothes & Furniture . . . The sight of so many thousand gallant Fellows, with all the Pomp & Glare of Warr yet undeformed with battle, those Scenes which England has for many years only beheld on Stages, may possibly invite your Curiosity to this place.[16]

The truth was that he had good reason to be worried. In the very same letter he eulogized Lord Oxford for his fortitude as enemies sought to dispatch him to the execution block. Pope referred less warmly to another ally, the Duke of Ormonde, who had also fled to France after being impeached, and stood ready to join the Rising as leader of a planned invasion of the southwest. While in power the Tories had appointed Ormonde commander-in-chief of the army, to replace the Whig hero John Churchill, Duke of Marlborough. It had been a brave measure on the part of Oxford and Bolingbroke to get rid of Marlborough and his formidable duchess, Sarah, as part of a strategy to end the War of the Spanish Succession. The government had persuaded the queen to dismiss 'her servant and counsellor of thirty years, and the builder of her fame and power', as Marlborough's descendant Winston Churchill put it with understandable fury. Now, however, this move would come back to haunt the ex-ministers.

Amid this uncertainty, Pope welcomed the chance to get away from the capital to the peace of the forest, spending some time at Binfield in the summer of 1715, unaware that he would soon lose this haven. In an amusing poem entitled 'A Farewell to London. In the year 1715', he complained that the bitter political infighting at Westminster and the literary squabbles at Button's coffee house were distracting him from his need to get on with the onerous work demanded by the *Iliad*: 'Why should I stay? Both Parties rage; / My vixen Mistress squalls; / The Wits on envious Feuds engage; / And *Homer* (damn him!) calls.'[17] He didn't really have a mistress, vixen-like or otherwise.

At the same time, there were more personal threats to the well-being of Pope and his Catholic friends, as the authorities tightened their grip in expectation of a Jacobite incursion. Street protests caused enough alarm for the government to bring in the famous Riot Act in early July, imposing tough penalties on anyone who failed to disperse when required. Whenever twelve persons or more were deemed to be assembling for an unlawful purpose, they could be arrested if they did not break up as soon as the Act was proclaimed 'in a loud voice'. It wasn't necessary for a riot to have taken place. Worse would soon follow. Papists were ordered to move out ten miles from the centre of London, and among other restrictions they were for-bidden in a curiously arbitrary diktat to own horses valued at more than £5. This was the prelude to other new laws that imposed extra taxation on the Catholic community and made its members regis-ter their estates as a basis for further swingeing imposts. As a result, Pope's family, who had no safe title to their property, were obliged to leave the home in Windsor Forest where the poet had spent his formative years. They sought out a more unobtrusive residence out-side the western fringes of London, at Hammersmith, which was deemed just far enough out to pass muster under the Ten Mile Act.

The largest set of problems posed by the Rising lay in another direction. Many of those who took up arms on behalf of the Pretender belonged to families with whom Pope had close relations. We have already seen that one of the leaders promptly dispatched after the defeat of the rebellion was the Earl of Derwentwater, connected by marriage to a number of the Thames Valley recusants who formed the nucleus of Pope's extended social circle. For example, among the Northumbrian gentry captured and sentenced to death (although they ultimately escaped or rotted in gaol until dying) were the Swinburnes, known to the poet chiefly through their matriarch, Lady Swinburne. She came from Berkshire and was an aunt of the Blount sisters. Two young women in her family served as couriers for the Jacobites. Even those not directly caught up in the military operations experienced close surveillance. This was the case with John Caryll, a lifelong intimate friend, dedicatee of *The Rape of the Lock* and godfather of Martha Blount. His relatives were engaged in the Stuart enterprise, and he seems to have decamped to the Continent for a time as he felt increasing heat from the authorities. Even Dr John Arbuthnot had to show politic skill to remain untouched, since his brother, a banker in France, was a confirmed Jacobite and actually became the paymaster for recruiting efforts mounted by the Pretender.

When the Harley ministry swept into power on a wave of euphoria in 1710, Swift had mentioned 'Triumphant Tories and desponding Whigs'.[18] Writing to John Gay a few weeks after the queen's death, Pope welcomed his friend back from a mission to Hanover with the words, 'Whether return'd a triumphant Whig or a desponding Tory, equally All Hail!'[19] Within four years British politics had turned full circle.

BELLS ARE RINGING

What of Curll? He could have ridden out the storm in 1715 quietly enough, since he lacked any personal stake in the violent struggle now playing out. Instead he stuck his nose into every controversial issue of the day, sensing the chance of quick profits. In consequence he had the most prolific year of his long career, producing more than eighty items – just ahead of the tally for 1714. The list gave full coverage of topical matters relating to politics, religion and military developments, in addition to the usual mixed bag of works in literature, drama, history, antiquarianism and many other areas. Among the pamphlets was one that called for restraints on 'the inferior high-flying clergy, [who] have occasion'd the late disorders in the state' – this was months before the Rising took off. There was a secret history of the late ministry, showing its hidden Jacobite plans. Curll naturally cashed in on the popularity of Nicholas Rowe's 'she tragedy', *Jane Gray*, which had its premiere in April, with items including a pamphlet entitled *The Life, Character, and Death, of the Most Illustrious Pattern of Female Vertue, the Lady Jane Gray, who was Beheaded in the Tower at 16 Years of Age, for her Stedfast Adherence to the Protestant Religion.* This claimed to have been 'collected from the best historians'. Well, from the most sturdily Protestant ones, perhaps. Charles Gildon brought out a fresh version of his *New Rehearsal*, with some comments on Rowe's play, and Curll naturally made sure the old strictures on *The Rape of the Lock* were reprinted.

Some timely reissues helped to bolster the available offerings. In this group comes a satire on Lord Oxford called *A Second Tale of a Tub*, written by the scapegrace son of Gilbert Burnet, recently deceased Bishop of Salisbury, who had been a leader of the Low Church and scourge of the Tories. Young Tom Burnet, as we shall see, soon joined in the clamour against Pope's Homer. Typically, Curll was still advertising this item fifteen years later. Most likely he was also behind a heavily ironic *Vindication of the Earl of Oxford*, often attributed to Defoe without the slightest show of plausibility. The death of members of the old guard of Whigs, including Burnet, Arthur Maynwaring, the Earl of Wharton and the Earl of Halifax, prompted eulogistic lives. Some of these came in for scornful mention the following year in Pope's *Full Account* of Curll's misfortunes. Predictably, the satire picked out the biography of Maynwaring for withering scorn, since Oldmixon had allotted many pages in this work to denouncing the Tory paper *The Examiner*, belabouring not just Swift as 'the greatest Hand' in its composition but also Bolingbroke, Prior and Atterbury for their supposed share. In fact, these shoddily produced lives went out of their way to express contempt for many of the individuals whom Pope regarded with the greatest affection. That alone supplied a basis for his increasingly bad relations with Curll.

Once the Rising had begun in earnest, there followed a flood of patriotic effusions in support of the Hanoverian cause. It was soon clear from his list where Curll stood. An early entrant was *A Full and Authentick Narrative of the Intended Horrid Conspiracy and Invasion*, with contents including 'A Particular Account of the taking Sir William Windham; and of his Escape, Surrender, and Commitment to the Tower', as well as 'Some Remarkable Circumstances relating to the Lord Lansdown'. Both these concerned men close to Pope. Another section is entitled 'The State of the Rebellion in Scotland and Northumberland; with a Compleat List of the Commanders of the Rebels', which was just as embarrassing potentially for the poet. The propagandist aims of the pamphlet are made clear by a helpful advertisement the distributor Roberts put into the newspaper: 'Those Gentlemen who see fit to disperse them among their Tenants in the Country, shall have them for 40s. a Hundred.'[20] Roberts is also named in the imprint of *Nixon's Cheshire Prophecy*, the supposed predictions of an idiot savant from the previous century. Oldmixon reprinted this traditional material as a warning against the dangers of a foreign invader, now identified as the Pretender. Curll very soon got in on the act, at least as early as November 1715, and by the end of his career he had published editions from the third right through to the twenty-first, issued in 1745 to counter the perceived threat of the Young Pretender.

Late in the year, there came crude bludgeoning of the Jacobites in an unperformed 'tragi-comical farce' called *The Earl of Mar Marr'd, with the Humours of Jockey, the Highlander*. The work is attributed to John Philips, but this is an obvious pseudonym. Curll published it on 3 December, a couple of weeks after news reached London of the inconclusive battle at Sheriffmuir. A piece of naked wish-fulfilment, the play ends with total defeat for the rebellion, as the captured leaders are led off in halters to the scaffold. One priest offers Mar a hundred thousand masses for his soul, in return no doubt for a sizeable donation. Another gives him a wafer and adds, 'Eat this, and you are sav'd.'[21] This gives the presiding officer the chance to launch into a tirade against Catholic rites and doctrines. How painful this would have been for Pope to read, knowing that real-life members of his faith were at imminent risk of death, imprisonment or exile! There was a character in the play called Sauny, a Scots abbreviation for Alexander – a frequent sobriquet for the poet. This man, a spy for Mar, is easily persuaded that he would do better to throw in his lot with the Hanoverian army.

Curll's list shows an increasing determination to invoke Pope's name whenever possible. Thus, in July he inserted the lines to a young lady, later identified as 'Miss (Martha) Blount', sent to her with the works of Voiture, at the head of his own edition of the French writer, brandishing the fact on his title page. A slender item called *The Bath Toasts for the Year 1715*, which came out in October, contained descriptions of Bath and Tunbridge Wells, the two great spa towns. Curll now had a shop open in Tunbridge during the season, while Pope was staying in Bath in the late summer with his friends Gay and William Fortescue. That is about the only way the publisher could justify the dedication of a poem about the reigning beauties at the resort 'To Mr. Pope'.

As one of the feared papists,[22] Pope certainly wasn't the toast of the town when he got back to London with the Rising now in full swing. Bath had been one of the expected centres of rebellion that the

Jacobites had targeted, with an arsenal built up there in the summer. Lansdowne's seat at Longleat lay very close, while Wyndham was knight of the shire for Somerset. According to one correspondent in the press, 'This Place has all the Summer been a Nest of Tories and Papists.' The church bells had rung out when Wyndham arrived to assume command. But the euphoria did not last long. A single company of horse made the town safe for the Hanoverians, and after the two leaders were arrested, it turned out that Bath was bent less on politics than on pleasure. The social round resumed.

HOMERIC BATTLES

Curll did not initiate the campaign against Pope's Homer, an attack that sought to portray the author as both incompetent and duplicitous as a translator. It was claimed that he perverted the Greek text in order to bolster the aspirations of the Stuart Pretender, and more generally to advance the cause of European Catholicism. However, the canny bookseller quickly saw the commercial potential. It was part of a Whig strategy to blacken the papist community at this fraught juncture, and Curll found a ready market for his slurs on the poet.

The nexus of this campaign was now the meeting place of Addison and his cronies, Button's coffee house off Covent Garden, where Pope no longer enjoyed a friendly reception. Here sundry men of letters gathered to swap bons mots and exchange their latest effusions. Among them was Ambrose Philips, known to posterity as 'Namby Pamby' from a withering description given to him for his feeble pastorals and poems for children. According to a story that went around town, Philips accused Pope one evening at Button's of entering into a 'cabal' with Swift to undermine the Whigs and destroy his own reputation. Pope denied that this ever took place.[23] Others in what the poet styled Addison's 'little senate' were the eccentric Eustace Budgell, a cousin of the great man who would ultimately commit suicide by throwing himself into the Thames; the poet-musician John Hughes; and the ambitious young writer Leonard Welsted. The ablest pamphleteers in the extended circle were the bishop's son Tom Burnet and his friend George Duckett. These men possessed a modicum of talent, but they looked up to their oracle for all their attitudes. This meant total allegiance in literary matters to Addison, as well as to the new Hanoverian regime in politics.

Key to developing events was the involvement of Thomas Tickell. He was a student and then a college fellow at Oxford, which by tradition leaned heavily on the Tory and High Church side. But the immense prestige that Addison now enjoyed was starting to make inroads into this solid rampart of conservatism. On his visits to London, Tickell made efforts to get the metropolitan elite to support his literary projects. By May 1714 these included a new translation of the *Iliad*, contracted with the greatest publisher of the day, Jacob Tonson. It will not have escaped attention that this was just two months after Pope had signed up with Lintot for his version. Such a coincidence could not have happened unless Addison had given at least his tacit approval. Certainly Pope believed that the suave *éminence grise* of the Whig party was behind the entire scheme. It can't have been sheer paranoia on his part.

The rival opening segments of the *Iliad* came out within two days of each other in June 1715, almost certainly another contrivance by Pope's enemies. Newspapers gave accounts of the 'Poetical War' between Tickell, supported by Richard Steele and Addison, heading the 'Party' at Button's, and his distinguished antagonist. According to a tale that John Gay picked up in early July: 'I am inform'd that at *Button*'s your character is made very free with as to morals, &c. and Mr A[ddison] says, that your translation and *Tickel*'s are both very well done, but that the latter has more of *Homer*.'[24] Pope, a good hater, never forgave Addison entirely, and not long afterwards he penned the earliest version of his silky, poisonous portrait of 'Atticus', from which we get such phrases as 'damn with faint praise', 'bear, like a Turk, no brother near the throne' and 'willing to wound, and yet afraid to strike'. Modern readers come across this in Pope's famous *Epistle to Arbuthnot* (1735), but it first saw print in a newspaper in 1722, three years after Addison died, and very soon afterwards in a miscellany produced by no less a figure than Edmund Curll.

Opposition by the Whig clique to Pope's translation began even before it saw the light. Burnet and Duckett led the way with the first of two pamphlets titled *Homerides*, issued under the imprint of Roberts in March. An amusing postscript has Punch deliver an epilogue recommending Pope's version to an audience of theatre-goers at Bath. Ever the snapper-up of unconsidered and forgotten trifles, Curll would reprint this item during the controversy over the *Dunciad* more than a decade later. Further censure appeared after the premiere at Drury Lane of a new farce, *The What D'ye Call It*, the first of 28 performances in the next two years, and its pub-lication soon afterwards. This play came mainly from the pen of John Gay, although opponents believed they could discern traces of Pope's hand. They may well have been right.

However, the Buttonians were flummoxed by Pope's next sally, which took the form of a pamphlet named *A Key to the Lock*. It was issued under the name of Roberts, but Lintot paid the author just over ten guineas for it at the end of April 1715 – about half as much as he got for *The Rape of the Lock* itself. The work promises on its title page to prove beyond all doubt 'the dangerous Tendency' of the poem 'to Government and Religion'. It is one of Pope's most delightfully witty productions, finding absurd clues in the text to show that it provides a hidden allegory to promote Catholic politics. This is easy to do, since the author is known to be 'professedly a *Papist*', and so suspected of wishing to 'spread Popish Doctrines'. Thus, the famous scene in which the heroine bedecks herself at a dressing table becomes 'an artful Recommendation of the *Mass*, and pompous Ceremonies of the *Church of Rome*'.[25] What were Addison and his junto of satirists to say? These coded references to Jacobitism were exactly the sort of thing they were bent on discovering in Pope's writing. On top of that, the entire method of the pamphlet serves as a ridiculous parody of the 'keys' to major works that Curll tossed out during his career. It was extraordinarily brave to bring out this daring subversion of counter-espionage efforts at a moment when the government was looking for the Pretender's agents under every bed.

Among the most considered statements that Pope made on the issues came in a letter to his Whig friend James Craggs on 15 July. In it he laments the current state of the nation: 'For the Spirit of Dissention is gone forth among us; nor is it a wonder that *Button*'s is no longer *Button*'s, when *Old England* is no longer *Old England*, that region of hospitality, society, and good humour. Party affects us all, even the wits, tho' they gain as little by politicks as they do by their wit.' Then follows a significant passage, anticipating the damning verses on Addison.

EXHIBIT 3.5

For they tell me, the busy part of the nation are not more divided about *Whig* and *Tory*, than these idle fellows of the Feather about Mr *Tickel*'s and my Translation. I (like the *Tories*) have the town in general, that is the mob, on my side; but 'tis usual with the smaller Party to make up in industry what they want in number, and that's the case with the little Senate of *Cato*. However if our Principles be well consider'd, I must appear a brave *Whig*, and Mr *Tickel* a rank *Tory*; I translated *Homer* for the publick in general, he to gratify the inordinate desires of One man only. We have, it seems, a great *Turk* in Poetry who can never bear a Brother on the throne; and has his Mutes too, a sett of Nodders, Winkers, and Whisperers, whose business is to strangle all other offsprings of wit in their birth.[26]

Of course, Curll's interests lay in dampening down such calls for moderation, and he did as much as anyone to see to it that conflict between the parties, over Homer or anything else, remained on the boil for as long as possible. He was almost certainly behind a notice in the press on 12 November:

> We hear that Mr. Oldsworth of Hants, the celebrated Author of a Poem call'd *Muscipula*, which is admirably well translated into English Blank Verse lately by a Gentleman, is preparing Amendments and Corrections for Mr. Pope's Homer, the Errors of which are already pleasantly display'd in a Pamphlet, call'd *Homer in a Nutshell*.[27]

Much of this is nonsense. In 1709 Edward Holdsworth did write a neo-Latin poem with this title for Curll, who reprinted it more than once. It was then translated by Samuel Cobb as *The Mouse-Trap* (1712), and both versions were included in a miscellany the bookseller brought out in 1714. But no such set of corrections ever emerged. Moreover, *Homer in a Nutshell* does not fit the context in any way. Published in July 1715, it consists of a travesty of the opening three books of the *Iliad* in a strange doggerel style, with some preliminary sections that clearly take Pope's side. They parody the Buttonians, not just Tickell but also Tom Burnet and especially his deceased father, the Bishop of Salisbury. The author was most probably Arbuthnot, or even Pope himself. Why would Curll get things so wrong? Either he had not really looked at *Homer in a Nutshell*, or he was simply stirring things again.

Needless to say, Curll would have liked to get hold of the Buttonian wits to augment his corps of writers. However, most of them were university men; and they were too close to the patrician at their centre, Addison, to wish to join the lower echelons of Grub Street. As a result Curll had to make do with people in a humbler station, such as Oldmixon and Gildon, although, as we shall soon find out, the combative old critic John Dennis was ready to enlist his aid in stoking up a feud with Pope that had been simmering for some time.

The starting point had been a pamphlet by Dennis, *Reflections Critical and Satyrical, upon a Late Rhapsody, Call'd, An Essay upon Criticism*, published by Bernard Lintot in June 1711. This made a series of accusations that were to become wearisomely familiar in succeeding years – the new poet on the block was a plagiarist, a cheat, a Jacobite and of course a misshapen creature ('a hunch-back'd Toad', with more along those lines).[28] Pope soon responded with *The Critical Specimen*, in which he spoofs the methods of a renowned figure, 'Rinaldo Furioso, Critick of the Woful Countenance'. This contrives in a few words to identify Dennis with a failed attempt at an English opera, *Rinaldo and Armida* (1697); with the headstrong and temporarily insane hero of Ariosto's epic *Orlando Furioso* (1532); and with the deluded Don Quixote. A synopsis of a proposed treatise has a chapter describing 'A Contention in Civility and good Breeding between the Critick and a little Gentleman of *Windsor Forest*, in which the little Gentleman had some Advantage.'[29] Two years later Pope returned to the fray with a blistering *Narrative* that was attributed to the quack doctor Robert Norris, but whose real target emerged in a subtitle, 'Concerning the Strange and Deplorable Frenzy of Mr. John Denn--'. Lintot also figures somewhat inconsequentially in the narrative. Now the veteran campaigner was up for revenge, and the new version of the *Iliad* gave him a fresh opportunity to belabour Pope for his lack of taste and discernment.

Curll managed to get some share in one of the pamphlets by Burnet and Duckett, along with an odd scrap from others. The assault on the Homer translation was thus conducted on two fronts. One was that of the Buttonians, which started in 1715. The other was that of the Curllians, who had to wait until the following year to make much impact. This campaign would now supply an excuse for the first sustained onslaught on Pope as a man and a writer.

4

Poisonous RELATIONS, 1716

The timing could hardly have been better for Curll. He launched his first serious attacks on Pope in the early months of 1716, just as the Rising sputtered to its hasty conclusion. The invading army had already been stopped in its tracks at Preston; most of the Highlanders who were not killed or captured went back to the safety of the glens, and the Pretender had slipped away from the small coastal town of Montrose on 5 February. He lived another half century, but he never again set foot on British soil. Nor did his unhappy choice to command the Jacobite army, the Earl of Mar, who accompanied him into exile and ultimate irrelevance. Those Jacobite leaders who had not been rounded up suffered the loss of their titles and estates as proscribed rebels. Among those caught, the most drastic fate lay in store for two of the rebel lords accused of treason. The Earl of Derwentwater was impeached by Parliament on 10 January, on a motion in the House of Commons by Nicholas Lechmere, a time-serving lawyer who would feel the lash of Pope's tongue in years to come. In company with five more of the leading rebels, the Northumbrian magnate Derwentwater and a peer from the Scottish Lowlands, the Earl of Kenmure, were brought from the Tower to face their accusers. They were rapidly dispatched through the grisly pageantry of a trial in Westminster Hall, followed by a march to the scaffold. For the two principal victims, it was all over by 24 February.

All this occurred in the midst of an exceptionally severe winter. The rebel prisoners had been driven down to London, their wrists pinioned, through a chilled landscape. The big freeze had started not long before the Jacobites saw their hopes dashed by the battles at Sheriffmuir and Preston. In the capital – which was in the grip of its worst period of cold for many years – a frost fair on the river began in November and lasted for almost three months. Newspaper reports chronicled the progress of events:

> The Frost, which we hoped in our last was gone, it having thaw'd two days together is set in again with more violence than ever, and the Thames continues like a Fair, Thousands of People crossing it every Day, and a great Number of Booths and Shops are set up, with Cooks shops, where they roast and boil all sorts of Meat with great Fires, just as if it was in the Street. Several poor people are found starv'd and frozen to death in the street.[1]

Among the booths that sprang up on the riverbanks were those of 'rowling press printers' and 'common press printers', ready to spread the latest news about the fate of the rebel lords. The rolling press was conveniently sited next to the 'first tavern built in Freezeland Street'. Writing to John Caryll on 10 January, Pope explains why he has had to defer a planned visit to Sussex: 'You see sufficiently the cause that prevents that satisfaction, whenever you look out of your windows, or put your nose out of doors. I very much wish the season had not exerted its severity before I had arrived among you.'[2]

As far as we know, Pope had not given any kind of active support to the rebellion. It is possible that the subscription campaign mounted on his behalf for the Homer translation acted as a cover for a fundraising exercise to bankroll the Pretender's adventure. A suspicious number of those who supported the Stuart cause were among the most ardent in promoting the *Iliad*, notably Caryll, while some individuals caught up in the Rising had been recruited as subscribers – and not just Mar and Derwentwater. A Jacobite commander, Lord Seaforth, was clan chief of the Mackenzies, who were connected by marriage to Pope's best friends, the Caryll family. Others on the list would have taken an active role if the military operations had gone as planned. These included the exiled Duke of Ormonde, the poet's own patron Lord Lansdowne, and Sir William Wyndham. Matthew Prior had managed to rustle up a few high Tory sympathizers in Cambridge to dilute the heavy Oxonian presence. But he was already in custody when the Rising began, and the attainted leaders of the former government, Oxford, Bolingbroke and Strafford, were likewise *hors de combat*. Pope wanted to attract as large an audience for his work as he could, so there were naturally large numbers of Whigs listed. But he believed that the Buttonian wit Ambrose Philips had deliberately blocked his venture by hanging on to money paid in by subscribers who belonged to a Whig group, the Hanoverian Club. Naturally Joseph Addison, keen to boost the rival translation of his protégé Thomas Tickell, did not offer any aid, as Pope had once hoped he might.

Here was a conjunction of events that brought together the impeachment of the Tory ministers, the appearance of the first portion of the *Iliad*, and the rise and fall of the Jacobite dream. Collectively, they made it possible for those who disliked or envied Pope (and there were many people in both categories) to expose him to scorn. Now he could safely be disparaged, in spite of the eminence he had already acquired by his poems, and the lofty social connections he had made. Still some way short of his thirtieth birthday, the young man was vulnerable on more than one account. Indeed, as early as April 1715 a journalist named Philip Horneck, who surprisingly never joined Curll's team, had linked Pope's writing (in particular his part in the Scriblerian comedy *The What D'ye Call It*) with the ongoing threat from the Jacobites: 'since Farces of *Popes* and *Pretender's* have taken such a Run alate'.[3] Horneck had in mind *The What D'ye Call It*, which had premiered on 23 February, and although it is now believed that John Gay was the main author, this mock-tragedy could be conveniently ascribed to the unpopular Pope by his enemies in the circle at Button's coffee house. They had good reason to be offended, since the burlesque of grand dramatic language in the play included parodies of Addison's *Cato* and Philips's *The Distressed Mother* (the biggest theatrical hit of each man).

In the wake of subsequent events, it was easy for Curll's writers to associate their target with a now unpopular religion, a would-be usurper, a turncoat peer who had led a fruitless invasion, a discredited ministry and a subscription project designed to enrich its author (as it would really do). Pope could not deny that he was a Catholic, or that many of his closest friends were loyal adherents of the faith and maintained contact with their co-religionists in hated France. As we have seen, his contacts extended to several individuals who participated in the Rising. He had openly enjoyed close personal relationships with the leaders of the former administration, Oxford and Bolingbroke, along with many lesser figures who had been involved in the peace negotiations that were now widely reviled.

Other criticism centred on his capacities as a translator, and it was true that Pope did not possess a deeply scholarly knowledge of Greek. The charge loses some force when we realize that most of his critics had even less acquaintance with the language and literature of the ancient world. Curll, for one, had a basic grasp of Latin, but little or no Greek. Nor could it be denied that Pope embarked on his Homer with the conscious desire to make a killing. The new Copyright Act had made that easier for a writer, with the right bookseller and the right contract. This naturally infuriated the scribblers dependent on the patronage of publishers such as Curll. They did not have the literary talent to follow in Pope's footsteps, and they had not been smart enough to put themselves in the legal and financial position he had managed to reach.

By the end of March, Curll had got into his stride in his attacks on the Scottish rebels. He produced an even more egregious sequel to *The Earl of Mar Marr'd*, another unperformed comedy that was again supposedly written by 'John Philips'. It boasted a title that may have been alluring to some, but was surely distasteful to folk such as Pope and his friends: *The Pretender's Flight, or, a Mock Coronation. With the Humours of the Facetious Harry Saint John. A Tragi-comical Farce*. This time the real-life characters (the Pretender, the Earl Marischal and Bolingbroke) were joined in the cast by two French nuns, traipsing about the Highlands in search of their hero the Pretender. They adopt a disguise, but risk being molested until they accept the protection offered by the notorious rake and infidel Bolingbroke. The recusant community were familiar with this kind of slur, since almost every family loyal to their historic faith had daughters who were sent at an early age to spend their days in a convent across the Channel. At the end of the action a cowardly Pretender flees from the Hanoverian army with the despairing Mar, now resigned to permanent exile.

How closely Curll had attached himself to the powers that be is evident from his booklist on the final page, where five out of nine recent publications are transparently anti-Jacobite and anti-Catholic. These are mostly sermons delivered by preachers anxious to show their loyalty not just to the Protestant religion but also to the Hanoverian dynasty. The most outspoken attack came from 'w.h.', identity unknown, in his poem *The Fate of Traytors*, which Curll sent out around 2 April. It contains a bitter onslaught on the Jacobites, but also condemns the Catholic Church in the most severe terms. Among individuals held up for denunciation are Jonathan Swift, Bolingbroke, Ormonde and Francis Atterbury, with the bishop pilloried under a nickname he had recently acquired, Scammony. If Pope did not have other things on his mind, this is the sort of text that would have caused him acute anxiety. It is hardly surprising that he came to look on the publisher as his enemy, when Curll regularly sent out such vicious personal abuse of friends and colleagues.

By now Curll was in a position to offer his first major challenge to a vulnerable opponent. When the chance came, it arose indirectly from the sequence of melodramatic events that had gripped the nation for the past six months.

CURLL PROVOKES

It happened in this way. Only one of the captured rebel lords pleaded not guilty to the charge of high treason when impeached by Parliament in January. This was George Seton, Earl of Winton, an eccentric young peer who had joined the forces of Lord Kenmure before being taken prisoner at Preston. His trial in Westminster Hall lasted two days, in a ritual colourfully described by Christopher Sinclair-Stevenson:

> Again the ceremonial mummery was lavished on the interested spectators. Processions, obeisances, uncovering of heads, impressive proclamations in Latin and in English, this ballet of etiquette seemed never-ending. At last. However, Wintoun, the Lieutenant-Governor of the Tower and the Gentleman Jailer with his axe made their appearance, and the charges were read; they referred to rebellion, regicide, murder and robbery. The verdict, of course, was a foregone conclusion.[4]

Nonetheless, the earl mounted a spirited defence. He disrupted proceedings and made strange interventions on procedural matters that led some people to regard him as simply insane. After a weekend break, the Lords reassembled on 19 March to consider their verdict. Winton's courtroom antics proved to have been of no avail. He was given the traditional means of execution reserved for traitors, to which the other rebel lords had been sentenced:

'You must be hanged by the neck, but not till you be dead; for you must be cut down alive, then your bowels must be taken out, and burnt before your faces; then your heads must be severed from your bodies, and your bodies divided each into four quarters; and these must be at the king's disposal.'[5] Such scenes were averted on this occasion, because the prisoner sawed through the bars of his gaol and got away to join the Pretender in Rome.

Pope could not have been unaware of this horrid outcome of a fiasco in which many of his co-religionists faced (and in some cases received) brutal retaliation. And we have two pieces of evidence to show that Curll, as usual, had his eye on the ball. The first concerns a publication that is generally seen as marking the start of full hostilities with Pope. It came out on 27 March. The title page reads as follows:

EXHIBIT 4.1

COURT POEMS.

Viz; 1. The Basset-Table. An Eclogue. 11. The Drawing-Room. 111. The Toilet.

Publish'd faithfully, as they were found in a Pocket-book taken up in Westminster-Hall, the Last Day of the Lord Winton's Trial.

Printed for J. Roberts, near the Oxford-Arms in Warwick-Lane. MDCC[x]VI. Six-Pence.

That was all innocuous enough, and, as often, the imprint concealed the identity of the true instigator of proceedings behind the name of the all-purpose distributor James Roberts. The real trouble, which arrived with the prefatory note that followed, looks to have come from the hand of Curll, even though he palmed off editorial responsibility on his willing day labourer John Oldmixon.

EXHIBIT 4.2

Advertisement.

The Reader is acquainted, from the Title-Page, how I came possess'd of the following POEMS. All that I have to add, is, only a Word
or two concerning their Author.

Upon Reading them over at St *James's* Coffee-House, they were
attributed by the General Voice to be the Productions of a LADY of
Quality.

When I produc'd them at *Button's*, the *Poetical Jury* there
brought in a different Verdict; and the Foreman strenuously insisted
upon it, that Mr. GAY was the *Man*; and declar'd, in Comparing the
Basset-Table, with that Gentleman's PASTORALS, he found the *Stile*,
and *Turn of* Thought, to be evidently the same; which confirm'd
him, and his Brethren, in the Sentence they had pronounc'd.

Not content with these Two Decisions, I was resolv'd to call
in an Umpire; and accordingly chose a Gentleman of distinguish'd
Merit, who lives not far from *Chelsea*. I sent him the Papers; which
he return'd to me the next Day, with this Answer:

'Sir, Depend upon it, these Lines could come from no other
Hand, than the Judicious Translator of HOMER.'

Thus having impartially given the Sentiment of the *Town*; I
hope I may deserve Thanks, for the Pains I have taken, in endeav-
ouring to find out the *Author* of these Valuable Performances; and
every Body is at Liberty to bestow the *Laurel* as they please.[6]

Everyone in the know would easily recognize that the 'Lady of
Quality' was none other than the formidable Mary Wortley Montagu,
and of course Pope the judicious translator. Curll obviously intends
to suggest that the distinguished gentleman was Addison, who is not
known to have had any part in the affair. But it helped to warm up
bad feeling lingering from the previous year over the rival translation
by Tickell. Things had gone a little quiet on that recently, and Curll

never liked such a lull in controversies. It needs no emphasis that what we have here is the language of a trial, a jury and a verdict – ominous words in the heady atmosphere of the previous few weeks, with the conviction and in two cases execution of the rebel lords.

Much later Curll explained that he had got the items from one Joseph Jacobs, 'the founder of a remarkable Sect called the Whiskers'.[7] He was a former linen draper who at the start of the century had become the minister of a congregational chapel that stood close to the site of Fenchurch Street station today. According to a contemporary observer, 'He that has the longest whiskers amongst them is by so much the better member; but Jacobs measures their profession by the Mustachio, and not by the ell and yard, as he used to do his linen. By their look you would take them to be of the Society of Bedlam.'[8] In a largely beardless age, beards were de rigueur for members of this sect. It was further revealed that Oldmixon had brought the material to the bookseller, and they agreed to share the profits with John Pemberton, a neighbour who often worked with them.

We can now be sure about the authorship of the three poems printed in the volume. They were all written by Lady Mary, as part of a series for each weekday (one for Friday was added by Gay). The newly fashionable 'town eclogues' had been pioneered by Swift and Gay, and their *raison d'être* lay simply in transposing the conventions of classical pastoral poetry, with its sheltered setting in remote Arcadia, to the busy social world of West End society. Not for nothing did the supposed editor begin by seeking the judgment of the cognoscenti at St James's coffee house, which stood on the west side of the street only a stone's throw from the palace, before appealing to the jury of *littérateurs* at Button's across town near Covent Garden, and finally searching out an impartial referee in the shape of the great oracle, Addison. (The writer's bolt-hole lay just on the far side of the stream dividing Chelsea and Fulham; it had once been the home of Nell Gwyn.) Pope copied out all

six eclogues, and they are preserved in an album lent out to Lord
Bathurst but eventually returned to Lady Mary.[9] She held on to it
after her violent rupture with Pope a few years later. Despite the
fact that Pope's role was seemingly confined to the most minor
adjustments, Curll went on regardless, and issued the three pieces
in various collections several times. He never had any compunc-
tion about attributing them to his enemy, and later he threw them
in with genuine items as *Court Poems . . . By Mr. Pope, &c.* (1726).

Pope Responds

The damage had been done. A frequent and bitter rebuke by his
antagonist is that Curll assigned works recklessly, to the damage
of the real writer but also the one to whom they were falsely attributed – a claim reiterated in a note to *The Dunciad*. From now open
hostilities were declared.

Supposedly, the retaliation came as early as 28 March. This
took the form of the notorious glass of sack (Spanish white wine,
beloved of Falstaff), laced with an emetic, administered by poet to
bookseller. It seems a puerile revenge, and it can be pardoned (if
at all) only by the uproarious comedy that Pope extracted from the
events in a pamphlet he published within a few days. For the first
time, Pope deliberately turned the methods of Grub Street back
against their usual perpetrators.

We can see this happening from the moment we survey the
title page:

EXHIBIT 4.3

A FULL and TRUE

ACCOUNT

of a Horrid and Barbarous

Revenge by Poison,

on the body of Mr. EDMUND CURLL, Bookseller;

with a faithful Copy of his

Last WILL and TESTAMENT.

Publish'd by an Eye Witness.

The whole style of this sensational headline constitutes a blow against Pope's target, mimicking as it does the formulas favoured by Curll and his kind. We have the claim to 'faithful' memoirs, the reproduction of the will, the absurd emphasis bestowed by the antiquated black-letter type, and above all the proud gesture with which the last will is announced. A few years before, Curll had started to print wills, which could be bought for a small fee at Doctors' Commons, the home of ecclesiastical lawyers, lying between St Paul's and the Thames. This branch of trade became one of his leading specialities, and by the early 1730s he was regularly advertising up to twenty volumes containing lives and last wills, with a premature name added at the end: 'Mr. Pope's Life is preparing for the press.' You could even buy a collected set of wills, although why anyone would wish to do that might tax the imagination.

After this, instead of the ennobling epigraph commonly found on a title page, Pope added three couplets of crude corporeal detail regarding the vomit, couched in the conventional diction of heroic verse. At least a potential buyer would be forewarned by a sort of spoiler alert that scatology was in prospect – title pages then served the function of the dust jacket today, and would be hung up as a point-of-sale display. Last comes the imprint, listing five booksellers, headed by James Roberts. All had been concerned in Curll's productions at one time or another. Two are women: Rebecca Burleigh and Sarah Popping, both, as we shall see, frequent agents of his business at this juncture. But there is no likelihood that they had any hand in Pope's mock-Curllian pamphlet.

The narrative gets quickly under way:

EXHIBIT 4.4

History furnishes us with Examples of many Satyrical Authors who have fallen Sacrifices to Revenge, but not of any Booksellers that I know of, except the unfortunate Subject of the following Papers; I mean Mr., *Edmund Curll*, at the *Bible* and *Dial* in *Fleetstreet*, who was Yesterday poison'd by Mr. *Pope*, after having liv'd many Years an Instance of the mild Temper of the *British* Nation.

Every Body knows that the said Mr. *Edmund Curll*, on Monday the 26th Instant, publish'd a Satyrical Piece, entituled *Court Poems*, in the Preface whereof they were attributed to a *Lady of Quality*, Mr. *Pope*, or Mr. *Gay*; by which indiscreet Method, though he had escaped one Revenge, there were still two behind in reserve.

Now on the Wednesday ensuing, between the Hours of 10 and 11, Mr. *Lintott*, a neighb'ring Bookseller, desird a Conference with Mr. *Curll* about settling the *Title Page* of *Wiquefort's Ambassador*, inviting him at the same Time to take a Whet together. Mr. *Pope*, (who is not the only Instance how Persons of bright Parts may be carry'd away by the Instigations of the Devil) found Means to convey himself into the same Room, under pretence of Business with Mr. *Lintott*, who it seems is the Printer of his *Homer*. This Gentleman with a seeming Coolness, reprimanded Mr. *Curll* for wrongfully ascribing to him the aforesaid Poems: He excused himself, by declaring that one of his Authors (Mr. *Oldmixon* by Name) gave the Copies to the Press, and wrote the *Preface*. Upon this Mr. *Pope* (being to all appearance reconcil'd) very civilly drank a Glass of Sack to Mr. *Curll*, which he as civilly pledged; and tho' the Liquor in Colour and Taste differ'd not from common Sack, yet was it plain by the Pangs this unhappy Stationer felt soon after, that some Poisonous Drug had been secretly infused therein.[10]

A striking feature here is the level of explicit detail, parodying a journalist's urge to give us the pure facts. We have the date, the time of day and the bookseller's business address – his shop sign acting as a corporate logo but also a navigating tool, since there were as yet no street numbers. We see Curll engaged in discussions over the all-important title page with his neighbour in Fleet Street; slyly, the narrator pretends to be vague about Bernard Lintot's involvement in the translation of Homer ('printer' here means what we should call publisher). The underlying joke is that Lintot needed help to devise the kind of attention-grabbing showbill that the great promoter regularly plastered at the front of his handiworks.

Characteristically, Curll tries to shift the blame by getting his associate Oldmixon into trouble; the phrase 'one of his Authors' quietly suggests a relation of master and men. The assignment is plausible, since we know from Lintot's accounts that Oldmixon did supply the index to the fairly unremarkable volume mentioned, the work of the seventeenth-century Dutch diplomat and double agent Abraham de Wicquefort. Curll himself never laid claim to any share in the book. It came out on 21 April, and Lintot put an advertisement in the *London Gazette* a week later, stating with a full sense of importance that he had 'lately publish'd with His Majesty's Royal Licence, Mr. Pope's Translation of Homer, Vol. ii. And Monsieur Wiquefort's compleat Ambassador.' Best of all in the excerpt is the throwaway line about 'this unhappy Stationer', hinting at one civic dignity that strictly didn't belong to Curll. In just three short paragraphs we have an astonishing range of evidence to show how bulky a file Pope had already assembled on his antagonist's movements.

Where There's a Will

The narrative proceeds. After Curll makes the short trip home, his condition has grown serious enough to alarm his wife. She is horrified to observe that the contents of his vomit are 'as green of grass' – a notion that Pope would poeticize to greater effect in *The Dunciad*. Lintot enters to spread further dismay by suggesting that his colleague has caught 'the vomiting Distemper', which kills a sufferer in half an hour. As the symptoms grow worse, Curll decides it is time he makes his will, an appropriate action for one who so often published the last testaments of others. Lintot goes to fetch Pemberton, and the two men commiserate with their friend. Despite great pain, he immediately proceeds to make a verbal will ('Mrs. *Curll* having first put on his Night Cap').

EXHIBIT 4.5

Gentlemen, in the first Place I do sincerely pray Forgiveness for those indirect Methods I have pursued in inventing new Titles to old Books, putting Authors Names to Things they never saw, publishing private Quarrels for publick Entertainment, all which, I hope will be pardoned, as being done to get an honest livelihood.

I do also heartily beg Pardon of all Persons of Honour, Lords Spiritual and Temporal, Gentry, Burgesses, and Commonalty to whose Abuse I have any, or every way, contributed by my Publications. Particularly, I hope it will be considered, that if I have vilify'd his Grace the Duke of *Marlborough*, I have likewise aspers'd the late Duke of *Ormond*; if I have abused the honourable Mr. *Walpole*, I have also libell'd the late Lord *Bolingbroke*; so that I have preserv'd that Equality and Impartiality which becomes an honest Man in Times of Faction and Division.

I call my Conscience to Witness, that many of these Things which may seem malicious, were done out of Charity; I having made it wholly my Business to print for poor disconsolate Authors, whom all other Booksellers refuse: Only God bless Sir *Richard Blackmore*; you know he takes no Copy Money.

The Book of the Conduct of the Earl of *Nottingham*, is yet unpublished; as you are to have the Profit of it, Mr. Pemberton, you are to run the Risque of the Resentments of all that Noble Family. Indeed I caused the Author to assert several Things in it as Facts, which are only idle Stories of the Town; because I thought it would make the Book sell. Do you pay the Author for Copy Money, and the Printer and Publisher. I heartily beg God's, and my Lord *Nottingham*'s Pardon; but all Trades must live."

The first paragraph outlines some of the common charges brought against Curll for his use of title pages and advertising to mislead potential buyers. The next sets up a bogus claim to impartiality, showing that Curll has slandered without principle leading figures on either side of the political divide. Ormonde had been the Tories' choice to succeed Marlborough as commander-in-chief, when they wished to run down the war by pensioning off the successful general. Robert Walpole was a rising politician with his mind already bent on the power he would eventually achieve. The aim here is not to defend either Tories or Whigs, but to expose the hypocrisy of Curll's publishing methods. Sir Richard Blackmore was a leading physician and the author of interminable epics on subjects such as King Arthur. Long a butt of Tory wits, from this time onwards Blackmore was one of Pope's most frequent targets. Some modern critics have tried to rehabilitate the Miltonic ambitions of his poetry, but it is an uphill task.

The fourth paragraph shows just how cunningly Pope sneaked into the private doings of his adversary. It concerns a book that was never published. Oldmixon had written a life of the Tory politician Nottingham, which the peer and his family wished to suppress. After some messy negotiations they succeeded, although it took another year. The work had been scheduled to appear in March 1716 under the imprint of Roberts. But we can tell from personal correspondence between Curll and the family that he was the real agent behind the scheme, while Oldmixon apparently bore most if not all of the costs himself, no doubt in return for a lion's share of the profits. The exchange of letters makes it abundantly clear that Curll had no intention of having to face the resentment of the family. He humbly agreed to dissociate himself from the project, and said that Oldmixon would withdraw if he were paid his expenses on print and paper. Should Lord Nottingham choose not to accept this deal, 'the Resentment must fall upon Mr. Oldmixon, for I shall take care not to incur the Guilt.' None of these documents was open to the public until long after the events; indeed, they surfaced as recently as 1970.[12] Pope somehow got to know what was going on almost as soon as trouble started to brew. Plainly he had enough sense of Curll's character to predict the line the bookseller would take when powerful individuals posed a threat to him.

The rest of the 'will' turns out to be a cross between a confession, an apologia and a cry for help. Like an accused who asks for other offences to be taken into consideration, Curll admits to having cheated numerous times: 'The second Collection of Poems, which I groundlessly called Mr. *Prior*'s, will sell for nothing, and hath not yet paid the Charge of the Advertisements I was obliged to publish against him.' The item by Prior was another one that had come hot from the press, having appeared on 17 March. In response, Prior had issued an indignant statement that some of the poems included were not genuine – in fact, most were – while others were 'imperfect'. Curll then invokes the name of the French critic of Pope's Homer, Anne Dacier, in respect of a rival version of *Cato* by François-Michel-Chrétien Deschamps. This had been advertised as forthcoming in February, but was delayed until 23 May: 'The *French Cato*, with the Criticism, showing how superior it is to Mr. *Addison*'s, (which I wickedly inscribed to Madam *Dacier*) may be suppress'd at a reasonable Rate, being damnably translated.'[13] The reference points at John Ozell, a competent translator from French and Spanish who worked regularly for Curll, even after they had a tiff in print two years later in 1718. Pope had once written a cutting epigram on a version of Nicolas Boileau-Despreaux's *Le Lutrin*, claiming that 'Those were slander'd most *whom Ozell prais'd*.'[14] In response, Ozell complained of the bookseller's 'Quack way' of inserting his words into newspapers without permission, despite promises not to do so. Curll retorted that he would always make use of Ozell's name 'in the most advantageous Manner I can, to promote the Sale of what Books I have printed for him'.[15]

The list setting out his previous form includes some of Curll's more notorious works of (generally mild) pornography:

EXHIBIT 4.6

I protest I have no Animosity to Mr. Rowe, having printed Part of his *Callipædia*, and an incorrect Edition of his Poems without his Leave, in Quarto. Mr. *Gildon*'s *Rehearsal*; or *Bays the Younger*, did more harm to me than to Mr. *Rowe*; though upon the Faith of an honest Man, I paid him double for abusing both him and Mr. *Pope*.

Heaven pardon me for publishing the *Trials of Sodomy* in an Elzevir Letter; but I humbly hope, my printing Sir *Richard Blackmore*'s Essays will attone for them. I beg that you will take what remains of these last, which is near the whole Impression, (Presents excepted) and let my poor Widow have in Exchange the sole Propriety of the Copy of Madam *Mascranny*.[16]

Blackmore's ponderous essays had been published as recently as 8 March. Here Pope suggests that they, and perhaps all serious literary fare, are worth less commercially than the sordid relation of a divorce case in Paris, which figured regularly in the much reprinted series of *The Cases of Impotency* (with alternative titles including divorce and sodomy). He also gets in a dig at one of the bookseller's foibles. Although his productions are seldom things of beauty, Curll took some pride in the elegant Dutch typeface he often used, especially for books in smaller formats. In 1714 he even called one of his raggle-taggle collections *The Elzevir Miscellany*, alluding to one of the fonts designed by the great dynasty of Dutch printers in the seventeenth century. The Elzevir family, famous for their handsome editions of the classics, would have felt no pride to see their name associated with such motley productions as *Court Poems*.

After a brief interruption when Pemberton objects to the terms proposed, and Curll's own speech becomes more indistinct as his vomiting grows worse, the confession resumes:

EXHIBIT 4.7

Dear Mr. *Pemberton*, I beg you to beware of the Indictment at *Hicks's-Hall*, for publishing *Rochester's* bawdy Poems; that Copy will otherwise be my best Legacy to my dear Wife, and helpless Child.

The Case of Impotence was my best Support all the last long Vacation.

In this last Paragraph Mr. Curll's Voice grew more free, for his Vomitings abated upon his Dejections, and he spoke what follows from his Close-stole.

For the Copies of Noblemen's and Bishop's *Last Wills and Testaments*, I solemnly declare I printed them not with any Purpose of Defamation; but meerly as I thought those Copies lawfully purchased from *Doctors Commons*, at *One Shilling* a Piece. Our Trade in Wills turning to small Account, we may divide them blindfold.

For Mr. *Manwaring's Life*, I ask Mrs. *Oldfield's* Pardon: Neither *His*, nor my Lord *Halifax's* Lives, though they were of great Service to their Country, were of any to me: But I was resolved, since I could not print their Works while they liv'd, to print their Lives after they were dead.[17]

In this short section Pope contrives to hit a number of targets. Curll is relieved as he sits on the toilet by his 'dejections' (an old medical term for evacuating the bowels). We learn that a threat of prosecution hangs over him at the Middlesex Sessions, held in Clerkenwell on a site later occupied by public toilets, but now used chiefly for parking motorbikes. Curll had begun to publish the scandalous poems of John Wilmot, Earl of Rochester, near the start of his career in 1707, and would go on issuing new editions as late as 1739, generally keeping his name well out of sight on the title page.

From 1714 he augmented their appeal by inserting in the volumes a section entitled 'The Cabinet of Love', obscene items mostly about dildos, with no known connection to Rochester.

The life of a Whig politician and follower of the Marlborough family, Arthur Maynwaring, had come out in July 1715, from the pen of the industrious Oldmixon. By way of a hook for potential buyers, Maynwaring's mistress, Anne Oldfield, happened to be perhaps the greatest actress of her time. Her death in 1730 would prompt several responses. Pope characterized her as 'dear charming *Oldfield*', and in a more backhanded way as a woman who 'with Grace and Ease, / Could joyn the Arts, to ruin, and to please'.[18] (Ouch!) Meanwhile Voltaire, in his *Lettres Philosophiques* (1733), observed that the English had been

> censured for interring the celebrated actress Mrs. Oldfield in Westminster Abbey with almost the same pomp as Sir Isaac Newton. Some pretend that the English had paid her these great funeral honours, purposely to make us more strongly sensible of the barbarity and injustice which they object to in us, for having buried Mademoiselle [Adrienne] Le Couvreur ignominiously in the fields. [The great French actress Lecouvreur was refused the last rites on her death in 1730 and buried in unconsecrated ground near the Seine (the exact location is not known).]

Immediately to the point, we find Curll devoting one of his egregious lives to Oldfield in 1731. As an appendix, this contains not just the actress's will, but also that of her protector. About two months after the biography of Maynwaring, in August 1715, the bookseller issued the life and works of the Earl of Halifax, a Whig but a generous patron of Pope, who is thanked in the preface to the *Iliad*. This time the book probably came from the hand of William Pittis, a miscellaneous writer who did occasional jobs for Curll.

If the unfortunate victim were present now, he would probably find himself reminded of the old saying 'Talk of the Devil'.

EXHIBIT 4.8

While he was speaking these Words, Mr. *Oldmixon* enter'd. *Ah! Mr.* Oldmixon (said poor Mr. *Curll*) *to what a Condition have your Works reduced me! I die a Martyr to that unlucky Preface. However, in these my last Moments, I will be just to all Men; you shall have your Third Share of the* Court Poems, *as was stipulated. When I am dead, where will you find another Bookseller?* Your Protestant Packet *might have supported you, had you writ a little less scurrilously. There is a mean in all things.*

Then turning to Mr. *Pemberton*, he told him, he had several *Taking Title Pages* that only wanted Treatises to be wrote to them, and earnestly entreated, that when they were writ, his Heirs might have some Share of the Profit of them.[19]

As well as harking back to the disreputable arrangements for the *Court Poems*, this section arraigns the hapless Oldmixon, not for the last time. We do not know how often Curll published Oldmixon's pamphlets on topical affairs, since the latter generally wrote anonymously and on many occasions Curll was acting behind a front such as Roberts. In fact, it was Roberts who was named in the colophon of the *Protestant Packet*, as ephemeral a journal as you could find. It ran for just four weekly numbers in January and February 1716, disappearing as the threat of the Rising receded. What mattered most to Pope is that Oldmixon was the most vehement and unrelenting proponent of the Hanoverian cause.

We have now reached the climax of the story. The account parodies scenes preceding noble and exemplary deaths in hagiographic works.

EXHIBIT 4.9

After he had said this he fell into horrible Gripings, upon which Mr. *Lintott* advis'd him to repeat the Lord's Prayer. He desir'd his Wife to step into the Shop for a Common Prayer-Book, and read it by the Help of a Candle, without Hesitation. He clos'd the Book, fetch'd a Groan, and recommended to Mrs. *Curll* to give Forty Shillings to the Poor of the Parish of St. *Dunstan*'s, and a Week's Wages Advance to each of his Gentlemen Authors, with some small Gratuity in particular to Mrs. *Centlivre*.

The poor Man continued for some Hours with all his disconsolate Family about him in Tears, expecting his final Dissolution; when of a sudden he was surprizingly relieved by a plentiful fœtid Stool, which obliged them all to retire out of the Room. Notwithstanding, it is judged by Sir *Richard Blackmore*, that the Poyson is still latent in his Body, and will infallibly destroy him by slow Degrees, in less than a Month. It is to be hoped the other Enemies of this wretched Stationer, will not further pursue their Revenge, or shorten this small Period of his miserable Life.[20]

This passage serves again to give the events a local habitation and a name, for dozens of books from this epoch carried the imprint 'printed for E. Curll at the Dial and Bible over against St. Dunstan's Church in Fleet-street'. Then comes a bitchy reference to the writer Susanna Centlivre. Best known today for her amusing plays, she was also a devoted follower of the Whig regime, producing poems in praise of the royal family and members of the government. She had even got out an item for the fleeting pages of the *Protestant Packet*. Married from the parish of St Paul's, Covent Garden, in 1707, she later lived with her husband in Buckingham Court at the top of Whitehall. This was a handy location, for Joseph Centlivre was a cook in the royal household, based at St James's Palace. Pope knew where to find her, as we shall see. The 'poison', we may assume, was antimony potassium tartrate, used as a powerful emetic since the Middle Ages.

To appreciate the full literary effects of the *Full and True Account*, it is best to read the entire pamphlet. It shows Pope's skill in creating a dramatic narrative rooted in detailed observation. Even the selections presented in abridged form here should be enough to illustrate its scabrous invention. As for its place within the quarrel, Curll would be certain from this moment exactly what he was taking on, whenever he entered into combat with this formidable antagonist.

CURLL FIGHTS BACK

In some ways, the *Account* backfired for Pope. Certainly, this riotously funny piece gave a damaging exposé of Curll's publishing methods, with abundant evidence from his current output. But one thing it did was to prompt retaliation. Like a cornered animal, the bookseller grew more aggressive. This was a lesson Pope had to learn more than once over the years.

The response came swiftly. We tend to think that this is possible only in the modern world of 24/7 communications and instant access to the news. But already in the early 1700s things were on the move. By the time of Pope's death, considerable improvements had been made to the Post Office, even on a national level, with better-organized mail services on the byways that reached most corners of the land. Some of these innovations were brought in by the poet's friend Ralph Allen, businessman and philanthropist of Bath. The growing volume of newspaper outlets followed these tracks. As for London, it had its own penny post scheme, which had been launched in 1680. According to the fulsome report of Daniel Defoe, forty-odd years later, 'it is come . . . into so exquisite a Management, that nothing can be more exact, and 'tis with the utmost Safety and Dispatch, that Letters are delivered at the remotest Corners of the Town, almost as soon as they could be sent by a Messenger, and that from Four, Five, Six, to Eight Times a Day . . . and you may send a Letter from *Ratcliff* or *Limehouse* in the *East*, to the farthest Part of *Westminster* for a Penny, and that several Times in the same Day.'[21] Present-day Londoners awaiting a traffic-delayed courier might envy the speed with which mail was delivered three hundred years ago.

Just days later, the Curllian side got in their first retort. It came in the shape of a notice in the Whig organ, the *Flying Post*, and was signed by Oldmixon, a regular contributor to the paper.[22]

EXHIBIT 4.10

Whereas Mr. *Lintot*, or Mr. *Pope*, has publish'd a false and ridiculous Libel, reflecting on several Gentlemen, particularly on myself, and it is said therein, that I was the Publisher of certain Verses call'd *Court Poems*, and that I wrote the Preface; I hereby declare, that I never saw a great part of those Verses, nor ever saw or heard of the Title or Preface to them till after the Poems were publish'd.

Witness, E. Curll.

J. Oldmixon.

The problem with this is that it conflicts with what Curll later said about the affair, when he clearly indicated that Oldmixon served as the 'Publisher', that is editor, of the volume. As we have seen, Curll stated in 1735 that the pieces were given by the Dissenter Joseph Jacob to Oldmixon, who passed them on to Roberts for publication. Curll also declared once more that he, Pemberton and Oldmixon took shares in the venture.

After just four more days Pope's adversary landed a further blow, and it was one of his keenest. On 7 April an advertisement in the *Flying Post* announced the publication of the second volume of Pope's Homer, the one that Lintot had issued on 22 March. It served two purposes: first, to bring in buyers to Curll's shop to acquire their copy of this much-heralded work, and second, to poke fun at the pretensions of the grandiose translation.

EXHIBIT 4.11

This Day is Publish'd,

The Second Part of Mr. *Pope*'s *Popish* Translation of Homer. The Subscribers having made great Complaint that there were no Pictures in the First Part: This is, to give Notice, that to this Second Part there is added a spacious MAP of the *Trojan* Tents and Rivers, finely delineated. Translated into *Copper* from the Wooden Original, as you have it in the Learned Dr. Fuller's *Pisgah Sight*; being the True Travels of Moses and the Children of *Israel*, from the Land of Goshen to the Land of Canaan. With an exact Scale. Sold by E. Curll, at the Dial and Bible against St Dunstan's Church in Fleet-street. Where may be had Mr. Pope's Court Poems, price 6d. * *N.B.* Mr. Pope has translated one Verse of *Homer* thus:

The Priest *can pardon, and the God appease.*

☞ Next Week will be publish'd, An Excellent New Ballad, call'd *The Catholick Poet*, or Protestant *Barnaby's Lamentation*. To the Tune of, *Which no body can deny.*

Tho of his Wit the Catholick has boasted,

Lintot and *Pope* by turns shall be roasted.[23]

This is a masterpiece among Curll's many inventive strokes of publicity. What immediately catches the eye is the bold description of the 'Popish' translation. The advertisement next draws attention to the disappointment of subscribers over the lack of pictures, a feeling not otherwise documented. Then comes an absurd passage indicating that a map found in the second volume had been lifted from Thomas Fuller's *A Pisgah-Sight of Palestine* (1650). In fact, two maps were specially engraved for the edition by the leading cartographer John Senex, at this time trading near the east end of Fleet Street, but later to move his business to 'the

Globe, over-against St Dunstan's Church, in Fleetstreet'. One map depicted Homeric Greece and Asia Minor, and the other the plains of Troy. We know that Pope took a close interest in their preparation, and even instructed the engraver on modifications that needed to be made to previous maps. In that biblically literate age, readers would be expected to have some familiarity with the Land of Goshen, from which the Israelites set out on their exodus to Canaan.

There is more to follow. First, a plug for *Court Poems*, the item that triggered everything that had subsequently happened. Then what must be a deliberate misquotation from the *Iliad* translation (Book 1, Line 116), where the text has 'the God may spare'. The obvious intention is to sneer at the quasi-divine power the Catholic religion bestows on its priests. After this comes what is meant to be a succulent treat in store, with an unflinching attack on the nation's most admired author in the form of a popular ballad, and a sub-title implicating Lintot, the fortunate member of the trade who had been able to snare Pope into signing up – although in the end the bookseller did not do as well from his deal over the *Iliad* as he might have hoped. We shall get to *The Catholick Poet* shortly. Last, but by no means least, an early example of one of Curll's favourite devices in combat with his enemy: a snappy two-liner in verse.

A MOST RIDICULOUS QUARREL

Not content with this attempt at a crushing démarche, the ever-resourceful publisher was back in the very next issue of the *Flying Post*, on 10 April. His increasing confidence is shown in the invitation for others to join his campaign.

EXHIBIT 4.12

To prevent any farther Imposition on the Publick, there is now preparing for the Press by several Hands,

HOMER defended: Being a Detection of the many Errors committed by Mr. Pope, in his pretended Translation of Homer, wherein is fully prov'd that he neither understands the Original, nor the Author's Meaning, and that in several Places he has falsified it on Purpose. To which is added, a Specimen of a Translation of the first Book of the Odysses, which has lain printed by Mr. Lintott for some Time, and which he intends to publish, in Order to prejudice Mr. Tickell's excellent Version. Any Gentlemen who have made Observations upon Mr. Pope's Homer, and will be pleas'd to send them to Mr. Curl, at the Dial and Bible against St Dunstan's Church in Fleet-street, shall have them faithfully inserted in his Work.

Much of this was pure invention. *Homer Defended* never appeared, although, as George Sherburn pointed out, it could be held *in terrorem* over the poet.[24] The purported version of the *Odyssey* was, and remained for almost a decade, nothing more than fantasy; and by the time the poet got around to the task, Tickell had renounced his feeble aspirations to shine in epic. For a time the Buttonians kept up their campaign in his support, but on the respective poetic abilities of the rival translators, reality finally sank in. Nevertheless, as we should anticipate from the products of Curll's shop, this is a rhetorically effective piece of advertising copy. Pope seemed cocky enough about the episode when he wrote to John Caryll on 20 April:

> Item, a most ridiculous quarrel with a bookseller, occasioned
> by his having printed some satirical pieces on the Court under
> my name. I contrived to save a fellow a beating by giving him
> a vomit, the history whereof has been transmitted to posterity
> by a late Grub-street author. I suppose Lewis [Erasmus Lewis,
> also a friend of Swift] has sent you the Pamphlet which has
> much entertained the town.[25]

For all his swagger, Pope too must have realized by now – if he did not know before – that he was dealing with an opponent of the highest calibre in the art of public relations.

VILEST WORMS

Curll's next enterprise is a bit of a puzzle. It may have been meant to draw more fire from the Buttonians, who lately had not been as active in their feud with the poet as the publisher would have liked. Most likely Pope himself leaked to Curll his ballad generally called *The Worms*, a short but virtuoso performance that plays around sayings and ideas associated with various species of the creature. Curll issued it at a price of twopence on 1 May under the title, 'To the Ingenious Mr. Moore, Author of the Celebrated Worm-Powder'. His notice in the press clearly labels Pope as the author. The title refers to John Moore, proprietor of a worming remedy sold from his base in Abchurch Lane in the City, and one of the quacks whom the Scriblerians delighted in mocking. His advertisements for his worming powder – to be used on humans, not animals – appeared in the press even more often than those for Curll's output.

The opening four quatrains set the tone:

EXHIBIT 4.13

How much, egregious *Moore*! are we
Deceiv'd by shows and forms!
Whate'er we think, whate'er we see,
All humankind are Worms.
Man is a very Worm by birth,
Vile reptile, weak, and vain!
A while he crawls upon the earth,
Then shrinks to earth again.
That woman is a Worm we find,
E'er since our Grandam's evil:

She first convers'd with her own kind,
 That ancient Worm, the Devil.
But whether Man, or He, God knows,
 Fæcundified her Belly,
With that pure Stuff from whence we rose,
 The Genial *Vermicelli*.[26]

'Genial' here means having generative power or seminal, but it also suggests enlivening or inspiring.

 Among several characteristic examples of wordplay that Pope uses in his ballads, one striking reference to the scriptures has been overlooked by editors: 'Ah *Moore*! Thy Skill were well employ'd / And greater Gain would rise, / If thou could'st make the Courtier void / The Worm that never dies!' This alludes to the Gospel of Mark 9:44 (repeated in verses 46 and 48), which reads in the King James version: 'Where their worm dieth not, and the fire is not quenched.' It was sometimes translated as 'never dies', because the Greek original has the particle οὐ, which can mean either 'not' or 'never'. The quotation looks back to Isaiah 66:24, 'for their worm shall not die'. Both passages refer to the corpses of unregenerate men who have turned their back on God. In other words, the fate of courtiers for their wrongdoing will be eternal torment.

 Another recollection of the Bible is that of Job 25:6: 'How much less man, that is a worm? and the son of man, which is a worm?' (in later translations, 'maggot' is substituted). The story of Job would be central to one of Pope's greatest works, the *Epistle to Bathurst* (1733). And, although Pope's critics don't seem to have fully recognized it, there is a blasphemous undertow to the entire poem: the second and third quatrains burlesque aspects of the story of Adam and Eve in Genesis 2:7, and 3:14–19, seen partially through John Milton's treatment of 'the false Worm' in *Paradise Lost*, Book 9. We may also hear the solemn incantation of 'dust to dust' in the Christian burial service. A typical salvo concludes the brilliant artillery display: 'Ev'n *Button*'s Wits to Worms shall turn, / Who Maggots were before.'[27] In this period a maggot was a whimsical or capricious person, given to strange habits or pursuits. But the root sense is present, too. The wits will revert to their previous state as larvae generated by flies buzzing around decaying bodies. They will always be agents of corruption.

The work occupied two sides of a broadsheet, with the colophon once more advertising the *Court Poems* and adding a note, 'N.B. Speedily will be Publish'd, some more of Mr. Pope's Pieces, and all his Writings for the Future, except Homer, will be Printed for E. Curll.' As far as the Homer is concerned, we might find it hard to tell, in James Thurber's words, whether he is boasting or complaining. Other versions quickly appeared in the press, and a 'second edition' was called for on 5 May – most probably this was just a reimpression with a new title page. This time Curll inserted in the advertisement a request: 'Mr. Curll hereby gives Notice, that he received a Letter on Wednesday last, sign'd Peter Pencil; If the said Peter will send Word how a Letter may be directed to him, he shall receive a satisfactory Answer to his Epistle.'[28] Was the name Peter simply a disguise for Pope, and what did the missive contain? We shall never know. At all events, *The Worms*, the name by which it generally goes, proved the most frequently reproduced poem in its author's own lifetime. It was a godsend to Curll, who printed it himself in at least eight separate collections. Not much profit was to be had on twopenny broadsides, even if they sold well; but there was money to be made from larger miscellanies.

One such publication hit the bookstalls on 19 May. It bore the unrevealing title *State Poems*, and its imprint names Roberts while adding a puff for *Court Poems*. As with many Curll items, the contents vary slightly from copy to copy. However, the core of the slim volume consists of a series of strongly Whiggish effusions, provided by such stalwarts as Nicholas Rowe, George Sewell (a physician and lapsed Tory who had switched sides after supplying

Curll with pamphlets in earlier years) and Susanna Centlivre, two of whose poems were reprinted in abbreviated form. The heroes of the collection are Walpole, lately recovered from a serious illness, his brother-in-law Lord Townshend, and James Stanhope, soldier turned statesman. Even an ardent Hanoverian might find some of the eulogistic language a bit much.

After wading through such unbroken signalling of political virtue, some purchasers of the volume must have found it a relief that the two last components are less high-minded. One is an epilogue to Addison's comedy *The Drummer*, which had been premiered at Drury Lane on 10 March. Despite the support of Button's faction, and the attendance of the Prince of Wales with Whig notables, it lasted just a week with three performances, never to reach the stage again during the author's lifetime. The unused epilogue centres on a meteor (technically an aurora) that had recently excited the nation after its appearance on 6 March, but also includes dismissive references to both Pope and the Pretender. The concluding item in the volume turns out to be our old friend 'The Worms, by Mr. Pope'. Nobody who has the slightest familiarity with Curll's methods will be surprised that this entire ragbag was transferred in whole or part as a makeweight to several later miscellanies. As long as he could find these more salacious products of the great man's pen, he was happy. As Paul Baines has said, the intent of publishing Pope's bawdier tavern pieces lay 'in an effort to discredit his "classic" pose'.[29]

Later in the month Curll was given something of his own medicine. It came in a twopenny broadside ballad issued by the obscure E. Smith, probably a woman named Elizabeth who sometimes worked with her fellow 'mercury' Anne Dodd in circulating the flood of newspapers round the city. The title is garbled, because the first word needs an 's' after the apostrophe – unless a pun on 'More Worms' is intended – but the drift is clear enough. A section of some of the best stanzas will illustrate the point:

EXHIBIT 4.14

Moore' Worms for the learned Mr. Curll, Bookseller; who, to be reveng'd on Mr. Pope for his poisonous Emetick, gave him a Paper of Worm-Powder, which caused that Gentleman to void a strange sort of Worms.

> Oh Learned Curll! thy Skill excells
>   Ev'n *Moore's* of *Abchurch-Lane* –
> He only *Genuine Worms* expells,
>   To crawl in Print for Gain.
> From a Wit's Brain Thou mak'st Worms rise,
>   (Unknown in the *Worm-Evil*)
> Fops, Silkworms, Beaus, and Butterflies,
>   With that old Worm the *Devil*.
> Ev'n *Button's Book-Worms* shall, with these,
>   (Like these with Dust decay'd)
> In *Grub-Street Rubbish* rest in Peace,
>   Till *Curlls* their peace invade.
> For Booksellers vile Vipers are,
>   On Brains of *Wits* they prey;
> The very *Worms* they will not spare,
>   When *Wits* to *Worms* decay ...
> From *Worms Erect* proud *Coquettes* arose;
>   Yet are but Baits for *Gudgeons*.
> The Rake a stingless Drone soon grows;
>   And Grub-Worms, Old Curmudgeons ...
> Ah *Curll*! how greedy hast thou fed
>   (E'er *Worms* gave Food to thee)
> Upon the late Illustrious *Dead*,
>   With Worms of thy Degree.
> For see! thy meagre Looks declare,
>   Some Poison in thee Lurks.

Let *Blackmore* ease thy restless Care –
Or who shall print his *Works?*[30]

Readers might know the use of 'worm', as in Dante's *Inferno*, to mean the serpent in the Garden of Eden. But who wrote this cleverly chosen series of wormy analogues? The strongest candidates must be either Pope or his associates. The key idea is that Curll caused Pope to produce a 'strange sort of worms', that is, the poem of that name. Much of the new poem parodies or restates material from the first, as in the line about fops, silkworms, beaus and butterflies, which derives wholly from the fifth stanza of the lines addressed 'To the Ingenious Mr. Moore'. But even if the latest contribution to the exchange came from an outside source, with no connection to the Scriblerian group, it does far more damage to Curll than to Pope, with allusions to the *Court Poems* and the bookseller's penchant for 'printing the lives and last wills of great men' cruelly highlighted in some marginal notes.

This was the situation as the year moved into the summer months. Pope had scored heavily with his *Account*, doing great damage with his revelations about the publisher's methods. But Curll had come back strongly thanks to his incisive wit and sheer chutzpah. For what remained of 1716, the contest would be no less keenly fought.

5

HORRID Wars, 1716

U nluckily for Curll, he had now become embroiled in another scandal of his own making. It had no relation to his ongoing feud with Pope, but it did happen to concern the same trial of Lord Winton that had cropped up in the preface to *Court Poems*. Soon after proceedings were over, Jacob Tonson, doyen of the book trade, announced that he was to produce the official record of what had taken place in Westminster Hall. Sure enough, an elaborate account running to seventy pages in large folio format appeared on 14 April. Curll always resented the hold on power that Tonson had acquired as a sort of *ex officio* publisher to the great and the good. On this occasion his valour outmatched his discretion, resulting in one of the first among many brushes with the law.

Some complex events ensued.[1] On 10 April the bookseller Sarah Popping advertised a scaled-down version of the trial proceedings. It amounted to just six pages and cost twopence. In an attempt to escape the rigours of the Copyright Act, it was claimed that the source was a French version printed in Amsterdam. Only two copies are known to survive, one in the House of Lords archives and one at Eton College, and the work was not described until 2007. As we should expect, the tone and tenor are strongly pro-Hanoverian. The pamphlet mentions Winton's apparently eccentric behaviour in court, suggesting that he was merely pretending to be non compos mentis.

The really interesting part of the story begins when the Lords lodged a complaint for breach of privilege. Popping was arrested on 13 April and summoned to appear before the peers the next day. She claimed through her sister that responsibility lay not with her but with Curll and John Pemberton, who had arranged for publication of the pamphlet. In this she was probably telling the truth. Evidence presented shows that Curll had asked her to pay £3 2s. 6d. to a journalist named Stephen Whatley on the account of – we might have guessed – 'Mr. Oldmixon'. The Lords duly ordered Curll and Pemberton to be taken into custody by Black Rod.

Events continued to move at a fast pace. Popping sent a petition to the Lords three days later, in which she protested her innocence. Soon afterwards she was brought back with her two colleagues under arrest. After questioning her, the House resolved that 'Ye sd Curle was only concerned in printing ye same and yt [that] ye said Popping was only ye publisher.' Translated into modern terms, this means that Curll was the sole publisher and Popping merely the distributor. Popping and Pemberton were now released, while Curll was joined in custody by the printer, Daniel Bridge. After a full examination, these two were once more committed to the charge of Black Rod. They then submitted a petition for leniency, and after undergoing a reprimand from the Lord Chancellor while kneeling at the bar of the House they were finally released on 11 May. Remarkably, Curll's business kept spewing out its usual torrent of pamphlets and advertisements while all this was going on.

Two documents that remained unpublished until the twenty-first century enable us to fill out the story. The first is a characteristic piece of servile Curllian language, as he petitions his captors on 3 May:

EXHIBIT 5.1

To the Right Honble, The Lords Spiritual and Temporal in Parliament Assembled.

Humbly Sheweth,

That your Petitioners are in the Custody of the Black Rod, by Order from your Lordships, For Printing and Publishing a Paper intitul'd, An Account of the Tryal of the Earl of Winton, which your Petitioners are now sensible, is contrary to a Standing Order of this most Honourable House.

That your Petitioners not knowing there was any such Order, did inadvertently cause the same to be printed and have thereby justly incurr'd your Lordships displeasure.

Your Petitioners for their Offence are heartily Sorry, and for the future do Promise to be more Circumspect, and resolve never again to offend your Lordships: and in regard your Petitioners have Families, which must inevitably be Ruin'd, unless your Lordships have Compassion on them, They humbly Beg that your Lordships will be pleas'd to Order them to be discharg'd from their Confinement.

And your Petitioners as in Duty bound shall Ever Pray. Edmund Curll Daniel Bridge.

The other document, surviving among the Cowper family papers, is a letter dated 17 April from John Oldmixon to the Lord High Steward, Lord Cowper, who had presided at the trial of the rebel lords.[2] Its tone is marginally less obsequious, although the writer does apologize for having incurred official displeasure, while explaining that he was 'entirely Ignorant' of the nature of the offence he had committed. He admits that he recommended the work to Curll and Pemberton, and sets out in his usual voluble style the manner in which he was misled into the error. A key passage is this: 'Mr. Pemberton has been my Bookseller & both he & Mr. Curl have printed above a Hundred Greater & Smaller Tracts for Me in the worst of Times & Since in Defence of the Revolution & Protestant Succession. In these I have always been concern'd both as to the Profit & Loss.' Here 'The worst of Times' means the years of the Oxford administration, 1710–14. Whether Oldmixon was exaggerating when he specified a hundred tracts, we don't know, but if so it cannot have been by very much. In a later account he would repeat that he was put to great 'Vexation and Expence' for suggesting that the account should be translated from the *Leyden Gazette*, with the significant addition of a barb directed at Tonson: 'I know very well that the Complaint came from a certain Bookseller, purely out of Apprehension that this Extract would prejudice his Market for the printed Trial.'[3] That bit is probably also true.

This episode has no direct bearing on Pope. However, it is highly relevant to the wider themes of this book. It illustrates the kind of risk Curll took, and his behaviour when caught. It demonstrates how closely public information continued to be regulated. It supplies a good instance of the bookseller's habitual practice, whereby Popping was the only named individual both in the imprint and in advertisements. It shows that Curll was slow to learn, since he was hauled before the Lords in another matter affecting breach of privilege, just four years later. It reveals the bad blood that could exist between operators at the top of the trade, such as Tonson, and those in a lower echelon, such as Curll. It exemplifies the huge range of Oldmixon's work on behalf of either Curll or Pemberton, or, as in this case, both.

A READY WRITER

We need to talk about Oldmixon, clearly. At the start of the quarrel, he was probably Curll's most important foot soldier.[4] He hailed from an old Somerset family, and as a boy in 1685 he had witnessed the Duke of Monmouth arrive in Bridgwater on the eve of the Battle of Sedgemoor, the last major battle on English soil. He moved to London when a young man, probably to work in the family business run by his uncle, a West Indies merchant. His ambitions originally lay in poetry and drama. Around the change of ministry in 1710 he was recruited by Arthur Maynwaring to write on behalf of the Whigs, and in particular the Duke of Marlborough, then under fire from the Tories. Together with Maynwaring, he opposed Jonathan Swift's paper *The Examiner* with his own vehement rhetoric. From this date on he made himself a constant thorn in the side of Oxford, Bolingbroke, Francis Atterbury and their allies, and in subsequent years he became known for his voluminous and violently Whig works on English history. At the same time, he was the strongest and most persistent critic of the political writings of Daniel Defoe.

In his own day Oldmixon was most widely known as a fearless propagandist for the Hanoverian monarchy and a bitter opponent of the Jacobite movement. Over a stretch of about eight years he wrote at least thirty pamphlets issued under the name of James Roberts, or the bookseller's mother-in-law Anne Baldwin. His first known work on behalf of Curll came in 1709, and although he felt he had been cheated over a translation of Nicolas Boileau-Despreaux, the pair were reconciled by 1712. Soon he had established himself as a key figure in the bookseller's corps of authors, something that Pope picked up on. One of Oldmixon's specialities was backstairs politics, exemplified by his *Secret History of Europe* in four volumes, *Arcana Gallica*, and the allegorical *Court of Atalantis*. A quick study, he wrote for journals such as the *Flying Post*.

Whenever Curll's new agenda required attacks on Pope, Oldmixon possessed the best credentials of anyone, having found many ways of badmouthing Oxford's principal authors.[5] Sometimes he did so in tandem: 'Here they are both coupled together, Foe [Defoe] and Swift, Fellow Labourers in the Service of the White Staff [Oxford, the Lord Treasurer], who however paid Foe better than he did Swift, looking on him as the shrewder Head of the two for Business.' More often he did it singly, however. Defoe, 'the bankrupt Hosier, and Apostasiz'd Independent [Congregationalist] and Republican', wrote 'against the Conviction of his own little Reason and large Conscience, to serve the Quondam Treasurer'; 'the most ignorant Rogue . . . that ever Scribled'; and who 'tack'd *de* to his Name, after he had stood in the Pillory . . . which he richly deserv'd afterwards, when he scribbled for the People that put him there [the Tories]'. Swift was described as 'that pious Divine, who had burlesqued all Religion, in his *Tale of a Tub*'; as one who 'prostituted his Pen' in the service of Oxford; as a libeller and a 'Hedge-Writer'; and as one who 'would, for a Pension, have written as much Falshood and Scandal against the new Ministers, as he did afterwards against the Old, if there had been Occasion for it'. Year after year, in pamphlet after pamphlet, the barrage went on. Not all these items came from Curll's press, but they indicate the kind of thing Oldmixon could do by way of assailing reputations.

Even after the Hanoverian accession, when Swift and Defoe lost most of their political influence, there was no let-up. Oldmixon's life of Maynwaring, mentioned by Pope in his *Account*, batters Swift without mercy, as does a biography of Lord Wharton, while he and Defoe are contemptuously linked once more in *Memoirs of Ireland* (1716). Can anyone doubt that the treatment doled out to the Tories led Curll to enlist Oldmixon in his campaign? Moreover, if Pope had any idea who wrote some of the items pouring abuse on his associates among the Tory party – and the *Account* shows that he kept his ear very close to the ground – we must expect that to feed into his hostility towards Curll's team. Self-evidently, Pope was not good at forgiving and forgetting. Storing up resentment for decades, he waited until he was ready to strike back at his assailant, naming him in *The Dunciad* 'that ready writer Mr. Oldmixon' and giving him an undignified role in the action.[6]

THE POPE-ISH CONTROVERSY

It was at this precise juncture, soon after Curll's release from custody, that he published the most effective of Oldmixon's satires on Pope, and one of the best that emerged during the feud. The bookseller had enough on his hands; his general list continued to grow, and the French *Cato* made its belated appearance on 23 May. Yet it's obvious that – for the time being, at least – it was the campaign to discredit Pope that engrossed his attention.

On the last day of the month came notice in the *Flying Post* of two new items. The first was *The Catholick Poet*, which, as we have seen, had been preannounced almost eight weeks earlier.

EXHIBIT 5.2

For the Diversion of the Town, this Day is publish'd, Two Pamphlets, I THE Catholick Poet; or Protestant Barnaby's Sorrowful Lamentation, an excellent new Ballad. To the Tune of, *Which no Body can deny*. Price 3d.

2 A True Character of Mr. Pope, and his Writings. In a Letter to a Friend, Price 3d.

A Lump Deform'd and Shapeless was he Born;
Begot in Love's Despight, and Nature's Scorn. – Roch[ester].
Aw'd by no Shame, by no Respect controul'd,
In Scandal *busy, in* Reproaches *bold:*
Spleen *to* Mankind *his envious Heart possess'd,*
And much he hated All, but most the Best. – Homer, Book 2.

Sold at the News Shops, and by all the Booksellers in England, Dominion of Wales, and Town of Berwick upon Tweed. Where may be had the WORMS, a Satyr, by Mr. Pope, price 2d. *N.B.* These Town Diversions will be continued Weekly, so long as the Pope-*ish* Controversy is on foot.

It will be immediately obvious that Curll's name is nowhere apparent. The list of anonymous sellers parodies the legal form in which the confines of England and Wales were stated. As well as the plug for *Court Poems*, we note the way that the 'disreputable' Restoration poet Lord Rochester, frequently reprinted in Curll's editions, is brought in as a guarantor of Pope's status. What wouldn't be so clear is that the four verses from the *Iliad* are actually two couplets from Pope's translation, separated by eight lines. The big point is that the passage describes Thersites, the crippled, abusive and low-born officer in the Greek army, who is killed by Achilles with a single blow. (He will be recalled as a colourful character in Shakespeare's *Troilus and Cressida*.) This was not the only time a parallel was drawn between Thersites and Pope in terms of deformity, scurrility and cowardice. Anyone who wished to argue that Curll had given Pope abundant provocation during the quarrel could plausibly introduce this advertisement into evidence.

When the six-page folio reached the public, its colophon gave a different source. It was stated to be 'printed for J. Morphew, J. Roberts, R. Burleigh, J. Baker, and S. Popping', and sold by the booksellers as before. John Morphew is an unlikely name here, because he distributed Tory pamphlets, including many by Swift. But all the others regularly issued material on the Whig side. Roberts, Rebecca Burleigh and the unfortunate Popping we have already met, while John Baker's imprint is habitually found in pamphlets by Defoe at this period. On 30 June the only name in a press advertisement is that of Burleigh, who may have done most of the dirty work for Curll. But no one has ever doubted the identity of the *éminence grise* behind the undertaking. The title is included in a large catalogue of his publications that Curll sent out near the end of the year. And long afterwards he was able to correct Pope's belief that Susanna Centlivre had written the ballad, and point to Oldmixon as the true author.

The verses are followed by four pages devoted to Bernard Lintot's supposed petition imploring mercy for all his wrongdoings. Although often discussed, the ballad seems never to have been reprinted, except in an expensive collection of Popiana some years ago, so it is worth quoting it in full to give a flavour of what Pope was up against.[7]

EXHIBIT 5.3

My Song is of *SAWNY*, The Poet of *Windsor*,
Whose *HOMER* will sell, when the *Devil is blind, Sir;*
And the *Hump* is before him, that now is *behind*, Sir;
    Which no Body can deny.
His *Muse* fed with Sack: Growing warmer, and warmer,
He *Ravish'd a Lock* from the pretty *Bell. Fermor,*
And thought with vile *Smut* to have charmed, the *Charmer;*
    Which, &c.
On the Stage *Collier* fell, long ago, and did maul it;
He cares not for that, he's more Bawdy than all yet,
Ev'n *Horner* Would blush at his Lewd *What d'ye call it;*
    Which, &c.
This Papist, this Atheist, this *FIGURE*, this Writer,
Feels his Purse to grow heavier, as *Lintott's* grows lighter;
Ah *Barnaby Bernard* Thou'rt *Bit*, tho' a *Biter;*
    Which, &c.
When he has undone thee, his Muse will be jaded,
And grinning he'll cry, thou hast traded, and traded,
But never did'st know what was *Greek* for a *Spade* yet;
    Which, &c.
From *Learned* and *Simple*, from Goers and Comers,
From *Oxford*, and *Cambridge*, from *Rome* and St *Omers*,
A Thousand Subscriptions I got for my *HOMERS;*
    Which, &c.
Quoth *Lintot*, G—d Z—ds, tho' you bully and vapour,
I value your *Pen*, Sir, no more than your Rapier;
What a Plague are your *HOMERS* to me but waste Paper?
    Which, &c.
'Tis a Lye by the Mass, cries the *Catholick* Poet,
To the Wall I will stick thee, – Quo' *Bernard*, aye do it;

I'm a *Protestant*, Z—ds, and I'll make you to know it;
   Which, &c.
Dear Bubble, the Poet reply'd, with some Kisses,
As dull, and as heavy a Bargain as this is;
You may thank me, I think, that I left the *Odysses*;
   Which, &c.
A Pox of your *Picture*, cries *Barnaby Bernard*,
Who the De'el would ha' Dealings with those they call
   Leamed,
'Tis eating one's Pudding before one has earn'd it,
   Which, &c.
Nay, prithee says *Sawny*, don't mutter and mumble;
Thou'lt ne'er get a Groat, if thou always dost grumble,
Come, pay, and Print on, and I'll be thy *most humble*;
   Which, &c.
I'm a Dog if I do, reply'd he, let me tell ye,
As bad as my Nose is, by G— I can smell ye;
Tho' I have no *Pope*, you've a *Chap* in your Belly;
   Which, &c.
Quoth *Sawny*, I'll burn my next Book, by St. *Peter*;
Quoth *Bernard*, I care not, G—d D—m yet, your *Metre*
Will make any Mortal a *Minter* or *Fleeter*;
   Which, &c.

I have left out some amusing footnotes, such as 'Mr. *Pope*'s Breakfast is Sop and Sack', but can't resist including the final jibe: 'Note, The Reader is desir'd to excuse the Swearing in this Ballad, without which, Mr. *Lintott*'s Character had been misrepresented, it being, as Mr. *Pope* has observ'd, his Essential Qualification.' This feature of the bookseller's speech is confirmed in a letter Pope wrote to Lord Burlington in 1716, although this account was not published for almost twenty years.[8] Oldmixon's source is the *Account*, to which the ballad makes sly allusion. Since he had been writing occasionally for Lintot in recent years, he ought to have known what he was talking about.

To be candid, the whole exercise rises far above Oldmixon's usual standard of name-calling. Its brilliance derives in large measure from the way it exploits the kind of device that Pope always used in his own ballads. There is snappy literary allusion to sources such as Jeremy Collier's notorious attacks on the immorality of the stage; and the lascivious behaviour of Horner, hero of *The Country Wife*, the best-known play by Pope's friend William Wycherley. There is precise observation of Pope's works other than the Homer, including *The Rape of the Lock* and its heroine, based on 'pretty Bell. Fermor', as well as *Windsor Forest*, and *The What D'ye Call It*, described as 'a ridiculous Farce, with Mr. *Gay*'s Name to it'. There is clever adaptation of proverbs and stock phrases, a favourite recourse of the Scriblerians in their demotic verse. This begins in the second line, which draws on the old saying 'That will come when the devil is blind' (meaning never), found in Swift's anthology of cliché named *Polite Conversation* (1738). The seventh stanza clearly glances at 'the pen is mightier than the sword' (but not in Pope's case, Lintot suggests). Some jokes need a bit of explanation today; the word 'figure' is used in a contemporary sense of someone cutting a ridiculous figure, a 'sight'. We have already come across the opprobrious reference to Rome, in other words the Catholic Church, and St Omers, the hothouse of Jesuit education. To vapour is to bluster. To stick to the wall is to drive someone to the last extremity. A bubble here is a dupe. The last stanza refers to debtors obliged to flee their creditors in the sanctuary of the Mint in Southwark, or else be incarcerated in the Fleet gaol.

Even though the focus is on Pope, Lintot does not emerge unscathed. Now aged forty, he had been apprenticed in the 1690s and became free of the Stationers' Company just before the turn of the century. At first he specialized in drama, but he really came to the fore around 1712 with miscellanies such as the one that introduced

The Rape of the Lock to the world in its earliest guise. He sometimes shared imprints with Curll, not surprisingly, since at the time he conducted business 'between the Temple gates', only a very short distance down Fleet Street from his colleague's shop. It is true that the *Iliad* did not make him as much of a fortune as he had hoped; the subscription money went to Pope, and his own trade edition suffered because of a pirated edition emanating from The Hague – this was probably the version that Curll advertised and sold. Lintot did not suffer unduly from his association with the poet; he ended up one of the most eminent members of the trade, while his son and successor did better still, marrying the daughter of a baronet and rising to the upper gentry as High Sheriff of Sussex. Still, Pope could not forbear ribbing his bookseller, with short poems such as 'Verses to be prefix'd before Bernard Lintot's New Miscellany', which predicts that his volumes will become waste paper in a particular sense: the final couplet runs, '*Lintot*'s for gen'ral Use are fit; / For some Folks read, but all Folks shit.'[9] Later he would play a starring role as Curll's rival during the stationers' fun and games featured in Book 2 of *The Dunciad*. He must have been a tolerant soul, because, unlike his fellow competitor, he avoided a lasting quarrel with Pope.

The prose section of the pamphlet follows. It opens in the mock-formal style of a petition, and it begins by asserting Lintot's standing in the trade:

EXHIBIT 5.4

To all Gentlemen, Authors, Translators, or Translating Poets, who are Protestants, and well affected to the present Establishment in the most Illustrious House of Hanover.

The humble Petition of Barnaby Bernard Lintott, *Living at the Sign of the* Cross-Keys *between the Two Temple-Gates in* Fleet-street, SHEWETH,

THAT your Petitioner having ever behav'd himself with great Industry in his Lawful Vocation, he thereby hopeth that all Bright

Gentlemen will now and then make him an Offer of their Productions, especially if they are *Humorous* for which he will give
them their own Price, rather than any other Bookseller shall Print
for them.[10]

Lintot's shop sign, the Cross Keys, was common enough on the
streets of London, but it sends ambiguous signals here, since this
was the emblem of the papacy, deriving from St Peter's keys.
Inevitably, *The Dunciad* picks up on that detail.

A rapid survey of the bookseller's career culminates in the suggestion that he was able to put in such a large bid for Pope's Homer
owing to a generous reward he had received for bribing voters in an
election for Sussex (his home county). Unfortunately, the deal went
sour, so that, having been 'in a fair Way of thriving by a *Protestant*
Parliament', as official printer of the votes at Westminster, he must
now 'inevitably be ruin'd by a *Papist* Poet'.

EXHIBIT 5.5

When he began this Work, he told your *Petitioner* he should have
great helps, and the Design indeed seem'd prosperous by the *Wits*
of the Town declaring in his Favour; but this true *Catholick*, after he
had got a Number of Subscriptions, by the Recomendation of our
Protestant Authors, who are Men of Honour; he immediately betray'd all their private Conversation to the Late Ministry, and at the
same time wrote GUARDIANS and EXAMINERS, for which Reasons these
Gentlemen have very justly forsaken him, and all the Books lye upon
my Hands.[11]

There is not a shred of evidence to support this charge. Pope did
write for Richard Steele's paper *The Guardian* in 1713, but always
on literary themes, not political. He had no connection with *The
Examiner*, a Tory journal once conducted by Swift. Behind this
paragraph there lies the split with Addison and Steele, which had

become an almost total rupture following the squabble over rival Homer translations in 1715.

The petition now rehearses a familiar charge, that 'Mr. *Pope* does not understand *Greek* thoroughly.' Some minor errors in the translation are highlighted, at least one spotted by Lintot's small son, whom he 'hath taken care to make . . . a Scholar'. As a postscript we find a reprint of Pope's verses to be prefixed to Lintot's miscellany (see p. 134 above). According to the pamphlet, 'your Petitioner took the Complement so kindly, that he was resolv'd upon any Terms to be Mr. *Pope*'s Bookseller.'[12] Of course, the feelings attributed to Lintot here, either positive or negative, are wholly invented. Principally Curll wanted to get at Pope; but he enjoyed stirring up dissention among the literary community, not least the 'Gentlemen, Authors, Translators, or Translating Poets' who flourished (or not) in the purlieu of Fleet Street and Covent Garden. All in all, *The Catholick Poet* was one of his smartest blows in the contest, especially for the wounds inflicted by the knowing allusiveness of the ballad.

NATURAL DEFORMITY

On the same day that *The Catholick Poet* emerged from the press, Curll let loose a further broadside against his enemy. It came from another veteran member of his assassination squad, John Dennis. Indeed, a note to *The Dunciad* links the two veteran authors: 'Mr. *John Oldmixon* (next to Mr. *Dennis* the most ancient Critick of our Nation)', a way of expressing superannuation if ever there was one.[13] The old campaigner had indeed been active since the 1690s as poet, playwright, critic and polemicist, although he came to the fore only after the turn of the century. Combative and outspoken, Dennis became notorious for bad-tempered exchanges with other writers, including Addison and Steele. These preceded his long-lasting battles with Pope, set off by a scornful reference to 'Appius' in

An Essay on Criticism. As we have seen, this provoked the first significant assault ever mounted on the poet, *Reflections Critical and Satyrical, upon a late Rhapsody, call'd, An Essay on Criticism*. Despite its title, Pope's rejoinder, *The Narrative of Dr Robert Norris* (1713), has Dennis as its principal target, while Lintot is awarded a minor role. Thereafter the participants declared full-scale war, with at least five major attacks on Pope from his antagonist. Some were more effective than others, but all must have wounded their object. There are further contemptuous citations from Dennis's works in *The Art of Sinking in Poetry*, prior to *The Dunciad*. Much later, however, when the aged warrior fell on hard times at the end of his life, Pope supported a benefit performance at the Haymarket Theatre and wrote a prologue for the occasion.

The new item that Dennis supplied to Curll was called *A True Character of Mr. Pope, and his Writings*. The title page carries the same epigraphs from Rochester and the *Iliad* that we saw in the advertisement (Exhibit 5.2). In the imprint only Sarah Popping gets a mention. At eighteen pages in octavo format, it was three times the length of the other pamphlet, but although it ranges over a wide tract of Pope's *oeuvre* it lacks the incisive wit that makes *The Catholick Poet* such an effective polemical work.

At various points Dennis mentions all the major writings for which Pope had become known, in addition to lesser items such as *The Worms*. In fact, he paraphrases a couplet from the last-named poem: 'They tell me, he has lately been pleas'd to say, *That 'tis doubtful if the Race of Men are the offspring of* Adam *or of the* Devil. But 'tis certain . . . at least, that his Origin is not from *Adam*, but from the *Divel*.'[14] This is a weak version by Dennis of the fourth stanza of Pope's lines (Exhibit 4.13), omitting the wordplay and wit in order to get in his own rejoinder. Much of the text is devoted to the 'character' of the writer, allegedly provided by a friend who might be Charles Gildon. This repeats all the familiar charges, and stands out mainly for the extreme violence with which these are pressed. Dennis asserts that he knows nothing for which Pope 'is so ill qualified as he is for Judging, unless it be for Translating HOMER'. The force of this comment is somewhat reduced when the pamphleteer goes on to say that he 'could never borrow the translation 'til this very Day, and design to read it over to Morrow'.[15] How scrupulous a critique is this likely to be?

Not for the first or the last time, Pope's physical appearance (as well as the convenient abbreviated form of his name A. P—E) leads the writer to portray him as a simian creature. For example, 'the Town, which supports him, will do by him, as the Dolphin did by the Shipwrack'd *Monkey*, drop him as soon as it finds him to be a Beast.' This refers to one of Aesop's fables, in which a shoal of dolphins rescue survivors of a wreck and a pet monkey tries to pass himself off as an Athenian citizen, until his pretences are exposed. Or again: 'Notwithstanding that Shape and that Mind of his, some Men of good Understanding, value him for his Rhimes, as they would be fond of an *Asseinego*, that could sing his Part in a Catch, or of a *Baboon* that could whistle *Walsingham*.' An asinego is simply a diminutive form of 'ass'; 'Walsingham' was a well-known ballad tune with many variant lyrics, set by the composer William Byrd. So it goes on:

> As he is in Shape a *Monkey*, is so in his every Action; in his senseless Chattering, and his merry Grimaces, in his doing hourly Mischief and hiding himself, in the variety of his Ridiculous Postures, and his continual Shifting, from Place to Place, from Persons to Persons, from Thing to Thing. But whenever he Scribbles, he is emphatically a *Monkey*, in his awkward servile Imitations.[16]

Out of kindness to Curll, let us withhold these comments from the list of exhibits to be presented to the virtual jury.

By comparison, some of the criticisms seem almost mild, although just as insulting personally:

Frontispiece to *Pope Alexander's Supremacy* (1729), engraved by
Herman Van Kruys. A typical simian caricature of the poet, 'A. P—E',
appears to be about to launch darts from his quill, while his beast
of burden, an ass, stands by.

EXHIBIT 5.6

But if any-one appears to be concern'd at our Upbraiding him with his Natural Deformity, which did not come by his own Fault, but seems to be the Curse of God upon him; we desire that Person to consider, that this little Monster has upbraided People with their Calamities and their Diseases, which are either false or past, or which he himself gave them by administring Poison to them; we desire that person to consider, that Calamities and Diseases, if they are neither false nor past, are common to all Men; that a Man can no more help his Calamities and his Diseases, than a Monster can his Deformity; that there is no Misfortune, but that the Generality of Mankind are liable to, and that there is no one Disease, but what all the rest of Men are subject to; whereas the Deformity of this Libeller, is Visible, Present, Unalterable, and Peculiar to himself. 'Tis the mark of God and Nature upon him, to give us warning that we should hold no Society with him, as a Creature not of our Original, nor of our Species. And they who have refus'd to take this Warning which God and Nature have given them, and have in spight of it, by a Senseless Presumption, ventur'd to be familiar with him, have severely suffer'd for it, by his Perfidiousness. By his constant and malicious Lying, and by that Angel Face and Form of his, 'tis plain that he wants nothing but Horns and Tayl, to be the exact Resemblance, both in Shape and Mind, of his Infernal Father.[17]

More than eighty years ago George Sherburn quoted part of this excerpt, and described it as displaying an 'insane glitter'.[18] It is hard to think of a better characterization.

For the rest, the abuse takes a predictable form. The rhetoric is at its most vehement when the writer comes to Pope's abilities as a translator, his skill in imitating poets such as Horace, and of course his Catholic and supposed Jacobite attachments ('He is a Professor of the worst Religion, which he laughs at, and yet has most inviolably observ'd the most execrable Maxim in it, *That no Faith is to be kept with Hereticks'*). This is an astonishing accusation to make, since the poet was known for his Erasmian version of the Catholic faith, his wide circle of friends among the Protestant community, and his avoidance of strict dogma. The canard is repeated that, as a 'virulent Papist' and 'a Jesuitical Professor of Truth, a base and a foul Pretender to Candour', he wrote political papers in favour of the Oxford administration.[19] The pamphlet contains many false claims and some erroneous attributions. Some would find it ironic that a recurrent charge is that Pope is guilty of libel.

A DRURY LANE BALLAD

Pope scarcely had time to recover from this assault before he was subjected to one of the most embarrassing mishaps he ever underwent. A press notice hoisted the red flag on 30 June, when Rebecca Burleigh inserted an advertisement for an intriguing new item. The title was 'A *Roman Catholick* Version of the First Psalm; for the Use of a Young Lady'. At the end of the notice came an obvious Curllian touch, with a promise of naked war: '*Bella horrida Bella.* Price 3d. Sold by all Booksellers. *N.B.* The *Pope*-ish Controversy continues.'[20] The quotation comes from the sixth book of *The Aeneid*, when the hero visits the sibyl at Cumae. She makes him a grim prophecy: 'I see wars – horrid wars – and the Tiber foaming with much blood.' A lot of blood would be spilt, figuratively at least, before either party allowed the controversy to lapse. In *The Dunciad* Curll and his fellows are left to contemplate the tapestry showing them black and blue from 'blanketings and blows' as they emerge from the stinking waves of the Fleet Ditch.

Also listed in the advertisement were *Court Poems*, *The Worms* and the two items from the end of May that we have just considered. At the end of the poem itself Burleigh (that is to say, Curll) advertised a further satiric offering by the obscure Francis Chute, masquerading as 'Joseph Gay', a name also used by another hack. This was *The Petticoat*, just published on 28 June. The writer claims to be a 'cousin german' of the real John Gay, and quotes from Pope's preface to the *Iliad*. Curll himself must have become confused sometimes about who had written what and when.

The poem by Pope that Curll had purloined, 'A Roman Catholick Version of the First Psalm', was a skilful but blasphemous parody of scripture. The host on to which it was grafted was not the received biblical text, but a widely used metrical transposition by the sixteenth-century hymnologists Thomas Sternhold and John Hopkins. It has been claimed that their collection long enjoyed a greater circulation than any other book in English, apart from the Bible and the Book of Common Prayer. Theirs remained the default psalter in the Church of England until it was replaced by the work of Nahum Tate and Nicholas Brady around the time the parody came out in 1716. Pope supplies a close line-by-line burlesque, sometimes citing phrases from the original to turn them to obscene purposes:

EXHIBIT 5.7

The Maid is Blest that will not hear
Of Masquerading Tricks,
Nor lends to Wanton Songs an Ear,
Nor Sighs for Coach and Six.
To Please her shall her Husband strive
With all his Main and Might,
And in her Love shall Exercise
Himself both Day and Night.
She shall bring forth most Pleasant Fruit,
He Flourish still and Stand,
Ev'n so all Things shall prosper well,
That this Maid takes in Hand.
No wicked Whores shall have such Luck

Who follow their own Wills,
But Purg'd shall be to Skin and Bone,
With *Mercury* and *Pills*.
For why? the Pure and Cleanly Maids
Shall All, good Husbands gain:
But filthy and uncleanly Jades
Shall Rot in *Drury-Lane.*[21]

No one can be surprised that the poem aroused hostile reactions. The seventh line traduces a verse in the original that refers to the blessed man exercising himself day and night in the service of the Lord. It was a bad miscalculation on Pope's part. We don't know how his enemy got hold of the material, but its appearance in print was to cause him lifelong distress. His prevarications on this point supplied a major reason that Victorian critics branded him a habitual deceiver. One of Curll's greatest hits, it was reprinted on at least twelve separate occasions, quite apart from appearances in miscellanies issued by other booksellers.

From the start, members of the Whig press saw their opportunity. Two weeks after the initial advertisement had come out, the *Flying Post* was back with a mocking response, including a reply in the same metrical form, parts of which are printed here:

EXHIBIT 5.8

The Eccho to *Pope*'s Drury-Lane Ballad.

The busy World can not agree,
Tho' sure, methinks, it should,
Whether the Pope or Devil be,
The better Friend of God . . .
We have a *Pope*, than both more vile,
Who dares God's Word Blaspheme,
By lewd, prophane, uncleanly Style,

In Terms, I dare not Name.
The Royal David's Harp he takes,
   To play his Wanton Song,
And screws and strains its Strings, so makes
   His smutty Notes sound strong.
No Atheist, Deist, Devil yet,
   Thus rudely touch'd that Lyre;
To prostitute thus Holy Writ,
   As do's this POPISH Squire . . .
May High-Church Fury seize the Wretch,
   And stop his filthy Tune,
Lest Heaven it self its Arm out stretch,
   And stop his Vitals soon.[22]

We cannot be sure who composed this retort, perhaps Oldmixon
or Curll himself. There are some cleverly infiltrated suggestions.
In appropriating 'Royal David's Harp' for his smutty lines based
on the psalter, Pope has committed not just blasphemy but a kind
of *lèse-majesté* against the ruling dynasty. The Curllians often
threatened to impose suitable punishment on their enemy, but
this may be the only time that anyone predicted God striking
down the poet.

No doubt about it, Pope felt rattled. On 31 July he composed a
less than candid notice for the press that fell just short of outright
denial of authorship:

EXHIBIT 5.9

Whereas there have been publish'd in my Name, certain scandalous Libels, which I hope no Person of Candor would have thought
me capable of, I am sorry to find myself obliged to declare, that no
Genuine Pieces of mine have been printed by any but Mr. Tonson and
Mr. Lintot. And in particular, as to that which is entituled, A Version of the first Psalm; I hereby promise a Reward of three Guineas

to anyone who shall discover the Person or Persons concerned in the Publication of the said Libel, of which I am wholly ignorant.

A. Pope.

Nobody claimed the three guineas, although Burleigh stated that she would show the manuscript written in Pope's hand to anyone who called at her shop. Long afterwards Curll reminded Pope that he had never paid up. Just conceivably the poet was uncertain about who had published the ballad; but it stretches credulity to suppose that he did not have a very good idea.

Pope must have hoped that this disclaimer, flimsy as it was on detail, would undo the damage. He wrote to Martha Blount's sister Teresa with obvious guilt, 'If you have seen a late Advertisement, you will know that I have not told a lye (which we both abhominate) but equivocated pretty genteely: You may be confident twas not done without leave from my Spiritual director.'[23] The phrase 'equivocated pretty genteely' has left a bad taste with many subsequent commentators. It lends support to the view that Curll was a no-nonsense kind of man, while Pope was a devious individual given to parsing simple statements so as to avoid having to admit the truth. The defence of the poem mounted by Norman Ault – that Pope was not burlesquing the scriptures, but rather making fun of the bad poetry of Sternhold and Hopkins – will seem disingenuous to most readers.[24]

A letter to Swift that Pope dated 20 June (it must really come from some weeks later) extends the story. The tone is more playful here, but some underlying anxiety shows through. Pope begins by comparing his state to that of the well-beneficed Dean of St Patrick's, Dublin:

EXHIBIT 5.10

As for me, I have not the least hopes of the Cardinalat, tho' I suffer for my Religion in almost every weekly paper. I have begun to take a pique at the Psalms of David (if the wicked may be credited, who have printed a scandalous one in my name). This report I dare not discourage too much, in a prospect I have at present of a post under the Marquess de Langallerie, wherein if I can but do some signal service against the Pope, I may be considerably advanced by the Turks, the only religious people I dare confide in. If it should happen hereafter that I should write for the holy law of Mohamet, I hope it will make no breach between you and me; every one must live, and I beg you will not be the man to manage the controversy against me. The Church of Rome I judge (from many modern symptoms, as well as ancient prophecies) to be in a declining condition; that of England will in a short time be scarce able to maintain her own family.[25]

Langallerie was an adventurer who had served many masters, including Louis XIV and the Sultan of Turkey. His probably spurious memoirs had been published in 1707 by a group of four booksellers – including Curll.

In Swift's reply to Pope from Dublin on 30 August, he set out what would become the Scriblerian party line:

EXHIBIT 5.11

And who are all these enemies you hint at? I can only think of Curl, Gildon, Squire Burnet, Blackmore, and a few others whose fame I have forgot: Tools in my opinion as necessary for a good writer, as pen, ink, and paper. And besides, I would fain know whether every Draper does not shew you three or four damned pieces of stuff to set off his good one? however, I will grant, that one thorough bookselling Rogue is better qualified to vex an author, than all his cotemporary scriblers in Critick or Satire, not only by stolen Copies of what was incorrect or unfit for the publick, but by downright laying other mens dulness at your door. I had a long design upon the ears of that Curl, when I was in credit, but the rogue would never allow me a fair stroke at them, though my penknife was ready and sharp. I can hardly believe the relation of his being poisoned, though the Historian pretends to have been an eye-witness: But I beg pardon, Sack might do it, though Rats-bane would not. I never saw the thing you mention as falsely imputed to you; but I think the frolicks of merry hours, even when we are guilty, should not be left to the mercy of our best friends, till Curl and his resemblers are hanged.[26]

This quick succession of attacks had clearly got under the skin of the two friends on either side of the Irish Sea. They saw Curll as their most potent enemy at this juncture, and a response was needed. However, the poet had other things on his mind.

6

The LOSS *of* EDEN,
1716

In many ways, this proved far from a happy year for Pope. It was not just that he had suffered more than one shrewd attack by Curll, to which his own caustic pamphlet *A Full and True Account* had gone only some way to rebuff. There was a bigger personal worry that arose from the continuing state of uncertainty on the political front. Mainly as a result of this situation, the Popes now underwent a family upheaval, behind which lay three factors.

First, the government had levied an extra property tax on Catholics, allegedly to meet the costs of putting down the rebellion, although really to encourage the others among the recusant community not to take up arms again. Second, it emerged that the title by which they held their house in Binfield was a legal fiction, and they could be turned out almost at a moment's notice. An act 'for the further preventing the growth of Popery' (1699) made it impossible for a Catholic such as Pope to inherit real property or to purchase it 'either in his or her own Name or in the Name of any other Person or Persons'.[1] He was in imminent danger of losing his horse, since it was worth more than five pounds – that strange measure from the time of Charles II was reactivated by an edict issued by George I in December 1714.[2] Third, Catholics were now obliged to take an oath of loyalty to the Hanoverian regime, or they might face severe sanctions. All this must have weighed heavily on Pope's mind, along with the sad aftermath of the Rising and the need to find somewhere for his parents to live out their lives in peace, what he described to Caryll as 'some asylum for their old age'.[3] By comparison, the quarrel with Curll may have seemed a minor distraction.

Perhaps there was a family conference, with Alexander junior using his more recent experience of metropolitan life to proffer advice. At all events, the decision was taken to up sticks. In the spring Alexander senior and Edith moved to the western side of London, in Chiswick, to a new home that their son had discovered and furnished. With some latitude it could be construed as observing the Ten Mile Act. It stood near where the Hogarth roundabout now directs a stream of traffic into and out of central London, and was near enough to the Thames for people at this time to make a boat journey in the same direction. The Popes stayed on there after the poet's father died the following year, until Edith and her son took up their Twickenham residence in 1719.

The move of 1716 was a decisive moment in Pope's life. It meant severance from his childhood home, and the place where he had forged his earliest ambitions as a writer. Just before his final departure, he passed a few days in the forest with Nicholas Rowe. As memories came flooding back, he wrote to his fellow Scriblerian Thomas Parnell, 'The Muse is driven, from those Forests of which she sung, the Day may shortly come, when your Friend may . . . look back with regret, on the Paradise he has lost, and have only the consolation of poor Adam, "The world lies all before him, where to chuse His place of rest, and Providence his Guide."'[4] The quotation from the close of Milton's great epic reminds us of a key fact: in how many ways *Paradise Lost* stimulated Pope's creative juices. One irritant tugging at his unconscious may have been his own feeling of dispossession, mirroring that of Adam and Eve on their expulsion from Eden. Soon afterwards he wrote to his friend and co-religionist John Caryll, 'I write this from Windsor Forest, of which I am come to take my last look and leave of [*sic*]. We here bid our papist neighbours adieu, such as those who go to be hanged do their fellow-prisoners, who are condemn'd to follow 'em a few weeks after.'[5] We cannot read this without detecting a vein of sympathy for the Jacobites, most of whom shared the poet's religion, who currently awaited their fate in prison.

When he wrote those words, Pope could not be certain whether his allies who were known or suspected to be Jacobites would follow Lord Derwentwater to the block or the hangman's noose – Oxford certainly, Bolingbroke and Ormonde if they returned, perhaps even Lansdowne, the Earl of Strafford or William Wyndham. The outlook seemed bleak on all sides. The Hanoverians had entrenched themselves more safely after the failure of the Rising (Pope may not altogether have minded that), and the Whigs had a total grip on the Commons, as they would have for almost half a century. The Tories could mount a small if often vociferous group in the House of Lords, but the bench of bishops had been purged of such support. It was the same with the magnates on the court of aldermen who dominated the affairs of the City of London. The big corporations lay in similar hands; even the South Sea Company, founded by Lord Oxford, had now come under the control of his former opponents – not that *this* would lead it to great financial triumph. As for Pope's old friends, they found themselves imprisoned, exiled, deprived of their offices, taxed and fined into poverty, or skulking in the backwoods.

This makes a stark contrast with Curll's situation. If his abilities or his fortune had been up to such things, the publisher had the right to a seat in Parliament, a vote, a sinecure at court, a professional or academic career, a role in civic government, a high rank in the army or navy, a leadership role in a trade guild, the ownership of land, a place on the bench of magistrates, and even a bishopric or a cosy nook in the Church hierarchy. Why, he could have sat on a grand jury as it indicted recusants, or given his verdict at the trial of some wicked fellow who had been charged with sedition. All these routes were closed to Pope. He might almost have been a woman.

A COLLEGE SALUTATION

Obviously Pope could have done with some good news, and he got some at the beginning of August. It happened in an odd way, when Curll found himself the victim of an archaic form of popular retribution, being 'tossed in a blanket' by a posse of schoolboy vigilantes. Sometimes the act was carried out in a spirit of loutish fun – as happens to Sancho Panza in the first book of *Don Quixote* (just after a scene in which the hero vomits after taking a poisoned drink). But things could get much more serious. When Falstaff says in the second part of *Henry IV* that he will 'toss the rogue [Pistol] in a blanket', he does not mean it in a jocular spirit. Nor is it much fun for Ben Jonson when he undergoes this punishment at the end of Thomas Dekker's *Satiromastix* (1602). His offence was to have produced nasty libels. That may be why the retribution seemed so apt in Curll's case.

The episode followed the death of a leading churchman, Robert South, a few weeks earlier. He was an alumnus of Westminster School, and the head boy delivered a funeral elegy. Unwisely, Curll had this oration printed on 26 July, using Rebecca Burleigh as a front. He evidently had access to some of South's materials, since he was about the publish the *Posthumous Works*. Incensed by the freedom he had taken, the scholars invited him to their historic lair, close by Westminster Abbey, and subjected him to the traditional punishment. The story was immediately leaked to the press:

EXHIBIT 6.1

King's College, Westminster. Aug. 3, 1716.

Sir, You are desired to acquaint the Publick, that a certain *Bookseller* near *Temple-Bar* (not taking warning by the frequent Drubs that he has undergone for his often pyrating other Men's Copies) did lately (without the Consent of Mr. *John Barber* present Captain of *Westminster* School) publish the Scraps of a Funeral Oration, spoken by him over the Corps of the Reverend Dr *South*. And being on *Thurs-day* last fortunately Nab'd within the Limits of *Dean's Yard* by the King's Schollars, there he met with a College Salutation: For he was first presented with the Ceremony of the Blanket, in which, when the Skeleton had been well shook, he was carry'd in Triumph to the School; and after receiving a Grammatical Correction for his false Concords; he was Reconducted to *Dean's Yard*, and on his Knees, asking Pardon of the aforesaid Mr. *Barber* for his Offence; he was kick'd out of the Yard, and left to the Huzza's of the Rabble.

I am, Sir, Yours, T.A.

This resembles nothing so much as the primitive horseplay of earlier centuries: a schoolyard rite, perhaps, or one of those communal punishments inflicted on people who broke the unwritten rules and had to submit to a ducking or worse.

There was more to come. An undermaster at the school was Samuel Wesley, brother of John, the founder of the Methodists, and Charles, the hymn-writer. He was a Tory, an ally of the Scriblerian group and a competent poet. His new offering, *Neck or Nothing*, pretends to be a 'consolatory' letter to Curll from the eccentric writer and bookseller John Dunton, remembered today chiefly for his half-crazy but informative autobiography, *The Life and Errors* (1705). *Neck or Nothing* goes through the bookseller's humiliation in excruciating detail. Much of the backstory is reiterated: the emetic; the ever-present threat to Curll of the pillory and the loss of his ears; the legend that he kept 'poor Bards' tied up in a garret; and the errors in the Latin version he had published. Many of the jokes relate to the blows administered to the victim's naked posterior ('their Rage goes farther, and applies/ More fundamental Injuries'). If the poor man was severely manhandled in the process, Wesley's Hudibrastic verses perform their own 'rough music'. The ending is particularly effective, offering cruel reminders of Curll's chequered history with the law. It also promises further indignities

Frontispiece to Samuel Wesley's *Neck or Nothing* (1716), showing Curll's ill-treatment by the Westminster schoolboys: at the top, he is tossed in a blanket; in the centre, he is flogged on a table; at the bottom, he is made to beg on his knees.

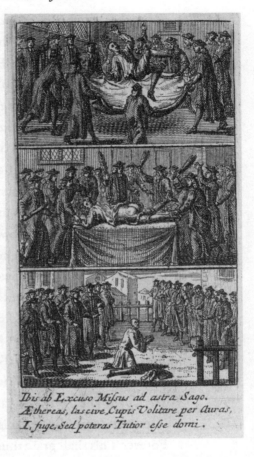

Ibis ab Excuso Missus ad astra Sago.
Æthereas, lascive Cupis Volitare per Auras,
I, fuge, Sed poteras Tutior esse domi.

that may be coming his way, with an emphasis on the names of individuals who might not be too sorry to see what had happened – Pope, Bernard Lintot, Jacob Tonson.

EXHIBIT 6.2

Hast thou not oft enough in Court
Appear'd, and often smarted for 't?
And dost thou not, with many a Brand,
Recorded for a Pirate Stand?
Glad that a Fine could pay th' Arrears,
And clear the Mortgage of thy Ears.
Then what Relief dost hope to draw,

From that which Still condemns Thee, Law?
And if from Law no Help there be,
I'm sure there's none from Equity ...
And since to rage will do no Good,
Pull in thy Horns, and kiss the Rod,
And while thou canst, retreat, for fear
They fall once more upon thy Rear.
Tho' 'tis vexatious, *Mun*, I grant,
To hear the passing Truants taunt,
And ask Thee at thy Shop in Jeer,
Which is the Way to *Westminster*?
Oh! how th' unlucky Urchins laugh'd,
To think they'd maul'd Thee fore and aft:
'Tis such a sensible Affront!
Why *Pope* will write an Epick on't!
Bernard will chuckle at thy Moan,
And all the Booksellers in Town,
From *Tonson* down to *Boddington*,
Fleet-street and *Temple-bar* around,
The Strand and *Holborn*, this shall sound:
Forever This shall grate thine Ear,
Which is the Way to *Westminster*?[6]

'Neck or nothing', an old phrase meaning to do something desperately, turns up in Jonathan Swift's *Polite Conversation*. 'Mun' is simply a familiar mode of address, a variant of man. Nicholas Boddington was a small fish in the booksellers' pool. As for Equity, Curll did have recourse to Chancery suits later on, but they do not seem to have done him much good.

Despite this reverse for the bookseller, it was not in his nature to back down in such circumstances. On 26 September a familiar shield, James Roberts, brought out a second part of *Court Poems*, this time with two authentic Pope items – *The Worms* and the 'Roman

Catholick Version of the First Psalm'. Until he could dredge out something new to use against his adversary, Curll would habitually content himself with recycling the ones he had already grabbed. Meanwhile, he carried on augmenting his general list with a variety of titles. Then, on 8 November, he joined with three other booksellers on a two-volume work, *Ovid's Metamorphoses. In Fifteen Books. A New Translation. / By Several Hands. / Adorn'd with Several Cuts.* There is nothing immediately remarkable about that, in an era when editions of the classics regularly shot from the press. But there are two noteworthy features. First, the work has some respectable authors, headed by Curll's frequent contributor George Sewell, but the biggest name by far is that of Pope, whose early translation of a single episode is included in Book xiv – probably without permission. Second, the enterprise was in competition with a separate translation 'by the most eminent hands', edited by Samuel Garth, which Tonson brought before the public in 1717. Here Pope had a brief presence in Book ix; there are more conspicuous sections executed by John Dryden, Joseph Addison and John Gay.

Soon after these events, Pope gave Teresa Blount a brief update in a letter quoted in the previous chapter, but he sounds relieved as much as delighted: 'Mr. Ed. Curll has been exercised in a Blanket and whipped at Westminster Schoole by the Boys, whereof the common Prints have given some account.'[7] Pope may have got rid of some anxiety by writing, or helping John Arbuthnot to write, a short squib called *God's Revenge against Punning* under the sobriquet of Sir James Baker. We can be sure he was plotting revenge, even if God wasn't.

A DEPLORABLE CONDITION

Pope had been looking for an opportunity to follow up on the *Full and True Account*, and in time it came his way. He dreamed up a sequel to carry on the story of Curll's misadventures, under the title

A Further Account of the Most Deplorable Condition of Mr. Edmund Curll, Bookseller, Since his being Poison'd on the 28th of March. We do not know the exact date of publication; it is set around Easter, but internal evidence suggests publication was delayed until the latter half of the year, perhaps in August. Now Pope could go on the offensive again with a rumbustious farce that put his campaign back on track.

After some thrusts at Richard Blackmore, parodying his grandiloquent style, the pamphlet gets down to the latest developments:

EXHIBIT 6.3

The Symptoms of his Departure from his usual Temper of Mind, were at first only *speaking civilly to his Customers,* taking a Fancy to *say his Prayers, singeing a Pig with a new purchas'd Libel,* and *refusing Two and Nine Pence for Sir* Richard Blackmore*'s Essays.*

As the poor Man's Frenzy increas'd, he began to *void his Excrements in his Bed, read* Rochester*'s bawdy Poems to his Wife,* gave *Oldmixon* a *slap* on the *Chops,* and wou'd have kiss'd Mr. *Pemberton*'s Arse *by Violence.*

But at last he came to such a pass, that he wou'd *dine upon nothing but Copper Plates,* took a *Clyster for a whipt Syllabub,* and eat a *Suppository* for a *Raddish* with *Bread* and *Butter.*

We leave it to every tender Wife to imagine how sorely all this afflicted poor Mrs *Curll:* At first she privately put a *Bill* into several *Churches,* desiring the Prayers of the Congregation for a *wretched Stationer* distemper'd in Mind. But when she was sadly convinc'd that his Misfortune was publick to all the World, writ the following Letter to her good Neighbour Mr. *Lintott.*

A true Copy of *Mrs. Curll*'s Letter to Mr. *Lintott.*

Worthy Mr. Lintott, You, and all the Neighbours know too well, the Frenzy with which my poor Man is visited. I never perceiv'd he was out of himself, till that melancholy Day that he thought he was poison'd in a Glass of Sack; upon this, he took a strange Fancy to run a Vomiting all over the House, and in the new wash'd Dining Room. Alas! this is the greatest Adversity that ever befel my poor Man since he lost *one Testicle* at School by the bite of a black Boar. Good Lord! if he should die, where should I dispose of the Stock? unless Mr. *Pemberton* or you would help a distressed Widow; for God knows he never publish'd any Books that lasted above a Week, so that if we wanted *daily Books*, we wanted *daily Bread*. I can write no more, for I hear the Rap of Mr. *Curll's Ivory headed Cane* upon the Counter. – Pray recommend me to your *Pastry Cook*, who furnishes you yearly with Tarts in exchange for your Papers, for Mr. *Curll* has disoblig'd ours since his Fits came upon him; – before that, we generally liv'd upon bak'd Meats. – He is coming in, and I have but just time to put his Son out of the way for fear of Mischief: So wishing you a merry Easter, I remain your most humble Servant, C. *Curll*.

P.S. As to the Report of my poor Husband's stealing a *Calf*, it is really groundless, for he always binds in *Sheep*.[8]

Sheepskin was naturally a cheaper binding than leather. As it happens, Curll's wife was named Anne, but we might excuse Pope for not knowing that.

The narrative continues with a virtuoso exercise in the use of satiric specifics. Curll wishes to rustle up his regular team of writers to instruct them on what needs to be done. A few sample directions he gives to a porter to locate them will show how much Pope knew about the environment of Grub Street.[9] One of these addresses is 'At the Bedsted and Bolster, a Musick House in *Moorfields*, two Translators in a Bed together'; another, 'At the Three *Tobacco Pipes* in *Dog* and *Bitch* Yard, one that has been a Parson, he wears a blue Camblet Coat trim'd with black: my best Writer against *reveal'd Religion*'. Then we have 'At the Laundresses, at the Hole in the Wall in *Cursitors* Alley, up three Pair of Stairs, the Author of my *Church History* – if his Flux be over – you may also speak to the Gentleman who lyes by him in the Flock Bed, my *Index-maker*.' ('Flux' here is a word for dysentery.) A final example: 'Call at *Budge Row* for the Gentleman you use to go to in the Cock-loft; I have taken away the Ladder, but his Landlady has it in keeping.' All these are genuine addresses, and most can be found on contemporary maps of London. They cover a good spread around town, with a dense concentration in the notoriously mean streets belonging to the parish of St Giles-in-the-Fields, on the northern edge of Covent Garden.

Not all the writers can be identified with certainty; it would spoil the fun if everyone had enough prominence for the description to be immediately transparent, for they are grouped in *The Dunciad* as 'ev'ry nameless name'. We can be sure that the only woman present, Susanna Centlivre, is 'The *Cook's Wife* in *Buckingham* Court', while the direction 'I don't much care if you ask at the *Mint* for the old Beetle-brow'd Critick' could lead the porter only to the debtors' sanctuary, there to summon John Dennis, ancient, glowering, impoverished – and a critic to his last breath.[10]

The chosen authors duly meet in Curll's drawing room. They gaze at each other with suspicion, said to be the result of '*Scorn, Solitude*, and *short Commons*', an unlovely but not altogether unpitying view of the hack's condition. Their employer now addresses them:

EXHIBIT 6.4

'*Whores and Authors* must be paid beforehand to put them in good Humour; therefore here is half a Crown a piece for you to drink your own Healths, and Confusion to Mr. *Addison,* and all other successful Writers.

Ah Gentlemen! What have I not done, what have I not suffer'd, rather than the World should be depriv'd of your Lucubrations? I have taken involuntary Purges, I have been vomited, three Times have I been can'd, once was I hunted; twice was my Head broke by a Grenadier, twice was I toss'd in a Blanket; I have had Boxes on the Ear, Slaps on the Chops; I have been frighted, pump'd, kick'd, slander'd and beshitten. – I hope, Gentlemen, you are all convinc'd that this Author of Mr. *Lintott*'s could mean nothing else but starving you by poisoning me. It remains for us to consult the best and speediest Methods of Revenge.'

He had scarce done speaking, but the *Historian* propos'd a History of his Life. The *Exeter* Exchange Gentleman was for penning Articles of his Faith. Some pretty smart *Pindarick*, (says the Red-Stocking Gentleman) would effectually do his Business. But the *Index-maker* said there was nothing like an *Index* to his *Homer*.[11]

It is obvious how each of the writers selects a mode of revenge that will bring him a job and a payment. Sadly, we don't have evidence of all the punishments Curll claims to have undergone. The most unusual way mentioned here was to be 'pumped', which refers to a milder form of waterboarding torture. Dunking the accused in hot or cold water had been part of medieval trial by ordeal, but it was not a judicial penalty in Britain, although one source in 1725 speaks of bailiffs dragging a debtor around 'every Pump within the Limits of the *Mint*, where he is pumped severely'. In her play *A Bold Stroke for a Wife* (1718), Centlivre, one of the assembled company, has a character say to a pickpocket, 'Don't you remember that the Mob pump'd you?'[12] If that really did happen, Curll must have incurred the resentment of someone holding a degree of power. Pope may just have made it up.

Those present now embark on a discussion of the steps they need to take against Pope. They pass fourteen resolutions in all, with eager unanimity. The first is to the effect that 'every Member of this Society, according to his several Abilities, shall contribute some way or other to the Defamation of Mr. *Pope*.' Among the others is an assertion that he has 'on Purpose in several Passages perverted the true ancient *Heathen* Sense of *Homer*, for the more effectual Propagation of the *Popish* Religion', although of course

they don't say which passages or how it was done. A further charge
is agreed, with an eye to the recent defeat of the Stuart rebellion:
'That the Printing of Homer's Battles at this Juncture, has been
the Occasion of all the Disturbances of this Kingdom'. To promote the familiar insistence that Pope's scholarship was defective,
it is resolved 'That a number of effective *Errata*'s be raised out of
Mr. *Pope*'s *Homer* (not exceeding 1746) and that every Gentleman,
who shall send in one Error, for his Encouragement shall have the
whole Works of this Society *Gratis*.' One relating to the items we
have just seen goes, 'That a Ballad be made against Mr. *Pope*, and
that Mr. *Oldmixon*, Mr. *Gildon* and Mrs. *Centlivre* do prepare and
bring in the same.'[13]

The meeting is now ready to break up, but not before the participants suggest remedies to return their employer to full health,
with conflicting proposals by Charles Gildon and John Oldmixon,
the most forthright of those attending. This minor altercation leaves
room for Curll's demented peroration, to close the session but also
the pamphlet. It is as brilliant a set piece as can be found in any of
Pope's prose works:

EXHIBIT 6.5

While the Company were expecting the Thanks of Mr. *Curll*, for
these Demonstrations of their Zeal, a whole Pile of *Essays* on a sudden fell on his Head; the Shock of which in an Instant brought back
his Dilirium. He immediately rose up, over-turn'd the Close-stool,
and beshit the *Essays* (which may probably occasion a *second Edition*)
then without putting up his Breeches, in a most furious Tone, he thus
broke out to his Books, which his distemper'd Imagination represented to him as alive, coming down from their Shelves, fluttering
their Leaves, and flapping their Covers at him.

Now *G-d damn* all *Folio's*, *Quarto's*, *Octavo's* and *Duodecimo's*!
ungrateful Varlets that you are, who have so long taken up my House
without paying for your Lodging? – Are you not the beggarly Brood

of fumbling *Journey-men*; born in *Garrets*, among *Lice* and *Cobwebs*, nurs'd upon *Grey Peas, Bullocks Liver*, and *Porter's Ale?* – Was not the first Light you saw, the *Farthing* Candle I paid for? Did you not come before your Time into *dirty Sheets* of brown Paper? – And have not I cloath'd you in double *Royal*, lodg'd you handsomely on *decent Shelves*, lac'd your *Backs* with *Gold*, equipt you with splendid *Titles*, and sent you into the World with the Names of *Persons of Quality?* Must I be *always* plagu'd with you? – Why flutter ye your Leaves, and flap your Covers at me? Damn ye all, ye *Wolves* in *Sheeps Cloathing; Rags ye were, and to Rags ye shall return.* Why hold you forth your *Texts* to me, ye paltry *Sermons?* Why cry ye – at every Word to me, ye *bawdy Poems?* – To my Shop at *Tunbridge* ye shall go, by G– and thence be drawn like the rest of your Predecessors, bit by bit, to the *Passage-House*: For in this present Emotion of my Bowels, how do I compassionate those who have great need, and nothing to wipe their Breech with?

Having said this, and at the same Time recollecting that his own was yet unwiped, he abated of his Fury, and with great Gravity, apply'd to that Function the unfinish'd Sheets of the Conduct of the Earl of *Nottingham*.[14]

We've long been aware how *The Dunciad* turns objects into animate forces, but even in his great poem Pope achieved nothing more imaginative than this, as the delirious publisher rounds on the volumes he has spawned. One aspect of the passage that stands out is the way the physical processes of bookmaking and binding are enlisted to characterize the publisher's output. The books return to rags, because paper was then made from scraps of old fabric. But the cadences recall the line in Genesis 3:19, 'For dust thou art, and unto dust shalt thou return.' In 1712 Curll had set up a business during the summer season on 'the Walks' at the spa town of Tunbridge Wells in Kent, but the venture lasted only a couple of years. Again we have the unsettling combination of great precision with regard to the specifics of Curll's life as a trader with a ludic and surreal quality in the scene. It is wonderfully funny, because it dramatizes Curll's career through the output of his supposedly starveling authors, but it is also a vivid enactment of the mores of Grub Street and a savage indictment of the seamier side of print culture. This, Pope might be saying, is what the Gutenberg galaxy has come to in the new era of freedom of the press.

For his own purposes, Pope wished to present Curll's troops as living in squalid circumstances across bad parts of town. (A passage-house was a shack used as an outdoor toilet.) It was not entirely fair to them, but since when has satire confined itself to the literal truth? In any case, it is piquant to note that the collection of essays that sets the farcical ending in motion is the product of a fully paid-up member of the great and good – Blackmore, a Fellow and eventually Censor of the Royal College of Physicians, alumnus of Westminster School and Oxford, an MD from the ancient medical school at Padua, a man knighted by William III, composer of a new version of the Psalms, and a widely published author on the treatment of several physical complaints (quite apart from his series of epic poems). You could not get more establishment-friendly than that.

The Stool of Repentance

We should not expect Curll to have sat idly on his hands while his opponent was attempting to regain the initiative, and he did not. He went on publishing and selling items critical of the late ministry and denouncing Jacobites. In fact, he maintained at this juncture a varied list even by his standards, and only a small proportion related directly to his ongoing feud with Pope. In December he issued a second edition of *The Court of Atalantis*, a feeble compilation from 1714 that attempted to follow Delarivier Manley's big hit, a *chronique scandaleuse* called *The New Atalantis*, by telling tales about the private lives of the famous. It now proved to have been edited by Oldmixon. Despite a rebranding of the work as *Court Tales*, and provision of a key to the persons disguised under fancy names, this effort to do for the Whigs what Manley had accomplished for the Tories came up a failure.

On top of this, Curll would now lose the services of his most diligent labourer. A paragraph in the *Weekly Journal* run by the Jacobite Nathaniel Mist reported that 'a noted Author, one J--n Oldm-x-n is lately retired from his Garret and Trade of drawing up Indexes, making Ballads, and writings of strange Relations; this is to give Notice that he now resides at Bridgw-t-r, in the County of Somerset, and is Intelligencer-General for that Place of that Writer to celebrated Fame and Veracity the *Flying Post*' (George Ridpath). There follows a list of new works to be expected from this noted author, among them 'A critical dissertation concerning the ety-mology, signification, and present use of the word shitsacks', and 'Observations upon the difference between lying in a gaol or a garret, and being in an office, gathered from his own experience'.[15] In reality, Oldmixon had been appointed customs collector of his native town. Pope got to know about that, too, because his note in *The Dunciad* remarks with cruel brevity, 'He was all his life a hired writer for a Party, and received his reward in a small place which he yet enjoys.'[16] Later Oldmixon came back to London, and wrote some voluminous histories, but he never again worked regularly for Curll.

Then came another haymaker, in the form of an advertisement placed on 10 December by Sarah Popping – but anyone who could tell a hawk from a handsaw knew the direction it was coming from. Obviously, Wesley's *Neck or Nothing* had drawn Curll's blood.

EXHIBIT 6.6

There is preparing for the *Press*,
A Satyr, entitled, *Pope* on the Stool of Repentance: Or, the Purge given to *Sir Alexander Knaw-post*, to prepare his Body for the New

Madhouse, erected for the cure of Atheists, Blasphemers, Liber-
tines, Punsters, Jacobites, and other prophane Lunaticks: To which
is added, a *Challenge* to this Rhiming Knight upon several nice and
curious Points in *Philosophy, Poetry, and Conversation*, which if he refuses to Answer, he'll be posted for a B–d. The *Purge* and *Challenge*
prescrib'd upon Reading a *Dogrel Poem* of Sir *Alexander*'s (called
Neck or Nothing or a consolatory Letter from Mr. *Dunton* to Mr.
Curll, upon his Being toss'd in a Blanket) and Dedicated to those
Noble and Illustrious Patriots that POPE basely (and undeservedly)
slander'd in his late infamous Libel, entitled, *God's Revenge against
Punning*. The whole *Satyr* written by Dr. *Dunton*, Physician to the
New Madhouse, and explain'd by a *Copper Plate*, representing (at
one View) Sir *Alexander's prophane Life and Writings*, which are all
Inserted in this *Purge*.

> *Deaf to all Means which might most proper seem*
> *Towards their Cure, they run stak Mad in Rhime.*

Oldham.

Note; That Dr. *Dunton's Purge* may want no Ingredient that is
necessary to bring this Patient (Sir *Alexander*) to his right Senses,
it will be compleated in a Book of 1s. price, or else will be inserted
in his Weekly Paper entitled, *Dunton's Madhouse*, till the whole is
compleated, but neither this *Purge* nor *Madhouse* will be publish'd,
till *Pope* has been lasht (both in Prose and Verse) by those First-rate
Wits that are to prove him a fit Patient for *Dunton's Madhouse*. DUN-
TON'S PURGE when ready for publication, will be sold by *S. Poping* in
Pater-noster-row.[17]

It is surely clear that all the details surrounding this retaliatory
'purge' are made up of the purest fiction. Why then was the name
of John Dunton used, since he had no claims to a medical title?
First, because Wesley had professed to write in his name. Second,
because Dunton did insert his own batty notices in the press.
Third, because the author's father, Rev. Samuel Wesley, was the

brother-in-law of Dunton, who had published his poems under the title *Maggots*; as noted earlier, this word was often applied to eccentric persons, and no one fitted that description better than Dunton. Fourth, because the title, *Neck or Nothing*, echoed one that Dunton had used in a pamphlet from 1713. Some of the notice parodies the language used by quacks to promote their own patent 'purges'. If Pope had needed some remedy for mental disorders, he could have nipped round to the shop of his neighbour, Mrs Cole, also opposite St Dunstan's church. She advertised incomparable drops to 'rectify all Disorders of the Head, Brain, Stomach and Blood'.[18]

Little needs to be said about *God's Revenge*, mentioned in the advertisement.[19] It is a trifle from the Scriblerian camp attributed to the non-existent Sir James Baker, and issued by Roberts in November. This mock prophecy suggests that punsters will come to a bad end if they do not heed the warning from the Almighty given in recent cosmic disturbances, notably the aurora that had been seen earlier in the year. In the advertisement, Pope is styled Sir Alexander Gnaw-Post because madmen were supposed to bite convenient objects in their despair: Cibber gnaws on his pen in *The Dunciad*. It also hints at the expression 'knight of the post', which meant a lying witness. There is a particularly effective touch at the start, where the posture Curll had been forced to adopt in the pamphlets – squatting on a close stool or toilet – is now transferred to his opponent. Pope is obliged to sit on the stool of repentance, an elevated chair in a church, often one belonging to Dissenters, as a mark of public shame. Naturally the other sense of 'stool' is there, to imply that the purgative medicine will cause him to evacuate his bowels, just as his victim had done in the *Further Account*. At least the poet now had a good idea what was coming: more lashings from such 'wits' as the publisher could assemble.

So a tumultuous year drew to its end. Curll had established his position as Pope's main antagonist and chalked up some incisive victories. The failure of the Rising had directed retribution against

the Jacobite leaders, while those with a share in the former government continued to face sanctions, and ordinary members of the
Catholic community suffered new curbs on their liberty. For Pope
it had been particularly difficult. On a more positive note, he had
largely seen off the threat from the Buttonians. He was still press-
ing ahead with the *Iliad*, although the next volume did not appear
in print until the following year. All in all, he might glimpse some
light on the horizon, but he would encounter fresh setbacks in the
coming months.

7

$\bullet$

The SECOND Aesop,
1717

The headlong pace of the feud slowed a little during the course of 1717, but elsewhere both principals kept up their usual busy schedule. In the summer Pope would reach a major landmark in his career, and achieve new recognition. Meanwhile Curll devised fresh ways of advancing his cause and thrusting his adversary into embarrassing situations.

It did not take long for the trouble to start. Around 5 January Curll issued under Rebecca Burleigh's imprint an impressive-sounding title, *Pope's Miscellany* – but this proved to be nothing more than an assemblage of the various pieces he had attributed to the poet over the previous twelve months, including *Court Poems*. A repeat advertisement on 10 January carried the addition of a promise or a threat, depending on where you stood on the quarrel: 'Yesterday I received a Letter signed Incognito, concerning Pope, and on Receipt of the Papers therein mention'd, they shall be immediately printed. E. Curll.'[1] This was the sort of running commentary on his publishing programme that Curll increasingly favoured as part of his advertising strategy.

THE FOOL'S CAP

A much juicier invitation soon opened up for the bookseller. On this occasion he had most of the public, and a good many of the cognoscenti, on his side. The episode centred on a new farce staged at Drury Lane on 16 January under the title *Three Hours*

after Marriage. The principal author was John Gay, but he acknowledged help from two friends, immediately recognizable as Pope
and John Arbuthnot. It ran for seven stormy performances, with
loud support and even louder denunciations in the playhouse.
Newspapers and pamphlets mounted a campaign to disparage the
play and its authors, with attacks from known members of the
Buttonian set. Some critics had apparently expected a partisan
offering on behalf of the Tories. This is not what they met with
in the theatre, but they still found abundant grounds for offence.
Obscenity made up a predictable charge, along with the far-fetched
nature of the action, which featured outlandish scenes involving a
mummy and a crocodile.

It was easy to spot real people in caricatured form among the
dramatis personae, and their defenders soon came along to point
out the scandalous libels acted out on the stage. No prizes would be
awarded for naming John Dennis as the model for a critic with a passion for the sublime, Sir Tremendous. Perhaps the most important
figure in the drama, Fossile, is a credulous antiquarian and virtuoso whose behaviour and affect were unquestionably drawn from
Dr John Woodward, an old antagonist of Arbuthnot. In my view
there are also references to two other great physician-collectors,
Hans Sloane and Richard Mead. The actor-manager Plotwell has
usually been identified with Colley Cibber, who actually played
this role in the early performances, although it seems implausible
that he should have innocently missed the self-portrayal. There is
less certainty about other persons, especially the women's parts,
one of whom was taken by Anne Oldfield.

Sensing that there was satiric capital as well as money to be
made out of the controversy, Curll was quickly on the spot. A
short pamphlet appeared on 31 January, entitled *A Complete Key to
the New Farce, call'd Three Hours after Marriage. With an Account of
the Authors*. The publisher was listed as Edward Berrington, who
usually put out material favouring the High Church or Catholic

viewpoint. However, we can be sure that Curll had an interest. The *Key* is generally bound up with Dennis's *True Character* of Pope, issued in the previous year. Moreover, it is one of the items in the *Miscellanies* of 'Joseph Gay', published by Curll in 1719, and the title is included in a booklist attached to a later compilation of *Court Poems*.

The key is altogether in the vein of the bookseller's other exercises along these lines. As for the supposed author, 'E. Parker, Philomath', his name is stolen from the Scriblerian lexicon – who else would have the knowledge, the desire or the nerve to pilfer such material? And by now it's not hard to recognize the source of familiar versicles that appear on the title page:

EXHIBIT 7.1

Why on these Authors shou'd the Criticks fall?
They've writ a *Farce*, but shown no *Wit* at all.
The Play is damn'd, and *Gay* would fain evade it,
He cries Damn *Pope* and *Arbuthnott* who made it;
But the Fools-Cap that on the Stage was thrown,
They take by Turns, and wear it as their own.

The last couplet refers to the prologue to *Three Hours*, in which the actor shows the audience a fool's cap with ears, and then throws it on to the stage with the words, 'Let him that take it, wear it as his own.'[2] Apart from an obvious allusion to the proverb 'If the cap fits, wear it', this goes back to the cap and bells worn by a court jester, which often featured asses' ears. Picking up a biblical reference in Gay's prologue to Jacob's son Issachar, 'a strong ass couching down between two burdens' (Genesis 49:14), the author of the *Key* awards this symbol of folly to the creators of the farce.

The dedication carries a sharp thrust at Bernard Lintot, who had paid the large but seemingly arbitrary sum of £43 2s. 6d. for the right to publish the play on 21 January. According to the *Key*,

Pope and Arbuthnot went along to Lintot's shop, only to find 'poor *Barnaby* in a Melancholly Posture' since there was no demand for the book. Lintot is reduced to tears by the realization that his ill-judged bargain for the *Iliad* has brought him to the verge of ruin. One of the accusations in the text is that the ladies of honour at court had made the authors a present of four hundred guineas 'as some small Encouragement for them to proceed in their *Dramatical Studies*'.[3] This too sounds like Curll.

The smartest riposte to *Three Hours* did not emerge until 30 March, with a shilling pamphlet under Burleigh's imprint. This took the form of a farce, unacted obviously, with the title *The Confederates*. Its author was 'Captain' John Breval, now establishing himself as a worthy member of the Curllian forces, although the dedication to Mrs Phoebe Clinket (a character in *Three Hours*) is signed by 'Joseph Gay', the all-purpose nom de plume adopted by Curll's team assaulting Pope and his friends. A coarsely drawn frontispiece depicts the guilty trio, with tiny Pope dwarfed by his heavy-set colleagues; Arbuthnot has a Scottish tam on his head as well as a sword and shield, perhaps hinting at a connection with the Rising. On the title page is a short quotation from a recent attack by the Buttonian Charles Johnson: 'These are the Wags, who boldly did adventure / To club a Farce by *Tripartite Indenture!*'

The cast list is brief, and comprises the three Scriblerians implicated in the affair, together with Lintot and Cibber, while the two female roles were played by Oldfield and Margaret Bicknell, who had likewise appeared in *Three Hours*. The three scenes are set in turn at the Rose Tavern, close to the playhouse; the green room at Drury Lane; and Lintot's home. Many of the barbs directed against the 'Triumvirate' have grown familiar by now; Pope has the opening speech, in which he states, 'With poyson'd Quill, I keep the World in Awe, / And from My Self a THERSITES draw.' In case anyone misses the point, a helpful note tells us that this refers to 'A Character in *Homer*, of an Ill-natur'd, Deform'd Villain'.

So the action rattles on, with a slanging match between Arbuthnot and Pope, each claiming supremacy as a satirist. Pope thinks to clinch his case by asserting, 'Not BUTTON's Wits from my Lampoons are free, / And Thou, and BLACKMORE are but *Worms* to me.' Unimpressed, the doctor reaches for his sword and threatens a duel, reminding the other man of his pygmy frame and thus his similarity to an ancient writer: 'The Second ÆSOP then, whose Neck was broke'.[4] The parallel draws on a traditional account of Aesop as a dwarfish and misshapen slave, who was eventually forced to leap to his death off a cliff at Delphi, after insulting the citizens. Seeing Arbuthnot's superior bulk, Pope quickly sues for a reconciliation. The friends plan to revive the play and pack the audience with their supporters, but Oldfield and Bicknell reject their overtures and decline to reprise their roles.

In the final scene Gay rushes off to Lintot's shop in search of a deal for the play that will salvage its fortunes. He finds Cibber there, likewise refusing point-blank to take to the stage again in *Three Hours*. Breval's aim is clearly to stir up a quarrel that was brewing between the actor and the Scriblerians. In desperation, the triumvirate throw themselves on the mercy of Lintot, claiming that what they need is 'Forty Pieces' – a little more than Judas was paid, but close enough to the sum they received from Lintot to raise suspicion of inside knowledge. The climax comes with the bookseller's denunciation of their methods, in two speeches that are interrupted only by a feeble pun that Breval allots to Pope:

EXHIBIT 7.2

Look on your HOMER, there, behind the Door.
Thou little dream'st what Crowds I daily see,
That call for TICKELL, and that spurn at Thee!
Neglected there, your Prince of Poets lyes,
By DENNIS justly damn'd, and kept for Pyes...
But your fam'd Heroes, with their warlike Bands,

Grace the same Shelf where OGILBY now stands,
And rot on mine, or on Subscribers Hands ...
For all your Puns, I shall not at this Age,
Turn *Bedlam* Commoner, or a *Gotham* Sage:
You may with CURLL your Quarrel now repent,
Or else to him you might for Help have sent:
But he with *Ballads* will debauch the Town,
And cloud your small Remainder of Renown.
Your *quondam* Vogue is now for ever lost;
As sure as on my Sign *Two Keys* are crossd.
Ev'n T[avene]R, whom you call *Senseless Drone*,
Trusts to your Comedy, to save his own.[5]

John Ogilby's translation of the *Iliad* (1660) was now regarded as crude and old-fashioned, but it had been the version that inspired Pope's love of the work as a small boy. 'Gotham Sage' refers to an old tale that the inhabitants of this village in Nottinghamshire were especially stupid, hence the ironic term 'wise men of Gotham' – it was this usage that led Washington Irving to apply the name to New York in 1807. William Taverner was a minor dramatist whose comedy *The Artful Husband* ran for fifteen nights in February, and thus far outstripped *Three Hours*.

At the end of the printed text of *The Confederates* occurs a short congratulatory poem addressed to Gay, 'on his Valour and Success behind Drury-Lane Scenes'. Metrically it's a bit wonky, but it scores a satiric hit in portraying Pope as a monkey dressed up in fine clothes:

EXHIBIT 7.3

So there our worthy Bards accord,
POPE finds the Pen, and Gay the Sword;
And may for SATIRE, and for COURAGE,
B' esteem'd the Champions of our Age.

'Tis true, they had a damn'd Miscarriage,
In their THREE HOURS AFTER MARRIAGE.
When kindly thinking to delight us,
They brought on Monsters, to affright us,
Wonders from *Ægypt*, and from *Nile*.
A Mummy, and a *Crocodile*.
Th' expecting Audience had hope,
Amidst the Monsters to've seen POPE:
So good a Jest how could they 'scape,
The Town would think't some merry Show,
Dress'd up in Masquerading Show,
To represent an awkward Beau.
Some People think most POPES are Evil:
But all agree, this POPE's the Devil.
Then, GAY, be kind, and cease to teize;
Forbear to Write, or learn to Please.[6]

To tease had a stronger sense then than it does now, meaning to annoy.

Few among the incessant attacks on Pope and his coadjutors reach the standard of this comedy. *The Confederates* is pointed and funny, with a keen eye for the missteps committed by the figures it targeted. After this, Pope never got involved in a play that was staged at a major London theatre. Perhaps Breval's farce about a farce deterred him.

REVENGE AND RETALIATION

The line about Dennis in *The Confederates* refers to the critic's latest offering. At the end of February he weighed in with one of the most wide-ranging onslaughts ever launched against his long-standing enemy, and this time Curll allowed his own name to appear on the title page. The extensive coverage is signalled immediately:

Remarks upon Mr. Pope's Translation of Homer. With Two Letters concerning Windsor Forest, and The Temple of Fame. Curll placed his first pre-announcement in an advertisement on 25 February, and publication was confirmed in the press three days later.[7] The same notice was printed in a different journal on 5 March. But there had evidently been a change of plan in the meantime. The *Flying Post* carried a strange notice:

EXHIBIT 7.4

Whereas Mr. Dennis's Remarks on the Senseless Popish and Jacobite Translation of Homer, were design'd to be publish'd on Thursday last, This is to give Notice to the Publick, That no such Book is to be expected. For the Popish and Jacobite Translator having got the foresaid Remarks into his Possession on Wednesday last, which was the Day before the intended Publication, made a smart, a surprizing, and a knock down Answer to them; that is, He immediately gave Orders to Bernard Lintott, to buy up the whole Impression.

No evidence has come to light to substantiate this story, which looks for all the world like a publicity stunt. The 'knock down' reply Pope is supposed to have produced has not left the slightest trace. In the event, the bookseller went on with publication untroubled, which may have been his intention all along.

The mixture is as before. Dennis gets straight down to deprecating Pope, both the man and his works: 'I regard him as an Enemy, not so much to me, as to my KING, to my COUNTRY, to my RELIGION, and to that LIBERTY which has been the sole Felicity of my Life.' This contrives to show Dennis at once as a Hanoverian, a patriot dead set against arbitrary foreign monarchs such as the recently deceased Louis XIV, a Protestant and a Whig. He feels he has a duty to show his adversary 'in his Natural Shape and Size, in spight of all his Malice, a quiet, harmless Animal' – a more nuanced version of what he has said on earlier occasions. He finds it amazing that

Protestants should have encouraged Pope 'to suborn Old HOMER to propagate his ridiculous Arbitrary and Popish Doctrines'. In the translation is found (deleting some repetitive phrasing) 'neither the Justness of the Original . . . nor any Beauty of Language, nor any Variety of Numbers [rhythms] . . . Instead . . . there is . . . Absurdity and Extravagance. Instead of the Beautiful Language of the Original, there is . . . Solecism and barbarous English.'[8]

Dennis can't stop himself from going back over the old complaints:

EXHIBIT 7.5

But 'tis no Wonder that this Translator, who in his *Rape of the Lock*, could not forbear putting Bawdy into the Mouth of his own Patroness, should put something like it into the Mouth of HOMER. If Mr. POPE had been a true Genius, he had been neither Wanton nor Impious. He had neither dishonour'd BELINDA, nor burlesqu'd the Sacred Writings. For, notwithstanding his Jesuitical Advertisement, it was He who burlesqu'd the *First Psalm* of DAVID. In that Jesuitical Advertisement, he does not deny it, but would appear to deny it. But supposing he had flatly deny'd it, can any one wonder, that one who has frankly and gayly, without any Provocation, and intirely against his Interest, done an Action by which he has disclaim'd all Pretence to Religion; would any one wonder, I say, that the Wretch should deny that Action, when all his Interest requir'd it. 'Tis apparent to me, that that *Psalm* was burlesqu'd by a Popish Rhymester. Let Rhyming Persons, who have been brought up Protestants, be otherwise what they will; let them be Rakes, let them be Scoundrels, let them be Atheists; yet Education has made an invincible Impression on them in behalf of the Sacred Writings. But a Popish Rhymester has been brought up with a Contempt for those Sacred Writings in the Language which he understands . . . Mr. POPE, I suppose, endeavour'd to make a Jest of God Almighty, out of a Spirit of Revenge and Retaliation, because God Almighty has made a Jest of

him. He has, indeed, a notable Talent at Burlesque: his Genius slides
so naturally into it, that he has burlesqu'd HOMER, without ever once
designing it.[9]

This passage, like others, displays a certain insight and a sort of
eloquence. But although the writing is a bit less hectic than before,
it is marred by damnable iteration.

The book moves on a little later to *Windsor Forest* as 'a wretched
Rhapsody'. It then turns to *The Temple of Fame*, Pope's recent mod-
ernization of Chaucer – not that Dennis seems to recognize the
source. A short appendix soon sees us back to personal recrimin-
ations, with assertions such as 'This little Author, who has lately
been so much in Vogue, has neither Sense in his Thoughts, nor
English in his Expressions.' Then comes a truly paranoid moment,
when Dennis talks of the story about Robert Norris, and expresses
his fears about further attacks from Pope: 'The Story is too long
to be told at present; the Reader who has Curiosity enough to be
acquainted with it, may have it from Mr. CURLL the Bookseller,
by whom he will hear of a Proceeding so black, so double, and so
perfidious, that perhaps a Villain who is capable of breaking open a
House, is not capable of That.' The writer ends his pamphlet with
a flourish, referring to what he has 'with a just Confidence, said,
in Defiance of his Two clandestine Weapons, his Slander and his
Poyson'.[10] It's easy to understand why even Pope's bitter enemy
Lewis Theobald called Dennis 'Furius'.

Over the past few decades, a number of commentators have
attempted to reinstate Dennis's standing as a critic of bold originality. Some of his productions may justify such an estimate. But
the *Remarks* enunciate few general principles, and they can only
be considered an aggressive intervention into the quarrel with Pope
that Curll was fomenting.

Not that the bookseller had a monopoly of retaliatory works. A
typical example of what was being passed around at this time occurs

in a poem published by Roberts in March 1717. This was an amusing account of the emetic episode and its aftermath, produced by a writer of minor talent, Leonard Welsted. Unfortunately, Welsted landed himself a spot in *The Dunciad* with effusions such as this work, *Palæmon to Celia*, which attacks the 'triumvirate' of Pope, Gay and Arbuthnot. The scene is set at Curll's business opposite St Dunstan's church. On its facade, the hours on the clock built in 1671 are counted out by the figures of the giants Gog and Magog, who strike the bells with their clubs (a sight that can still be seen). It is a fitting emblem, perhaps, for Curll's activity.

EXHIBIT 7.6

Near Dunstan's rising pile, where crowds repair,
The young for assignations, th' old for prayer;
Where two grim giants strike the vocal blow,
While damsels sell their toys and love below;
A noted Bibliopole great cares sustains,
Fam'd for his sufferings, envy'd for his gains,
Who venal Learning courts with low rewards,
And hires with promis'd pence ill-fated Bards,
A Mercury in ingenious frauds expert,
Renown'd for witty wiles and stealths of art . . .
This harmless Artist fell a destin'd prey
To the Triumvirs' unrelenting sway;
By secret stratagem they subtly wrought,
And couch'd their satyr in a purging draught;
The poisonous juice, with vellicating pains,
Successful Wits! ferments in all his veins;
He speaks his anguish in distorted looks:
Ah! what avail his copies or his books!
At length, the dwindled Hero rais'd his head:
'O frolic Bard, severely blythe', he said,
'What Patriot shall from pungent pains be free,

If such facetious drugs are known to thee?
Keen thy resentments are, and operate soon:
O say, is this a Protestant lampoon?
Now, Dennis, learn, learn from your foe to write;
Mix jalap with your satyr, and 'twill bite.'

'Jalap' was a purgative drug, once widely used. At this point the victim assumes that no remedy will save him, since 'The Quack prescrib'd the purge the Poet gave.' But he starts to recover, and addresses Pope, with side remarks on Gay and Arbuthnot. When the effects of the poison wear off, Curll is 'Restor'd at length to Learning and his Shop'. Immediately he plans revenge against his tormentor, and 'seeks the support of Protestant Allies', such as the editor of the Whig *Flying Post*, George Ridpath. The poem makes a vigorous contribution to the simmering debate, as one of the few which do not take sides openly.[11]

Behind the Scenes

By this time the bookseller had managed to lay hands on more of the poet's occasional verse, and again it didn't do Pope's reputation much good to have his name plastered over Curll's productions. The most substantial item was *The Court Ballad*, a broadside advertised by Rebecca Burleigh on 31 January. Wherever he obtained this, Curll assuredly felt grateful for the gift; he reprinted it in six places over the next twenty years. It is too allusive to make ready sense to most readers these days, which is a pity, because it illustrates beautifully Pope's skill in using the demotic form of the ballad to explore complex issues and sophisticated feelings.[12]

The poem concerns intrigues at court, both political and amatory. It centres on three ladies-in-waiting to the Princess of Wales, later Queen Caroline. Pope had become friendly with several of these women since the arrival in England of George I and his family.

This was facilitated by the fact that the Prince of Wales had quarrelled with his father, which was par for the course among the early Hanoverians. The junior branch of the royal family established a virtual court of their own when they moved to what is now Leicester Square at the start of 1718, and they had already cultivated a different circle of acquaintances.

In the political world this was mirrored by a bitter feud between two factions of the governing Whigs, which had created a fissure at the centre of the party. The ballad works around one of the latest developments in this struggle, which had sidelined Robert Walpole; his colleague Townshend was first instructed to go out and govern Ireland as Lord Lieutenant, and then dismissed from this post, as well. At the same time came the relegation of a one-time hero in crushing the Rising, the Duke of Argyll, who lost his place in the Prince's household. In June Pope wrote to Lady Mary Wortley Montagu, now on a mission to Constantinople with her husband: 'The Political State is under great divisions, the Parties of Walpole and Stanhope as violent as Whig and Tory. The K. and P. continue Two Names: there is nothing like a Coalition, but at the Masquerade; however the Princess is a Dissenter from it, and has a very small party in so unmodish a Separation.'[13] This situation naturally absorbed the keen interest of many of Curll's readers. On 28 March the bookseller advertised *An Impartial Enquiry into the Conduct of the Right Honourable Charles Lord Viscount T-----*, a long defence of Townshend, published by Anne Dodd, and once attributed to Defoe on very slender grounds.

Power was now in the hands of Lord Sunderland and Lord Stanhope, whom the king trusted much more than the outgoing ministers. The former was a son-in-law of the Duke of Marlborough, by now elderly and ailing; this connection would not have endeared him to Pope, who still disliked the duke. In passing, the verses of the ballad touch on the king's imminent return from a spell in Hanover, which had in some respects become a holiday home. There are also oblique hints of the princess's latest confinement, and of the forthcoming marriage of Argyll to a former maid of honour, Jane Warburton (the duke had been separated for many years from his first wife, before her death in January 1717).

All this may suggest a heavy work dominated by politics. In fact, it has quite as much to do with sexual intrigue and court scandal, and to be honest, its language at a surreptitious level is simply dirty. The ballad was to be sung to a tune that had been associated with a jaunty Restoration number, 'To all you ladies now on land'; Pope switches this to read, 'To one fair Lady out of court', probably implicating a maid of honour named Mary Bellenden, whom the prince was pursuing. There may not be many readers today who need, or perhaps wish, to look at more than one stanza to understand the point:

EXHIBIT 7.7

What passes in the dark third row
    And what behind the Scene.
Couches and crippled Chairs I know,
    And Garrets hung with green;
I know the Swing of sinful Hack,
    Where many a Damsel cries oh lack.
        With a fa, la, la.'⁴

The first two lines relate to clandestine activities going on at the theatre. Women did not usually sit in the pit, but occupied the boxes, with 'Ladies of Quality' in the first row, 'Citizens Wifes' in the second, and in the third 'the common People and Footmen'. Perhaps this row was darker because it was further from the chandeliers that hung over the stage to illuminate the auditorium (there were no house lights). The latent idea of a 'green room' was a recent coinage, first recorded in the work of Cibber as lately as 1701: 'I do know London pretty well, and the Side-box, Sir and behind the

Scenes; ay, and the Green-Room, and all the Girls and Women-Actresses there.'[15] 'Swing' might suggest the jolting motion of a carriage, but there must be a sexual undertone. In the same way, 'hack' could refer to a coach, but with the epithet 'sinful' a colloquial sense of prostitute must be suspected, as in a contemporary definition as 'a common horse, coach, strumpet'. The garrets might be not the abode of hack writers, as in Hogarth's *Distrest Poet*, but rather the secluded quarters of kept women. In political coding, green had no Irish connection then; it meant support for Protestants and the Glorious Revolution. The last line defies commentary. (Nor is this the filthiest portion of the poem.)

Three weeks later the *Court Ballad* was reissued in a volume with the come-on title *The Parson's Daughter. A Tale. For the Use of Pretty Girls with Small Fortunes. To which are added, Epigrams, and the Court Ballad, By Mr. Pope. From Correct Copies*. This time the supposed publisher was the virtually unknown 'J. Harris near St James' Bagnio', but he was no doubt a front for Curll. Soon the item was advertised by Burleigh, in the middle of a Curll announcement. He kept reprinting the title poem for several years, sometimes attributing it to a shadowy figure named Wyvill. The generally reliable *Monthly Catalogue* dubs the volume 'by Mr. Curll'. Both the ballad and the newly added epigrams by Pope would soon be recycled in *Pope's Miscellany, Part 2*, which came out in August. The bookseller could claim that he was using correct copies, because his text of the *Court Ballad* is close to the poet's holograph, which survives in the British Library, while the epigrams don't stray very far from the readings found in a contemporary transcript.

Someone with links to the poet was passing the materials on, possibly with his cooperation. A feature of the quarrel that may surprise us today is Pope's readiness to connive in illicit publications by his enemy, if it suited his purposes. He never admitted authorship, but nor did he deny it, even when the items went into the controversial *Literary Correspondence* in 1735. A few months later Curll would include the recent offerings by Breval and Giles Jacob (coyly described as 'the most eminent hands') in a collection called *The Ladies Miscellany*. The sting came in a subtitle: 'To which are added, Court-poems, on several occasions'. It is amazing how much recyclable material Curll was able to extract from his stock.

The publisher's affairs went well for him generally in the opening months of the year. True to form, he did manage to involve himself in a foolish tiff over rights with the pioneer horticulturalist Richard Bradley and the engineer John Theophilus Desaguliers – but that is another story. He received more saleable items from the prolific Breval, and then dug up a poem that would long sell in various guises, entitled *The Rape of the Smock*. It was written by Giles Jacob, otherwise known mainly for industrious compilations on legal and literary subjects. In common with better and worse writers than himself, Jacob ended up in *The Dunciad* after praising *The Confederates*. The *Smock* doesn't have much to do with the masterpiece whose title it twists, other than aiming at a mock-heroic style. Jacob launches one salvo against 'that stupid Farce, called *Three Hours after Marriage*'.[16]

After this came a fresh reprint of Dennis's *True Character*, twelve months on from its original appearance. But the main area where Curll had gained ground lay in his ridicule of *Three Hours after Marriage*, and in his new ability to dabble in court gossip, always a saleable commodity. He had his antagonist to thank for that.

APOLOGIA

Meanwhile, things had started to look up for Pope. The summer of 1717 was generally propitious for the Tories. This was thanks less to their own strength in Parliament than to the opposition movement sparked by the split in the Whig ranks. One result was that an Act of Indemnity was passed in July, granting a pardon to Jacobites, but Lord Oxford and Matthew Prior were meanly exempted. Oxford did not care, because he had just been released from the Tower after two years in captivity. The opposition of dissident Whigs, led by Walpole in the Commons and Townshend in the Lords, had successfully blocked the impeachment process. Friends of the peer greeted his return to liberty with enthusiasm. In May, Pope managed to get out a work by his fellow Scriblerian Thomas Parnell, who had translated *The Battle of the Frogs and Mice*, an anonymous Greek burlesque epic. This contained a life of Zoilus, the carping critic of antiquity, known as the scourge of Homer, and it was not hard to decode its implied references to Dennis – starting with the epigraph from the Latin poet Martial: 'I wish to see Zoilus hanged.'

From Pope's point of view, the larger achievements were still to come, involving two considerable projects. Both works appeared on 3 June. The third volume of the *Iliad* reached the public on time, although Pope was currently unwell and found his labours on the next segment of the translation increasingly burdensome. One of the factors may have been the threat of further onslaughts from Curll's party, if not from the now dwindling forces of the Buttonians. Joseph Addison had been seconded to become Secretary of State, a post for which he was barely qualified. He was intelligent and methodical, but had no presence in the parliamentary chamber, no oratorical gifts and no strong interest in the diplomatic wrangles going on in the Mediterranean region – yet these had become his responsibility, along with Ireland, a nation that fortunately he did know well at first hand.

An even more lasting contribution to literature emerged alongside the Homer instalment. Pope accomplished a great innovative stroke when he produced almost the first collected edition of the works of a living writer in English. Moreover, its author had not yet reached his thirtieth birthday. The original publisher was Lintot, but Jacob Tonson complained that he held the right to some items, so that the title page was changed to incorporate his name. It was a handsome volume, printed by the noted William Bowyer. The text is adorned with several decorative tailpieces, while the frontispiece is an engraving of a portrait of Pope by his friend Charles Jervas, executed in 1714. Although this is not the most frequently reproduced image of the poet, it is one of the best. It shows him in a deliberately upright posture, with one hand across his body, long fingers slightly spread. There is no attempt to hide his large, straight nose.

What of the contents? There are five main divisions. First come complimentary poems by friends, including Lady Winchelsea, Parnell and William Wycherley; that was a fairly usual element. Next we have the preface, followed by an essay on pastoral writing, never published before. The major works are then printed, with everything that had already seen the light apart from the Homer volumes. A final group is made up of new items, notably the elegy on *An Unfortunate Lady* and *Eloisa to Abelard*, two of Pope's most emotionally expressive productions that appealed more strongly to Romantic taste than most of what he wrote.

In this collection, Pope attempted to define his achievement up to this point and to establish his credentials as a writer of classic status. The preface sets out a considered view of his career and his role as a poet, in the nearest he ever came to an *apologia pro sua vita*. It also served as his most decisive answer to Curll, exemplifying a range of literary skills far beyond even the ablest writers of his contemporaries. Apart from the preface and the essay on pastoral, it contains no prose, so we do not have any of the racy pamphlets, or the salacious poems for that matter. This is Alexander Pope, Esquire, on his best formal manners. Critics of his role in the quarrel view such behaviour as deceit and hypocrisy, or a way of concealing his underlying urges towards nasty and destructive lampoons. Admirers see it as proof of his true stature, a revelation of his immense gifts and an extraordinary dedication to his art. The jury will have to decide.

It is worth recalling here a key passage at the end of the preface to the *Iliad*, which had appeared back in 1715. This reveals

Pope's sense of indebtedness to those promoting his work, but it also gives an idea of the company he wished to keep. Here he lists his acknowledgements, ending with the eminent patrons who had supported him, including the Duke of Buckingham, Lord Halifax and the later Duke of Chandos. But before that he expresses his gratitude to his fellow writers:

EXHIBIT 7.8

What I have done I submitted to the Publick, from whose Opinions I am prepared to learn; tho' I fear no Judges so little as our best Poets, who are most sensible of the Weight of this Task. As for the worst, whatever they shall please to say, they may give me some Concern as they are unhappy Men, but none as they are malignant Writers. I was guided in this Translation by Judgments very different from theirs; and by Persons for whom they can have no Kindness, if an old Observation be true, that the strongest Antipathy in the World is that of Fools to Men of Wit.

Then the roll call of the great and the good:

EXHIBIT 7.9

Mr. *Addison* was the first whose Advice determin'd me to undertake this Task, who was pleas'd to write to me upon that Occasion in such Terms as I cannot repeat without Vanity. I was obliged to Sir *Richard Steele* for a very early Recommendation of my Undertaking to the Publick. Dr. *Swift* promoted my Interest with that Warmth with which he always serves his Friend. The Humanity and Frankness of Sir *Samuel Garth* are what I never knew wanting on any Occasion. I must also acknowledge with infinite Pleasure the many friendly Offices as well as sincere Criticisms of Mr. *Congreve*, who had led me the way in translating some Parts of *Homer*, as I wish for the sake of the World he had prevented me in the rest. I must add the Names of Mr. *Rowe* and Dr. *Parnell*, tho' I shall take a farther Opportunity of doing Justice to the last, whose Good-nature (to give it a great Panegyrick) is no less extensive than his Learning. The Favour of these Gentlemen is not entirely undeserved by one who bears them so true an Affection. But what can I say of the Honour so many of the *Great* have done me, while the *First Names* of the Age appear as my Subscribers, and the most distinguish'd Patrons and Ornaments of Learning as my chief Encouragers.[17]

A noble tribute to fellow members of the literary profession, generously admitting his debt to some former colleagues with whom he had ceased to be on good terms? Or a name-dropping exercise, with ill-concealed self-satisfaction and a desire to bask in reflected glory? We know what Curll would say. But either way – let the record show this exhibit.

8

♦

An *Abominable* CATALOGUE, 1718–19

Almost at the moment of his greatest triumph so far, the poet suffered a crushing blow. On the night of 23/24 October 1717 Alexander Pope senior died from an unexpected heart attack, at the age of 71. His son wrote to the Blount sisters, 'My poor Father dyed last night. Believe, since I don't forget you this moment, I never shall.' To John Caryll, asking for prayers, he added, 'His death was the happiest to himself imaginable; but I have lost one whom I was even more obliged to as a friend, than as a father.' And to John Gay he gave a few more details:

> I shall not enter into a detail of my Concerns and Troubles, for two reasons; because I am really afflicted and need no Airs of grief, and because they are not the concerns and troubles of any but my self. But I think you (without too great a compliment) enough my friend, to be pleas'd to know he died easily, without a groan, or the sickness of two minutes; in a word, as silently and peacefully as he lived.[1]

Nobody who has read the messages he exchanged at this time can doubt his tender feelings towards his parents.

Pope's first care now had to be for his mother, who had reached the age of 74. Still a member of the household, and only a few years younger, was his old nurse, Mary Beach. He started to look around for a new place to live, since Chiswick had never been more than a convenient resting place and had never replaced the beloved family home. It took him another twelve months to find the Twickenham villa. He had to wind up his father's estate, the bulk of which passed to him after small bequests to relatives. In the meantime he grew less willing to leave his mother alone, and refused many opportunities to carry out his favourite 'rambles' in the country, which took him to see friends such as Caryll and Lord Bathurst. He felt additional pressure in case he should fall behind on his self-imposed task of producing a volume each year on the Homer project.

Keys and Clues

It is natural that in the following year, 1718, Pope should have had a much quieter time on the Curll front, as he scaled back his other literary endeavours. There were only two serious passages of arms in the ongoing combat. The first occurred very early on. Colley Cibber had just made a big splash with his comedy *The Non-Juror*, which premiered at Drury Lane in December 1717. The play ran for sixteen consecutive performances with two benefit nights for the dramatist, who enjoyed a huge payday of over £1,000. The king permitted an obsequious dedication offered by 'the lowest of Your Subjects from the *Theatre*'.[2] A tremendous cast included the star performers Robert Wilks and Anne Oldfield, later to be subjects of Curll biographies, as well as Barton Booth, whose intended biography the publisher aborted for some unknown reason. The prologue was supplied by the Poet Laureate, Nicholas Rowe.

The naked Whig sentiment expressed in the drama elicited a variety of responses. It was the biggest theatrical event for a long time, and its notoriety made the reception of *Three Hours after Marriage* the previous year seem like a tame episode. *The Non-Juror* was now published by Bernard Lintot on the second day of the new year, the first of five editions in a short time. The central character, Dr Wolf, is a Jesuit posing as an Anglican priest. He may be based on a real-life High Church clergyman, but no one can agree on who that might be. Wolf is a hypocrite in the line of Tartuffe, but if anything more dislikeable, since he lacks the shreds of humanity that Molière bestows on the hero in his more rounded character-ization. On top of the duplicity of the French original, Cibber later claimed, 'I ingrafted a stronger Wickedness, that of an *English* Popish Priest, lurking under the Doctrine of our own Church, to raise his Fortune, upon the Ruin of a worthy Gentleman, whom his dissembled Sanctity had seduc'd into the treasonable Cause of a *Roman Catholick* Out-law.'[3] At the end of the play the worthy gentleman Sir John Woodville is restored to his estate, which Wolf was planning to seize by means of a fraudulent document, and the papist spy is exposed by a former Jacobite, now pardoned for his services. It turns out that Wolf actually served in the rebel army during the Rising, in favour of the Roman Catholic outlaw.

Right on cue, Curll was able to deliver his response to the play when the sheets of Lintot's edition had scarcely dried. Perhaps the motive for an attack was the identity of the publisher, rather than the author. At all events, the pamphlet was available to buyers for sixpence on 6 January. It was called *A Compleat Key to The Non-Juror. Explaining the Characters in that Play, with Observations thereon*, and attributed to our old friend Joseph Gay, who may or may not be John Breval. Unlike most Curll keys, it does not take the form of a close line-by-line comparison, but rather detects similarities with Molière in features such as the characterization. It is not until the final pages that 'Gay' offers the conventional 'key' material. No really big names are involved. The pamphlet ends with a list of borrowings, including works by Pope, Susanna Centlivre and George Ridpath of the *Flying Post*. The *Key* proved popular enough to warrant two further editions that Curll brought out in quick succession.

Only a few glancing allusions in Cibber's comedy point at Pope and his associates, but the poet could hardly be expected to take much comfort from that, in view of the virulent anti-Catholicism that pervades the text. He may have attended a performance at Drury Lane, which would have been brave, but probably he merely subscribed for tickets to a benefit night without troubling to go along to the playhouse. But he had a comeback ready. This was *A Clue to the Comedy of the Non-Juror. With some Hints of Consequence Relating to that Play. In a Letter to N. Rowe, Esq; Poet Laureat to his Majesty*, a sixpenny pamphlet smuggled to Curll (who would print anything he was sent, regardless of its ideology) in time for publication on 15 February – Pope, for his part, was often willing to put the quarrel aside, if this gave him a chance to intervene slily in a current war of words. This joined a veritable flood of attacks from the Tory side, notably in Nathaniel Mist's *Weekly Journal*, but the *Clue* was by far the cleverest and funniest among them. The author pretends to have discovered that the play is really a satire from the opposite quarter – in fact, a concealed skit on a Whig hero, Benjamin Hoadly, the Bishop of Bangor, whose views on the independence of Church and state had provoked a furious war of words generally known as the Bangorian controversy. The true author comes from the Tory camp, this writer claims, and the praise of the Hanoverian regime is ironic, but people on both sides of the political divide have been too stupid to realize this: 'I am at a Loss which to admire [wonder at] most, the noble, free Spirit of our Friend the Author; the insensibility of those whom the Satire is *really Aim'd at*, or the ignorant Rage of those *disaffected Jacobite Wretches* who cry out when they are not hurt.' The 'friend' is of course Cibber, here exposed as a crypto-Jacobite, the last thing this studious follower of the party line would have wished to seem.

The pamphlet goes on to analyse various characters and themes, adducing 'evidence' to show that Wolf must be a bishop, who professes great zeal for the Church while betraying it. The argument is one of deliberately shortcut logic:

EXHIBIT 8.1

This premised, let us observe the principal Figure that presents it self to our View; I mean Dr. *Wolf*, whose Character answers to *Moliere's Tartuffe*, who is known to have represented a *certain puritanical Bishop in France*.

We next are to take Notice, That *Wolf* in the Stile of *Ecclesiastical Allegory* constantly signifies the *Presbyterian Party*: You know it is thus in the *Hind* and *Panther* [by Dryden], and most other Pieces of Controversial Divinity or Poetry. So Dr. *Wolf* is a *Presbyterian*.[4]

Plainly the aim is to ridicule facile 'keys' that interpret works so as to reveal a putative subtext that undermines the surface meaning. Pope had already made fun of this desire to find subversive elements hidden in his work, as we know from *The Key to the Lock*.

As for Curll, he was obviously glad to have the chance to take a share in an ongoing squabble that had rocked the town. In a postscript, doubtless of his own contriving, he even got in a plug for one of his own dramatic offerings, Centlivre's *The Cruel Gift*, published in January 1717, and to which Rowe had contributed an epilogue. But he may not have realized at first that the source of his new work was his old enemy. Three days after his original notice, he placed a fresh advertisement in the *Evening Post*. This supplied a new title, *The Plot Discover'd*, and adds one of Curll's ineffable asides in square brackets: '[The Manuscript of this Pamphlet was sent to me on Tuesday last, and I was this Morning given to understand, that this signal Favour was conferr'd on me by Mr. Pope for which I hereby return my most grateful Acknowledgment for the same. E. Curll].' The same advertisement lists other gems sent out by Curll's chaste press, among them *Eunuchism Display'd*, published on 6 February (see p. 196), and stated to be occasioned by an episode in which a young lady was decoyed into an amour with Nicolini (Nicolò Grimaldi), the star castrato at the Haymarket.[5]

No one could deny that Curll was quick on his feet. By 20 March he had a second edition prepared, now using the revised form of the title. Several small changes have been made to the text. The most engaging of these concerns a new set of verses added on the verso of the half-title:

EXHIBIT 8.2

To Mr. POPE.

Be Gen'rous *POPE*, nor strive to be conceal'd,
Since your own *Clue*, it's *Author* has reveal'd;
Go on, the Frauds of *Cibber* to explain
And prove him, what he is, a --- in grain.[6]

The missing word in the last line is 'fool'; the expression 'a fool in grain' was proverbial to mean someone confirmed in their idiocy. Curll went on advertising the *Clue*, and Pope made no effort to contradict the ascription. More than twenty years later Cibber remembered the affair and mentioned the pamphlet as a stage in the developing animosity between poet and playwright. It was the start of a feud that would almost rival those involving Pope, Curll and John Dennis among the quarrels of authors.

A MEETING AT WILL'S

Hostilities resumed in April, when Charles Gildon's *Memoirs of the Life of William Wycherley* came from the press. The dramatist had died in 1715; since he was an early mentor, Pope thought of himself as in some measure a guardian of Wycherley's reputation. The brief biography contains some of the nastiest things yet said about Pope. This extract starts in the early years of the century, when Pope came up to town aged about sixteen:

EXHIBIT 8.3

About this time there came to Town, and to *Will's*, one *Pope*, a little diminutive Creature, who had got a sort of Knack in smooth Vercification and with it was for setting up for a Wit and a Poet. But unknown as he was, furnish'd with a very good Assurance, and a Plausible, at least Cringing Way of Insinuation, first got acquaint- ed with that Ingenious Gentleman and excellent Critick Mr. *Walsh*, who was pleas'd to bear with his Impertinence, and suffer his Com- pany sometimes to divert himself either with his Figure or forward [pushy] Ignorance. For a Man of Wit may find an agreeable Div- ersion in the Company of a pretending Fool sometimes, provided that the Interviews are short and seldome. But this gave this young Poetaster an Opinion of himself, and that he must have something extraordinary in him to be admitted to such a Conversation . . .

From this Acquaintance he advances to that of Mr. *Wycherley*, then disgusted with the Wits; him he follows, attends and cringes to in all Places, and at all Times, and makes his Courtly Reflections on such as he found not very much in his good Graces.

I remember I was once to wait on Mr. *Wycherley*, and found in his Chamber this little *Æsopic* sort of an animal in his own cropt Hair, and Dress agreeable to the Forest he came from. I confess the Gentleman was very silent all my stay there, and scarce utter'd three Words on any Subject we talk'd of, nor cou'd I guess at what sort of Creature he was, and shou'd indeed have guess'd all the Pretences of Mankind round before I shou'd have imagined him a Wit and Poet. I thought indeed he might be some Tenant's Son of his, who might make his Court for continuance in his Lease on the Decease of his Rustick Parent, but was sufficiently surpriz'd, when Mr. *Wycherley* afterwards told me he was Poetically inclin'd, and writ tolerably smooth Verses.[7]

William Walsh, another sponsor of Pope as a boy, was a poet and a member of the influential Whig society known as the Kit-Cat

Club. It will be noticed that Gildon harps less on the young man's physical appearance than does Dennis, but his malice grows no less clear as the passage goes on. In subsequent years Pope would come back to his dealings with Wycherley, deprecating the way in which Curll and the dunces had treated the old man's literary remains.

After this, Curll put the quarrel on the back burner for a while. In July, he did reprint *The Worms* at the end of a small publication that carries various names. The title page says *Love's Invention: or, the Recreation in Vogue. An Excellent New Ballad upon the Masquerades*, with one of the bookseller's defiant mottos, *Honi soit qui mal y pense* (Shame on anyone who thinks badly of it), as an epigraph. However, the half-title reads *Mr. Pope's Worms: and a New Ballad on the Masquerades*. The same item was later advertised as *Heidegger's Masquerade: or the Ball*. Curll never made things easy for bibliographers.

Nor had the disputes surrounding *The Non-Juror* been forgotten, when they still could make money. A strange little opusculum issued in July had no title other than the salutation *To Mr. Cibber. Dear Colley*. It consists of a letter from Curll to Cibber; a reprint of Rowe's prologue to the controversial drama; a parody of this by the ever-willing Joseph Gay, in the shape of an epilogue for a revival of *Tartuffe* at the Lincoln's Inn Fields playhouse; and a former epilogue by the Earl of Dorset. The Molière adaptation had opened on 20 June as a rival to the hit production at Drury Lane. This could all be a hoax, although if that is the case the parodist took off Curll pretty neatly.

The letter refers to a comedy that Breval had recently written for Drury Lane, called *Play Is the Plot*. It was staged on 19 February, with Cibber in one of the major roles as Peter Pyrate, a bankrupt bookseller. Jacob Tonson published the play on 6 March. Most of the way the character of Pyrate speaks doesn't suggest Curll very directly, but parts of a speech near the end of the second act unmistakably point in that direction, while the misadventure with Mr Dactyl suggests Lintot's experiences with Pope:

EXHIBIT 8.4

You will pardon' me, Madam, but a malicious Rogue of a Wit gave me a Dose of Antimony about two Years ago in a Glass of *French* Claret, and I have never been my own Man again since – But to the purpose – I had as Flourishing a Trade, Madam, as any Man of my Profession in City or Suburbs, till the famous Mr. *Dactyl* put it into my Head, that I should get an Estate by publishing his Works: *Hinc illæ Lacrymæ*; from Penny Ballads, he drew me in for Octavo's, from Octavo's to Quarto's, from Quarto's to Folio's: I neglected my Business, built Castles in the Air, brought my Noble to Nine Pence, bought a Brush as the Saying is, and had a Statute awarded against me; this is the Sum total of the Life and Disasters of your Ladyship's most humbly devoted and obedient Servant *Peter Pyrate*.[8]

To bring a noble (6*s*. 8*d*.) to ninepence meant to dissipate your fortune by idle spending (it's a proverb used by Jonathan Swift in *A Modest Defence of Punning*, 1716). To buy a brush, also proverbial, meant to decamp, here to get away from creditors. In the play, Peter Pyrate tricks a spinster into marrying him in the belief that he has discovered the elusive secret of finding the longitude, for which the government had awarded a prize of £20,000 in 1715. Preposterous schemes to accomplish this discovery were a favourite target of the satirists, particularly John Arbuthnot, as a mathematician and good friend of Edmond Halley, the leading expert on navigational science. In 1714 Curll had been one of the booksellers advertising a pamphlet attributed to 'Jeremy Thacker', a philomath otherwise unknown, who touted an absurd scheme in competition for the prize.[9]

THE ROLL OF SODOM

Another quarrel was now festering. Although it did not go on as long as the great Popian feud, it caused Curll some trouble. This time his antagonist was Daniel Defoe, already an established author known for his poems, pamphlets and tracts on history, politics, morality and economics. Within a year he would make his bid for literary immortality and universal fame with the first of his novels, the opening instalment of *Robinson Crusoe* (the part dealing with the hero's desert island existence). It also enriched the publisher William Taylor, Curll's sometime colleague in the trade.

Back in 1715 Defoe had labelled his antagonist with heavy irony 'that Conscientious Bookseller, so celebrated for his Honesty, Mr. *Edmund Curl* in *Fleet-street*', and stigmatized the practice 'of Mr. *Curl*, and his Associates, Writing for and against' – fair enough, but with his record Defoe was the last person to blame anyone for doing just that.[10] The real clash came in 1718, when Curll began his series of works on the wider spectrum of sexual activity. On 6 February he published *Eunuchism Display'd. Describing all the Different Sorts of Eunuchs*, translated by a new figure on the Curll scene, Robert Samber, who would become one of his most reliable helpmates.

A month later came *Onanism Display'd*, Curll's bid to cash in on the popularity of a famous admonitory work, *Onania: or the Heinous Sin of Self-Pollution* (1710), which reached its nineteenth edition before mid-century. As we would expect, *Onanism Display'd* presented itself as a work of righteous indignation, partly at the sin and partly at the excesses of its competitor, while allowing wide latitude in prurient speculation. In the preface, the writer (possibly Curll himself) attacks his successful rival as a mere 'Empirick' (quack):

EXHIBIT 8.5

I shall make it my Business to set forth the Absurdity, inconsistency, imposture of this supercilious Scribler in every part; to prove that his

Treatise tends to the encouragement of Lewdness and Debauchery; that his own Medicines promote the very Sin, he, for interest sake, takes upon him to Discountenance; and to demonstrate, that he is really ignorant of what was the Crime of ONAN.[11]

These books prompted a bitter attack by Defoe on 'Curlicism' in Mist's *Journal* dated 5 April. The writer contends that the age is 'running into the highest Extream of the worst Part of verbal Lewdness, which, for want of a more extensive Word, I call *printed Bestiality*'. Although Rochester and Chaucer were now forgotten because of their bawdy talk, there was a new threat: 'Whither will the lewd Writers, and lewder Booksellers, of this Day lead the People, and what numerous odious Things will our Children find in the Libraries of their Fathers?' In his frenzy, Defoe launched into a violent attack on publishers. Of course, he had a particular individual in mind:

EXHIBIT 8.6

O Mist . . . hast thou ever heard among the roll of Sodom, crimes of the Sin of CURLICISM? Know then, this is the Sodomy of the Pen; 'tis writing beastly Stories, and then propagating them by Print, and filling the Families, and the Studies of our Youth, with Books which no Christian Government that I have read of, ever permitted. The Cry of the Sins of Sodom reach'd up to Heaven, yet they had not printed Bestiality among them, that we read of; but we have outdone Gomorrah, and all the Cities of Europe may be Challeng'd to match us in this Particular.

There is indeed but one Bookseller eminent among us for this Abomination; and from him, the Crime takes the just Denomination of *Curlicism*: The Fellow is a contemptible Wretch a thousand Ways: he is odious in his Person, scandalous in his Fame, he is mark'd by Nature, for he has a bawdy Countenance, and a debauch'd Mein [mien, facial appearance], his Tongue is an Echo of all the beastly

Language his Shop is fill'd with, and Filthiness drivels in the very Tone of his Voice.

Defoe wondered how 'this Manufacturer of Sodomy' could be permitted to promulgate his 'abominable Catalogue'; how could the Stamp Office take its twelve pence tax 'for the Advertisement of his infamous Books, publishing the continual Encrease of lewd, abominable Pieces of Bawdy'.

In a Word, *Mist*, record it for Posterity to wonder at, that in four Years past, of the Blessed Days we live in, and wherein Justice and Liberty are flourishing and established, more beastly and unsufferable Books have been published by this one Offender, than in thirty years before by all the Nation; and not a Man, Clergyman or other, has yet thought it worth his while to demand Justice of the Government against the Crime of it, or so much as to caution the Age against the Mischief of it.

A week later Defoe returned to his diatribe. This time he put some of the blame on authors as well as publishers, and wound up his argument in this way: 'There is only one Thing to be wish'd, viz., that all Booksellers who sell stinking books, such as Blasphemous, Bawdy, Lying, Treasonable Books, should like the Tomturdmen be obliged to open Shop only by Night, and then I doubt [believe] there would be very few Booksellers to deal with by Daylight.'[12]

About the end of May Curll published another volume in his series, a translation by George Sewell of *De Flagrorum Usu in Re Medica et Venerea*, compiled by Johann Heinrich Meibom in 1643. This carries one of Curll's resonant titles: *A Treatise of the Use of Flogging in Venereal Affairs: also of the Office of the Loins and Reins. Written to the Famous Christianus Cassius, Bishop of Lubeck, and Privy-Councillor to the Duke of Holstein. By John Henry Meibomius, M.D. Made English from the Latin Original by a Physician. To which is added, A Treatise of Hermaphrodites.* Years afterwards, when arraigned for obscene publications, he asserted that the book on flogging was issued 'on Occasion of the untimely Death of Mr. *Peter Motteaux* (who lost his Life in a Brothel through an Act of *unnatural Lewdness*). No Objection was made to it in Eight Years *Time*, nor was it published with the least immoral Intent.'[13] Motteux was a Huguenot author and journalist who had died in a brothel three months before, allegedly strangled by the girls during an act of erotic asphyxiation. As for *Tractatus de Hermaphroditis*, this was translated by one of Curll's diligent men, Giles Jacob, whom we shall soon meet again.

The inevitable riposte to Defoe came on 31 May with a pamphlet called *Curlicism Display'd. or, An Appeal to the Church: Being Just Observations upon some Books publish'd by Mr. Curll, viz. The Cases of Impotency, &c., Eunuchism Display'd, Onanism Display'd, A Treatise on Flogging, &c. In a Letter to Mr. Mist.* The imprint omits Curll's name, but since he signs the text at the end and writes in the first person (as well as advertising it in the press) there is no mystery about the work's origins. It is not clear how he thought the Church would welcome a detailed analysis of the contents of nine obscene books, but that is essentially what he gives us.

In the course of the pamphlet, the bookseller thanks his adversary for the free publicity and for what could be an excellent promotional label. Moreover, 'Your super-annuated *Letter-Writer* was never more out, than when he asserted, that CURLICISM was but of Four Years standing . . . I do sincerely assure you, Mr. Mist, that CURLICISM (since it must be so call'd) dates its Original from that ever memorable *AEra* of the Reign of the first Monarch of the Stuartine Race'. He then supplies a rundown of some of the *Cases of Impotency and Divorce* for which he had become well known, comparing them with the cases of conscience that Defoe had written about for Mist. There follows a rebuttal of the charge that such impious works would not have been published under Queen Anne, when allegedly 'none but *Persons of exemplary Piety and Virtue*, such as the *Ormonds*, the *Marrs*, the *Bolingbrokes*, &c. and their Agents the *Swifts*, the *Oldisworths*, the *Sacheverells*, &c. shar'd the *Royal Favour*.'[14] This is shifting the grounds of the discussion, since the writers listed had all earned fame on account of their Jacobite activity or High Church sentiments, and not for obscene writings.

Curll was equally unrepentant about *Eunuchism Display'd* and other recent publications on sexual matters:

EXHIBIT 8.7

They cannot by the *Laws of Nations and Nature* be term'd *Bawdy* Books, since they treat only of Matters of the greatest Importance to *Society*, conduce to the mutual Happiness of the *Nuptial State* and are directly calculated for *Antidotes* and against *Debauchery* and *unnatural Lewdness*, and not for *Incentives* to them. For which Reasons I shall not desist from printing such Books, when any Occasion offers, nor am I either concern'd or asham'd to have them distinguish'd by the facetious Name of CURLICISM.

In his usual fashion, Curll was entirely brazen about what he had done. He would not have replied at all, 'had not an Opportunity thereby offer'd it self to me of publishing to the World the Contents at large of these several PIECES, which have of late been so severely inveigh'd against' by one who had 'never read a Syllable in either of them beyond the Title Page'.[15] In addition, he took the opportunity to remind Defoe that the majority of his list consisted of works of history, divinity, antiquities or poetry.

A final flourish gave rise to other consequences. Picking up Defoe's habit of inventing 'isms', Curll accused him of 'MISTICISM and POPERYISM' (a neat touch), and wheeled the attack round to the politics of Mist's journal, which Curll, with every reason, denounced as Jacobite. This caused Defoe some uneasiness, and he wrote to his contact in the ministry, Charles Delafaye, on 4 June 1718:

> Here has been a Very Barbarous attempt made by Curl the
> Bookseller upon Mr. Mist (Viz) to Trepann him into Words
> Against the Governmt with a Design to Inform against him; I
> think Mist has Escaped him but if he brings it into your office
> I shall Lay a Clear state of the Matter before you. I kno' the
> Government is Sufficient to it self for punishing Offendors,
> and is Above Employing Trepanns to Draw men into offences
> On Purpose to Resent them.[16]

At this time Defoe was writing for Tory journals such as Mist's on
the instructions of his Whig paymasters, and he may have guessed
that Curll was looking for opportunities to act as a government
informer.

In any case, Mist had his own solution to the matter, according to two letters purporting to come from him that were printed in
the rival Whig paper, Read's *Weekly Journal* of 14 June. The first
requires Curll to retract by advertisement the accusation of sedition.
The second issued a full challenge: 'I have heard you have offered
to meet me at Sword and Pistol. Be assur'd I won't be trifled with.
I have been inform'd of your Insolencies in a certain Company this
Afternoon. I'll be at Six to-morrow Morning on the Bridge, the
lower end of Ludgate-hill, at Fleet-ditch.'

Mist is said to have ducked out of the contest. In response he
printed two further letters, one accusing himself of moral rather
than physical cowardice in failing to pursue the campaign against
Curll, and one restating his contempt for 'that Monster of unclean
Things, who you have so often, so justly, and so victoriously exposed
for Curlicism, I mean the Bookseller with a bawdy Countenance,
near Temple-Bar'. This writer objected to Curll's annoying habit
of 'insinuating as if no Body should have the Privilege of publishing
Bawdy or Blasphemy, but they that were for King George; or as if
being on King George's Side gave the Authority to write against
God and good Manners'.[17] Curll had thus made one more enemy

in Mist, who continued to keep an eye on his activities. In the issue of 28 June Mist's *Weekly Journal* referred with a sneer to a correspondent who 'by his writing seems to be in a condition to be ty'd down; he raves, and bellows, and talks much of Mr. Curll.' It is not certain whether the whole noisy affair was a publicity stunt. But it assuredly took Curll's attention in another direction for a while, and that left Pope with more time to get on with his more serious literary endeavours.

For the poet, the summer had brought some respite. The fourth volume of the *Iliad* did make its appearance promptly on 14 June, and he was able to get away to the seclusion of country seats owned by his friends to make progress on the next instalment. Thomas Parnell came to England for his first visit in a long time, but sadly he died on his return trip to Ireland. He left behind many unpublished works that Pope would include in a collection to follow in 1721. Naturally Curll had managed to scrape together a few fugitive pieces by the deceased that he would optimistically label *Original Poems upon Several Occasions*. At the end of the year Rowe, a regular victim of Curll's depredations, also went to his grave, creating a vacuum that provoked a contest among volunteers anxious to succeed him as Poet Laureate. A large group of wannabees emerged, who could be thought of as candidates by themselves or others, realistically or otherwise. Among them were Dennis, Gildon, John Oldmixon, Leonard Welsted, Thomas Cooke, Charles Beckingham, Aaron Hill, Eustace Budgell, John Hughes, Richard Steele, Ambrose Philips and Nicholas Amhurst. Then there were Lewis Theobald, whom Pope christened Laureate in the first version of *The Dunciad*, and Cibber – who got the real-life job next time round, in 1730. Obviously, Curll could have picked out of his stable of authors an excellent slate from which electors might choose. If the field does not look very strong, we should recall who was actually awarded the laurel in 1719. His name will not ring many bells: Laurence Eusden, anyone?

By now Pope had other things on his mind. He had decided not to go ahead with a plan to build on land made available by Lord Burlington, close to the peer's mansion off Piccadilly. This would have made him a neighbour of friends such as Arbuthnot and Erasmus Lewis; not far off stood the residence of Charles Jervas, where he had often stayed on trips to the capital. But it would have breached the restrictions on Catholics imposed by the Ten Mile Act; and maybe it would have allowed the denizens of Grub Street too easy access. Instead, he had found the villa on the Thames that he would call home for the rest of his days. Around December he made preparations for a move that would take place in the early part of the following year. Someone well aware of current developments was the vigilant Curll. From this time he always kept an eye cocked towards Twickenham.

An Inoffensive Writer

As he settled into his new environment, Pope must have been aware of many changes. Twickenham had come to prominence as a resort of those sufficiently jaundiced with the city to covet, and prosperous enough to acquire, a Thames-side retreat. It was not a backwater, for the road to London ran past the rear of the villa and the busy river flowed by at the bottom of the garden. Pope had never had a home of his own in such an opulent milieu. His landlord was a wealthy merchant and MP; his neighbour almost next door from 1722 was an earl; and not far off stood a house where Lady Mary Wortley Montagu came with her husband in 1719 to rent (and later buy) the property from the artist Sir Godfrey Kneller, whose main residence lay in the adjoining village of Whitton. A fellow incomer was James Craggs, Secretary of State and a good friend of Pope. Downriver, the grand mansion of Marble Hill took shape a few years later, with Pope's active involvement in its design and embellishment. This was the home of Henrietta Howard, a great lady at the royal court, and one of several well-heeled residents who welcomed the poet on social occasions.

This could not have been much more different from the world Curll inhabited around Fleet Street and Covent Garden. As we saw at the start of the book, this was crowded, crime-ridden and notorious for its red-light district; but it was also lively and diverse, with a great charge of cultural electricity. All the same, we can be misled by Pope's decision to seclude himself from the world of business, since Twickenham was more than just a *buen retiro*. The villa, as well as a sheltered haven for his mother, became his principal workplace, where many of his finest productions were laboriously brought to life. Without it, we probably should not have had many of the undertakings that most provoked Grub Street into febrile responses. Equally, Pope devoted a lot of energy to his garden, 'as busy in his three inches of Gardening, as any man can be in three score acres'.[18] He never forgot that his property was tiny compared to those of his rich friends and neighbours. As Maynard Mack has said, 'he drew amusement from considering himself a minuscule inhabitant of a world tailored to fit him.'[19] In 1720 the court of the manor of Twickenham granted him a licence to begin work on his famous grotto (partially restored in recent years), and this would occupy his attention for the rest of his life. Despite Curll's obvious curiosity about the way Pope lived in his retreat, the poet did not set up for a country gentleman. Twickenham was a place where he could get things done.

Understandably, Pope was not very productive in this phase of resettlement. For the first time he did not manage to get out his annual segment of the *Iliad*. In March 1719 a fine edition of the poems of Matthew Prior, fit to rival his own collection, was published. It had been set up at a meeting two years before, after Prior's release from house arrest. Those attending along with Pope were the prime movers, Bathurst and Lord Harley (son of Lord Oxford), Arbuthnot, Gay and Lewis. The subscription list outdid Pope's in many respects, which may have been a source of private discontent for him. Among the deaths at this time were those of two leading Whigs, with Samuel Garth following Nicholas Rowe. Each had remained a trusted friend, but Joseph Addison's departure in June after a long period of illness must have stirred mixed emotions.

That same month brought a minor scare, when the Jacobites launched another ill-fated expedition in Scotland, but it was easily seen off. Meanwhile, Curll was up to some of his old tricks. He advertised a sequel to or imitation of *The Court Ballad* entitled *News from Court* under Pope's name, but after persevering with the sham for a while, he retracted the attribution soon afterwards, ungraciously remarking, 'The Gentleman, whose Name by mistake, was prefix'd to this Edition, denies being the Author.'[20] He kept on selling the poem, of course, with the unknown 'Mr. Caley' listed as author. Subsequently he included it in the *Miscellanies* of the indefatigable Joseph Gay, along with several of the items we have already come across, notably *The Confederates*, selected *Keys* and Dennis's *True Character*. It would have been unlike him to jettison anything that might conceivably help his campaign against Pope. Curll took advantage of Addison's death to reissue a number of the pieces written by the deceased that he had been selling for years, legally or otherwise. He quickly got out a life by Giles Jacob, but uncharacteristically had to wait until a second edition five years later before he could append the will.

Jacob was involved in another project that had more lasting consequences. This was a compilation that he produced and to which Curll gave various titles. It was advertised in December 1718 as *The Poetical Register: or, the Lives and Characters of the English Dramatick Poets*, and it was joined the next year by a second part subtitled *The Lives and Characters of the English Dramatick Poets. With an Account of their Writings*. Together they made up one of the first guides to the history of English writing, from the Renaissance onwards, anyway (medieval authors are not very well represented, excluding 'Sir

Geoffrey Chaucer'). Among the Curllians awarded an entry are Centlivre, Dennis, Gildon, Delarivier Manley, Oldmixon, John Ozell and Theobald, not to mention Breval, who, according to the writer, 'has writ several very entertaining Poems' – well, he would say that, wouldn't he? Also present are Joseph Gay, 'author of an excellent Farce, call'd *The Confederates*', and 'John Philips', although goodness knows their master must have been fully aware of their indeterminate status. Let no one say he did not look after his own.[21]

The second volume contains a long and highly favourable account of the works of Pope. One issue relates to a claim Curll made in his responses to *The Dunciad*, to the effect that this entry 'was drawn up by Mr. *Pope* himself, and by him given to Mr. *Jacob*, with a Brace of *Guineas* to insert in it'. Jacob himself asserted that he sent Pope the printed proofs of the account, when 'by his Alterations and Additions therein, he entirely made the Compliment his own.'[22] That may or may not be true. What we can say for certain is that Pope read the *Poetical Register* with care. James McLaverty has shrewdly suggested that *The Dunciad*, through its text and notes, provides an alternative literary history to the one that Jacob's volumes offer.[23] This would not be the only occasion that the bookseller's productions gave the poet a stimulus to his own creativity.

Otherwise, Pope was left alone for the most part this year. He made a joke to Caryll of having fallen outside the loop: 'I have not the least knowledge of any poetical affairs; I have not seen a play these twelve months, been at no assembly, opera, or public place whatever. I am infamously celebrated as an inoffensive unenvied writer, even by Curll himself.'[24] The nearest the bookseller came to an antagonistic gesture was when he reprinted a Dublin pamphlet on the art of punning as the work of Swift, though it was really by the Dean's friend Thomas Sheridan. In April Curll must have felt some bitterness when *Robinson Crusoe* appeared and made the fortune of William Taylor. Defoe had triumphed without any need for Curlicism.

9

CRIMES *and* PUNISHMENTS, 1720–24

The coronavirus epidemic of 2020 spread fears and caused economic damage throughout the world. Three centuries earlier, the year 1720 brought the people of Europe not just the Great Crash, but the Twin Crashes. In France an ambitious scheme that involved reordering national finances on the basis of credit came to an abrupt halt in the summer. The so-called 'system' was launched by the Scottish adventurer, economic projector and gambler John Law. At its heart lay the Compagnie des Indes, a joint stock firm often known as the Mississippi Company since its main assets derived from land in what is now the southern United States. Scholars today praise Law's efforts to introduce a modern way of regulating investment and public entities, but corruption and exaggerated profit forecasts led to an all too predictable loss of confidence. By May the price of shares had started to plummet, the national bank Law had created was forced to stop payment, and there were riots in the streets of Paris as investors panicked. The Regent of France, who had formerly backed the innovations, now dismissed their promoter. Law fled the country by night and passed the rest of his life in exile, having returned for some time to Britain to reverse the banishment imposed on him years before (in his youth he had killed a man in a duel). While in London he was in contact with leaders of the opposition to Robert Walpole, as well as with John Arbuthnot, who had got to know the financier in Paris before the crash.

The story of the British bubble is more familiar. Again it centred on a company nominally trading to the South Atlantic and

Pacific regions. However, the South Sea operation, founded in 1711 by Robert Harley (soon to be Earl of Oxford), was a device to take over much of the growing national debt in return for favours from the government. The early enthusiasm of Tories, reflected in the optimistic vision of Pope's *Windsor Forest* (1713), dwindled as the Whigs gained control and the royal family became more deeply implicated, along with courtiers and politicians. The Company took on ever deeper obligations, and offered new subscriptions at intervals. At first it seemed the value of shares could only rise and rise, until the inevitable reckoning came in the autumn of 1720. Many investors, lured by the prospect of quick gains, were stripped of almost everything when the bubble burst. Among the biggest losers were huge tycoons such as the Duke of Chandos (a generous patron of Pope), as well as leading figures in the City who had built up great fortunes over their lifetime and were reduced to comparative penury. But there were also many humbler individuals who were driven to bankruptcy, some as far as suicide. Pope was unduly sanguine about share values until the eve of the collapse, but he seems to have escaped without too much damage. The unworldly John Gay had less luck, frittering away on a South Sea gamble the gains he had made from a well-supported subscription for his collected poems.[1]

Meanwhile, public anger vented itself on those responsible for the debacle. The leading ministers, Stanhope and Sunderland, died in the aftermath of the affair, as did Pope's friend James Craggs, a neighbour in Twickenham. The directors of the Company and senior officers were heavily fined, but several individuals got away with the full extent of their crimes. The entire episode sent shock waves through the economy, although these eventually lessened in part through the repairs instituted by the new prime minister, Robert Walpole, who took advantage of the weakened political establishment to grasp a hold on power that he would not relinquish for twenty years. It took Pope more than a decade to produce his measured but still devastating response to the fiasco in the *Epistle to Bathurst* (1733), one of his greatest poems.

We have no idea whether Curll invested in South Sea; if he did, either it was on a small scale or he got his money out in time. Instead, he sought to profit from the affair by devising come-hither titles to feed the public fascination with the topic, seen chiefly in a widespread desire to pin the blame on as many guilty men and women as possible. It is enough here to list some of these works. Writing just before the collapse, Susanna Centlivre had produced an amusing poem addressed to the deputy governor of the Company, wondering whether she should subscribe; Curll had put this out by 20 August, the eve of Armageddon. After the blow fell, there was *A Detection of the Whole Management of the South Sea Company. From the First Rise of their Stock to its Present Declension*, a serious but unremarkable compilation with a quotation from Jonathan Swift's biting satire *The Bubble* on the title page. (Curll later claimed to have issued the poem; this can only mean James Roberts's edition of January 1721, published days before the *Detection*.) Another of his contributions to the post-mortem on the Bubble was an impassioned speech made by the always erratic Eustace Budgell to the Court of the South Sea Company.

One of the earliest treatments in verse of the crisis was by 'Hugh Stanhope' (not coincidentally, the surname of a leading minister, adopted perhaps by Curll's frequent henchman William Bond). It was called *An Epistle to his Royal Highness the Prince of Wales, Occasion'd by the State of the Nation*, and didn't pull many punches: 'See here Two ruin'd Countesses in Tears; / While there a *South-Sea* Upstart's Strumpet wears / Two *Pendants*, worth two *Mannors*, in her Ears.'[2] It was popular enough for Curll to issue a stern warning: 'If any Person shall presume to Pyrate this Poem, they shall be prosecuted as the Act of Parliament directs, by H. Stanhope.'[3] This was most probably a bluff, since Stanhope was a legal fiction. The epistle was praised in an effort entitled *The Directors* from the equally suspicious 'Mr. Arundell', who added some verses at the end naming Curll as 'a Friend to *Poets*'.[4] Well, some might have agreed. These items were included in a collection of *South-Sea Pills to Purge Court Melancholy*. We may doubt whether they greatly assuaged the depression of those who had lost their shirts, at court or elsewhere.

A Conversion Narrative

Among the continuing aims of the bookseller was his desire to keep the quarrel with Pope in people's minds, even when he had little or nothing new to bring to their attention. On 22 March he mischievously attributed a poem on Lady Mary Wortley Montagu to his antagonist, as he would do in several later volumes.[5] Then, soon after the appearance of a third pamphlet attack on Curll, entitled *A Strange but True Relation*, the publisher provided a conspectus of the main exchanges to date in an advertisement on 12 April:

EXHIBIT 9.1

Next Week will be publish'd, adorn'd with the Effigies of Mr. Pope, *curiously engraven;*

The pope-ish Controversy compleat, viz.

I. An Account of the poysoning of Mr. Curll the Bookseller in Fleet-street; with a true Copy of his Last Will and Testament. II. The humble Petition of Barnaby Bernard Lintot to the Town. III. The Catholick Poet; a Ballad. IV. The Westminster Expedition successfully perform'd by Mr. Curll. V. A Relation of Mr. Curll's Conversion to Judaism, and of his Circumcision. VI. Proper Notes and various Readings to the whole. Dedicated to Mr. Pope; wherein are recited the Surprizing Adventures of his Bookseller, who, in one Campaign, ventur'd Drowning, Hanging, and Starving; with the Secret History of the Translation of Homer by Mr. Pope, and his Assistants. Written by Mr. Curll. *Nemo me impune Lacessit.* Printed for the Author.[6]

This gives us a great deal in a short space. For instance, we see that the bookseller was now appropriating the poet's image, something he would do for the rest of his life, culminating in the use of Pope's head as his business logo. It is also apparent that he is bundling together his attacks, such as *The Catholick Poet*, with responses from the other side. Seemingly he has already started to sell the circumcision pamphlet, although we do not know of any edition before 1732. Most significantly, the publisher threatens to bring out a new item, which will include a satire on Bernard Lintot as well as a full exposé of events surrounding the Homer translation; he already knows that Pope received help from scholars on the *Iliad*, but Pope had not yet embarked on its sequel, and so the secret over the multiple authorship of the *Odyssey* volumes would not break for a few years. With characteristic jauntiness Curll turns Samuel Wesley's *Neck or Nothing* into a triumphant exploit on his part. A favourite maxim, 'No one gets away with it if they provoke me,' was the motto of Scottish royalty.

One bit of the description that will puzzle us is item v, on the conversion of Curll to Judaism. This relates to an obscure pamphlet that had just come out, around Easter. Its full title, indicating its contents, is *A Strange but True Relation How Edmund Curll, of Fleetstreet, Stationer, Out of an Extraordinary Desire of Lucre, went into Change Alley, and was Converted from the Christian Religion by certain Eminent Jews: And How he was Circumcis'd and Initiated into their Mysteries*. The phrasing suggests, plausibly enough, that this is a sequel to the devastating assaults Pope had launched in 1716, *A Full and True Account* and *A Further Account*. However, the new work has been neglected on account of several factors. All copies of the original issue are lost, so that we have to rely on a reprint in the Swift–Pope *Miscellanies* from 1732. The pamphlet then appeared for several decades in collections of Swift's works (a totally untenable ascription), and not in those of Pope. It has never been edited. Even by Scriblerian standards, it has an awful lot of topical references, to financial, political and historical matters. It employs the device of a foolish narrator, as did other satires the group produced, and introduces many garbled references and blunders. In addition, there are unsettled questions over the authorship: Arbuthnot clearly took some part, and may be primarily responsible.[7]

The main reason the *Strange but True Relation* has been overlooked, however, lies elsewhere. On the surface it looks like an anti-Semitic tract, and indeed it has been read that way. Beyond doubt, the pamphlet does make use of stereotypical aspects of Jewish lore and rites. But the villains of the piece are not the stockjobbers who entice Curll to join their community. It is the greed and ignorance of the bookseller himself that come under the strongest fire. Written at a time when the boom in the stock market was still on the rise, the piece portrays the readiness of a nominal Christian to abjure his faith at the prospect of lucre. Unwittingly, he goes through experiences that mirror the temptations of Christ – and this is not the only place where we are reminded of passages in the Gospels. Some of the language echoes the Anglican prayer book, and it mixes allusions to Jewish customs and diet with parodies of Christian theology.

As the absurd conjunction at the end of a final prayer ('*Satan, Papists, Jews*, and *Stock-jobbers*') makes clear, the targets that Pope and/or Arbuthnot had lined up were of a diverse character. The tract parodies journalistic tales of wonders and sensational events. It sports with the craze for get-rich-quick schemes as the Bubble year moved ever closer to its catastrophic climax. Its farcical plot manipulates traditional associations of the Jewish community with wealth, either well- or ill-gotten. It offers some brazen passages that burlesque the devotional canon of Western Christianity. If the pamphlet is making fun of Protestant fears of the dangerous papists (as Pope had done in *A Key to the Lock* five years before), the author is equally amused by the linkage of Jews with Satan. He probably recalled the message of the collect for Good Friday, read in churches at the time the events are set, asking that Jews and infidels should be saved and brought home to God's flock.

All in all, *A Strange but True Relation* continues Pope's joyous if often indecent campaign against Curll. It must be read in conjunction with his earlier pamphlets exposing the bookseller to ridicule. This was a man whom Pope may have regarded with contempt, but whom he delighted to pillory in print. (I say 'Pope' here to keep things simple, despite the signs of Arbuthnot's involvement.)

Two passages indicate the tone and temper. Be warned that this is strong stuff, for all its comic exuberance. The first describes the efforts made to persuade Curll to convert:

EXHIBIT 9.2

They now promis'd if he would poison his Wife and give up his *Grisking*, that he should marry the rich *Ben Meymon*'s only Daughter. This made some Impression on him.

They then talk'd to him in the *Hebrew* Tongue, which he not understanding, it was observ'd had very great Weight with him.

They, now perceiving that his *Godliness* was only *Gain*, desisted from all other Arguments, and attack'd him on his weak side, namely that of *Avarice*.

Upon which *John Mendez* offer'd him an Eighth of an advantagious Bargain for the *Apostles Creed*, which he readily and wickedly renounced.

He then sold the *Nine and Thirty Articles* for a *Bull*; but insisted hard upon *Black-Puddings*, being a great Lover thereof.

Joshua Perrara engag'd to let him share with him in his *Bottom-rye*, upon this he was persuaded out of his *Christian Name*; but he still adher'd to *Black-Puddings*.

Sir *Gideon Lopez* tempted him with *Forty Pound* Subscription in *Ram's Bubble*; for which he was content to give up the *Four Evangelists*, and he was now compleated a perfect *Jew*, all but *Black-Pudding* and *Circumcision*; for both of which he would have been glad to have had a Dispensation.

'Bottomrye' refers to marine insurance, while Ram's Bubble was a recent financial scheme that evolved into the durable London Assurance (absorbed by Sun Alliance in 1965).

Soon afterwards Curll is prepared for his ordeal:

EXHIBIT 9.3

At his Entrance into the Room he perceived a meagre Man, with a sallow Countenance, a black forky Beard, and long Vestment. In his Right Hand he held a large Pair of Sheers, and in his Left a red hot Searing-Iron. At Sight of this, Mr. *Curll*'s Heart trembled within him, and feign would he retire; but he was prevented by six Jews, who laid Hands upon him, and unbuttoning his Breeches threw him upon the Table, a pale pitiful Spectacle!

He now entreated them in the most moving Tone of Voice to dispense with that *unmanly* Ceremonial, which if they would consent to, he faithfully promis'd that he would eat a Quarter of *Paschal Lamb* with them the next *Sunday* following.

All these Protestations availed him nothing, for they threatned him that all Contracts and Bargains should be void unless he would submit to bear all the *outward* and *visible* Signs of *Judaism*.

Our Apostate hearing this, stretched himself upon his Back, spread his Legs, and waited for the Operation; but when he saw the High-Priest take up the *Cleft Stick*, he roared most unmercifully, and swore several Christian Oaths, for which the *Jews* rebuked him.

The Savour of the *Effluvia* that issued from him, convinced the Old *Levite* and all his Assistants that he needed no present *Purgation*, wherefore without farther *anointing* him he proceeded in his Office; when by an unfortunate Jerk upward of the impatient Victim, he lost five times as much as ever Jew did before.[8]

The sequel may easily be imagined. One notable feature here is the profusion of puns, which deliberately mingle Jewish, Catholic and Anglican vocabulary. There's room to doubt whether even contemporary readers got all the jokes. Still, Pope knew Curll would, and that may have been enough.

Undeterred, the bookseller mounted a further slashing attack in mid-June. It was advertised as *The Paralell* [*sic*]: *A Poem. Comparing the Poetical Productions of Mr. Pope with the Prophetical Productions of Mr. Campbell. By Mr. Stanhope.* As noted earlier, the name of the author was probably a pseudonym for William Bond, one of the ablest members of the Curllians. The poem appeared in a collection called *Mr. Campbell's Packet*, which contained material about the deaf-and-dumb fortune teller Duncan Campbell. In turn the writer pours scorn first on *The Rape of the Lock*, damned as before for obscenity, its derivation from *Gabalis* and the poet's '*Monkish*' origins; and then on *Windsor Forest* for internal contradictions and feeble attempts to make the sound of the verses mirror the sense. Curll liked this item enough to reuse it in *The Progress of Dulness* eight years later, when a lot more material was available to him.

There may be one more unsuspected dig by Pope at Curll. It occurs in *An Answer to Duke upon Duke*, a response published in August 1720 to Pope's clever ballad of that name. The original poem concerns an abortive duel between a minor politician named Guise, known to Pope, and the vehement Whig Nicholas Lechmere, who led the prosecution of the Jacobite lords in 1716 and that of the hapless young printer John Matthews in 1719. Previous commentators have seen the *Answer* as an attack on the poet, but it seems to me more likely that this was a joke from the Scriblerian side, parodying the language usually found in such assaults. It is written in the voice of Lechmere, who is the chief butt of *Duke upon Duke*. He emerges as an even more ridiculous bigot this time round. Here is the way the *Answer* opens:

EXHIBIT 9.4

Thou *POPE*; oh *Popery* burning hot,
For none but *Papists* wou'd,

Enter into a cursed Plot
'Gainst *Protestant* so good.

For this have I, O Libeller,
As 'twill be made appear,
For the Succession kept a stir,
And *Speech'd* it Year to Year.

For this, thine *Homer* have I bought,
All thy smart Things on *Curle?*
With a Sham *Dukedom* set at nought,
Who thought to be an Earl.[9]

The joke about the sham dukedom refers to the title bestowed in the ballad on Lechmere's opponent, Sir John Guise, but also to the former's ambitions to go beyond his role as Chancellor of the Duchy of Lancaster – a government sinecure he had managed to retain even when fired as Attorney General in early 1720.

Inadvertent Errors

Quite apart from the Bubble, and the things Pope did to him, Curll had some self-induced troubles. At the end of 1719 he had made one of his quixotic or simply foolish gestures when he published a book alleging fraud in the operations of the customs service. It was written by a man lodging with him, Robert Loggin, who held a junior post in the organization. The commissioners who oversaw this branch of government revenue took umbrage and dismissed Loggin. After reading Curll's book, the board grew shirty and recommended to the Treasury that the publisher should be prosecuted, but the charge was dropped after he appeared before them and agreed to apologize. This came by way of a grovelling press notice on 17 February 1720 that admitted his share in 'the

said false scandalous and malicious Libel', which he had published 'thro' Inadvertency'. He ended by claiming that he would
'always be more proud of retracting an Error than persisting in
one', which does not really match his record as far as the quarrel
with Pope goes.[10]

Soon another rash decision would provoke the threat of litigation. A Presbyterian minister named William Clark had been
accused by members of his church of fornication with a certain
Widow Coleman. Somehow Curll had got hold of some old depos-
itions relating to the affair. Having no other convenient vehicle, he
had tacked these on to the end of a juicy narrative of rape, under
the title *The Backsliding Teacher*. Clark understandably reacted
with fury. His reply in May 1720, *Party Revenge*, sought to restate
his innocence, and to lambast Curll for having rooted out the old
accusations:

EXHIBIT 9.5

It cannot but be acceptable to the sober Part of Mankind, to acquaint
'em, that *Edmond Curl*, Bookseller is now under a severe prosecution by the Reverend Mr. *William Clarke* a Dissenting Minister,
near *Shadwell*, for publishing a flagrant, malicious, and scandalous
Libel against that Gentleman's Character. A Bill of Indictment has
been found against the said *Curl* at the *Old Bailey*; accordingly it was
design'd he should have taken his Trial there last Sessions ... but the
Case not being call'd, it is deferr'd till next Sessions, when 'tis hop'd
that Wretch (who hath given out that he never did any thing he had
reason to be asham'd of) will receive his just Deserts.

As it has been his continu'd Practice for many Years to Print de-
faming, scandalous and filthy Libels, particularly (of late) against
the Honourable Commissioners of his Majesty's Customs, to be seen
by his Recantation in the Daily Courant *Feb.* 17. 1720, so he has rak'd
up the Scandalous Accounts of some Perjur'd Testators (an old Devilish Plot contriv'd by the High Church Party in the late Reign, to

bring the Dissenters into Contempt) which Mr. *Clarke* hath clearly confuted about 12 or 13 Years ago.

Since Clark had been 'barbarously abus'd in his Character', he resolved to prosecute his detractor to the utmost extent of the law. After the trial at the Old Bailey he would bring 'a swingeing Action against the said *Curl* for the great damages sustain'd by the said Libel', in the hope that the 'Honourable Court will adjudge him as a common Nuisance to Mankind'.[11]

Here Clark is asking for two remedies: a government trial for sedition and a civil suit for what we call libel today, that is, personal defamation. Neither action seems to have survived in the official archives. Clark was a zealous Hanoverian who offered to reveal to the authorities some treasonable words uttered by Jacobites. Such episodes should remind us that it was not only Pope who would have liked to see someone clip Curll's wings.

One of the biggest distractions for Pope was the unveiling of a Jacobite invasion plotted by conspirators with his close friend Bishop Francis Atterbury at their head. Walpole's operatives were able to nip the plan in the bud. Several of those involved had taken some share in the Rising of 1715, and the poet had some acquaintance with almost all these individuals. After Atterbury's arrest and imprisonment in the Tower in August 1722, Pope remained a loyal friend and agreed, despite misgivings, to testify on behalf of the bishop when the Lords arraigned him for high treason the following May. By his own admission Pope flunked the task of reporting his conversations with the bishop: 'Though I had but ten words to say, and that on a plain point, (how that bishop spent his time whilst I was with him at Bromley) I made two or three blunders in it: and that notwithstanding the first row of lords, (which was all I could see) were mostly of my acquaintance.'[12]

The aftermath was chilling: lifelong banishment for Atterbury, and the death sentence for a hapless understrapper named

Christopher Layer (Curll had been asked by Lord Townshend, according to his own testimony, to extract some incriminating documents held by Layer's clerk). There were lengthy sentences for mere foot soldiers in the cause, although one of them, a Nonjuring parson from Ireland named George Kelly, managed to escape from the Tower. He got as far as the Pretender's court at Avignon, and took part in the no less futile invasion of Scotland in 1745. Curll brought out memoirs of his life after his flight in 1736, as he had done with Atterbury just three months after the trial in the Lords ended. Over the next few years he also took the opportunity to get into print whatever odd items composed by the bishop he could lay hands on. But he had a more direct interest that has lain unobserved in the government files. On 20 March 1723 he wrote to the Secretary of State, Lord Townshend, enclosing a message he had 'intercepted' that morning. It concerned 'Two of the chiefest Agents in the Bp. of Rochester's Secrets'.[13] Pope could not possibly have known just how active Curll was as a government spy, but if he had, this would just have confirmed the opinion he had long held about his great adversary.

Meanwhile Walpole's ministry heaped up the pressure on Catholics by imposing further new taxes. Not only had Pope seen one friend exiled to France, but he had also lost his long-time patron and ally the Earl of Oxford, who died in May 1724. It was hardly the most propitious background for work, in particular his edition of Shakespeare, which he characterized as 'the dull duty of an editor'.[14] But at least Curll was not stalking him quite so regularly – for the time being, that is.

DIRECTOR OF WIT

For the next few years, something of a dampening down in hostilities took place: not a complete lull, because sporadic outbursts showed that the quarrel had not gone away, but each participant had other distractions to occupy him. To a degree, their careers went on in parallel, without as much direct interaction as before or indeed after. Each in turn faced sanctions for attempting to publish the allegedly treasonable writings of the Duke of Buckingham. In 1720 Pope successfully completed the *Iliad*, breathing an almost audible sigh of relief when he dedicated the work to a fellow professional, William Congreve: 'Let me leave behind me a Memorial of my Friendship, with one of the most valuable Men as well as finest Writers, of my Age and Country.'[15] Wisely or not, he soon agreed to follow up with a version of the *Odyssey*, a task for which he would need to recruit two aides as his secret co-translators. This, together with his edition of Shakespeare, ate up much of his time and energy into the middle of the decade. The renovation of the villa at Twickenham went on for some time, while his collection of works by Buckingham brought him into conflict with the authorities for the first time.

As we have seen, Curll's legal troubles began in earnest during the South Sea year, and mounted steadily afterwards. He was devoting much of his list to substantial antiquarian works. As always, he tried to capitalize on current events, such as a scare caused by the spread of bubonic plague as far as Marseilles, resulting in hasty quarantine provisions by the government and many panicky articles in the press. Arbuthnot was one of those called in to advise on the matter, along with fellow luminaries in the Royal College of Physicians, Richard Mead and Hans Sloane, while Daniel Defoe found an admonitory parallel with the events of 1665 in his *Journal of a Plague Year*, a book frequently recalled during the equally troubled year of 2020. Curll also wanted to turn to his advantage the Atterbury affair, and cause Pope fresh embarrassment. But none of these efforts brought him huge returns, and he had to depend more than ever on his sleazier productions. Financial turmoil and political upheaval might come and go, but rapes and eunuchs would always sell.

Curll did continue to pursue Swift. This involved printing under the dean's name a number of dubious items that are no longer believed to be from his hand. In April 1720 Swift wrote wearily to his old friend Charles Ford about this:

EXHIBIT 9.6

I cannot help the usage which honest Mr. Curl gives me, I watched for his Ears in the Queens time, and was I think once within an Inch of them. There is an honest humrsom Gentleman here who amuses this Town sometimes with Trifles and some Knave or Fool transmitts them to Curl with a Hint that they are mine. There is one about Precedence of Doctors, we do not know who writt it; It is a very crude Piece, tho not quite so low as some others; This I hear is like-wise a Present of Curl to me. I would go into any Scheam you please with Mr. Congreve and Mr. Pope and the rest, but cannot imagine a Remedy unless he be sent to Bridewell for Life.[16]

Part of the joke here comes from the fact that Bridewell was known most widely for the incarceration of prostitutes. Pope has his dunces troop past the gaol 'as morning-pray'r and flagellation end'.[17] Whipping was a punishment administered in the 'house of correction' for crimes such as petty theft. It might seem apt for a man notorious for pillaging literary property, and who had recently published a book on flogging.

In the same year Swift made a passing thrust in verses to his friend and amanuensis Stella (Esther Johnson), regarding the dread-ful poems in Curll's collections. But, of course, that would never have discouraged his tormentor. In late 1721 came a new assem-blage of *Miscellanies Written by Dr Jonathan Swift, D.D. Dean of St Patrick's Dublin*. Except that most of them weren't. Also adver-tised was 'a very curious print of Dr Swift', taken from a portrait by Godfrey Kneller.[18] Around the same time John Gay produced a neat couplet with a jokey eye-rhyme: 'Were Prior, Congreve,

Swift and Pope unknown, / Poor slander-selling Curll would be undone.'[19] When Matthew Prior, almost an associate member of the Scriblerus group, died in September, the publisher enjoyed something of a bonanza. Within weeks he had out a life, a supplementary volume to the poems he had formerly pirated, a will and a 'curious' print. How must Pope have squirmed, in anticipation of what might happen if Curll survived him – as ultimately transpired!

Curll had given cause for irritation when he misattributed to Prior a small poem, 'The Female Phaeton', in 1718, as indeed he continued to do for years to come. The item concerns the young socialite Lady Catherine Hyde, later a fervent supporter of Gay. Prior denied the claim in a typically graceful ballad-style 'Answer'. It opens with a reference to the ceremony of the Royal Maundy before Easter, when alms are handed out to elderly people. The money was then bestowed by the Lord High Almoner on behalf of the king:

EXHIBIT 9.7

As Almoner in Holy Week
Dealing George's good Cloth and Bread
Sends forth his Officers to seek
The People who stand most in need.
So Thou Director Great of Wit
Amongst Us Authors Rule'st the Roast
Distributing as Thou think'st fit
To those that seem to want the most.
Thou did'st to Me a Bard half Starv'd
A Plenteous Dole of Fame Provide
And gav'st Me what I ne'er Deserv'd
Something of Phaeton and Hyde . . .
By adding to my fame
Dear Curl, thou hast undone Me.
Making me richer than I am
Thou drawst My Creditors upon Me.

> From Blanket and from Physic free
> Thou long sha't Live and We'll be friends,
> Put out my Name and We'll agree
> Make me at least this smal Amends.
> Then Curl for Mine and for Truths sake
> Thy righteous Printing Press employ,
> To prove I never did Mistake
> A Lady for a Boy.[20]

Although ironically dubbed great director of the world of literature, Curll is not allowed to forget the emetic or the blanket toss. Unfortunately, this charming retort to irresponsible marketing was not published until long after Prior and his friend Pope had died.

BREACHES OF PRIVILEGE

Another death, that of the Duke of Buckingham in February 1721, affected the plans of both the major players in the quarrel. Buckingham was a former minister and courtier, a poet and an early patron of Pope. Without delay Curll produced a work by the diligent William Bond entitled *Buckingham House*, about the duke's mansion, which would later be converted into the royal palace. An advertisement in the *Daily Post* on 18 May announced that 'This poem was approv'd of by the Duke, (who made the Author a handsome Present, but desir'd that it might not be publish'd till after his Decease).' By the end of the year plans for a full edition were complete, and on 22 January 1722 Curll gave notice in the press of the works in prose and verse, with a life by Lewis Theobald and, naturally, a true copy of his Grace's last will and testament. This immediately alerted the House of Lords, ever jealous of its privileges, whether historic or freshly minted. Within hours the publisher was ordered to attend the House on the following day. No one will be surprised to learn that the outcome was another dressing-down for Curll. His fate is tersely described in the official *Journal* of the Lords:

EXHIBIT 9.8

E. Curll examined, about his Advertisement for publishing the late D. of Bucks' Works, &c.

The House being informed, 'That *E. Curll* attended (according to Order):' He was called in. And so much of an Advertisement inserted in the News Paper, intituled, '*The Daily Journal, Monday, January* 22d, 1721–2,' as gave Notice, That the Works of the late Right Honourable *John Sheffield* Duke of *Buckinghamshire*, in Prose and Verse, with his Life (compleated from a Plan drawn by his Grace) by Mr. *Theobald*, and a true Copy of his last Will and Testament, will speedily be published by the said *Curll*,' being shewed to him; he owned, 'That he caused the same to be printed; that he had not the Consent of the Executors or Trustees of the said late Duke, for publishing his said Life, Works, or Will.' And being further examined in relation to the printing the said Advertisement; he was directed to withdraw.

And being accordingly withdrawn.

Motion, that it is a Breach of Privilege to print the Works, &c. of any Lord, after his Death, without Leave:

It is Resolved and Declared, by the Lords Spiritual and Temporal in Parliament assembled, That if, after the Death of any Lord of this House, any Person presume to publish in Print his Works, Life, or last Will, without Consent of his Heirs, Executors, Administrators, or Trustees, the same is a Breach of the Privilege of this House.

And it being moved, 'That the same be entered upon the Roll of Standing Orders of this House . . .

Then it was agreed by the House, 'That the said *Curll* should be again called in, and reprimanded by the Lord Chancellor, for causing the said Advertisement to be printed; and forbidden to publish the Book so advertised.'

And the said *Curll* being again called in; and, on his Knees, reprimanded by the Lord Chancellor accordingly; and forbidden to publish the said Book: He was directed to withdraw.[21]

Not for the first time, Curll had ended up on his knees before the Chancellor, with the peers in attendance. A committee was appointed to look into the advertisements. On 31 January the full House reviewed the issues and determined that a breach of privilege had been committed:

EXHIBIT 9.9

The House (according to Order) proceeded to take into Consideration the Motion made the Twentythird Instant, for entering upon the Roll of Standing Orders the Resolution and Declaration then made, against publishing in Print the Works, Life, or last Will, of any Lord of this House.

And the same, being read by the Clerk, was, with some Additions, agreed to by the House, as follows:

Notice being taken, That the Works, Lives, and last Wills, of divers Lords of this House, have been frequently printed imperfectly, and published after their Deaths, without the Direction or Consent of the Heirs, Executors, Administrators, or Trustees, of such Lords: It is therefore Resolved and Declared, by the Lords Spiritual and Temporal in Parliament assembled, That if, after the Death of any Lord of this House, any Person presume to publish in Print his Works, or any Part of them not published in his Life-time, or his Life, or last Will, without Consent of his Heirs, Executors, Administrators, or Trustees, the same is a Breach of the Privilege of this House.

Ordered, That the said Resolution and Declaration be entered on the Roll of the Standing Orders of this House, and printed and published, and affixed on the Doors of this House.[22]

No such rule had previously been in force, and no precedent was cited. It could be said that the offender was being punished retrospectively, but the standing order survived through all the troubles of the Revolutionary era and was not countermanded until 1845.

In the event, Curll being Curll, he ploughed on – not exactly regardless, but with a keen sense of how far he could go without further retribution falling on his head. He brought out a slightly cut version of the book, leaving out the life and the will. He added a note, 'The Reader may be hereby assured, that the PIECES which compose the following *Collection*, are the Chief of what were published by his GRACE in his Life Time, they were revised and corrected for the Press by himself, and delivered for that Purpose to Mr. *Gildon* in the Year 1721, all which Corrections and Alterations made by his GRACE, have, in this Edition, been Faithfully observed.'[23] He took the further precaution of dating the volume 1721, although it does not seem to have been issued until the following year. The dedicatory verses to the Duke of Argyll are signed by John 'Orator' Henley, a frequent butt of the Scriblerian group. The last item in the collection is the duke's poem commending Pope, especially the Homer, originally written for the *Works* in 1717.

But Curll's adversary had to tread lightly himself. Although the duke was a good friend as well as a valuable supporter to Pope, and a royal patent had been obtained in April 1722 by the publisher John Barber for an authorized set of his works, his connections with the Stuart line made him a dangerous ally in the new Hanoverian world. In particular, his wife was a natural daughter of James II, the result of a liaison between the king and the court lady Catherine Sedley. This meant, of course, that she was a half-sister of the Pretender. The vigilant Walpole government discovered what they considered seditious passages in the *Works*, with the result that immediately after the publication of two sumptuous volumes in January 1723 the official watchdogs, known as messengers of the press, arrived at the printer's shop and seized copies. The *London Journal*, strongly Whiggish and government-subsidized, went so far as to report on 2 February 1723 a rumour that 'Mr. P---' had been taken into custody on account of Buckingham's *Works*, but it was not true.

The work attracted suspicion because Barber, alderman of London and a leading member of the trade, was an undisguised Jacobite accused of involvement in the Atterbury plot; he would shortly make his way to Rome to carry funds from Britain to support the Pretender's planned rising. He had been a good friend of Swift since the days of the Oxford administration, and he remained on excellent terms with Pope too. In 1741 Curll, who had a long memory, returned to the fray with a life of Barber, most probably of his own contrivance, featuring the inevitable will and also some details that still had the power to embarrass Pope.

Soon, all the elements in the press hostile to Pope heard all about the seized volumes. They accused him of bad faith, implying that he had gained the licence by suppressing the existence of the more offensive portions of the text. One writer, perhaps George Duckett, a Buttonian who sometimes produced items for Curll, fanned the flames of the latest controversy by bringing up an epitaph the duke had written for himself. It concluded with a statement in the decent obscurity of Latin, claiming that Buckingham was always for the republic and often (*just* often) for the king. This was easy to interpret as a slur on George I, and possibly a bit of Pope's handiwork – it wasn't. A second imaginary letter from Pope to the departed Buckingham appeared in the same journal a week later. This forces him to admit to having submitted only pieces that would pass the 'Test' of legality. He acknowledges that 'he is obliged *to keep no Faith with Hereticks*; an Article of my Religion (as much as I have ridiculed most others) I have constantly been very punctual.' That at least was a palpable hit by the journalist, even though the article mentioned was never strictly part of Catholic doctrine; some popes, such as Gregory IX, had enunciated the principle. The supposed letter goes on to make obvious allusion to the recently uncovered plot, listing among its leaders 'Cardinal Francisco', a transparent code name for Atterbury.[24]

Eventually the copies were returned to the printer with the offensive bits removed from the second volume. The edition was republished in February 1724, now with some booksellers of a less controversial kind, such as William Taylor and John Innys, named in the advertisement along with Barber (who was probably in Italy at this time). Pope expressed his discomfort about going ahead with the project, once suggesting that he would abandon his *Odyssey* subscription if the authorities went on hounding him: 'Let the Odyssey remain untranslated, or let them employ Mr. Tickell upon it.'[25]

This was one of the most fraught junctures in Pope's entire life. His less than glorious witness statement in support of Atterbury before the Lords prompted sneering references from his critics. Once more the writer in the fiercely Whig *Pasquin* took the lead, with a mock confession by Bishop Atterbury: 'As a farther Proof of my Innocence, I have produced the worthy Mr. *P-pe*, a professed *Roman Catholick*, who has deposed that he used frequently to visit me, and that I never mentioned this *Scheme* to him; but constantly entertained him with agreeable Panegyricks upon the *Protestant Religion*; and the *Church of England* as by Law established.'[26] George Sherburn once wondered whether 'the same sly Curll was active against Pope when, in 1723, Pope's edition of Buckingham's *Works* was suppressed'.[27] We cannot be sure, but it would be highly imprudent to bet against the possibility.

LOVE AND INTRIGUE

You might suppose that anyone would desist, having just gone through the experiences Curll had done. Most people who had been on the end of a formal rebuke from the highest powers in the land, as well as the threat of further court action, would surely decide to assume a lower profile for a while. But Curll's nature made that impossible, and he went on as recklessly as ever. There had been a warning in the hearings before the Lords over the Buckingham *Works*. After issuing their new standing order, their lordships had slipped in an ominous addition: 'The Lords following were appointed a Committee, to consider of an Advertisement in the same News Papers, intituled, "*The Daily Journal, Monday, January* 22, 1721–2," of Six Books, just published, all printed for *E. Curll*, over-against *Catherine Street*, in *The Strand*; and to report to the House.'[28] The books in question were almost all concerned with sexual matters. They include the ones on eunuchs and onanism, plus the manual on flagellation, the Latin love poems of the sixteenth-century writer Jean Bonnefons (translated and marketed under titles such as *The Pleasures of Coition, or the Nightly Sports of Venus*) and two little pieces in the style of the more ribald Chaucerian tales. According to the advertisement, they were all 'just published', in the conventional but misleading formula. In reality the first three items here had been out since 1718. But Curll never worried about details of that kind.

The committee members listed included several friends of Pope, such as Bathurst, Lord Islay and the still unprosecuted Atterbury. We don't know if they attended meetings, since only five were needed to make up a quorum. It is hard to fathom what qualifications the reprobate Duke of Wharton or the sadistic bully Lord Coningsby had to serve on this court of morality. But in any case, nothing more seems to have been done about the matter for the time being. Perhaps some of the five bishops on the panel dissuaded their colleagues from perusing such lubricious titles. So the threat hung over the publisher for two more years.

The feud remained quiescent, most of the time. Curll made a point of getting a translation of the *Remarks upon Mr. Pope's Homer* by the French classical scholar Anne Dacier; but this was criticism, not naked abuse, and could be shrugged off. On the other hand, Pope may have felt some anger when the portrait of Addison as 'Atticus' got into one of his opponent's miscellanies. It had appeared in a newspaper some months earlier, but anonymously, with a covering note signed from Button's coffee house. That would not cause the poet to lose much sleep. However, when it was printed in *Cythereia: or, New Poems upon Love and Intrigue* on 6 April 1723, the poem was given a whole new slant. The title read, 'Verses Occasioned by Mr. *Tickell*'s Translation of the First *Iliad* of HOMER. By Mr. POPE'. This was explicit enough to leave no doubt. It was almost as if the controversy over the rival translators had never ceased. The passage is justly celebrated, with some familiar phrases that have become almost proverbial; but it's worth citing the early version as it stood in 1723:

EXHIBIT 9.10

If *Dennis* rhymes and rails in furious Pet;
I'll answer *Dennis*, when I am in Debt:
If meagre *Gildon* draws his venal Quill,
I wish the Man a Dinner, and sit still;
But should there *One*, whom better Stars conspire
To form a Bard, and raise a Genius higher:
Blest with each Talent, and each Art to please,
And born to Write, Converse, and Live, with Ease;
Should such a *One*, resolv'd to rule alone,
Bear, like the *Turk*, no Brother near the Throne;
View him with Scornful, yet with Jealous eyes,
Hate him for Arts, that caus'd Himself to rise;
Damn with faint Praise, assent with civil Leer,
And without Sneering, teach the rest to Sneer;
Alike reserv'd to blame or to commend,
A tim'rous Foe and a suspicious Friend:
Fearing ev'n Fools, by Flatterers besieg'd;
And so obliging, that he ne'r oblig'd:
Willing to wound, and yet afraid to strike,

Just hint a Fault, and hesitate Dislike;
Who, when *two Wits** on rival *Themes* contest,
Approves them *Both*, but likes the *Worst* the *Best*:
Like CATO, give his *little Senate Laws*,
And sits attentive to his *own Applause*;
While *Fops* and *Templars* ev'ry Sentence raise,
And wonder with a foolish Face of Praise:
Who would not laugh, if such a Man here be?
Who would not weep, if ADDISON were He?[29]
　　*Pope *and* Tickell

This is a devastating, even cruel revelation of a very precise psychological type. But we should remember that in *Cythereia* this was surrounded by assorted ribaldry, with pieces from writers such as Chaucer and Boccaccio, and titles such as 'Kissing' and 'The Nymph's Rapture'. How it looked in that company, it is not easy to guess. Following Pope's poem, Curll printed 'An Answer', presented to Addison's widow. It begins, 'When soft Expressions Covert-Malice hide'.

This was the situation when the quarrel entered its second decade. Pope would run into two new storms, first with the publication of his edition of Shakespeare, provoking a sharp response from Lewis Theobald, and then after it was revealed that he had performed the translation of the *Odyssey* in tandem with two collaborators. Both incidents provided handles for Curll and his minions to renew their attacks. But it would not all be plain sailing for the publisher, either. On his side, he was in the throes of his most protracted and damaging encounter with the law.

10

PRISON,
1724–7

The epithet Pope applies to Curll in *The Dunciad* is 'dauntless', but the one he used about Daniel Defoe, 'unabashed', would do just as well. Curll had been hammered from various directions by the House of Lords, the Commissioners of Customs, the office of the Secretary of State, a Presbyterian minister and very probably others we don't even know about. The prospect of further action by the Lords loomed over his obscene books. He had been sued by Jacob Tonson for a breach of copyright. All this came in addition to the heavy blows his reputation had suffered at the hands of Pope. What did he do? He carried on as before.

The next threat arose out of an eight-page pamphlet entitled *Heydegger's Letter to the Bishop of London*, which came out around Easter 1724. We met the impresario John James Heidegger in Chapter One, and we can expect that he would have had influential protectors as the man who ran opera as well as masquerades at the Haymarket Theatre, an establishment patronized by the great and the good. The poem written in his name purports to defend masquerade as a 'harmless Pastime'. Its recipient was the mighty Edmund Gibson, appointed Bishop of London not long before, and the effective leader of the English Church throughout Robert Walpole's long reign. Gibson had preached a vehement sermon before the Societies for the Reformation of Manners on 6 January, in which he inveighed against masquerades on account of the opportunity for misbehaviour they gave to lascivious persons of both sexes. To say that this was a bold move on the part of the publishers is a gross understatement.

Moreover, the text suggests that prominent men and women in society may be hiding their true selves behind a mask, in effect adopting masquerade costume: 'Oft has a *Garter* and a *Star* / Conceal'd a surly sawcy *Tar*: / Many, misled by Shews, miscall / A Butcher *Captain-General*. / Thus Scriv'ners seem *Prime-Ministers*, / And *Oyster-Women, Barristers.*' These lines could obviously be read as indicting grandees who had been decorated with the Order of the Garter, but the most damaging reference is to the 'butcher', who might be either the recently deceased Duke of Marlborough (always portrayed by Tories as a callous blood-hunter) or his successor as head of the army, General William Cadogan. The 'Tar' might well be George Byng, Lord Torrington, an adherent of the ministry. Then come still more flagitious lines that might point to the Bishop of London himself: 'And sure it will be no hard Task, / To prove a M[itr]e is a Mask.'[1]

The imprint is that of the usually inoffensive Nicholas Cox, who, along with other booksellers, was named in press advertisements. A different ad carried a mysterious note, stating that a bookseller's name had been appended to the work 'and the said Bookseller utterly denies the Knowledge or Meaning of the same', with the hope that information will be supplied of the author, to avoid such a scandalous practice.[2] Had Curll simply foisted the book on to a rival in the trade? Whatever the case, he was arrested by the king's messengers in May on a charge of publishing a libellous pamphlet. Also taken into custody were Cox, the notorious Jacobite agent provocateur Thomas Power (for writing it, presumably) and Samuel Aris for printing it. Subsequently a pamphlet-seller called Richard Macey was also taken up.[3]

Curll was bailed to appear at the King's Bench court on a steep surety of £100. After this he sought clemency from Charles Delafaye, the official who handled most of the day-to-day business for the Secretary of State. In a letter of 8 May, Curll denied all knowledge of the pamphlet, and proclaimed his 'Affections to the Government'.

He assured Delafaye that, 'as to the pamphlet, I have not any concern therein; neither was there one ever seen or sold in my Shop.'
It seems unlikely that this is true. In a hopeful aside, he pleaded
not to be detained for long, because he had a great deal of business
on his hands at the time – a consideration that had little chance of
influencing the ministry. The subsequent disposition of the case
remains unknown. In August the *Flying Post* would pose the question, 'Why is poor *Curl* hunted down by the *Society for Reformation
of Manners* for his unprofitable starving Bawdry?'[4] Indeed, Curll
seems to be the only one of the group who was actively pursued.
The facts indicate that he was high on the government's hit list.

ENTERTAINMENT AND INSTRUCTION

All this may have been no more than a mild irritant to Curll. It
was the prelude to a much more serious chain of events that began
to unfold in the coming months. For a time the battle with Pope
became a secondary aspect of his life; but we should be aware of
what was going on, because his antagonist certainly was – and
made good use of what he knew in the later satires he wrote on
Curll. Sordid details that came before the courts gave the poet his
strongest material to blacken his opponent's character.

The trigger for the bookseller's struggles with the law was *Venus
in the Cloister, or the Nun in her Smock*, a translation of a work by
'the Abbé du Prat', probably a pseudonym of Jean Barrin, published in 1683. As the title indicates, it is openly erotic in nature.
Two nuns converse, an older one giving an initiation to a younger
one on the most common variants of sexual behaviour. While it
would not be considered grossly titillating today, in an age when
pornography is so freely available, it was hot stuff in its time. The
translator, Robert Samber, had already worked several times for
Curll, including producing renditions of *Eunuchism Display'd* and
The Praise of Drunkenness, which came out in the previous year.

Later, Samber claimed that the latter work was ironic and should be read in the same way as *The Praise of Folly* by Erasmus.[5] Once again, this was not the sort of argument that was calculated to impress the courts, as Curll found to his cost when the authorities caught up with him. Samber, incidentally, was paid four guineas for his pains, plus twelve bound copies – quite a munificent reward, although the book is of moderate length.

In February 1725 Curll was arrested by the messengers in connection with the obscene books and bailed on a recognizance of £200 – as much as an ordinary worker would make in four years. At the same time an order went out from on high to indict him in the King's Bench court. He was charged in the cumbersome legal jargon (Latin was still used until 1733), naming him as a wicked, impious and roguish fellow. Initially the accusations related to *Venus* and the flogging pamphlet, but when the Secretary of State, the Duke of Newcastle, took a hand, the total went up to four 'Lewd and Infamous Books'. The additions were the volume of Chaucerian poems from 1721 and a fresh publication, *De secretis Mulierum: or, The Mysteries of Human Generation fully Revealed*, which was hot off the press. Unlike some of the other items, this bore Curll's name on the title page. In an effort to give it credibility, he attributed it to the medieval German philosopher and Dominican friar known as Albertus Magnus, but this was fantasy. On 3 April Newcastle instructed the Treasury solicitor to go ahead with the prosecution.[6]

For the next three years the case and its branches shuffled in and out of the courts, with the defendant making repeated bids to stay their progress. Curll's main recourse was to offer information against various seditious writers. While on bail he wrote a series of letters to Delafaye and a colleague, Charles Stanhope, referring vaguely to a deal he had made with Lord Townshend and suggesting that his arrest breached it. He claims to be able to reveal some libels that have lain dormant for as much as fifteen years, and to expose widespread disaffection with the government. There is no doubt that Curll was acting as an undercover agent, since a few of his letters dishing the dirt on individuals thought to be disloyal are still to be found in the archives of the Secretary of State. By now *The Praise of Drunkenness* had been added to the roster of his books facing prosecution. He claims that *Venus* was printed and published by Thomas Edlin, 'who I am informed is to be a Witness against me'.[7] He adds exculpatory notes on all the items under suspicion, pointing out, for example, that the work attributed to Albertus Magnus had been licensed by the Bishop of London on its first appearance in 1636. So what, the authorities might have asked?

PHYSICAL BOOKS

In spite of all the defendant's efforts, the government decided to proceed against the 'lewd and obscene' books, and the first hearing was set for 30 November. Notes on Curll's defence are preserved in a document in the Bodleian Library, Oxford. It shows that he was adopting a common strategy, that is, seeking to prove that the work (here especially the one on flogging) was medical rather than pornographic:

EXHIBIT 10.1

Not Guilty is pleaded.

Case.

This Prosecution appears to be malitious for the following Reasons – in being brought Seven Years after the Publication of the first Book which will be proved a Physick Book ex professo by Dr Rose of the Coli of (Physicians) – we no [*sic*] of no Law prohibiting the Translations of Books either out of Latin or French or any other Language neither we presume can such Transactions be deemed Libels.

The originalls of both Books will be in Court.

To prove that the Treatise of the use of Flogging is a Physicale book – Call Dr Rose.[8]

Dr Rose can be identified as Philip Rose, MD, a licentiate of the
Royal College of Physicians, and a relative by marriage of the great
man at the head of the profession, Sir Hans Sloane. He was probably in need of some fees as an expert witness, because he once
had to plead to be forgiven a debt of £12 to the College. Rose wrote
An Essay on the Small-pox; Whether Natural, or Inoculated, which
Curll published in 1724. His skill in the relevant area of medicine
does not appear.

At some point Curll compiled a printed justification of his behaviour, which he called *The Humble Representation of Edmund Curll;
Bookseller and Citizen of London, Concerning Five Books Complained
of to the Secretary of State*. Naturally it is far from humble, since it
mounts a spirited defence of the books (six of them, actually). He
uses the arguments we have already encountered, such as the debt
to Erasmus, the serious medical import of the works and the relevance of the one on flogging in view of 'the unfortunate End of Mr.
Motteux, who was found Dead in a Brothel'. He gets in thrusts at his
rivals, as on the heavy promotion of *Onania*: 'This lewd Pamphlet,
though pretendedly wrote against the *Sin* of *Self Pollution*, has
throughout a Tendency to encourage that *Vice*: and . . . yet passes
uncensured, though it be the Production, as is universally believed,
of a *Secular-Priest* of the Church of *Rome*.' There is just one glancing blow directed at Pope. Curll argues that the bawdy poems he
printed were no more criminal than several recent modernizations
of Geoffrey Chaucer, as those by John Dryden and Pope:

EXHIBIT 10.2

Among which is the *Wife of Bath*'s Tale, but the *Prologue* to it *Dryden*
declared he could not attempt on Account of its Obscenity; yet this
lewd Prologue has been modernized by Mr. POPE, and likewise published by Mr. *Tonson*. And the whole Works of CHAUCER, have been
lately given us in their *native Obscenity*, after the most *correct Manner*, by the Society of *Christ Church* College *Oxford*, in a pompous

Folio Edition, published by Mr. *LINTOT*; the Profits arising from the Sale of which, he assured me are to be applied to the Finishing of *Peckwater* Quadrangle, belonging to that College.[9]

Here the reference is to the posthumously published edition of Chaucer (1721) by John Urry. The tale goes that when fewer subscriptions came in than had been hoped, the college obliged all new entrants to buy a copy. In any case, the quad did get finished, and it still stands there in handsome pride.

None of these manoeuvres on Curll's part worked. The court found him guilty in respect of *Venus* and *Flogging*. He entered a motion for an arrest of judgment, which the judges granted. This was on the grounds that one claim by the defence needed further investigation – namely, that the trial should have been held in an ecclesiastical court as an offence *contra bonos mores*. A precedent did exist for that in the case of *Regina* v. *Reid* (1707), when the respected Lord Chief Justice John Holt had ruled that obscenity ought to be treated not under common law, but rather as a breach of ecclesiastical law. According to court reports, the Attorney General, Philip Yorke (later Lord Chancellor Hardwicke, who gave his ruling in the major copyright case of *Pope* v. *Curll*), pressed hard for a conviction. But a number of the judges were unsure, notably the Lord Chief Justice John Pratt. On top of that, counsel for the defence, John Strange, hinted darkly that his client 'had something material to offer' and asked for further time to bring this forward. By pursuing such delaying tactics Curll managed to get his sentence postponed for an entire year.[10]

How quickly did this welcome news reach Pope? We don't know, but he was an assiduous reader of Mist's *Journal*. This paper got the items wrong, stating that Curll had been convicted of publishing two vile and scandalous books, *Flogging* and '*A Poem in Praise of Drunkenness*, or *The Nun in her Smock*'. In fact, the one on drunkenness had now disappeared from the charges, exempt perhaps because it was 'a physical book'. But Curll had already lined up his next moves. On 3 December he let loose a bombshell in the press:

EXHIBIT 10.3

Having been found Guilty of publishing two Books, (1. A Treatise of the *Use* of Flogging, &c. 2. *Venus* in the *Cloister*; or the *Nun* in her *Smock*. This last not bearing my Name; but only a Copy of it was sold by me, as it might have been by any other Bookseller) I hereby most humbly ask Pardon for these Offences; but being resolved never more to offend in the like Manner, I give this Notice, that so soon as two Books, now in the Press, are finish'd, (viz. 1. The Miscellaneous Works of that Memorable Patriot *Andrew Marvel* Esq.; in Prose and Verse. 2. The *Case* of *Seduction*; being the late Proceedings at Paris against the Rev. Abbé des Rues, for committing Rapes upon 133 Virgins. Written by himself) I am resolved to retire from all Publick Business, with this Satisfaction, that whatever Human Frailties I may either unwarily, or wilfully, have committed, no Person can charge me with the Guilt of any dishonourable Action; and I will therefore do myself Justice against who have libelled me upon this Occasion."

E. CURLL.

It is not clear where the libels appeared, but we can guess their substance. In any case, although the two books mentioned in the notice did appear (*The Case of Seduction* as soon as 20 December), the main story lay in Curll's supposed retirement.

Flak rained down on the bookseller for some time on this issue, not all from the Popians. Once it provoked a long poem entitled *Hereditary Right Exemplified: or, a Letter of Condolance from Mr. Ed---d C--l to his son H---y, upon his late Discipline at Westminster*. Here Curll adjures his son to stay away from the school where he had been tossed in a blanket a decade earlier. He also advises Henry on how to conduct business:

EXHIBIT 10.4

If I may counsel, *Hal*, depend
Solely for Wit upon thy Friend.
Let that thine Author's Province be,
For thine, 'tis only Piracy.
Steal all comes near Thee, Bad or Good,
Thou'lt pick a pretty Livelihood.
No matter how Thou fobb'st the Town,
How coarse the Paper, or how brown;
No matter tho' the wretched Stuff,
Is not like *Lintot*'s wiping Proof.
Tho' Patience 'self it would enrage,
To foul ones Fingers with thy Page.
What tho' Thou rak'st in every Nook
Of private Life, or Pocket-Book?
Like me still careful to display,
The Deeds of Mid-night in Mid-day? . . .
The Rascal swings that steals a Purse,
A scabby Sheep, or found'red Horse;
While he goes scotfree with his Prey,
Who steals our Fame or Friend away.[12]

The last words of the poem mention in a rueful tone '*Edmund Curll*,
late Bookseller'.

To no one's surprise, the bookseller's threatened retirement from
business proved as short-lived as many another exit from the stage.
On 10 February 1726 came a message from his current address in
gaol. Curll's notice appeared next day in the *Daily Journal*, advertising no fewer than seven books. The first of these titles was the
egregious volume on *Seduction*, with its account of the mass rape
of the unfortunate virgins. A postscript followed:

EXHIBIT 10.5

King's Bench, Southwark

Feb. 10, 1725–6

Having been last Term found Guilty of vending two Books, I. *A Treatise of Flogging*, &c. II. *The Nun in her Smock*; And having asked *Pardon* of my *Superiors*, both in Private and Publick for the *Offence* taken at these Pieces: I hope, as I resolve never more to offend in the like manner, it will be a sufficient *Atonement*. In Justice to my own *Character*, which I defy any Man upon Earth to stain with one *dishonest*, or *dishonourable* Action of any *Kind*, I think my self obliged to declare, that my present *Confinement* is neither occasioned thro' *Debt*, or *Disaffection* to the Government; and therefore all those with whom I have had, or yet have any Dealings, shall be paid in full in a very short Time.

E. CURLL[13]

This paragraph obviously functions to supply further publicity for the two books that had given offence. No one surpassed Curll at appearing to grovel while advancing his own interests; Uriah Heep could have learned from him.

THE PRISONER'S ADVOCATE

It's a little hard to believe, but things got even worse on the legal front. For the past few years Curll had been publishing tracts by a former Chancery clerk named William Staunton. They exhibited some unorthodoxy on controversial theological points, notably the Trinity. While they do not look all that incendiary to a modern eye, the authorities did not have a modern eye. They sent a posse of messengers to raid the bookseller's premises in the Strand. Soon they emerged, having seized nine books and pamphlets, including the Staunton items. Curll was arrested and bailed in the sum of £200, with two sureties of £100 each. Among those providing a recognizance was the author Thomas Cooke, soon to be given a minor role in *The Dunciad*, and often employed by Curll, most recently as editor of the works of Andrew Marvell. The officials reviewing the file determined that Cooke was 'only a Lodger, and a Man of no good Character as to his Substance'.[14]

The King's Bench was far from the most squalid prison in the capital, or even among the five main gaols in Southwark. But it was no holiday camp. Its buildings dated from the time of Henry VIII, and they had grown so cramped that it would move in 1758 to much more spacious accommodation constructed down the road near St George's Fields, in the vicinity of the modern Elephant and Castle. It lay in an alley off Borough High Street, just south of the more fearsome Marshalsea prison, in a small group of buildings surrounded by a brick wall. Debtors made up most of the inmates, but there were also people convicted at the King's Bench court of serious offences, such as those for which Curll had now been arrested. He was probably transported from the court in Westminster Hall to his new abode by boat, since it was quicker to go by water than by the clogged London Bridge, the only road crossing in the capital, with a usable carriageway just 3.7 m (12 ft) wide.

For the time being Curll remained in custody, perhaps because he could not raise the bail money at short notice. In desperate letters to Delafaye and others, he claimed he had made a full submission to the Bishop of London, indicating that punishment for the Heidegger pamphlet of two years earlier was still hanging over him. He further declared that he had resolved 'never more to advertise any Book that shall give Offence either by its Title or Contents', an optimistic vow even assuming it was sincere. In his most pathetic accents, he lamented that his wife was lately dead, his apprentice had served out his time, and he had just one servant to help him carry on the business. But where was his son Henry? We have no idea. Henry appears regularly in the imprint of books in 1727, but he went missing at this juncture. Meanwhile his father renewed his appeal from his confinement; a letter to Delafaye on 21 February 1726 mentions an enclosure, a copy of which had also been sent to Walpole. A sinister warning points to a danger facing the nation if some 'Private State Memoirs' were allowed to reach publication.[15] This must refer to the memoirs of John Ker, which Curll was shortly to issue. If so, he thought better of releasing them, and he remained in prison until June.

While languishing in captivity, Curll found a new outlet for his energy. He co-published and advertised a jeremiad on the state of the gaols, which came out in about August 1726, and he is thought to be the 'Philalethes' (a favourite pseudonym) who signed the dedication, bizarrely dated 31 April 1726. Who wrote the main text is anybody's guess, although he had obvious knowledge of the King's Bench prison. It must be admitted that Curll was well qualified to embark on this task. The work was entitled *The Prisoner's Advocate, or, a Caveat against Under Sheriffs and their Officers, Jayl-keepers and their Agents*. Less than three years later a major scandal occurred when the warden of the Fleet prison was convicted of barbaric treatment of inmates, after the atrocities had been exposed by a parliamentary committee. The historian John Strype, in his magisterial update of Stow's *Survey of London* (1720), had noted that the King's Bench was 'a Prison wherein great Abuses are committed by the *Marshall* or *Keeper* and his Underlings, and much complained of in Parliament'.[16] The *Advocate* does not chronicle enormities on quite that scale, but it does specify in excruciating detail the corrupt practices of the keeper of a spunging-house in Southwark (a halfway house, prior to full confinement) to which the writer had been sent. It can be identified as an establishment known as the Golden Lion, which operated close to St George's church. We don't know if Curll suffered the indignities that are described, but he may well have.

At the beginning of June Curll wrote an abject appeal to Walpole. It contains some of his trademark features, notably some cocky verses: 'From the King's Bench where I still am, / Where if I stay, 'twill be a shame.' He offered his usual fulsome compliments to the great: 'When you cease to deserve well of your country, I will cease to proclaim your merits.'[17] He got what he wanted – his release on 2 July – but it was a brief respite, for the worst was yet to come. Curll was immediately remanded back to the prison, on a totally separate charge.

THE FICTION OF A NAME

In the middle of all his battles with the law, Curll took an extraordinarily bold decision at one fraught moment. He chose to print an affidavit he had sworn before Sir Robert Raymond, the chief justice who would preside at his trial the following year. It relates not to the books under prosecution, but to one of the bestsellers in his backlist, *The Case of Impotency as Debated in England*, first published in 1715. This was a follow-up to an earlier success, *The Case of Impotency Debated, in the late Famous Tryal at Paris; between the Marquis de Gesvres . . . and Mademoiselle de Mascranny his Lady* (1714). The notice replies to a letter by 'A.P.' that appeared in the *London Journal* of 12 November. There the writer had castigated the publisher (unnamed), who had attributed the *Impotency* volumes to Sir Clement Wearg, a lawyer who had died on 6 April. A.P. goes on to complain about the deceptive practices used in the book trade, and adds a paragraph clearly aimed at Curll's use of phoney names:

EXHIBIT 10.6

This Practice, if it went no farther than the Fiction of a Name, or the Invention of a Character, would be only foolish and idle; but as it is carry'd on, it becomes bad and immoral. How often are the works of such Anonymous Authors of no Merit, ascribed to some Dead Men of Reputation? An Injury both to the Writer and the Reader. How often imposed on the World, as the Productions of some Living Gentlemen, whose Fame is universally allowed? What a Burden of such Stuff does the celebrated Doctor SWIFT's Name labour under? By the Number of their Writings, there ought to be at least Three Mr. POPE's; and for Mr. GAY, they have hatch'd a Kinsman and a Namesake, from whom he cannot defend himself . . . Thus the real Poet is unhappily toiling hard to raise a Reputation, which the Phantom is pulling down. I say *Phantom*; for tho' Mr. JOSEPH GAY be a very voluminous Author, yet no one living can bring any manner of Proof that there is or ever was any such Writer really in being.[18]

This may or may not have come from Pope himself, although we should note that in *The Dunciad* a phantom poet appears in a section involving Joseph Gay and other fabrications by Curll.

We can be quite certain that Curll was responsible for the notice that appeared in the press four days later. The statement attributed to Wearg simply reproduces the preface to the volumes of 1715.

EXHIBIT 10.7

AFFADAVIT concerning the Publication of The CASES of IMPOTENCY and DIVORCE, by *Sir* Clement Wearg, *late Sollictor-General*, Printed for H. Curll. *over-against* Catherine-Street, *in the* Strand.

To invalidate the notorious and scandalous Falshoods contained in the *London Journal* of the 12th Instant, *Edmund Curll* maketh Oath, That a Book by him produced, Intitul'd, The CASE OF IMPOTENCY. *as Debated in England*, was published by *Clement Wearg*, Esq; and printed from an Original Manuscript by him given to this Deponent, and the following Advertisement by the said *Clement Wearg*, Esq; thereto prefixed, 'The Publick having been given a general Approbation of the late Tryal between the Marquis *de Gesvres* and his *Lady* at *Paris*, as indeed so nice and curious a Subject deserved; I was inclined to search our own Law-Books and Historians, to see what adjudged Cases and Precedents we had of the same Nature.

That which is the most considerable in our English History, was, the Case of the Earl of *Essex*, and the Lady *Howard*; a Case that engaged the Politicks of the greatest Statesmen, and the Casuistry of a Monarch himself. There has as yet been a great Defect of Information concerning this Case, which the Reader will now find supplied from an Original Manuscript of Archbishop *Abbot*'s, written in his own Hand. This Manuscript contains an exact Account of all the Artifice and Stratagems used in that Affair, and is not only very full and articular upon the Case, but lets us into a considerable Part of the Secrets and Politicks of King *James*'s Reign. To make a Collection of this Nature as perfect as I well could, there is added the Lord *Audley*'s Tryal, and the Proceedings upon the Duke of *Norfolk*'s BILL of *Divorce*; which, as they bear some relation to this Subject, so they are now very rare and valuable. The Duke of *Norfolk*'s Case, in particular, employ'd some of our greatest Lawyers, who have made since very eminent Figures in their Profession; and contains all that can be said upon the Article of *Divorce. Inner Temple, Oct.30. 1714.*

This Deponent further saith, that when the abovementioned Book was printed, he returned the Original Manuscript to *Clement Wearg*, Esq; at his Chambers in the *Temple.*

Jurat apud Serjeant's-Inn
Chancery-Lane, 14 *Die*
Novembris, 1726.
Coram me
R. RAYMOND   E. CURLL[19]

Neither of these documents seems to have been reprinted before. Their importance lies partly in the way that the case rests on the authenticity of manuscript sources, but principally in the fact that Curll was able on this occasion to enlist the law in his own interests. Unfortunately, this did not help him to avoid facing trial on the items under prosecution.

A Spy Comes Out

Not content with the slender array of misdemeanours laid at his door, Curll had decided to do something even more hazardous. While he was in gaol he encountered John Ker, also known as John Crawfurd, a Scottish double agent and informer who had been given licence to infiltrate the Jacobites during Queen Anne's reign. He came to be regarded as untrustworthy by both sides. After this he engaged in a number of dodgy exploits on the Continent, which suggest that a good name for him would be the misadventurer. Ker subsequently moved to London in quest of more undercover employment. None being forthcoming, he was forced to sell his paternal estate in Ayrshire, but despite that he ended up in the King's Bench prison on account of mounting debts. Curll might have been attracted to the bold character of his fellow gaolbird, but what really grabbed his attention was the fact that Ker had compiled his memoirs. Their content was likely to include incriminating material about the past actions of those in power. The sales potential of these revelations was obvious. It was also a huge risk to bring them in front of the world, something that would have been apparent to most people – but not to Curll.

The *Memoirs* came out in three volumes. The first, carrying an obsequious dedication to Walpole, was issued on 9 June 1726, 'with the Authority of a Privy-Seal from her Majesty Queen Anne', whatever help that might be thought to give. It bears no bookseller's name on the title page, but this cautious manoeuvre was undone by a list of publications by Henry Curll included among the prelims. Within a week Lord Townshend directed that a prosecution should be launched against Ker and also Curll senior. According to the press, 'several' messengers duly showed up at the prison and seized the papers of both parties. The memoirist objected to news reports of this event, and managed to elicit an apology from George Parker, author of a *Penny Post*, who stated that Ker had

ordered a prosecution of the *Daily Journal*. Parker asked to be forgiven for propagating 'a Rumour so notoriously Groundless and
Malicious'. Unfortunately, the rumour seems to have been entirely
true. You would not know the seizure had taken place from a notice
Curll placed in one of the papers on 4 July, at a time when he was
remanded back to gaol:

EXHIBIT 10.8

In Gratitude to my Friends, the most Obscure, and in Contempt of
my Foes even the most Mighty, (if an. such there be) I think my
self obliged to declare, that I have Strictly kept my Word with the
Publick in not concerning my self either in printing or publishing
any Book since the finishing of *Marvel's* Works. And that notwithstanding what has been inserted either in (those *Daily-Legends*) the
News-Papers, or from the Assertion of *any Person whatever*, that I
had not any Papers seized in the *King's-Bench-Prison*, nor am I the
Publisher of Mr. Ker's *Memoirs*, as my Superiours are well assured by
the Author himself. *Magna est Veritas & prevalebit.*
From my House in the *Strand*.
July 4, 1726.   E. CURLL.[20]

Perhaps truth is great and will prevail; but the notice exercises
great economy with the facts. Despite what he says, Curll had been
involved, openly or clandestinely, in at least three other books since
the turn of the year. Regardless of considerable evidence, he denies
any share in the *Memoirs*; but he would, wouldn't he?

Fortune was not on Curll's side. Very soon after these incidents,
on 8 July, Ker died in prison, aged fifty-two, and he was buried
at nearby St George's church. Curll now had to face the music
alone. Rash as ever, he elected to produce two more volumes of
the *Memoirs*, with affidavits that confirmed the accuracy of the
material in the first part. The government found these equally
objectionable. It would be tedious to go through all the legal

machinations that followed, with desperate measures adopted by the two Curlls, Edmund and Henry, to ward off the prosecution. This is the sort of thing that they used in their attempts at justifying publication:

EXHIBIT 10.9

Tomorrow will be Publish'd, upon Oath, The MEMOIRS and SECRET NEGOTIATIONS of JOHN KER, of Kersland, esq; The THIRD and LAST PART. To which is added, A Copy of the Information exhibited by the Attorney-General against the FIRST PART of these Memoirs.

AFFIDAVIT. This Informant being intrusted with all the Papers of John Ker of Kersland, Esq; deceased, (intended to be made publick) hereby deposeth, That this Third and Last Part of his Memoirs and Secret negotiations, &c. is faithfully printed from the Original Manuscripts of the said John Ker, esq; and other Authorities, serving to illustrate the said Work; prepared for the Press by his express Direction. S. GRAY. jur' undecimo Die Januarii, 1726–7, (apud Serjeants-Inn, Chancery Lane) coram RO. PRICE.

Printed for J. SMITH in Cornhill; and sold by all Booksellers: Where may be had, The FIRST and SECOND PART of these Memoirs.[21]

To the uninitiated, this might have seemed plausible. Robert Price was a real Welsh judge, whose biography Curll later published, and whose estranged wife, Lucy, managed to set up chambers in Gray's Inn and, against all law and custom, practise as a lawyer.[22] But such affidavits rarely stood up in court.

As enquiries went on during 1726 and 1727, Henry Curll claimed at one point that a mysterious woman had inveigled him into ordering five hundred copies for sale. The copies he sold in the shop he disposed of as an agent of this shadowy person. He did not know who she was, or who had printed the work. Alas for this defence, the authorities had found members of the trade who bought immunity by admitting that they had printed the book at Curll's direction. As for Edmund, he continued to insist that he had not kept a shop for two years, and that the premises were not his but his son's. However, Susanna Gray, who was apparently Curll's live-in companion and who had sworn the affidavits, complicated the picture. According to Henry, he kept the shop but his father paid the rent.[23] None of it sounded very convincing.

The hard-headed minions at Walpole's disposal would not buy any of these stories. After the publication of the second volume, both father and son were charged and bail for each set at £200. In a heartfelt message written probably on 14 February 1727, Curll *père* begged Delafaye to show pity on him:

EXHIBIT 10.10

Sir. Glad I should be to know what is determined concerning me, because I am every way incapacitated from serving my Self, or my Family. If Bail be insisted upon for my Son, it cannot be procured unless I have the liberty to sollicit Friends for that Purpose. As to my Self, Lord Chief Justice Raymond told Mr. Paxton (when I was bailed out of Prison on my former Recognizances) that he would take my own Appearance as to Ker's Memoirs, since I was under Twelve hundred Pounds Bail already, & was thereby sufficiently Secured.

Therefore Sir in the midst of Judgment I hope Mercy will be remembered. My Son in one Messenger's Custody – and my Self in Another – My Family without a Servt. – and my Lodgers going out of the House – my Landlady tho' I do not owe half a Years Rent has seiz'd my Goods which may all be torn from me in four and twenty hours. These Distresses, I hope Sir will move that Compassion which beats in the breast of every Man of Honour. I have been with Mr. Roberts ever since Saturday and no one comes to near me to let me know your commands.

Tuesday 3 o'clock.

I am Sir Yours E. Curll.[24]

Even those generally unsympathetic towards Curll may feel inclined to cut him a little slack in the light of this appeal – and that might have included Pope, assuming he had an inkling of what was going on.

THE CAMBRIDGE CHATTERTON

There was one promising new recruit to the bookseller's stable. Sadly, he was to flash across the literary sky like a comet for the briefest of moments. This was William Pattison, a farmer's son from Sussex, who had quit Cambridge at the age of twenty to seek fame if not fortune in the capital. According to legend, he went looking for encouragement at Button's, although the coffee house was now a shadow of its once influential self. His short life invites comparison with those of greater prodigies; and while Pattison lacked the talent of a Chatterton, let alone the genius of a Keats, he possessed some ability in a range of poetic genres. Much of his extant work was written before he left the university, and even when he got to London he cast regular glances back at his former home.

Most of what we know about Pattison is owing to Curll, who quickly spotted some potential and took the young man under his wing. The poet had already assembled enough verses to fill two volumes; the first appeared in September 1727 and the second, grandiloquently styled *Cupid's Metamorphoses*, in December. They indicate that the author was destined, if not for greatness, at least for a high level of professional competence. Curll probably never got much of a return on his investment, since the hastily mounted subscription for Volume I attracted an exiguous tally of 120 buyers. Only a few familiar names are apparent, such as Lady Mary Wortley Montagu, but one individual stands out, Mr. Pope, and this is where the story re-enters the narrative of the quarrel.

The *Poetical Works*, as the first volume is entitled, begin with a memoir of forty-plus pages. From internal evidence, this can be assigned to no one except Curll. Pattison spent the last month of his life at the bookseller's house, and since he was dying of small-pox in the final days this reflects great credit on his host. There are only a few references to the poet in the preface, with one charac-teristic puff: 'Shortly after, calling at Mr. *Curll*'s to buy Mr. *Pope*'s Letters, I found Mr. *Pattison* putting [sitting?] in a Chair.' Later we are told, 'He earnestly sollicited a Friendship with Mr. *Pope*, of the Success of which I cannot say any thing.'[25] If that sounds cold, in view of the admiration for Pope expressed in Pattison's poems, we must take note of a startling accusation, prompted by a single phrase in *An Author to be Lett* (1729), generally thought to be by Richard Savage. Here the hireling author refers to an occasion when he was able to outsmart Curll: then, 'some Years after (just at the time of his starving poor *Pattison*) the Varlet was revenged.'[26] The pam-phlet is a comic exaggeration of the works of hack writers, and it pretends to come from one bitterly opposed to Pope and his allies. Not a shred of evidence exists to support this tale.

Pattison's amusing address to Curll appeared in the first volume of the all-embracing *Miscellanea* that the publisher brought out in July 1726. Gentler than most of its kind, it is dated from Cambridge in 1715, but, since he was then only nine, the contents indicate that we should read 1725 here:

EXHIBIT 10.11

> While spurious Poems daily vex us,
> And cannot please, but must perplex us;
> While Tonson builds on Dryden's Name,
> And flourishes in Wealth and Fame,
> By swelling Volumes *three to six*,
> And other *miscellaneous* Tricks,
> By stuffing them with Rhymes on Trust,
> (Well, Things by standing will get Dust.)
> Then pr'ythee Curll, e'er 'tis too late,

(For Mortals must submit to Fate)
Collect, correct, and eke produce
The scatter'd Labours of *thy Muse*,
I'm sure they'll make a pretty Volume,
And every Body will extol 'em;
For Fame you'll have a double Venture,
As Author first, then next, as Printer:
So shall you *prove* by that you've writ,
What Tonson *passes* for a *Wit*.
  But this observe, Sir, let your *Letter*
Be good as *Lintot*'s, if not better:
As for the *Title*, on the Shelf,
I'll leave *that Matter* to *your self*.
The Binding, ay, the Binding tho' –
You know fine Trappings make a *Beau*-----.
For if that shine thro' *Chrystal-Case*,
'Twill wound the *Ladies* as they pass:
And then the *Toy*, 'tis so *uncommon*,
Of being *handled* by a *Woman*!
Commended almost out of Measure,
The Pride of giving *Ladies* Pleasure!
  Thus happier than Apollo, *you*,
Shall gain the Nymph and *Laurel* too.[27]

At some point Pattison might have had to choose between the support of Pope and the patronage of Curll, but that day would never come. Nor did Curll ever collect his fragmentary verse, which would have made a slight but entertaining volume.

For all his troubles, there was no sign that the publisher had abandoned his campaign. In March Henry issued the strangest gallimaufry that even the Curlls ever let loose on the world. It was called *The Altar of Love*. Not many copies survive, and every single one is different as regards its array of reprinted items from the firm's backlist, each of which may appear in any old order. They often have no relation to the subject of love. Typically, the volume might contain two short items by Pope that had recently been dredged up by Curll and printed for the first time, 'A Receipt for Soup. Address'd to Dean Swift' and an epitaph for the tomb of James Craggs in Westminster Abbey. In any given copy, these may or may not be followed by 'Popiana', a series of choice extracts from the full range of the poet's works – needless to say, Curll didn't hold the rights to any of these. One of the few poems reproduced in full is *The Worms*. Some copies have the Atticus lines, drawn from one source or another. It was a reminder to Pope that, whatever scrapes Curll got into, his foe would always be lying in wait around the next corner.

In that light, Curll was lucky to get away with just a single slap in the manual of bad poetry, *Peri Bathous: or The Art of Sinking in Poetry*, which came out in the Scriblerian *Miscellanies* in March 1728. The writer observes that 'There is no question but the Garret or the Printer's boy may often be discern'd in the compositions made in such scenes and company; and much of Mr. *Curl* has been insensibly infused into the works of his learned writers.'[28] Writers who did earn their own entries in the text of this work, signalled by initials, were John Dennis, Charles Gildon, John Oldmixon, Leonard Welsted, George Sewell, Aaron Hill, Lewis Theobald, Laurence Eusden, Defoe, Richard Blackmore and possibly Pattison. By now there were rumours that Pope had a major work on hack authors in the pipeline. At this prospect, a few of those just indicted in *Peri Bathous* must have passed that spring quaking in their boots.

II

PILLORY,
1725–8

In 1720 Pope could look on the accomplishment of his project on the *Iliad* with some satisfaction. It had received praise in the literary world, and the noise that had surrounded its inception was now muted, if not altogether silenced. He had seen off the Buttonians. The Whig cenacle had dispersed following the death of its high priest, Joseph Addison, in 1719. Richard Steele was now mainly preoccupied with managing the Drury Lane theatre, and not long afterwards ill health and debt forced him to retire to Wales. His active life in Parliament and the playhouse was over. Thomas Tickell, Ambrose Philips and Eustace Budgell each took a middle-level administrative post in Ireland. Wild young Tom Burnet grew mellower in early middle age, on his way ultimately to a judgeship. Plump Charles Johnson passed from the theatrical scene, although he was eventually elected to the fellowship of the Dunces, as 'a Martyr to obesity' and thus 'too large an object to be missed'.[1] As a result, Curll's forces were thinned, and although he gradually replenished their numbers, the new team generally lacked the clout that Addison had managed to assemble at Button's.

Now this period of Pope's seeming invulnerability came to an abrupt end. His major undertakings in the early years of the decade were his edition of Shakespeare and his translation of the *Odyssey*. The former got under way in about 1721, the latter in 1723. Each was published by subscription, but on a markedly different basis. The plays were edited for the benefit of Jacob Tonson, and Pope received £217 for his work – a tidy but not princely sum, and far less than the thousands he had picked up for the *Iliad*. Moreover, the list of subscribers was shorter and less distinguished. By contrast, the new translation yielded another impressive roster of names, although this time there was a more naked Tory colouring to its members. Ultimately the Shakespeare appeared in six volumes in 1725, and the Homer in five spread over two instalments in 1725 and 1726. But even before they reached completion, signs of public unease had surfaced.

Restoring Shakespeare

In both cases, the poet had been guilty of a costly miscalculation. True enough, he had made a serious effort to carry out due diligence in his work on Shakespeare. Evidence from the poet's letters shows that he embarked on his task with the intention of producing a solid scholarly job, in an era before Shakespeare became a full-blown industry. We must project ourselves into an age when very little of the information we take for granted was available to lovers of the dramatist; to take a single example, the chronology of his works was still very hazy, and it was not unknown for informed readers – even John Dryden – to suppose that *Pericles* came not late but early. A major scholar of theatre in this period, Robert D. Hume, has argued that Shakespeare was then, by our standards, an 'inaccessible' writer to many.[2]

As part of his research, Pope put notices in the press, requesting that collectors who owned copies of early editions might loan them to him. In addition, he sought out the advice of interested friends, and reclaimed an early copy, most probably the third folio of 1663–4, that he had lent to Francis Atterbury. But he found the labour required was more than he could satisfactorily handle. Again he asked for help, enlisting the young poet Elijah Fenton, as he would do on the *Odyssey*, and dragging in his friend John Gay; both were remunerated quite well by Tonson for their assistance.

Pope also paid an unknown man at Oxford £35 to relieve him of some of the drudgery.

It did not fully avail. The compilation has some virtues; it draws unfashionable attention to some lesser-known plays, and it involved some sound textual decisions, although the notes are scanty and the collations Pope performed were mostly perfunctory. Easily the most impressive feature of the work to a modern reader is the preface, which dilates in warm language on Shakespeare's human-ity and originality, topics on which not even Samuel Johnson did much better. But the defects were soon apparent. Immediately on publication, newspaper articles complained about the price of the volumes, accusing Tonson of 'exorbitant Demands'. As George Sherburn observed, 'being a bookseller, [he] was probably no more dear to Grub Street than was Pope.'[3] As for the scholarly value of the editor's work, very few were competent to form an opinion. Unluckily for Pope, one man who hated him was.

The failings of the edition were duly pointed out by Lewis Theobald, in a book titled *Shakespeare Restored: Or, A Specimen of the Many Errors as well Committed, as Unamended, by Pope in his Late Edition of this Poet*, published in March 1726. Theobald knew more of the background in Elizabethan drama than almost anyone then alive, and as we'd expect he showed greater accuracy in his references. Pope had set out the duties of an editor pretty well in his preface, but he was more capricious in his handling of textual matters than his claims would suggest. On top of that, he had little to add to Nicholas Rowe's edition of 1709 on the dramatist's biog-raphy. Forced to acknowledge the justice of Theobald's points, he adopted without much grace some of the suggested improvements in a second edition, which came out in 1728.

Pope's more lasting response was to appoint his critic the great laureate of Dulness in the guise of 'Tibbald'. Up to this point, little had been heard from Theobald in the course of the quarrel, apart from a possible attack on *The What D'ye Call It* back in 1715. His work had been published from time to time by Curll, who advertised a reprint (not now accessible, if it existed) of Theobald's adaptation of *Richard II* in early 1722. But from this date he was among the most valuable sidemen for the bookseller. One outcome was a new edition of *Shakespeare Restored* in 1740, as well as some shorter items. Starting out as an attorney, that is, in the lower ranks of the legal profession, Theobald originally planned to translate the *Odyssey*, but this fell through because Bernard Lintot was overextended on Pope's *Iliad*. After this he turned to the theatre and became prominent for his 'pantomimes', actually spectacular entertainments involving dance, music, mime and special stage effects. Aside from his dealings with Pope, he is now best remembered for *The Double Falshood* (1727), which was allegedly based on a lost play named *Cardenio* by Shakespeare. The present state of knowledge is summarized in Wikipedia in this way:

> Theobald's claim of a Shakespearean foundation for his *Double Falshood* met with suspicion, and even accusations of forgery, from contemporaries such as Alexander Pope, and from subsequent generations of critics as well. Nonetheless Theobald is regarded by critics as a far more serious scholar than Pope . . . There appears to be agreement among scholars that the 18th century *Double Falshood* is not a forgery, but is based on the lost *Cardenio* of 1612–13, and that the original authors of *Cardenio* were John Fletcher and possibly William Shakespeare.[4]

Be that as it may, there is no doubt that Theobald had given Pope a bloody nose. Retribution would inevitably follow.

The Undertaker

The other mistake Pope made played right into Curll's hands. Pope had embarked on the *Odyssey* hoping to capitalize on his success with the *Iliad*. But this time around, he embarked on the task with less alacrity. He had a lot on his plate: the need to work on Shakespeare concurrently; lesser projects with Buckingham and Thomas Parnell; rebukes from the prominent classicist Anne Dacier; being dragged into the public spotlight when his friend Atterbury was arrested; and renovations of his villa and garden. The previous translation had exposed him to endless personal abuse from Curll and his kin. Now that he had escaped from the shoals of the South Sea affair more or less unscathed, he had less urgent need to make money. When he started work, he obviously wanted to get it done as quickly as possible, in the hope of returning to his own creative projects after a long interval.

In an unlucky hour, Pope made a decision that he must have regretted for the rest of his life. He made an agreement to share work on the translation with two poets, Fenton and the slightly younger William Broome. The plan was for Broome to be responsible for eight books, while Fenton took on four. This left half of the books to Pope himself. The collaborators may have started in 1722, but Pope not until a year later. As we might expect, rumours soon began to circulate about what was going on. To placate subscribers, a feeble attempt at damage limitation was mounted, with Broome admitting to three and Fenton to just two. Newspapers were quick to point out that this was to engage in the seamiest of Grub Street tactics. One journalist, very probably Daniel Defoe, wrote ironically of the unjust treatment bestowed on 'a certain Author', who had produced 'a Translation, or Version, of your old Friend *Homer* under his own Name', when it seemed that 'he *could not have been* the real Operator.'[5]

It took Pope several years, and then not until after Fenton's death in 1730, grudgingly to concede the truth. By that time the damage was done. As often happens in attempts at a cover-up, the explanations caused as much outrage as the original suspicions. The collaborators were decent poets, and Broome in particular has his moments, even though neither could match Pope's contribution in terms of verbal energy and metrical dexterity. But what caused the furore was the subterfuge involved. 'Pray keep the utmost secrecy in the matter,' Pope had instructed his colleagues, and if there is one thing Curll enjoyed it was spilling a secret.[6] It emerged in time that the idea was to conceal the nature of the scheme until after publication; once success was assured, the identity of the co-translators would be revealed. That seemed even more underhand.

Equally devious was the mechanism for admitting that Pope had been helped. He allowed Broome to sign a long note at the end, which praised Pope in extravagant terms and set out a fraudulently low count of books for which he and Fenton were responsible. The explanation falls into a Curllian device, too, when Broome – clearly a mouthpiece for Pope – states that 'it was through inadvertency only' that Anne Dacier's name was sometimes omitted from notes that quoted her opinions.[7] There are shades here of the apology to the House of Lords that the bookseller made back in 1716.

The biggest single blunder from the point of view of public relations occurred in the royal licence printed at the start of each volume. In this the king acknowledges a petition by Lintot that he was 'now printing a Translation, undertaken by Our Trusty and Well beloved *Alexander Pope*, Esq'.[8] The poet had never been universally beloved, and now few would call him trustworthy. A writer in the *London Journal* soon smelled a rat, having noticed that the formula differed from that used in the patent for the *Iliad*. He then advised the public to look on Pope not as the translator but only as the publisher (that is, editor), or, 'as it is expressed in his Patent, *the Undertaker of this Translation*'.[9] This joke depends on the ambiguity of the key word. Our modern sense of 'funeral director' was only just emerging; the main usage was that of someone who undertakes an enterprise, but this could shade into less favourable terms such as 'projector'. In the Bubble era, that expression suggested the authors of crooked investment schemes, and it had also been applied to tax farmers, that is, the unpopular private contractors collecting levies for the government. This was a bit unfair, because in his proposals for the *Iliad*, Lintot had explained that subscribers must pay down a sum in advance (as was normal) 'in regard of the Expence the Undertaker must be at in collecting the several Editions, Cricks, and Commentators'.[10] This refers to Pope, but the word sometimes meant a publisher: thus, Lintot appeals for contributors to a volume named *Love's Academy* to send in material to him as 'the Undertaker'.

Regardless of that, the expression immediately caught on. One epigrammatist found a way of praising Pope while borrowing the damaging epithet:

> If *Homer*'s never-dying Song, begun
> To celebrate the Wrath of *Peleus*' Son;
> Or if his opening *Odysseys* disclose
> A patient Hero, exercis'd in Woes:
> Let undertaking *Pope* demand our Praise,
> Who so could copy the fam'd *Grecian* Lays,
> That *still Achilles Wrath* may *justly* rise,
> And *still Ulysses suffer* in Disguise.[11]

But most of those who picked up the expression had hostile intent – and naturally Curll was among them. At the end of 1725 he published a book by a certain Thomas Pope, and proclaimed its origins on the title page with the words, 'By Mr. Pope; not the Undertaker'. He issued around the same time a work called *The Adventures of Pomponius*, which contains the sentence, 'As a Parallel to this Management of Authors by *Cabal*, may be mentioned that late Jobb of Journey-Work, the Translation of *Homer*'s

ODYSSEY, *Undertaken* by Mr. POPE.' For this and the 'mutilated' edition of Shakespeare, a subscription has been carried on, 'purely through the sycophantick Meanness of the *Undertaker*, who crawls under the *Toilet* of every *Court-Lady*'.[12] This is the poet as voyeur. In one of his replies to *The Dunciad*, Curll twice harked back to the coinage, calling Broome 'one of the Journeymen employed by Mr. *Pope*, as *Undertaker-General*, in Translating the *Odyssey*', and stating that John Ogilby was 'no Author; but an *Undertaker* of other Men's Labours, (as Mr. *Pope* was *of the Odyssey*)'.[13] This thrust goes deep, because Pope had portrayed Ogilby as 'the great fore-father' of the dunces. Never again did Curll find such an apt way of aligning Pope with the exact practices that earned a place among the dunces for his enemies in Grub Street.

TRIFLING REMAINS

As we are aware by now, Curll was always one for surprises. In the midst of his troubles, with spells in and out of gaol, interrogation by the authorities and repeated court appearances, he somehow achieved his greatest coup yet. Actually, we shouldn't think of it as a matter of mere chance. His success, as usual, was owing to his vigilance as a snapper-up of unconsidered trifles. This talent showed itself even while he festered in the King's Bench, now without a helpmate, since his wife had died and Henry was not much help. At the height of his legal battles, in July 1726, he brought out the first two volumes in a series of miscellaneous collections. Later ones carry fancy titles, but the opening set was given the misleadingly bland label *Miscellanea*. This disguised the explosive nature of one ingredient in the brew, which naturally concerned Pope. Everything else in the set was secondary to this big find, even some letters by Dryden and a reprint of Jonathan Swift's *Cadenus and Vanessa: A Law Case* in the first volume. In the second volume a few small items by the Scriblerians are included, with the sheets of *Court Poems* present in some copies (rarely do we find identical copies of such miscellanies). We don't know the source of these items, but the Nonjuring clergyman Richard Rawlinson must be a suspect.

The meat of the compilation is found at the start of the first volume. Curll had managed to lay hands on a good selection of Pope's early letters, and had done so by the oldest commercial stratagem – he had bought them from the owner. They were written to the poet's friend Henry Cromwell, an elderly *flâneur* thirty years Pope's senior. The stripling author tries to appear worldly and sophisticated, but he achieves the opposite effect. Like other young men putting on the style, he comes across as coltish, brash, bawdy, pedantic, smug, pretentious and vain. While nothing very dreadful emerged from the letters, they stood in contradiction to the self-image Pope had cultivated so assiduously over the years.

Cromwell had undertaken to school the young poet in rakish attitudes. A bachelor, he posed as a critic, a man about town and a flirt. The correspondence had surfaced through sordid means. In about 1714 Cromwell had passed the letters on to a mistress by the name of Elizabeth Thomas. Her early verse had attracted the notice of Dryden, who gave her the sobriquet 'Corinna'. The index to the Twickenham edition of Pope identifies her simply as a 'poetaster', which is a bit harsh. Some years later, poverty compelled her to sell the letters to Curll for ten guineas. Not long afterwards she was committed to the Fleet debtors' goal. Worse, she found herself punished for her actions by being allotted an undignified role in the booksellers' sports in *The Dunciad* as 'Curll's Corinna'. In his disingenuous note to this passage, Pope stated that he had not meant to reflect on Thomas, adding that 'he has been inform'd she is a decent woman and in misfortunes.'

At the same time Pope admitted the cause of his anxiety over this affair: 'We only take this opportunity of mentioning the manner in which those Letters got abroad, which the author was asham'd of as very trivial things, full not only of levities, but of wrong judg-ments of men and books, and only excusable from the youth and inexperience of the writer.'[14] In October 1727 he wrote to his old friend John Caryll: 'I have greatly before my eyes the fear of a ras-cally bookseller who has printed some [letters], very unfit to see the light in many regards.' In February 1729 he told Caryl, 'how-ever glad I might be of expressing my respects, opening my mind, or venting my concerns to my private friends, I dare not, while there are Curlls in the world.'[15] Unconvincingly, he assured Swift soon afterwards, 'I smile to think how Curl would be bit, were our Epistles to fall into his hands, and how gloriously they would fall short of ev'ry ingenious reader's expectations?'[16] From now on, Pope would take a lot more care over the disposition of his letters.

The simmering quarrel now moved to a different level. Curll had often got under Pope's skin before now, but this episode would ini-tiate the most serious battles between the two men. Some damaging explanatory notes to the letters also rankled with their author. On top of that, the ease with which Curll had purloined the Cromwell letters may have posed a threat to Pope's fragile hold on his iden-tity. Later, Curll insolently retorted to Pope's strictures that he saw 'no reason [Mrs Thomas] had to ask either Mr. *Cromwell*'s or Mr. *Pope*'s leave' to dispose of the letters as she thought fit.[17] For his part, Cromwell maintained that he had not seen the letters Curll published, and that he had had no contact with Mrs Thomas for seven years. He also reported that Curll had used the poet William Pattison as an intermediary.

For Pope to find his private self exposed in this public way pre-sented a serious challenge. As a result, he started asking his friends to return letters he had written to them, in case they should be mis-appropriated as had been the correspondence with Cromwell. In this spirit the poet wrote to Caryll on 5 December 1726:

EXHIBIT II.I

I will begin by entreating of you to consult my fame, such as it is, and
to help me to put out of Curl's power any trifling remains of mine. If
therefore you have preserved any verses or letters, I beg you to send
them to me (as I will desire every man to do whom I know to be my
friend). I will review them, and return whatever can do no hurt to
either of us, or our memories, or to any other particular man's character; but so much, as would serve to bear testimony of my own love
for good men, or theirs for me, I would not but keep on all accounts,
and shall think this very article more to my reputation than all my
works put together.[18]

Here we have the basis for the heavy editing that Pope carried out
on the letters he eventually allowed into print. Needless to say, he
did not let Curll have this one.

Since he never did return the items Caryll gave him, and actually used them as the basis of doctored texts in subsequent editions,
Pope's words here cannot have been completely honest. It looks
as if Curll's initiative had given him the idea to edit his earlier
correspondence and publish it in a form that would enhance his
reputation. On occasion he may have been genuinely irritated by
his persevering adversary, as when he complained to the bookseller Benjamin Motte on 30 June 1727 about a press notice for the
Cromwell letters:

> The advertisement of Curl is a silly piece of Impertinence,
> & it serves to tell every body what makes for my purpose &
> reputation, 'That those Letters to Mr. Cromwell were printed
> without My Consent or knowledge.' The fact of *Cabinets
> being broke open, & dead people's Closets ransacked . . . is never-
> theless true*, which this Scoundrel wishes to have applyd to
> *Cromwells* Letters, *only to advance their Sale.*[19]

The advertisement referred to here has not previously been recovered. However, it is clearly a notice that Henry Curll put in the *Evening Post*, which survives in the issue of 8 July. This is one of the family firm's cheeky replies to the great – even the opening lines, which have no direct relevance to the quarrel, illustrate the way Curll treated those in authority:

EXHIBIT 11.2

This Day is publish'd,

COFFEE. A TALE ECCLESIASTICK.

Harping upon several untoward Matters, wherein every Freeborn Briton is concern'd; more especially tender Parents, and all Conscientious Guardians of Infants: With an irrefragable patch'd-work'd preface. [The Author of this just Satire is ready to own it, to those who have a proper Authority for asking the Question.] Printed for H. Curll over against Catherine Street in the Strand. price 1s.

N.B. To Mr. POPE.

Sir, Since you have asserted a most flagrant Falshood (in the Preface to a late revived Collection of party-pamphlets, printed about sixteen Years ago) I must . . . retort the Lye upon its Inventor. You say, you have been extreamly ill-treated by some Booksellers, especially me, and that 'the Cabinets of the Sick, and the Closets of the Dead, have been broke open, and ransacked, to publish your private Letters, and divulge to all Mankind the most secret Sentiments and Intercourses of Friendship.' Your Letters to Mr. Cromwell, there hinted at, were given to him by a Gentlewoman, to do with them as she pleas'd. The Truth of which is hereunder confirmed; and to which, your Guilt of this most notorious Calumny must oblige you to be silent.

E. CURLL.

Extract of a Letter to Henry Cromwell, Esq; June 27, 1721.
Sir, It is doubly injurious In Mr. Pope, to treat me with the opprobious Name of Thief, when I am certain you will do me this Right of

owning, you made me a free Gift of his Letters, and therefore I came honestly by them.   E. T[HOMA]S.

June 8, 1727. I waited upon Mr. Cromwell this Morning, who acknowledg'd that he gave the Letters (written by Mr. Pope to him) to Mrs T[homa]s, above fifteen Years ago.

W. PATTISON.

These Letters of Mr. Pope are printed in two neat pocket Volumes price 5 s.

Who the mysterious W. Pattison was, we already know. As for the remark about dead people's closets, that comes from the preface to the *Miscellanies* of Pope and his friends, to which we now turn.

A JUST REPRISAL

Curll's new volumes had another effect. They helped to trigger the publication of the *Miscellanies* of the Scriblerus circle, which appeared in four instalments up to 1732, beginning with two issued in June 1727. Although Swift and Pope had come up with the idea of such a collection years before, it took Curll's productions to galvanize them into action. The plan had originally been to include *The Dunciad* in the series, but ultimately this was dropped in favour of *The Art of Sinking*. Several of the satirists' best works were reprinted, and some new ones added. For our present purposes, the most important section is the preface that Pope contributed to the first in the series, speaking also on behalf of Swift. Dated 31 May 1726 from Twickenham (where Swift had just been staying on his last visit to England), the document sets out the official Scriblerian line on the progress of the quarrel, as it dramatized larger issues relating to book history. It does not take Pope long to get to the villain of the piece:

EXHIBIT 11.3

Having both of us been extremely ill treated by some Booksellers (especially one *Edmund Curll,*) it was our Opinion that the best Method we could take for justifying ourselves, would be to publish whatever loose Papers in Prose and Verse, we have formerly written; not only such as have already stolen into the World (very much to our Regret, and, perhaps, very little to our Credit,) but such, as in any Probability hereafter may run the same Fate; having been obtained from us by the Importunity, and divulged by the Indiscretion of Friends, although restrain'd by Promises, which few of them are ever known to observe, and often think they make us a Compliment in breaking.

But the Consequences have been still worse: We have been entitled, and have had our Names prefixed at length, to whole Volumes of mean Productions, equally offensive to good Manners and good Sense, which we never saw nor heard of till they appeared in Print.

For a *Forgery*, in setting a false Name to a Writing, which may prejudice another's Fortune, the Law punishes the Offender with the Loss of his *Ears*; but has inflicted no adequate Penalty for such as prejudice another's Reputation, in doing the same Thing in Print; though all and every individual Book so sold under a false Name, are manifestly so many several and multiplied Forgeries.

Indeed we hoped, that the good Nature, or at least the good Judgment of the World, would have cleared us from the Imputation of such Things as had been thus charged upon us, by the Malice of Enemies, the Want of Judgment in Friends, the Unconcern of indifferent Persons, and the confident Assertions of Booksellers.[20]

As we have noted, forgers were scarcely ever subjected any more to such draconian punishment, but that is beside the point for Pope. The preface goes on to specify further injustices perpetrated by the trade, among them this:

EXHIBIT II.4

Those very Booksellers who have supported themselves upon an Author's Fame while he lived, have done their utmost after his Death to lessen it by such Practices: Even a Man's last *Will* is not secure from being exposed in Print; whereby his most particular Regards, and even his dying Tendernesses are laid open. It has been humorously said, that some have fished the very Jakes, for Papers left there by Men of Wit: But it is no Jest to affirm, that the Cabinets of the Sick, and the Closets of the Dead, have been broke open and ransacked, to publish our *private Letters*, and divulge to all Mankind the most secret Sentiments and Intercourse of Friendship. Nay, these Fellows are arrived to that Height of Impudence, that when an Author has publickly disowned a spurious Piece, they have disputed his own Name with him in printed Advertisements, which has been practised to Mr. *Congreve* and Mr. *Prior*.[21]

No prizes would go to the sagacious reader in 1726 who identified the culprit responsible for such deception.

The series was published by Benjamin Motte, successor to Benjamin Tooke, who had put out many of Swift's earlier works. Motte had no previous association with Pope, but he had been responsible for *Gulliver's Travels* in the previous year. Swift had smuggled the manuscript across to England, fearing – with some reason – that it might have been intercepted if sent through the post, in the continuing state of heightened alarm following the Atterbury scare. Indeed, the authorities would likely have confiscated it on account of the 'seditious' ideas it contained. With an excess of caution, Swift entered into a series of mystifications to establish contact anonymously with Motte. 'To his own gifts for impersonation and deceit', says Irvin Ehrenpreis, 'were added the subtleties and financial cunning of Pope.'[22] In fact, the elaborate byplay around publication, with a letter from Gulliver's cousin 'Richard Sympson' sending a portion of the manuscript by messenger, may have given Pope the idea for the preposterous arrangements, eight years later, by which he tried to conceal the way his letters reached the public.

Motte makes plain the connection between Curll's project and that of the Scriblerians in a letter to a certain Mr Woodford in March 1728:

EXHIBIT II.5

The dispute with Mr. Curll stands as follows: – For many years past he has made it his business to pick up straggling and imperfect Copies of Verses, which he has father'd upon Dr Swift or Mr. Pope, or some other name of reputation. Some of these were really written by these Gentlemen, but publish'd by him without their knowledge and against their consent; and many Pieces were laid to their charge which they knew nothing of, and were so worthless that they had reason to be ashamed of them. To vindicate their Reputation they made a Collection of such things as were genuine, and have just now published them, having before for a valuable and substantial consideration made a formal Conveyance of the Copyright of them to me in May last. On the Publication of them I receiv'd the following Letter from Curll: –

> Mr. Motte, – I have carefully examin'd your new last volume of old Miscellanies; in the Art of Sinking, your Authors have printed the Project for advancing the Stage, which is my copy; and most of the other pieces in the Volume have been by me published many Years ago. To-morrow night you'll find I have in some measure undeceiv'd the Town. And to do myself justice, will reprint whatever is *New* in this last Volume as a just reprizal for what they have taken from me that is *Old.* | Yours, | E. Curll.

However Swift and Pope agree,
Nor they nor you shall bubble me.

Q. Whether, in case he be in execution in the Court of King's Bench, that Court has not a power to curb him in such enormities?[23]

The answer to this final question is that the court was doing its best. But whether even this august body had the power to curb the enormities is a matter of doubt. The bookseller knew how to find and exploit loopholes in the law.

What may have added to Motte's displeasure is the fact that Curll had reverted to his old ways. Within weeks of the publication of Swift's masterpiece, he had provided *A Key, being Observations and Explanatory Notes, upon the Travels of Lemuel Gulliver*– in fact, the first of four instalments working through the text, voyage by voyage. Before 1726 was out, the parts were collected in a single volume, *Lemuel Gulliver's Travels into Several Remote Nations of the World. Compendiously Methodized, for Publick Benefit; with Observations and Explanatory Notes throughout.* It's clear that the title was designed to trick buyers into thinking they were purchasing the original book. The supposed author is absurdly identified as 'Signor Corolini, a noble Venetian now residing in London', evidently Curll's long-lost Italian cousin of whom nothing had been heard until now. Even Pope, anxious as he was for the success of his friend's work, may have smiled at this barefaced impudence.

Grub Street writers soon responded to the *Miscellanies* on behalf of Curll, who could almost be seen as their champion. An Irishman named Matthew Concanen, active in the London prints and so destined for an appearance in *The Dunciad* on various counts, described the Preface in this way:

EXHIBIT 11.6

The first Thing we meet with here (and indeed half the Work is taken up with it) is a Page or two of severe Satire upon Booksellers, particularly one *Edmund Curll.* I won't enter into the Occasion or the State of the Controversy, or the Strength of these Gentlemen's Raillery and Reasoning; but is it not truly pleasant to see two of the greatest Genius's of our Age *set their Wits* to a paltry Bookseller? . . .

Your Triumphs, O ye Bards, proclaim, and all your Flags unfurl,
For Doctor *Swift* and Mr. *Pope* have conquer'd *Edmund Curll*.
Henceforward let no little Under-Wits disdain to write against
Curll, if he provokes them, (as I have known several give themselves
such Airs) since the two Leaders of the Muses Bands have put their
Names to a Libel against him. Rejoice therefore, O *Edmund Curll*,
and let thy Gladness know no End, since thou hast had the Honour to be Satirized by the same Pens, which have been employed in
lampooning the Duke of *MARLBOROUGH* and Mr. *ADDISON* ...

It is an easy matter to keep the dullest Stuff alive by the Art of
multiplying Impressions, which consists only in the Variation
of Types, Title-Page, Size and Paper. Mr. *Curll* is so great a Master
of this, that I don't wonder at his falling under the Resentment of
such People as intended to make a Monopoly of it.[24]

Although this is a backhanded compliment to the crafty publisher,
Curll may have been glad to receive it. He certainly got few plaudits
from his colleagues in the trade.

A STATION AT CHARING CROSS

At length the government began to grow impatient. There had been
delays when Edmund Curll was granted further bail, for which
he sent thanks to Charles Delafaye, and pleaded for the release of
Henry, who had been arrested in connection with the memoirs
of John Ker. But the Attorney General was anxious to proceed,
not just with the Ker trial, but also with the suspended proceedings in the case of obscene libel. A trial date was fixed for 18 May
1727, but it was again stood over for a further term, 'being a case
of great consequence'. In the Michaelmas term it finally reached
court, with the fearsome Judge Francis Page now among the justices of the King's Bench. Curll's lawyer John Strange asked for yet
another deferral, because the bookseller had not consulted him in

time. Since the latest failure was caused by the defendant's own neglect, the court rejected this plea. Towards the end of November Curll at long last got his day in court. It did not go well.[25]

In his opening address, with regard to the obscenity case, the Attorney General maintained that there was no way other than common law for punishing the defendant, since if there was a remedy in the spiritual courts this had never been used – a slightly specious argument, perhaps. In any event, there were precedents for regarding the temporal law as the place in which offences *contra bonos mores* were to be tried. The Attorney General moved to set aside Lord Chief Justice Holt's verdict in 1707, when the publishers of pamphlets entitled *Sodom* and *The School of Love* were acquitted on the grounds that they had committed no temporal crime. It had also been laid down that a libel must involve defamation of a person. That last decree would be challenged in 1727, and effectively countermanded. This time the moderate Justice John Fortescue Aland was not on the bench to oppose conviction, whereas he had previously held out against the majority. He stated later that although *The Nun in her Smock* contained some bawdy expressions, it 'did contain no Libel against any Person whatsoever'. Going further, he thought it should be published, 'on purpose to expose the *Romish* Priests, the Father Confessors, and Popish Religion'.[26] Curll could not have put it better.

News of the prosecution quickly reached the ears of the highest in the land. Just after Swift returned to Ireland for the last time, John Arbuthnot wrote to him to say that he had been with 'our friend' (the king's mistress Henrietta Howard) at St James's Palace, and had spoken to the queen: 'The first part of our discourse was about yow [a Scots form of 'you'] Mr. Pope Curle & myself.'[27] This was just a day after the verdict was announced.

All the defendant's attempts at rebuttal had fallen on deaf ears. He had to wait until 5 February to receive judgment, when he 'pleaded his own Cause, and submitted himself wholly to the Mercy of the Bench'. He was to receive sentence 'both on his Amatory and Political Offences' a week later, as Nathaniel Mist put it with a sneer. The outcome proved to be this: on the amatory side, a fine of 25 marks (£16.66) for each book, to be paid before he could be released from prison, and on the political, 20 marks (£13.33), plus a stint of one hour in the pillory at Charing Cross. He also agreed to be bound over in the sum of £100 for his good behaviour.[28] These were not small sums, but it will be noticed that the most conspicuous punishment was imposed in connection with Ker's *Memoirs*, not the obscene items. The pillory was of course a long-lasting mode of public humiliation, whose ramifications have been explored in a brilliant recent study by Thomas Keymer.[29] So it was that on 23 February 1728 Curll was lifted on to the rostrum at a spot often seen as the very centre of London, halfway between his home in the Covent Garden area and the seat of justice and power at Westminster.

We have no contemporary image of Curll in the pillory. From his elevated position, he must have been able to see the bronze equestrian statue of Charles I in the centre of what was then a Y junction (Trafalgar Square had yet to be built, of course). The king gazes down Whitehall towards the site of his execution and the home of the parliamentarians who tried him. But, since the victim's head was so tightly constricted in the pillory frame, Curll probably had no sight of these things. Depending on the exact location of the contraption, he might have got a glimpse of the entrance to the Strand, down past the massive Jacobean frontage of Northumberland House in the direction of his own business.

It's important to recognize that people were not sent to the pillory for any old reason. As the crime historian J. M. Beattie explains, there was a selection process:

The offenses that judges and magistrates were anxious to punish by the pillory were acts that aroused deep public

anger and hostility, either because of the vulnerability of the
victim (a child, for example) or because the offense was both
damaging and difficult to prevent. The point of punishment
by public exposure was in those cases not only to chastise
the offender and to deter him and others from such behav-
ior in the future, but also quite simply to make his identity
known so as to forewarn potential victims – 'to mark him
out to the public,' as was said in 1730, 'as a person not fit to
be trusted, but to be shunned and avoided by all creditable
and honest men.'[30]

Both men and women were pilloried for various kinds of fraud,
such as pretending to tell fortunes or cheating at cards, and making
false accusations. Sometimes women were pilloried for keeping a
bawdy house.

However, the sentence was increasingly imposed for sedition,
after the government lost some of its ability to censor publications
deemed to attack public institutions and morals. Keymer explains
it this way: 'Within a few years of the 1695 lapse [of the Licensing
Act], prosecution for seditious libel had become central as never
before, and with it the shame and hazard of the pillory.'[31] Hazard
there certainly could be. The historian of the London mob Robert
Shoemaker reports an instance:

> When John Middleton stood in the pillory in 1723 for attempt-
> ing to earn rewards by making false accusations of treasonable
> practices, such was the popular hostility against him that
> the high constable summoned twenty constables and 104
> assistants to protect him, though even this number could not
> prevent the crowd from smothering him to death with dirt.[32]

According to newspaper accounts, Middleton was a young Irishman
who had mounted the pillory while drunk, and threw down the

stool on which he stood, so that in Mist's cruel estimate, 'he was thereby his own Executioner.'[33] An inquest jury brought in a verdict of accidental strangling, but the Lord Justices acting during the king's absence in Hanover were sufficiently concerned to summon those responsible for carrying out the sentence. Possibly the Justices were anxious in case this brutal punishment should deter people from tipping them off about renegades. Middleton left a wife and two small children. It was a scene that Curll could have witnessed if he had taken a short walk down the Strand, since it took place at Charing Cross, as did his own penance five years later. As a regular informant to the ministry on seditious publications, he may have felt a few tremors of apprehension.

It could certainly be a frightening experience to stand on the rostrum for an hour in full public gaze, especially if your offence was unpopular with the mob. Some of the perils are enumerated by V.A.C. Gatrell:

> It is not easy to ignore such scenes as those enacted at the Charing Cross pillory, with miscreants exposed at the dinner hour when streets were most crowded. Overlooked by a sheriff, the crowd was expected to bring cats, eggs, decayed cabbages, and dung with which to pelt the victim, women being allowed to throw from the front if they tipped the constables first. Eyes were lost, blood flowed in mud on these occasions, and some died – usually those pilloried for 'unnatural' crimes.[34]

A quarter of a century earlier, another man accused of sedition, Daniel Defoe, had been raised on what he called the 'hieroglyphick state machine' at three different locations – the last of them Curll's stamping ground, Temple Bar. 'Instead of having his head spattered with yolks of eggs and stinking fish,' his biographer James Sutherland wrote, 'he had seen his pillory garlanded with flowers and heard his health drunk by crowds of good fellows in the streets below.'[35] But recent authorities, notably Keymer, have shown that this was a Victorian invention, and the evidence for such kindly treatment is thin.[36]

Still, it did happen in a few cases, and perhaps that explains why, according to Strange, the miscreant got off so easily. The *State Trials* report:

EXHIBIT 11.7

This Edmund Curll stood in the pillory at Charing-Cross, but was not pelted, or used ill; for being an artful, cunning (though wicked) fellow he had contrived to have printed papers dispersed all about Charing-Cross, telling the people, he stood there for vindicating the memory of queen Anne: which had such an effect on the mob, that it would have been dangerous to have spoken against him: and when he was taken down out of the pillory, the mob carried him off, as it were in triumph, to a neighbouring tavern.[37]

Defoe had prepared a handout for the crowd in the shape of his *Hymn to the Pillory*. Curll was no less savvy in terms of street theatre, and he got out an address to the spectators, rather like a candidate distributing election publicity, although today it would be on social media:

EXHIBIT 11.8

GENTLEMEN,

I Hope you'll consider, that this Gentleman who now appears before you, is not guilty of any base or villainous Crimes; he has indeed been found guilty of publishing three Books, and that for which he is thus exposed, is called, *The Life and Actions of* JOHN KER, *of Kersland*, and who had from Her late most gracious Majesty Queen ANNE, of immortal Memory, the under-written Royal Leave and Licence, which will shew you the Trust SHE had in him, and which he faithfully discharged: Likewise did this Gentleman, who now stands before you, perform his Promise to him on his Death-Bed, in publishing the Two last Books, he himself having published the First in his Life-time.[38]

The last part is untrue, although Ker may indeed have sent out the first volume at his own expense, using Curll as a paid distributor.

Was this a good marketing strategy? Years later Henry Fielding wrote in his *Covent-Garden Journal* recommending that booksellers should mount 'the wooden machine' for an hour and proclaim their goods to the populace: 'This was practised with much Success by the late Mr. Curl, Mr. Mist and others, who never failed of selling several large Bales of Goods *in this Manner*.'[39] We have to suspect some exaggeration here.

AN OPERA AND A HOTCHPOTCH

There was one other big event at this moment, although it did not totally eclipse public awareness of Curll's misfortunes. This was the premiere of Gay's *Beggar's Opera* on 29 January 1728. At first the success of the play hung in the balance, but, thanks partly to audible encouragement from the boxes by the Duke of Argyll, the atmosphere warmed, and there was a torrent of applause at the final curtain. It has continued to wow audiences round the world, despite the fact that much of its satire, drawn from the world of opera, politics and crime, has lost its immediate topical edge. *The Threepenny Opera* (1928) by Kurt Weill and Bertolt Brecht, an adaptation that came out on the bicentenary of Gay's work, is perhaps even better known today. We might, however, recall the astringent judgement of Percy A. Scholes: '*The Beggar's Opera*, after struggling through thousands of performances over a period of exactly two centuries, at last had life put into it by Kurt Weill.'[40] In his broken-backed life of Gay (1733), Curll has little to say

about *The Beggar's Opera* and its sequel *Polly*, doubtless because
his son Henry had been named in an injunction preventing him
from publishing the later play.

Not everyone loved the new hit play. But according to legend,
Walpole managed to conceal his true feelings and applauded vigorously when he came to a performance, even though his features
were readily apparent under the mask of Peachum, the thief-taker.
One quick response was a work attributed to 'Caleb D'Anvers', a
pseudonym adopted by Nicholas Amhurst. Its title tells us most of
what we need to know: *The Twickenham Hotch-Potch, for the Use
of the Rev. Dr Swift, Alexander Pope, Esq; and Company. Being a
Sequel to the Beggars Opera, &c.* The imprint names James Roberts,
but Curll advertised this item in his list, and internal evidence
confirms his involvement. The first piece among the varied contents billed on the title page is 'The State of Poetry', in which the
writer complains about the way ministers of our most august monarch have been ridiculed under the characters of a thief-catcher
(Peachum), a gaoler (Lockit) and a highwayman (Macheath). Is
this ironic? It's hard to be sure, especially since the writer goes on
to attack 'an impertinent *Scotch*-Quack, a profligate *Irish*-Dean,
the Lacquey of a Superannuated Dutchess, and a little virulent
Papist', an easily decoded allusion to Arbuthnot, Swift, Gay and
Pope. Elsewhere in the collection, we have a letter from Theobald
reinforcing his criticism of the Shakespeare edition, with a few
tired thrusts at Pope and Swift, one in an advertisement for a
poem called *The Knight of the Kirk*. This was written by a minor
Scottish author named William Menston; but Curll had been
involved in its republication in London at the end of April, and
used the dedication to insert a puff for *Miscellanea*. The introduction to the *Hotch-Potch* ends with a passage twisting Pope's
verse on Longinus and the sublime in *An Essay on Criticism* to fit
the bathos of 'this *Twickenham*-Club'.[41] But the crafty publisher
had already thought of that one.

What would be in store for Curll, as he climbed down off the pillory? From this time forwards everyone knew about his disgrace, although to be fair Pope does not make undue capital from the episode in *The Dunciad*. That famous production was now on its way, and the world would get to see the form that the poet's long-expected response to his enemies took.

12

A Confederacy of DUNCES, 1728–9

*T*he *Dunciad* was more than a work of literature. Its appearance constituted an event, or, in the language of the 1960s, a happening: that is, a staged performance intended to shock and disorientate all beholders. It took the world of letters more than a generation to get over its impact, and the relations of booksellers and authors were never quite the same from this moment. In a passage dating from 1732, one author (probably Richard Savage, although Samuel Johnson and others have suspected Pope himself) refers to the War of the Dunces, running from 1727 to 1730, and describes publication day in somewhat lurid terms:

EXHIBIT 12.1

On the Day the Book was first vended, a Crowd of Authors besieged the Shop; Entreaties, Advices, Threats of Law, and Battery, nay Cries of Treason were all employed to hinder the coming out of the *Dunciad*: On the other Side the Booksellers and Hawkers made as great Effort to procure it: What could a few poor Authors do against so great a Majority as the Publick? There was no stopping a Torrent with a Finger, so out it came.

Many ludicrous Circumstances attended it: The Dunces (for by this Name they were called) held weekly Clubs to consult of Hostilities against the Author; one wrote a Letter to a great Minister, Mr. *Pope* was the greatest Enemy the Government had; and another brought his Image in Clay, to execute him in Effigy; with which sad Sort of Satisfaction the Gentlemen were a little comforted.[1]

There is room to doubt whether there was in sober truth 'a Confederacy of Dunces', a phrase that is now well known because it was adapted from Jonathan Swift by John Kennedy Toole for the title of his novel (1980). Clear signs exist, however, that victims of the satire did band together to forge a concerted reply to Pope.

Rather like *Ulysses*, the poem is composed in a multilayered form, except that James Joyce's book is a little simpler in construction. Along with parody of classical epic, the defining attribute of mock-heroic writing, it draws in a sustained way on a variety of cultural and artistic models. These include the Bible, *Paradise Lost*, paradoxical encomiums such as Erasmus's *In Praise of Folly*, Ovidian myths, theories of historical development, antiquarian lore, pastoral ancient and modern, earlier English sources such as John Dryden's *Mac Flecknoe*, snatches of Shakespeare, Newtonian physics, popular shows in playhouses and fairs, and a great deal else.[2] We can observe a steady undertow of jokes deriding the court of George I and his son, who had recently succeeded to the throne, as well as the government of Robert Walpole. The rule of Queen Dulness mimics the sovereignty of Hanoverian royals. As may have become clear, it is centrally a poem concerned with London – its history, topography, traditions, legends, civic pageantry, theatrical life and even its sanitation system. The action takes place on Lord Mayor's Day, the biggest event on the municipal calendar. As a fully fledged citizen and member of an ancient livery company, not to mention a tradesman operating at the heart of the inner parishes close to the Thames, Curll could hardly escape the firing line.

For these reasons, it is apt that the depiction of Grub Street in its broad sense – the world of commercialized writing and publishing – occupies a key place in the design. In 1728 the king of the dunces nominated was Lewis Theobald, journalist, contriver of pantomimes, but crucially here a representative of what Pope regarded as narrow pedantry in criticism. This connects with another target of the satire, namely the kind of minute textual scholarship

Illustration to *The Dunciad* by Francis Hayman, engraved by Claude Grignion, *c.* 1750, showing the 'ample presence' of Queen Dulness and the 'veil of fogs' that surrounds her, while her laureate Colley Cibber turns his head away from his futile works.

F. Hayman inv. et del.   C. Grignion Sculp
Her ample Presence fills up all the Space,
A Veil of Fogs dilates her anfull Face.
Dunciad, Book I.

associated both with the real Richard Bentley and the imaginary Martin Scriblerus. Bentley had been a leader of the Moderns in the great Battle of the Books against Swift's allies in Oxford. His influential editorial methods are parodied in the notes appended to the poem by Scriblerus. When Pope revised the work in 1743, Theobald's role was taken over by Colley Cibber, a dramatist, an actor-manager, but most relevantly a despised Poet Laureate.

The history of *The Dunciad* is littered with bibliographical complexity that we need not explore. In outline, the story runs in this way. The first edition, anonymous as was its successors, was published on 18 May 1728; the only name on the title page is that of the 'mercury', Anne Dodd, whose identity served as a flag of convenience. Very soon followed a piracy that used to be attributed to Curll, without any good evidence. An extended version of the poem appeared as *The Dunciad Variorum* in April 1729, now attributed to 'A. Dod'. In it the text of the poem, in three books, was augmented by an elaborate critical apparatus, with new prefatory material including 'Testimonies of Authors' (citing the nasty things the dunces had said about Pope), and appendices including a list of attacks in pamphlets and journals. But the most important change was the addition of lengthy footnotes that redouble the damage already inflicted by the verse. A new vignette on the title page shows an ass carrying a heavy burden of duncely volumes, with the authors' names visible on the top edge of the pages; we can pick out almost all the usual suspects. Was Curll relieved not to be chosen as one of the rogues' gallery here, or miffed that he missed out on the publicity?

The copyright was assigned to Pope's aristocratic friends Bathurst, Oxford and Burlington for protective reasons. Nevertheless, Pope kept real control and pocketed most of the proceeds that did not go to the young bookseller Lawton Gilliver, who handled most of his publications from then on. An advance copy was presented to the queen on 12 March by Walpole, a gesture of immense daring that is hard to fathom, since both the king and the prime minister are targets of the satire.

Untaught to Fear

There are sporadic references to Curll throughout the text of *The Dunciad*. However, the two main sections where he takes centre stage both occur in the course of the mock-heroic games that dominate Book II. These interconnected passages occupy about 130 lines, describing contests in which Curll is pitted against his fellow booksellers Bernard Lintot and William Chetwood, the former a rival and the latter a sometime partner.

First, the dunces are summoned by the presiding deity, Dulness, to the area near St Mary's church in the Strand, almost on the doorstep of Curll's shop. They are to take part in 'high, heroic Games', parodying the sports found in both Homer and Virgil, with the footrace in Book 5 of the *Aeneid* the most immediate model. Some impressive contests between finely appointed chariots in Book 23 of the *Iliad* are replaced here by a kindergarten romp. The opening challenge is to run in pursuit of a phantom poet who plays the role of a hare to greyhounds. 'Lofty Lintot' is quick to enter the fray, but he soon has a formidable competitor. At first it looks as if Curll's supreme confidence is well placed:

EXHIBIT 12.2

Fear held them mute. Alone untaught to fear,
Stood dauntless Curl, 'Behold that rival here!
The race by vigor, not by vaunts is won;
So take the hindmost Hell.' – He said, and run.
Swift as a bard the bailiff leaves behind,
He left huge Lintot, and out-stript the wind.
As when a dab-chick waddles thro' the copse,
On feet and wings, and flies, and wades, and hops;
So lab'ring on, with shoulders, hands, and head,
Wide as a windmill all his figure spread,
With legs expanded Bernard urg'd the race,
And seem'd to emulate great Jacob's pace.[3]

'Urge' is used in an obsolete sense, that is, to gather speed. The last line glances at Jacob Tonson's awkward gait; in later versions it becomes 'left-legged Jacob'. But pride literally goes before a fall here. It is introduced with a particularly bitchy comment about Elizabeth Thomas under her nom de plume, Corinna. She was

Scene from the dunces' games in *The Dunciad*, set near a bridge across the Fleet Ditch. Curll may be one of the bystanders on the bankside. Engraving by Charles Grignion after Francis Hayman, *c*. 1750.

living handily close to Curll, and she happened, poor woman, to suffer from unpleasant digestive problems after swallowing a chicken bone.[4]

EXHIBIT 12.3

> Full in the middle way there stood a lake,
> Which Curl's Corinna chanc'd that morn to make,
> (Such was her Wont, at early dawn to drop
> Her evening cates before his neighbour's shop,)
> Here fortun'd Curl to slide; loud shout the band,
> And Bernard! Bernard! rings thro' all the Strand.
> Obscene with filth the Miscreant lies bewray'd,
> Fal'n in the plash his wickedness had lay'd;
> Then first (if Poets aught of truth declare)
> The caitiff Vaticide conceiv'd a prayer.
> 'Hear Jove! whose name my bards and I adore,
> As much at least as any God's, or more;
> And him and his if more devotion warms,
> Down with the Bible, up with the Pope's Arms.[5]

Here the last line cleverly plays on the two booksellers' shop signs; it will be recalled that Lintot used the papal emblem of crossed keys, while Curll's had been the Dial and Bible (he promptly complained, in his pernickety way, that this was no longer the case). 'Vaticide' is a pompous mock-heroic term for one who kills a prophet, applied in this case to the poet (Latin *vates*) as a prophet. In an earlier draft, the fifth line began, 'Here slidder'd Curl,' which comes across as more evocative today.[6]

At this stage in the race, it looks as if Curll has missed his chance. But providentially he is able to call on aid from Cloacina, goddess of the sewers. As happens throughout the poem, we are at once in mythical space and also in real-life London, where human waste piled up in the street and stagnant waterways such as the

Fleet Ditch acted as the main sewage disposal lines. His appeal to Cloacina does the trick, and Curll emerges the victor:

EXHIBIT 12.4

> Oft, as he fish'd her nether realms for wit,
> The Goddess favour'd him, and favours yet.
> Renew'd by ordure's sympathetic force,
> As oil'd with magic juices for the course,
> Vig'rous he rises; from th' effluvia strong
> Imbibes new life, and scours and stinks along,
> Re-passes Lintot, vindicates the race,
> Nor heeds the brown dishonours of his face.[7]

Once more, sordid events are described in epic language ('dishonours', and 'vindicates' in the sense of the Latin *vindicare*, meaning to claim the race). Curll finds, though, that he is unable to grasp his prize, since the phantom poet whom he pursued will not release his works – he is a physical embodiment of 'Joseph Gay' and the other non-existent names the bookseller had used. Instead, the goddess appoints him her stationer, that is publisher, with licence to engage in identity theft as he wishes: 'Cook shall be Prior, and Concanen, Swift' (Matthew Concanen we have met as a journalist, and he would become heavily involved in the aftermath of *The Dunciad*). Curll's further reward is a tapestry displaying the fate of the votaries of Dulness, including Daniel Defoe, 'Earless on high' (we've seen that bit about the pillory is not true), and the writer John Tutchin 'flagrant from the scourge below', once sentenced to be whipped through the streets.[8] This is one of Pope's slick etymological puns, since 'flagrant' means conspicuous, as it can today, but also 'burning red from a flogging'; the *OED* adds that this is an obsolete sense, to which we might add 'Thank goodness.' Also portrayed on this visual memorial of punishment is the much-battered bookseller himself:

EXHIBIT 12.5

The very worsted still look'd black and blue:
Himself among the storied Chiefs he spies,
As from the blanket high in air he flies,
'And oh!' (he cry'd,) 'what street, what lane, but knows
Our purgings, pumpings, blanketings and blows?
In ev'ry loom our labours shall be seen,
And the fresh vomit run for ever green!'[9]

Pope was never going to allow Curll to forget these shameful episodes, and in case anyone missed the point a note spells out the grisly particulars.

A second contest now begins. The prize is no less than the novelist Eliza Haywood, now much more highly regarded than she was in her own day. The note claims that this passage depicts the 'profligate licentiousness of those shameless scribblers . . . who in libelous Memoirs and Novels, reveal the faults and misfortunes of both sexes, to the ruin or disturbance, of publick fame or private happiness'. Needless to say, modern readers would not find this a very convincing justification for what follows. A china jordan (chamber pot) will be used as part of a pissing competition, with the prize to go to whoever can send his urinary spout highest. It is not much of a defence that in the *Iliad* a woman is carried away as the joint first prize, along with an impressive three-footed cauldron.

EXHIBIT 12.6

Chetwood and Curl accept the glorious strife,
(Tho' one his son dissuades, and one his wife)
This on his manly confidence relies,
That on his vigor and superior size.
First Chetwood lean'd against his letter'd post;
It rose, and labour'd to a curve at most:

So Jove's bright bow displays its watry round,
(Sure sign, that no spectator shall be drown'd).
A second effort brought but new disgrace,
For straining more, it flies in his own face;
Thus the small jett which hasty hands unlock,
Spirts in the gard'ner's eyes who turns the cock.
Not so from shameless Curl: Impetuous spread
The stream, and smoaking, flourish'd o'er his head,
So, (fam'd like thee for turbulence and horns,)
Eridanus his humble fountain scorns,
Thro' half the heav'ns he pours th' exalted urn;
His rapid waters in their passage burn.

    Swift as it mounts, all follow with their eyes;
Still happy Impudence obtains the prize.
Thou triumph'st, victor of the high-wrought day,
And the pleas'd dame soft-smiling leads away.
Chetwood, thro' perfect modesty o'ercome,
Crown'd with the Jordan, walks contented home.[10]

Curll, as we know, had lost his first wife, so it would be up to Henry to try to 'dissuade' his father from his habitually rash decisions. Eridanus was the name of a mythical river, sometimes identified with the Po, and supposed to flow through the skies.[11] The obscene overtones of some words are obvious, as with 'size', 'cock' and 'burn'. We shall see presently that the innuendo concerning a burning sensation is taken up more openly in Pope's note.

One aspect of this section has generally been missed. The events have a special propriety because Haywood was one successful writer ('Authoress and Translatoress of many Novels', he calls her) whom Curll had never nabbed for his list.[12] He would assuredly have been happy to have her for his own. But Chetwood was an equally good choice. In his *Key* to the poem, Curll revealed that 'Among other Pranks played, in a Drunken-Debauch, Mr. *Chetwood* was sent

Home with a Jordan, *alias*, a Piss-Pot on his Head.'[13] So he too got what – as the satire pretends, anyway – were his deserts. Throughout Book II, Pope manages to find concrete instances to support his comic allegory, where journalists engage in mud-diving, authors tickle their patrons and plunge into foetid waters, poets jabber and echo each other's cacophonous 'songs', while booksellers strive to outdo one another in purloining stray manuscripts. It is an exposé of Grub Street, but one contrived in an expressive vehicle that was beyond the powers of any Grub Streeter to match, thanks to its learned wit, its range of idiom from the classical to the demotic, and its malicious attention to detail.

MARKS OF DISTINCTION

What, then, of the notes, an equally destructive weapon of the satire? On his first full appearance in the text, Curll is awarded a substantial entry, in which many compromising facts are disclosed with an air of good nature. Although the ironic note is transparent, there is considerable delicacy in its execution; a whole history lies behind the use of words such as 'many lengths', 'taken notice of', 'marks of distinction' and 'unmerited':

EXHIBIT 12.7

Stood dauntless Curl, &c.] We come now to a character of much respect, that of Mr. *Edmond Curl*. As a plain repetition of great actions is the best praise of them, we shall only say of this eminent man, that he carried the Trade many lengths beyond what it ever before had arrived at, and that he was the envy and admiration of all his profession. He possest himself of a command over all authors whatever; he caus'd them to write what he pleas'd; they could not call their very names their own. He was not only famous among these; he was taken notice of by the *State*, the *Church*, and the *Law*, and received particular marks of distinction from each.

It will be own'd that he is here introduc'd with all possible dignity; he speaks like the intrepid *Diomed*; he runs like the swift-footed *Achilles*; if he falls, 'tis like the beloved *Nisus*; and (what *Homer* makes to be the chief of all praises) he is favour'd of the Gods: He says but three words, and his prayer is heard; a Goddess conveys it to the seat of *Jupiter*. Tho' he loses the prize, he gains the victory; the great Mother her self comforts him, she inspires him with expedients, she honours him with an immortal present (such as *Achilles* receives from *Thetis* and *Æneas* from *Venus*) at once instructive and prophetical: After this, he is unrival'd and triumphant.

The tribute our author here pays him, is a grateful return for several unmerited obligations: Many weighty animadversions on the Publick Affairs, and many excellent and diverting pieces on Private persons, has he given to his name. If ever he ow'd two verses to any other, he ow'd Mr. *Curl* some thousands. He was every day extending his fame, and inlarging his writings: witness innumerable instances! but it shall suffice only to mention the *Court-Poems*, which he meant to publish as the work of the true writer, a Lady of quality; but being first threaten'd, and afterwards punish'd, for it by Mr. *Pope*, he generously transferr'd it from *her* to *him*, has now printed it twelve years in his name. The single time that ever he spoke to C. was on that affair, and to that happy incident he owes all the favours since received from him. So true is the saying of Dr *Sydenham*, that 'any one shall be, at some time or other, the better or the worse, for having but *seen* or *spoken* to a good, or a bad man.'[14]

The publisher's name crops up in several other places, as when a gloss is provided for the reference in Book I to 'Curl's chaste press, and Lintot's rubric post'. Two further examples must suffice. One is where chapter and verse are provided for a line mentioning the pillory, 'where on her Curlls the Public pours / All-bounteous rains, and golden showers.' Pope originally dated the event March 1728, but when it was pointed out that this was incorrect, he supplemented his entry: 'N.B. Mr. *Curl* loudly complain'd of this Note as an Untruth, protesting "that he stood in the Pillory not in *March* but in *February*"; And of another on Verse 144. Saying, "he was not tost in a Blanket, but a *Rug*." *Curliad* in 12°. 1729.'[15]

The most damaging addendum to the text may be the one supplied to the line we just saw in Book II, concerning the 'burning' passage of Curll's water during the pissing contest. It is a beautiful example of appearing to take back an imputation while reinforcing it:[16]

EXHIBIT 12.8

I am aware after all, that *burn* is the proper word to convey an idea of what was said to be Mr. *Curl*'s condition at that time. But from that very reason I infer the direct contrary. For surely every lover of our author will conclude he had more humanity, than to insult a man on such a misfortune or calamity, which could never befal him purely by his *own fault*, but from an unhappy communication with another. *This Note is partly Mr.* THEOBALD, *partly* SCRIBLERUS.[17]

The note, purportedly written either by the leading dunce or by the foolish pedant Martin Scriblerus, says just enough. It is not much of an excuse for Curll to say that he can have contracted venereal disease only by having sex with a woman who was already contaminated. In addition, a few passages in the prelims and appendices of the *Variorum* mention aspects of the feud, but the damaging blows came in the text and footnotes.

It is hardly a surprise that few writers rallied to Pope's cause. However, he got an immediate boost just after the *Variorum* text came out. This was a pamphlet called *An Author to be Lett. Being a Proposal Humbly Address'd to the Consideration of the Knights, Esquires, Gentlemen, and other Worshipful and Weighty Members of the Solid and Ancient Society of the Bathos. By their Associate and Well-wisher Iscariot Hackney*. Savage later claimed to have written it: if so, it would cement his reputation as Pope's inside man among the Grub Street fraternity. The editor states that in a back street off Charing Cross he came across a packet of letters addressed to 'Hackney', sent by Theobald, James Moore Smythe, Curll, John Dennis, Thomas Cooke and the dunce Bezaleel Morris, the last remembered (if at all) on account of his name. One of the items he picked up was Hackney's own apologia. Although the victims and the charges are familiar, many of the jokes still strike home. For example: 'My Pamphlets sell many more Impressions than those of celebrated Writers; the Secret of this is, I learned from *Curll* to clap a new Title-Page to the Sale of every half Hundred; so that when my Bookseller has sold Two Hundred and Fifty Copies, my Book generally enters into the *Sixth Edition*.'[18]

In a previous chapter we were told of Hackney's attempt to bilk Curll, but we did not hear of the sequel. Here the hireling author, named 'Iscariot Hackney', relates how he 'was employed by *Curll* to write a merry Tale, the Wit of which was its Obscenity'. This they agree to 'palm upon the World for a posthumous Piece of Mr. *Prior*'. A lady wishes to meet the author, at which '*Curll*, on my promise that if I had a Present, he should go Snacks [share it with him], sent me to her.' He was admitted when she was getting dressed, and the maidservant sent away. At this point all looks promising for the hack, but things then go awry:

EXHIBIT 12.9

What passed between us, a Point of Gallantry obliges me to conceal; but after some extraordinary Civilities, I was dismiss'd with a Purse of Guineas, and a Command to write a Sequel to my Tale. Upon this I turn'd out smart in Dress, bit *Curll* of his Share, and run out most of my Money in printing my Works at my own Cost. But some Years after (just at the time of his starving poor *Pattison*) the Varlet was reveng'd. He arrested me for several Months Board, brought me back to my Garret, and made me drudge on in my old, dirty Work. 'Twas in his Service that I wrote Obscenity and Profaneness, under the

Names of *Pope* and *Swift*. Sometimes I was Mr. *Joseph Gay*, and at others Theory *Burnet*, or *Addison*. I abridg'd Histories and Travels, translated from the *French*, what they never wrote, and was expert at finding out new Titles for old Books. When a notorious Thief was hanged, I was the *Plutarch* to preserve his Memory; and when a great Man died, mine were his Remains, and mine the Account of his last Will and Testament. Had Mr. *Oldmixon* and Mr. *Curll* agreed, my Assistance had probably been invited into Father *Boheurs* Logick, and the Critical History of *England*.

For the most part, Curll did not deal extensively in Tyburn hangings. It's also the case that John Oldmixon's version of Abbé Dominique Bouhours's *Arts of Logick and Rhetorick* (1728) and his fanatically Whig *Critical History* (1724–6) had nothing to do with Curll. We recall that the bookseller did not really starve his promising find, William Pattison. But everything else rings true. The theologian Thomas Burnet was the author of an influential *Sacred Theory of the Earth*, and his other works were a staple of the bookseller's list. The coverage is eerily accurate.

PUDDLES AND MIRE

The storm broke quickly. Within eighteen months at least thirty pamphlets appeared, containing a direct response to *The Dunciad* in either incarnation. Among the participants were Oldmixon, Dennis, William Bond, Cooke, Concanen and Orator Henley, to list some frequent labourers on Curll's behalf. Theobald, who bore the brunt of the satire, did not come out with his own contribution at this stage. These attacks were matched by scores of articles in newspapers and journals; some may still be untraced. 'All I could hear of you of late,' John Gay wrote to his friend in August 1728, 'hath been by advertisements in news-papers, by which one wou'd think the race of Curls was multiplied.'[19] Only a few bold refuseniks took Pope's side. He must have been expecting as much. In one way the poem supplied the equivalent of clickbait: replies to the text of 1728 are used in the revision of 1729, as we have just seen in the case of Chetwood. Even so, as the tide of hostile commentary rose higher, Pope must have dreaded the prospect of being swamped by an enchafed flood.

Within the range of pamphlets, eight can be linked to Curll as their open or surreptitious progenitor. The most noteworthy can be mentioned briefly here; it would take a hefty tome to explore the entire collection. Bond's miscellany *The Progress of Dulness* rashly attempts to meet Pope on his own ground, since the title poem in couplets is a reprint of *The Paralell* from 1720, which we looked at in Chapter Nine. Various hunks of old charges are recycled. In a note signed from Twickenham by A.P. and J.S., a forthcoming item entitled *The Popiad* is announced. Then comes 'The Evidence summ'd up', a quatrain in jaunty triple metre that looks very much like Curll's handiwork: 'Nor Rimer is *Theobald*, nor Critic is *Pope*, / Nor does *Gay* for a Conjuror pass; / *Arbuthnott* and *Swift* may join Forces, I hope, / And 'tis Easy to find out the Ass.' ('No conjuror' meant 'not very bright'.) Finally, a mysterious notice headed 'Covent Garden, June 8th. 1728' describes an altercation over a rival to Curll's *Key to the Dunciad*, in the possession of William Lewis, a schoolfellow of Pope and a bookseller in Covent Garden. The alternative key is unknown. A concluding triplet, directed to Mr. William Lewis 'at his shed under Tom's coffee house', has all the hallmarks of Curll's style: ''Tis well for C—L his Character is known,/ Thou'rt but a Mute at Dulness' Throne/ Thy Style and faulty Spelling are thy own.'[20]

The Female Dunciad is another miscellany, printed for the fringe operator Thomas Read but advertised by Curll. The title is misleading, since, apart from one contribution by Haywood that has no bearing on the poem or the quarrel, there is little about women. The work deals first with the 'profligate and profane Pen' wielded by Pope in his letters to Henry Cromwell, supposedly to reveal his 'Intrigues, Gallantries and Amours'. It is again stressed that the author's original manuscripts may be seen 'under his own Hand at one *Edmund Curll*'s, a Bookseller in the *Strand*', something also noted in newspaper advertisements. We find the entire *Court Ballad* reprinted, to illustrate just how immoral Pope's verse is, as well as two stanzas from our old friend *The Worms*. The writer refers to the publication of some further papers 'in my Custody' – who else can this indicate but Curll? A competent poem by Thomas Foxton, a regular in the bookseller's team, chastises Pope for spoiling his reputation: 'A Poet renown'd for Politeness, and Fire,/ Has stain'd all his Laurels in Puddles and Mire.'[21]

That does not exhaust the flow of retorts from the aggrieved bookseller. A further item, from September 1728, is *Codrus: Or, The Dunciad Dissected*. Pope assigned it to Elizabeth Thomas and Curll, which may or may not be correct. The title item is accurately described by J. V. Guerinot as 'a fantastic biography of the poet', which absurdly portrays his father as a husbandman in Windsor Forest, and Pope himself as a rustic hand who took advantage of others to climb out of his lowly station.[22] This is followed by a fable, 'Farmer Pope and his Son', which versifies a similar narrative. However, on this occasion the young Pope is a toad, enabled to rise in the world thanks to a bard, identified as William Wycherley, on whom the horrid reptile spews noxious effluvia. But even this proves his impotence:

EXHIBIT 12.10

The stinking Venom flows around,
And nauseous Slaver hides the Ground.
Yet not one Mortal, whom it hit,
'Twas just as harmless as his Wit.
For take away the filthy Part,
Of Turd, and Spew, and Mud, and Fart:

(Words which no Gentleman could use,
And e'en a Nightman would refuse.)

So we are back again with Tom Turdman – a reflection of the importance these sanitary workers once had in the life of cities.

At the end, the toad challenges Apollo's sacred herd for possession of the pastures of the gods, but, in attempting to puff himself into a more heroic stature, he bursts in two: 'A loathsome Stench does all surround, / Malignant Vapours spread the Ground.' All that remains is 'a Splatch of solid Gore'.[23] It is hard not to think of Mr Creosote from Monty Python. If anyone doubts that Pope had to face some disgusting abuse, these verses should be recalled. We needn't concern ourselves with further efforts, such as *The True Peri Bathous*, which is simply a reissue of Nicolas Boileau-Despreaux's *Art of Poetry*, published in 1714, with an insulting note at the start.

Of course, Curll would have been ready to sell in his shop the productions of other publishers. The most substantial of these include Jonathan Smedley's *Gulliveriana*, an uninvited 'sequel' to the three volumes of the Swift–Pope *Miscellanies*. This was issued by James Roberts in August 1728, and is mainly directed at Swift. However, it collects a number of the newspaper attacks on Pope, and has one good thrust at *Gulliver's Travels*: 'Poor *Curll*'s Head was stuck in a Pillory, for a Book which could not do a hundredth Part of the Mischief, as not having had a hundredth Part of the Readers.'[24] The work has a clever allusive frontispiece, which shows Swift and Pope surrounded by a satyr and a harlequin, with a star labelled 'Stella' in the heavens. Smedley had also written a vicious attack called *The Metamorphosis*, in which Swift and Pope have been transformed into dogs and are savaged by sundry dunces, along with their employer: '*Curll* next advanc'd and full of Sight, / Swore, that they never more shou'd bite; / And falling to his Work, like mad, / He kick'd out every Tooth they had.'[25]

We must not assume that victims of Pope's lampoons were always ready to acknowledge Curll as their leader. On 15 June 1728 Mist's *Weekly Journal*, which was generally favourable to Pope and always hostile to Curll, gave an account of skirmishes in 'the present unnatural War betwixt the Sons of Parnassus', including a plan by the 'Allies of Charing-Cross' to besiege Twickenham. A postscript follows: 'There is a Rumour, that the Allies having discovered one Edmund Curl lurking about their head Quarters, they seiz'd him, and found him to be one of the *Pope*'s Spies; upon which, according to the Law of Arms, they hang'd him up immediately; he died very hard, and no Body pittied him.' But a more neutral source, the *London Evening Post*, included this paragraph on 27 June:

EXHIBIT 12.11

We hear that since our last the contending Poetical Powers have agreed upon certain preliminary Articles, to facilitate Matters in the ensuing Congress of Neutral Bards, to whom their several Pretensions and Disputes are referr'd; It is also said, that Mr. Dennis stands fairer than Mr. Theobald for the Honour of first Plenipo from the Allies of Charing-Cross; and that Mr. Moore Smyth will be third; but it is uncertain whether Mr. Savage is to represent the Allies of Twickenham or not, as has been rumour'd: Men are much divided in their Sentiments and Expectations on this important Occasion; but the Prospect of Peace among Poets is desir'd by all Lovers of Harmony. N.B. Mr. Curl is not to be admitted, either in person or by Proxy, at the Congress, for nineteen Reasons. Both Parties have protested against him in the Preliminaries.

We can easily come up with at least nineteen reasons. Even the adversaries of Pope thought Curll was unreliable; but this was a bit hard, because he had certainly been responsible for more effective blows against their common enemy than anyone else.

POPPING AT POPE

In the midst of this torrent of pamphleteering, three pieces stand out because of their importance to the quarrel. Each is unquestionably the work of Curll, and each examines the text of *The Dunciad* with minute attention. The bookseller might lay claim to the title of the poet's most attentive reader. In a backhanded way, this fact could even have appeared flattering to Pope; as do authors in general, he knew that his books were often skim-read, if they were perused at all.

The earliest of the three came off the press on 28 May 1728, ten days after the wooden horse suddenly appeared before the eyes of citizens inside the walls of London. No one could accuse Curll of sitting around idly. It took a familiar form, that of *A Compleat Key to the Dunciad*. Matching Pope, Curll has the imprint bearing the name A. Dodd. His epigraph derives not from an ancient source, but from his own fertile poetic imagination: 'How easily Two Wits agree, / One finds the Poem; One the Key.' The opening letter to the public is in Curll's most aggressive vein. He starts by addressing Pope's claim that nobody has stood up in his defence with the retort that no one with a vestige of honour or conscience could defend 'a *Scoundrel*, or *Blockhead*, who has, at one Time or other, *Betrayed* or *Abused* almost every one he has conversed with'. The tone does not get any gentler:

EXHIBIT 12.12

By a dull Pun, from the Word *Duncia* in *Statius*, the *Dunciad* is formed; and as Mr. *Publisher* is *informed*, has been the Labour of full Six Years of the Author's Life. But in my simple Opinion, to pursue this agreeable Metaphor, He must be a very great DUNCE, who, from a Plan so extensive, could not have raised a much nobler Structure in Six Days.

However, not to keep the Reader any longer in Suspence, he may be assured that Alexander Pope Esq; is both the Publisher and Author of this Patch-Work Medley.

Had the Hero, *says Mr.* PUBLISHER, been called *Codrus*, how many Would have affirmed him to be Mr. *Welsted*, Mr. *Dennis*, Sir *Richard Blackmore*, *&c.* but now all that unjust Scandal is saved by calling him THEOBALD, which by good Luck happens to be the Name of a *real* Person.

A notable Discovery![26]

The third paragraph is a quotation from the introductory letter from the publisher (editor) in the first edition of *The Dunciad*, but it acquires a different slant here. Curll is at his vituperative best, with a neat allusion to the six days that God took to create the world.

Most of the work consists of detailed glosses that identify references in the text. Once more, a comment by Guerinot is to the purpose: 'There is very little direct abuse of Pope; Curll is too busy annotating.'[27] Some of these guesses were off the mark, but in the majority of cases Curll got it right. In the *Variorum*, Pope's notes are heavily indebted to the *Key*, as he more or less admitted in a prefatory section of the work: 'In some Articles, it was thought sufficient barely to transcribe from *Jacob*, *Curl*, and other writers of their own rank . . . Most of them had drawn each other's Characters on certain occasions; but the few here inserted, are all that could be saved from the general destruction of such Works.'[28] You can almost see the dunces wincing as they are forced to contemplate the mass extinction of their prized products. A second edition of the *Key* appeared on 4 June and a third on 2 July, with many alterations and updates. In a familiar ruse, these brandish on their title page the presence of Sir Richard Blackmore's character of 'Mr. Pope's Prophane Writings', in reality a short excerpt from an essay in which Blackmore denounced the 'Roman Catholick Version of the First Psalm'. This gives the bookseller a chance to tell the story of the three guineas reward that was never paid to Rebecca Burleigh, back in 1716.

By this date Curll had his latest salvo ready to fire off, the previously announced *Popiad*. One of his advertisements appeared naming five other booksellers along with himself; the imprint simply uses the common evasive formula, 'printed in the year . . .' It adds that, 'to keep Pace with Mr. Pope', the third edition of the *Key* is also published.[29] Six titles that supposedly bear on the quarrel are listed, going back as far as the *New Rehearsal* and *Court Poems*; Curll did not allow the stock of his old favourites to be depleted while they could still embarrass his antagonist. *The Popiad* again consists of previously published items, and reprints Giles Jacob's coverage of the poet from the *Poetical Register*, with the old canard that Pope (who had now attacked Jacob in *The Dunciad* as the 'Blunderbuss of Law', alluding to his legal manuals) had paid the compiler two guineas to insert a laudatory entry.

The most abrasive section is a reissue of a short pamphlet that had been published by the invisible 'A. Moore' at the start of June, and that would shortly find another home in *Gulliveriana*. It describes what seems to be an entirely mythical assault on Pope, although there's little doubt that it depicts the kind of retaliation that his enemies would have liked to exact. The full title says it all: 'A POPP upon *Pope*; Or, A true and faithful Account of a late horrid and barbarous Whipping committed on the Body of SAUNY POPE, a Poet; as he was Innocently walking in *Ham-Walks*, near the River of *Thames*, meditating Verses for the Good of the Publick. Supposed to have been done by two evil-dispos'd Persons, out of Spite and Revenge, for a harmless Lampoon which the said Poet had writ upon them.'

The narrative explains how the attack occurred as Pope took his evening promenade:

EXHIBIT 12.13

Two Gentlemen came up to him, (whose Names we cannot certainly learn) and knowing him perfectly well, partly by his Back, and partly by his Face, walk'd a Turn or two with him; when, entring into a Conversation (as we hear on the *Dunciad*, a pretty Poem of the said Poet's writing) on a sudden, one of the Gentlemen hoisted poor Master *Pope* the Poet on his back, whilst the other drew out, from under his Coat, a long Birchen Rod, (as we are inform'd, made out of a Stable Broom) and with the said long Rod, did, with great Violence and unmerciful Hand, strike Master *Pope* so hard upon his naked Posteriors, that he voided large Quantities of Blood, which being yellow, one Doctor *Arbuthnot* his Physician, has since affirm'd, had a great Proportion of Gall mix'd with it, which occasion'd the said Colour . . .

Mrs *Blount* a good charitable Woman, and near Neighbour of Master *Pope*'s at *Twickenham*, happening to come by, she took him up in her Apron, and buttoning up his Breeches, carried him to the Water-side, where she got a Boat to convey him home.

We hear that Master *Pope* has ever since been greatly disordered; occasioned, as it is supposed, by the said Whipping, which has driven the Humours upward, and affected his Head in such a Manner, that the poor Man continually raves for Pen, Ink, and Paper; and although they have been allowed him by his own Physician Dr *Arbuthnot*, who entirely mistook his Case; yet he is now strictly forbid the use of them, by the learned Dr *Hale* of *Lincoln's-Inn-Fields*, under whose Care he is at present, and who doubts not (God willing) but to restore the poor Man to his Senses.

Although compassion is expressed for 'this unfortunate Poet', the conclusion is more sombre: 'we cannot too much admire the Wisdom of Providence, which brings this Man to the Lash, whose wanton Wit has been lashing of others.'[30]

The piece has all the hallmarks of fiction, since neither John Arbuthnot nor Martha Blount (who was staying at nearby Petersham around this time) corroborated the story, but Pope was obliged to place an advertisement in the paper on 14 June to refute this 'malicious and ill-grounded Report', stating that he had not stirred from his house on the day in question.[31] Curll duly reprinted this at the end of the *Popp*. Richard Hale (1670–1728) had indeed become a respected member of the Royal College of Physicians and treated patients with mental-health problems at Bedlam and Bridewell, despite a setback early in his career when he was accused of the excessive use of opiates. However, no connection with Pope is known. It looks as if the writer were trying to pay back the poet for the way he had punished his opponents. This is one of the most incisive retorts the Curllians ever mustered. It cleverly mimics the style of both Pope and Arbuthnot, in their mock-sympathetic accounts of a victim's descent into madness, notably Dennis, Dr John Woodward, William Whiston and Curll himself.

In its conclusion, *The Popiad* sets out one of Curll's most imaginative ideas. It relocates the home of Dulness at Twickenham, and dubs Grub Street, represented by Curll's shop in the Strand, the new Parnassus:

EXHIBIT 12.14

The most partial *Popeling*, or *Dunciadier*, cannot but allow, upon an impartial Perusal of what Mr. *Dennis*, and Madam *Dacier* have herein advanced, that the present Residence of the *Goddess* of *Dullness* is at *Twickenham*.

The Publick may now behold the Regularity of her *Sway*, and the great Progress She has already made in *Windsor-Forest*, the *Temple of Fame*, and the *Iliad*. The next Mail that arrives from our Camp on *Parnassus*, when opened at Mr. CURLL's in the *Strand*, will bring certain Advices, as the Vulgar phrase it, that, *the Enemy's Head is turn'd*, For as Mr. *Dennis* lately observ'd in Conversation, nothing could be a greater Act of Lunacy, than that Mr. *Pope* could not be content with the *Enjoyment* of a *Fame* to which he has not the least *Title*, but that he Himself must call in the *right Owners* to assert their *Claims*.[32]

It was a bold stroke by Curll to identify Dennis and the rest of his crew as the modern-day Parnassians, but then he had never lacked self-confidence. The new mail from Parnassus would not arrive until the early part of the next summer.

THE SECOND CAMPAIGN

The Variorum edition of *The Dunciad* elicited a fresh burst of pained commentary from its victims. Little more than two weeks later Curll had his response before the public, in a pamphlet entitled *The Curliad*. As part of an advertisement he placed in the *Daily Journal*, announcing 'a Mail from Parnassus', he promised various goodies, for example 'Ignorance, Absurdity, and Falshood', proved upon Pope and his pseudonymous helpers. There are also 'The crimes and case of Mr. Curll, fairly stated' and Pope's meeting at the Swan Tavern 'set in a true light'.[33] Would those confounded *Court Poems* never go away?

There was quite a bit more. Combative as ever, on 9 May the bookseller announced with all the emphasis of black-letter type, 'This Day is open'd The Second Campaign of the Dunciad-War.'[34] This time we must see the full title page, which enlists all of the bookseller's accumulated craft as a publicist:

THE

CURLIAD.

A HYPERCRITIC

UPON THE

DUNCIAD *Variorum.*

WITH

A farther Key to the New Characters.

Pope, has less Reading than makes Felons *'scape*,
Less human Genius than God gives an *Ape*.
DUNCIAD. B. I. V. 235, 236

O may his Soul still Fret upon the Lee,
And nought attune his Lyre but Bastardy;
May un-hang'd *Savage* all *Pope*'s Hours enjoy,
And let his spurious Birth his Pen employ.

Incerti AUTH.

LONDON:

Printed for the AUTHOR. 1729.

(Price One Shilling.)

The opening lines blazon the name of the target work, which happened to be available at Curll's shop. By mentioning the 'farther Key', he draws attention to its predecessor, which is advertised at the head of a list of Popiana on the verso of the title page. The first epigraph subverts a passage from the poem by substituting 'Pope, has' for 'How, with' in the text. Here the joke relates to the legal device of 'benefit of clergy', by which persons convicted of a capital offence could escape death by showing their literacy in court. The traditional test was to read aloud the 'neck verse': that is, the start of Psalm 51, 'Have mercy upon me, O God, according to thy loving kindness.' It was easy for criminals to memorize the words and thus receive a lesser sentence.

The second epigraph is directed at Richard Savage, the struggling poet reviled by the dunces as a fifth columnist who spied on them for Pope. As some may recall from the famous life written by Samuel Johnson, at this date his friend and ally in poverty, Savage claimed to be the illegitimate son of an earl. He maintained that after he was born his mother rejected him. Recently the 'wild young man' – not so young; he was rising thirty – had got into a tavern brawl near Charing Cross, and thrust his sword into a man named Sinclair. In those days the wheels of the criminal court turned with remarkable sped. Within three weeks Savage was tried at the Old Bailey and found guilty of murder. With the notorious Judge Francis

Page on the bench, he faced the inevitable sentence of death, but also a sneering address to the jury. As Johnson expressed it, his friend was now due to lose his life 'by the Evidence of a Bawd, a Strumpet, and his Mother'.[35] In the end Savage gained a pardon after an appeal to Queen Caroline. The lines on this episode must have been freshly written, most probably by Curll.

Within the pamphlet, we encounter the usual miscellaneous efforts to blacken Pope's reputation. Curll brings out several old charges. One is that the poet wrote verses in praise of himself and pretended they were the work of Wycherley (Pope continued to resent adverse material reissued by Curll). A second accusation is that he betrayed his immoral character in *The Worms* and the '*Burlesque* of the first *Psalm*'; a third is that he took money to get Jacob to include him in the *Poetical Register*; a fourth is that he plagiarized *Paradise Lost*, which is true if we take plagiarism to include parody and allusion.

Curll goes through the three books of *The Dunciad*, pausing to indicate a number of references to earlier writers that Pope had failed to signalize in his notes. Reaching the passage in Book II that concerns his own career, Curll launches into a long defence of the allegedly obscene works, repeating much of what he had said in the *Humble Representation of Edmund Curll* some four years earlier. Once more he makes implausible claims for the medical value of these books. This time, he goes on to vindicate the publication of John Ker's memoirs. As to the pillory, he refers flippantly to 'the corporal Punishment . . . of mounting the Rostrum for one Hour, which I performed with as much Alacrity as Mr. *Pope* ever pursued his Spleen against Mr. *Theobald*'.[36] Then we are back to *Court Poems*, with Curll's most detailed account of what exactly happened in 1716.

Elsewhere he gets in some of his accustomed hits, as with a touch of doggerel on the prefatory material that is attributed to the obscure William Cleland:

EXHIBIT 12.15

Mr. *Cleland* tells us, out of Respect to the present Royal Family, that
Mr. *Pope* has Panegyrized some noted *Papists* also, *Robert* late Earl
of *Oxford, Henry* late Viscount *Bolingbroke*, and eke some *South-Sea*
Heroes, who were his Factors in carrying on the Subscription for his
Homer in the memorable Year of Honesty and Wisdom 1720.

And, since several of Mr. *Pope's* Operations are to be seen in
French, it must be confessed that the same Language is adorned with
The Writings of *Bunyan* and *Daniel de Foe,*
Viz. The *Pilgrim's Progress,* and *Robinson Crusoe.*[37]

It would not do for such a pamphlet to end without verses ridiculing Pope and his friends, along with some nakedly anti-papist
comments:

EXHIBIT 12.16

Is it not very merry, in the Notes, to observe, that Mr. *Henley* is
rebuk'd for breaking *Bread*, and *Jests*, in one and the same room;
whereas, the Articles of Mr. *Pope's* Creed, oblige him, and all true-
blue *Catholicks*, to *worship* their GOD, and *devour him* at one and the
same Time?
Persisting in Idolatry, un-aw'd
They must be Dunces! who thus eat their God.
(*So much for* religious Parody, *all fair; next hear a* Lamentation sad,)
Of some, so very hard the Fate, the Luck is,
Gay has no Pension, tho' his Friend's a Dutchess.
Hibernian Politicks, O *Swift*, thy doom,
And *Pope* now owns, he did translate with *Broome*.
Drawlers, like *Savage*, fix on him their hopes,
Thinking that Rhime and Sneer will make them *Popes*.
Thus easy 'tis, in Parody to shine,
Pope shares the *Dunciad*, and the *Curliad's* Mine;

Alike too, next the Road our Houses lye,
Backward he views the Thames, and so do I.
Strand, April 25.1729.   E. CURLL.[38]

That was more or less it for the year, apart from a few scattered
shots. One or two can be found in a typical biographic ragbag called
Memoirs of the Life, Writings, and Amours of William Congreve, Esq;,
published in August 'in Opposition to all ridiculous Messages and
Threatnings'. The author is named as 'Charles Wilson', a name that
might mask Jacob, Oldmixon or (most probably) Curll himself, as
comments in the newspaper advertisements quote the bookseller's
favourite motto, *honi soit qui mal y pense*. Even though Pope himself emerges from the proceedings without much harm inflicted,
the preface contains a bitter attack on Dr Arbuthnot ('much more
remarkable for *Politicks* than *Physick*, and for *Wit* than *Wisdom*'), for
his efforts to stop the publication of personal material. Separately
the bookseller issued Congreve's will, with a promise on the title
page of a 'character' of the dead man by Pope, in reality just a short
paragraph from the postscript to the *Iliad*. Back files were always
kept ready for use in this way. Elsewhere in the volume, the author
criticizes a comment by Pope on the actor Thomas Betterton, and
adds, 'I only wish Mr. *Pope* may live to repent of his malevolent
Spleen.'[39] Whose voice do we hear in these words?

At the close of 1729, Curll could look back on two years of
hyperactivity. Pope had set the agenda with his successive editions of *The Dunciad*, but no one had reacted more often or more
vigorously than the bookseller. The controversy went on without
any real interruption, although for some of the time the principals
refrained from confronting one another directly.

13

The PUBLIC Ear,
1730–34

For both contestants, the next four years held substantial importance. Pope reinvented himself as a political and philosophical writer, and in the process he forged an enhanced reputation throughout Europe. Curll moved the site of his shop three times and experimented with a new form of business model (or at least promoted it in this way). He also remarried and made his will. As just noted, the feud never went into abeyance, but it would occupy a less central place than it had in recent years – that is, until the quarrel entered its most fervent phase, in 1735.

On Pope's side, we can sum up the main events in a short space. At the beginning of the new decade his allies embarked on a project that allowed them to act as a scourge of the dunces. This was a weekly paper called the *Grub Street Journal*, which ran for over four hundred issues until the close of 1737. Pope kept at one remove from its day-to-day operations, but most people thought he was a hidden presence if not a prime instigator. From the very start, Curll became a frequent target.

Late in 1731 the poet launched a series of works connected in one way or another with his grand scheme of an *Opus Magnum*, which would be left incomplete at his death.[1] These comprised four *Moral Essays*, each addressed to a friend and dealing with a particular issue. Thus, the first is directed to a major patron of the arts, Lord Burlington, and subtitled *Of Taste*; its contents relate to the interests of the dedicatee, mainly architecture and landscape gardening. Perhaps the best known today is the *Epistle to a Lady*,

'The Art and Mystery of Printing Emblematically Displayed', from the
Grub Street Journal, 26 October 1732. Curll is the two-faced figure standing
in front of the window.

subtitled *Of the Characters of Women*, a subject that has naturally
attracted the attention of many feminists, who have detected more
or less concealed sexism in Pope's approach to the topic.

Simultaneously, there appeared *Imitations of Horace*, a series
of bold modernizations of poems by the great Latin author. These
items went on until 1740, if we include an epilogue in two parts: the
famous *Epistle to Arbuthnot* is sometimes included as a prologue to
the group. Lastly, *An Essay on Man* came out in 1733–4, and immediately provoked fierce debate; indeed, for the next century it was
the most fully discussed work in Pope's canon across the North
Atlantic world. One of the poem's assertive critics was the Swiss
philosopher Jean-Pierre de Crousaz, and Curll duly advertised a
translation of his commentary in 1738, with an ambiguous preface
that pointed out failings in the work without attacking Pope openly.
Neither the *Essay on Man* nor the set of *Moral Essays* has anything
to say about Curll, but it is different with the *Imitations*, in which
the bookseller is named from time to time.

What sets the Horatian items apart is that they show Pope for
the first time as an openly political writer, adopting the rhetoric of
the Opposition movement to Walpole's government. He positions

himself as a kind of guardian of the realm, whose task was 'to rouse the Watchmen of the Publick Weal', and to speak up boldly for truth and honesty in the face of a corrupt oligarchy.[2] Pope joined a motley assembly of those opposed to the ministry, who numbered in their group unreconstructed Tories, dissident Whigs and independents. They had cells dotted around southern England, where leaders such as Lord Cobham at Stowe, Bathurst at Cirencester and Bolingbroke at Dawley near Uxbridge regularly gave Pope a warm welcome. But their power was limited, and although they enjoyed an occasional victory – as when they joined with City interests to defeat an unpopular plan to increase the excise duty in 1733 – the truth was that more often than not Robert Walpole had the means to outmanoeuvre them.[3]

On the surface, this situation has little to do with the quarrel, because not all the dunces took Walpole's part (or money), even if some did. However, Pope managed to link the court with literature and the theatre, since Colley Cibber had now been elevated to the unlikely dignity of Poet Laureate. As he had done in *The Dunciad*, the poet depicts George II after his succession to the throne in 1727 as the epitome of misdirected patronage, and singles out Lord Hervey, a crony of both the queen and Lady Mary Wortley Montagu (now a bitter enemy of Pope), as performing Curllian functions: 'Let the *Two Curls* of Town and Court abuse / His Father, Mother, Body, Soul, and Muse' (*Epistle to Arbuthnot*).[4]

Not many changes occurred outwardly in the poet's life at this stage, apart from the death of Edith Pope in June 1733, around the date of her ninetieth birthday. Alexander felt the loss of his mother severely, but he now had fewer responsibilities at Twickenham. If he imagined that he might be secure from wounds inflicted by his main oppressor, he would soon learn differently.

A Pamphlet in the Morning

By this time Curll had been forced to confront a new critic. This was Henry Fielding, later a celebrated novelist and notable London magistrate. In 1730 he was in his early twenties, and had just embarked on his career as a dramatist, when his play *The Author's Farce* was put on at a fringe off-Drury house, the Little Theatre in the Haymarket. It was advertised as 'a new Comi-Farcical Opera, call'd the Pleasures of the Town'. In the printed version issued by James Roberts, the author is named as 'Scriblerus Secundus', which immediately lets us know where his loyalties lay. The work took the form of a ballad opera, one of a seemingly endless conveyor belt of such pieces since the success of *The Beggar's Opera* two years before. There are twenty-five songs, with fresh words set to familiar tunes, mostly drawn from folk music.

The farce begins in the garret of a young writer named Luckless, who stands in for the aspiring playwright Fielding. It moves to a tavern for the second act, and ends with a miniature rehearsal comedy, performed at the playhouse, much in the way of the old Hollywood musicals set around 42nd Street. Here Luckless directs a run-through of his puppet show, which takes place in the shades on the other side of the River Styx, where the Goddess of Nonsense falls in love with the ghost of Signior Opera. The cast list gives a good idea of the satirical targets: Marplay (a cover name for Cibber); Sparkish (the actor Robert Wilks); Bookweight, a bookseller whom we need not bother to identify; and Quibble, a scribbler, who could be any old dunce. In the pantomime, backing up the roles of Punch and Judy, we find among those arriving in the other world a bookseller with the even more transparent name of Curry, described as the 'Prime Minister of Nonsense' – Curll is to true literature what Walpole is to real statesmanship. Others alleged to be recently deceased are Signior Opera, probably the much-ridiculed castrato Senesino (Francesco Bernardi); the self-promoting preacher

Dr Orator (John Henley); Monsieur Pantomime (the impresario John Rich); Mrs Novel (Eliza Haywood); and Don Tragedio (Lewis Theobald). A ragged poet whose body lay unburied for a fortnight might remind us of the death of poor William Pattison, but the six folios of his works must belong to a living hack such as the prolific Thomas Cooke. Even though the play contains topical references that easily go over our heads today, its absurd travesties of theatrical effects give it a stageable vitality. With an imaginative producer, it could still delight an audience.

In the first act Bookweight refuses to publish the play that Luckless has shown him, a thrust at Curll's not altogether merited reputation for stingy payments:

EXHIBIT 13.1

BOOKWEIGHT.

I do think writing is the silliest thing a man can undertake.

LUCKLESS.

It is strange you should say so, who live by it.

BOOKWEIGHT.

Live by it! Ah, if you had lost as much by writers as I have done, you would be of my opinion.

LUCKLESS.

But we are losing time. Will you advance fifty guineas on my play?.

BOOKWEIGHT.

No, nor fifty shillings, I assure you.

LUCKLESS.

'Sdeath, sir! Do you beat me down at this rate?

BOOKWEIGHT.

No, nor Fifty Farthings. Fifty Guineas! Indeed your Name is well worth that.

LUCKLESS.

Jack, take this worthy Gentleman, and kick him down Stairs.

BOOKWEIGHT.

Sir, I shall make you repent this.

JACK [a servant].

Come, Sir, will you please to brush?

BOOKWEIGHT.

Help! Murder! I'll have the Law of you, Sir.

LUCKLESS.

Ha, ha, ha!⁵

In current slang, the invitation to brush meant 'get lost'. Fifty guineas was of course an impossible sum for an unknown writer to ask of a publisher; most professional authors would have struggled to make much more than that in a year. Still, it's not hard to imagine that there were some ambitious authors, fully conscious of their own abilities, who would have liked to kick Curll out of the house.

The second act gives Bookweight some broad comic moments, and a few speeches that hint at trade practices not confined to Curll. He is addressing hacks whose job it is to produce a political tract and a tragedy for him:

EXHIBIT 13.2

BOOKWEIGHT.

Fie upon it, gentlemen! What, not at your pens? Do you consider, Mr Quibble, that it is above a fortnight since your Letter from a Friend in the Country was published? Is it not high time for an Answer to come out? At this rate, before your Answer is printed your Letter will be forgot. I love to keep a controversy up warm. I have had authors who have writ a pamphlet in the morning, answered it in the afternoon, and compromised the matter at night.

QUIBBLE.

Sir, I will be as expeditious as possible.

BOOKWEIGHT.

Well, Mr. Dash, have you done that murder yet?

DASH.

Yes, sir, the murder is done. I am only about a few moral reflections to place before it.

BOOKWEIGHT.

Very well. Then let me have the ghost finished by this day sevennight.[6]

In the final act Curry asks the poet, recently arrived in the shades, what has happened in the other world. The answer he gets, 'Authors starve, and Booksellers grow fat, *Grub-Street* harbours as many Pyrates as ever *Algiers* did', is not the one he wants, since it links publishing with the notorious Barbary corsairs.[7]

Some believe that the puppet show in *The Author's Farce* influenced the design of the last book of *The Dunciad*. Certainly Pope never spoke a truer word about his adversary than Fielding's line, 'I love to keep a controversy up warm.'

VARIANT READINGS

Of course, Curll had not been sitting on his hands at this juncture, in spite of his supposed plans for retirement. However, he was side-tracked by a number of distractions. He moved from his long-time home opposite Catherine Street a short distance down the road to a site near the Exeter Exchange, a kind of enclosed shopping mall where the Strand Palace Hotel now stands. That did not last long, and he soon chose to up sticks once more, setting up a warehousing operation to which he gave the impressive name of the Literatory. Customers would find it on the corner of Bow Street and Russell Street – very close to Button's coffee house, and almost adjoining the two big patent theatres. As we saw in the first chapter, the publisher reached his final premises in 1734, on the other side of Covent

Garden. It is possible that the last move was connected to his marriage in February of that year to Elizabeth Bateman, the widow of
a builder. What had happened to his former housemate Susanna
Gray, we have no idea. As is the case with so many women in the
past, she disappears from the records.

The first item in Pope's new series of poems, the *Epistle to
Burlington*, elicited a good number of commentaries at the start of
1732. Among the most substantial was a volume generally supposed
to be edited by Matthew Concanen, *A Miscellany on Taste. By Mr.
Pope, &c.* The imprint lists three publishers, headed by 'G. Lawton,
in Fleet Street'. No such figure is known in the trade, and we can
be sure that this is simply a transposition of the name of Lawton
Gilliver, Pope's usual agent at the time. If we add to this a couplet on
the title page, plucked from John Gay's *Fables* in the usual Curllian
manner, we may feel confident of the true source. Then we find a
reprint of the verses parodying the first Psalm, now styled 'Of Mr.
Pope's Taste of Religion', and *The Worms*, labelled 'Of Mr. Pope's
Taste of Original Sin'. The volume opens with a key to the poet's
new *Epistle* under the guise of 'Clavis'. Should any doubts remain,
we find Curll advertising the work within a very short period. The
Grub Street Journal harboured no misgivings on the issue, dubbing
it simply '*Curlean Grubbism*'.[8]

Quite as much to the point is an advertisement by Thomas
Payne, a frequent partner of the bookseller, placed on the last day
of 1731. This reads: 'Next Week will be published, *In Octavo, to
bind up with the Dunciad*, Mr. POPE's Poem on TASTE. Cum Notis
Variorum. Wherein the Text will be carefully preserv'd, and some
Variae Lectiones [variant readings] added.' The two lines from
Gay are then quoted, plus a couplet that encapsulates the entire
thrust of the campaign: 'It is impossible they e'er should part, /
POPE has the Publick Ear, and CURLL their Heart.'[9] This jaunty note
is carried through the *Miscellany* into the notes, among which are
some that look like vintage Curllian touches and offer incisive, if

literal-minded, observations on the verbal texture of the *Epistle*. But then the conclusion is routine abuse, mouthing the usual party line on the merits of Pope's works in comparison with those of authors of recent years:

EXHIBIT 13.3

Thus have I given my Readers a few plain Remarks upon Mr. *Pope*'s last doughty Performance: I shall now add Mr. *Congreve*'s Epistle to the Lord Viscount *Cobham*, (on a Subject not much different) whereby the World will easily perceive that this Work falls as far short of Mr. *Congreve*'s, as his Ode on *Music* did of Mr. *Dryden*'s; His *Pastorals* of Mr. *Philips*'s; His *Windsor Forest* of Sir *John Denham*['s] *Coopers Hill*; His first Book of *Homer*, of that done by Mr. *Tickell*, or his *Dunciad* of the *Dispensary*.[10]

Few students of literature today would agree with these rankings, except perhaps in the case of John Dryden. They were necessary to keep the flag flying.

It scarcely needs to be added that Curll went on advertising his old attacks on Pope, and attributing anything he could, plausible or not, to the poet. However, he was not able to get much traction on his enemy in his bread-and-butter productions, such was the string of biographies that kept coming. These included books on the actress Anne Oldfield (not enough evidence of personal contact); on the actor Robert Wilks (demolished in the *Grub Street Journal*); and amazingly even the life of Pope's beloved colleague John Gay. Not much could be done when Mr. Joseph Gay, energetic as ever, versified Hogarth's popular series of prints, *The Harlot's Progress*, shortly after the real Gay had died, although the writer (probably John Breval) did manage to slip in a short quotation from the still notorious version of the first Psalm.

318

Mr Kirleus

As we have seen, the attacks on Pope began very early in the run of the *Grub Street Journal*. The fullest onslaught appeared in the fourth issue of the paper, in January 1730. It's clear immediately that the editors, like Pope himself, had kept a close eye on the publisher's activities over several years. In the lead story for this number, we read a letter dated 23 January from 'Kirleus' at Covent Garden, in which he puts in for the role of bookseller by appointment to 'the learned Society' of Grub Street. As his application is vetted, it emerges that he believes he has been harshly treated throughout his career. He blames the poisoning episode on 'a profest Papist', while the blanket-tossing incident at the school was 'approved, if not incouraged by a late Bishop, who once made a bitter invective against me in the House of Lords, and was since banish'd for holding a treasonable correspondence with the Pretender', a clear reference to Francis Atterbury. Kirleus says that he made his 'utmost endeavours to get some satisfaction for this violence: but as if Justice was fled from Westminster-Hall, as well as piety from Westminster-Abbey, I could meet with no Lawyer who would undertake my cause.' He goes on to boast of the range of his accomplishments in the trade:

EXHIBIT 13.4

Those who have made the greatest figure in our way have generally run chiefly upon some single branch of Science, as Divinity, Physic, Law, Poetry, &c. and have frequently raised an estate, by going on servilely and stupidly in one track of business. But, moved by nobler views, and having a laudable ambition to become famous in the Commonwealth of learning, I scorned to confine my self to anyone of its parts, but endeavoured to the utmost of my power to promote it in all. And tho' Biography, secret History, natural Philosophy, and Poetry were my chief favourites; yet no part of literature can complain, that it has been disregarded, much less intirely neglected by me. And, I believe, a perfect *Encyclopædia* of Arts and Sciences may be collected solely from the books which I have published.

This may seem a paradox to those, who form a judgment of the number of books printed for me, by seeing my name in the Title Page; and may thence be apt to conclude, that where that does not appear, I was not at all concerned. This is a very uncertain way of judging: there being a great many cases, in which it is not at all proper, either for an Author, or a Bookseller, to put his name to the book he publishes. And I can evidently prove, whenever it shall be deemed necessary, that I have actually printed and sold as many books under fictitious names, or under none at all, as under my own.

'In short,' he continues, 'I may venture to affirm, that the mystery of bookselling has been carried to a greater height by me, than by any, either of my Predecessors, or Contemporaries.'[11] Exactly so, the Popians would respond.

Alas for the hopes of poor Kirleus, we find out in a subsequent issue that he has not got the job. Instead it has gone to Captain L. Gulliver, the hero of Swift's *Travels*, who has now opened a shop near Temple Bar. It is no coincidence that this was where Pope's protégé Lawton Gilliver operated. Why is Kirleus rejected? One member of the society deplores his activity in lewd books: 'In this sort of trade he became so eminent, as to give occasion to the inrichment of our language with a new term, filthy discourse having now for several years been called, by the polite part of the world, *Curlicism*.' The Scriblerians had not invented this word, but they got a lot of use from it as time went on.

At this point a supporter of Kirleus mounts an absurd defence of bawdy works, arguing that they justify the practice of booksellers in general and his friend in particular:

EXHIBIT 13.5

For the design of some of them is to give a true historical account of former transactions, which may serve as precedents in determining the like cases which may happen, such as *Cases of impotency and divorce, &c.* Others are designed to promote natural knowledge, as *The use of flogging, Art of kissing, Art of getting pretty children, Mysteries of conjugal love, &c.* which all tend very much to the good of the public, by inciting to the propagation of a sound and vigorous offspring. And Books of Novels, if the events are unfortunate, are useful to deter young persons from following the like lascivious courses. Now if the abuse of writings of this kind be an argument against the use of them; it will hold equally strong against books of Anatomy, Surgery, Midwifery, &c. which are all perverted by the natural corruption of some readers to the promoting of lewdness and debauchery.

All these titles are recognizable Curll offerings.

It is no good. The society votes against Kirleus as their bookseller, but a case is made to allow him to become a member in the capacity of an author:

EXHIBIT 13.6

As it would be great pity to deprive the world of the ingenious lucubrations of Mr. KIRLEUS, by his confining himself to the employment of a bookseller; so I am very certain, that he will never consent to do it, much less to deprive himself of the annual profit arising from the sale of diverting books.

There are three branches of literature in which he has distinguish'd himself, *Natural History* and *Philosophy* (called by some *Obscenity*) and *Antiquities.* In labours relating to the 2 former he spent the vigour of his years: to the latter he has applied himself in his more advanced age, as a subject more suitable to his maturer judgment. The testimony of a learned Antiquarian relating only to his collections in one of these sciences may be justly applied to him in respect of all, *that no Bookseller in Town has been so curious as he.* Twenty volumes of *Antiquities,* and more than twice twenty of *Natural Philosophy* and *History* are a noble stock for one Book-seller, sufficient to enable him to carry on in his *Literatory* a very profitable business, with ease and dignity in his old age.[12]

Captain Gulliver is duly elected.

It appears from an issue in June that Kirleus had not taken his failure well. He is accused of having written a hostile article in the *Daily Journal* on 23 May. In fact, this was an attack on Pope and his friends, written by 'Philalethes' (lover of truth), which was Curll's favourite pseudonym. This claims that the paper has been inclined 'to do Justice to the Gentleman libell'd in the Dunciad'. To allow a critical description of Pope to appear would confirm its impartiality 'in the present Poetical War now raging in Great-Britain'. The verses chosen are taken from a pamphlet published by Roberts on 28 April, *One Epistle to Mr. Pope.* This contains some vicious lines on the poet, followed by a harsh portrait of his collaborators, starting with Dr Arbuthnot:

EXHIBIT 13.7

Let his weak, wilful Head, unrein'd by Art,
Obey the Dictates of his flattering Heart;
Divide a busy, fretful, Life between
Smut, Libel, Sing-song, Vanity, and Spleen . . .
Let him with all his Might, and all his Will
His unabating Thirst pursue – to scribble still.
Giv'n at his Birth! The Poetaster's Gust,
False and unsated as the Eunuch's Lust . . .

And here! a Groupe of Brother Quill-men see,
Co-witlings all, and Demi-bards like Thee;

Such whom the Muse shall pass with just Disdain,
Nor add one Trophy to thy mottly Train:
But Quack *Arbuthnot* shall Oblivion blot,
That puzzling, plodding, prating, pedant *Scot*!
The grating Scribler! whose untun'd Essays
Mix the *Scotch* Thistle with the *English* Bays,
By either *Phoebus* pre-ordain'd to Ill,
The Hand prescribing, or the flattering Quill,
Who doubly plagues, and boasts two Arts to kill![13]

The conclusion skilfully blends Arbuthnot's multiple avocations, by referring to Apollo, god both of the arts and of healing, as well as the deity who brought plagues with his arrow.

After commenting further on Mr. Kirleus's failure to win the election, the paragraph in the *Grub Street Journal* ends with some advice. The members 'very much approve his having lately cleared his Literary of Books of Antiquities . . . and retaining only such as relate to Biography, secret History, natural Philosophy, and Poetry, subjects much more suitable to the brightness of his parts'.[14] They then suggest that he should look at these books, ignoring their spurious title pages, and reflect on the real authors, who were responsible for creating 'all his wealth and reputation in the world'.[15]

A FIGURE WITH TWO FACES

Throughout its run, the paper found regular opportunities to besmirch Curll's reputation in the world. The most cutting took the form of a piece entitled 'The Art and Mystery of Printing', which came out in October 1732. This features an allegorical scene set in a printing house, with a bizarre Janus-faced figure presiding in the centre of the picture. A detailed gloss is provided next to the illustration. Another segment of the print shows a devilish figure hanging up on a rack what may be proof sheets of *Cases of*

Impotency. Higher up we can see sheets of books entitled *Onania, Rochester's Poems, Sessions Papers* – and *Manual of Devotion.* The editor is able to explicate this, too:

EXHIBIT 13.8

The grand figure I take to be a bookseller, who has as much occasion for two faces in the way of trade, as persons in any other business . . . What was sayed in relation to the same printer's being concerned in printing weekly papers, pamphlets, or books, written in direct opposition to each other, is equally applicable to booksellers: Nay, they have frequently employed persons to write answers to books printed for themselves, in order to make them sell the better, and sometimes an author has been employed to answer himself. The same bookseller has frequently printed, at his own charge, religious and impious, godly and lewd books. This sufficiently justifies the application of the figure with two faces – In the attitude in which he is placed, he may be supposed as giving his order to his slaves the printers, who work like horses, grunt like hogs, and fawn upon him like dogs. Or else he may be considered as giving directions to his authors, to write poetical, political, historical, theological, or bawdy books; which authors are properly represented by the gentlemen who have the heads of a dog, a horse, or a swine, and are accordingly treated by him like spaniels, hackneys, and hogs.

The devil in the last division of the picture, seems to denote a particular bookseller, stripped of all his false ornaments of puffs, advertisements, and title pages, and in propria persona, putting up his own and other peoples copies, books, some of pious devotions, and others of lewd diversion, in his literatory.[16]

There can have been very few readers who didn't instantly know what devil was depicted here.

One last thrust may be mentioned. By 1735 Curll had adopted an image of Pope's head both as his shop sign and as a logo to use within a cartouche on promotional material. The *Journal* found this amusing, comparing him to a counterfeiter:

EXHIBIT 13.9

Curst CUR, besieg'd by Duns, to raise the cash
With POPE's immortal busto stamps his trash:
So squandering *Coyners*, to retrieve a loss
Imprint their monarch's image on their dross.[17]

Similarly, when the bookseller started to use an elaborate monogram made up of whirling lines (Curlicues, you might call them), he was the object of a supposed defence by 'D.D.' (not Defoe; he was long gone):

EXHIBIT 13.10

Gentlemen   *Jan.* 8, 1735 [/6].
I have read in your Paper . . . complaining of C--- a *Bookseller*, as guilty of imposing on the Publick in certain Volumes published with the Title of Mr. P---'s *Literary Correspondence*. As I take this to mean a reflection on the *candid* Mr. E----- C---, I beg leave to say a few words in defence of that eminent Stationer; who, far from attempting to impose upon any one, hath ingenuously prefix'd *his Name* to every Book which he hath published, besides a pretty Picture of the *Initial Letters* E.C. curiously interwoven in Cyphers; and who cannot be said to have deceived any *one* Purchaser, Since who is there in the Kingdom that sees Mr. C---'s NAME in the Title Page, and is not from that circumstance enabled to form a perfect judgment of the Book?
I am your humble servant,   D.D.[18]

'Candid' here means kindly or well disposed, and 'ingenuously' in an honourable way.

Over its span of seven years, the *Grub Street Journal* maintained the pressure on Curll, as his most regular assailant from Pope's side.

Others felt its sting, such as Theobald for his Shakespeare, Richard Bentley for his edition of Milton, and John Henley for his madcap oratory, together with John Dennis, Cibber, Eustace Budgell, James Moore Smythe, Aaron Hill and even Henry Fielding for various offences committed while loitering in Grub Street. None of these men can have been quite as well prepared for what was coming as the bookseller was. He now had an assured position as a standard-bearer for free speech in defiance of the courts. A minor poet named James Bramston put it this way in 1733:

EXHIBIT 13.11

Long live old *Curl!* he ne'er to publish fears,
The speeches, verses, and last wills of Peers.
How oft has he a publick spirit shewn,
And pleas'd our ears regardless of his own?
But to give Merit due, though *Curl*'s the fame?
Are not his Brother-booksellers the same?
Can Statutes keep the *British* Press in awe,
While that sells best, that's most against the Law?[19]

Actually, Curll's ears were no longer under great threat, since that punishment for libel was now used infrequently. But he might have been proud of the endorsement these verses provided.

HARD WORDS OR HANGING

Curll's hand had not lost its cunning. Early in 1733 he responded to a pair of works emanating from his opponents. First came the premiere of *Achilles*, the last play written by John Gay, who had died in the previous year. It took place at Covent Garden playhouse on 10 February, and according to some accounts Pope supervised the rehearsals. It was not a great success in the theatre, a fact that gave Curl an early opportunity to respond. Soon afterwards, on 15

February, Pope had brought out his imitation of the first satire of the second book of Horace. We touched on this in the Introduction as a particularly good example of the poet's ability to parody a forensic argument, or rather here dialogue, in verse. There are passages of great venom, but also extraordinary virtuosity: 'Slander or Poyson, dread from *Delia*'s Rage, / Hard Words or Hanging, if your Judge be *Page*: / From furious *Sappho* scarce a milder Fate, / *Pox'd* by her Love, or libell'd by her Hate.'[20] The personal animus here is unmistakable, with rapid allusions to stories of the day – Lady Deloraine's alleged attempt to poison another maid of honour at court; Francis Page's rough treatment of Richard Savage in the murder trial; Lady Mary's efforts to introduce inoculation against smallpox, and her bitter verses supposedly against her one-time friend.

Yet this passage loops back at the end to libel, and that is a running theme of the poem: Pope's need to go on writing the truth, even if his satires offend powerful people and risk his being prosecuted for sedition. Just like Curll, although for slightly different reasons, the poet had constantly to watch his back, as Walpole's surveillance team hunted down unacceptable material. His interlocutor, William Fortescue, advises restraint with a genuine lawyerly caution, foreseeing a knighthood in prospect if he would consent to turn out panegyrics on the king. But for Pope this seems like time-serving in the manner of Blackmore: 'What? Like Sir *Richard*, rumbling, rough and fierce, / With ARMS, and GEORGE, and BRUNSWICK crowd the Verse?'[21] Blackmore was famous for his rumbling coach, as well as his cumbrous lines, and for celebrating the Hanoverians (the king was also Duke of Brunswick) against 'Popish Bigots, and Protestant Jacobites'.[22]

Both the new Scriblerian items met with a swift reaction. As early as 2 March, there came a pamphlet under the imprint of William Mears, Curll's most frequent partner around this period. The title was *Achilles Dissected: Being a Compleat Key of the Political Characters in that New Ballad Opera, Written by the Late Mr. Gay.*

THE POET AND THE PUBLISHER

An Account of the Plan upon which it is Founded. With Remarks upon the Whole. By Mr. Burnet. To which is added, The First Satire of the Second Book of Horace, Imitated in a Dialogue between Mr. Pope and the Ordinary of Newgate. The author is named in a reissue twelve months later as 'Alexander Burnet, Esq.' Either way, he is just a convenient fiction. The writer claims that the work was left unfinished by Gay, and that Pope and Arbuthnot have botched their attempt to complete it, especially as regards the songs. He then quotes a hostile report from the *Daily Courant*, which suggests that a claque including Pope were present at the first night to support a play in which they had no confidence. 'Burnet' offers a weak rebuttal of this case. Subsequently he devotes several pages to reproducing *Homerides*, the pamphlet we encountered in 1715, when Thomas Burnet and George Duckett made fun of Pope's *Iliad*, and offered a travesty of the first book. 'Burnet' concludes that Pope first burlesqued the story by his translation; Duckett carried the process further, turning Achilles into a clownish figure, and Gay has completed the transformation of the hero into a mere ballad singer.

The real strength of the pamphlet emerges in its second half. This is a response to Pope's Horatian verses, in which 'I have, according to his Manner of ridiculing the *best Poets* of our Nation, presented him with a Parody of his *vain* Imitation of this *Satire*, and which is a more faithful *Mirrour*, than any of the Bits of Looking-Glass that reflect the Beauties of his *Subterraneous Grotto*' – one of the earliest references to the cave of curiosities that was under construction at Twickenham.[23] What follows is a dialogue, as in the *Epistle* by Pope that serves as its model, and now said to be conducted between Alexander Pope, a poet, and the chaplain of Newgate, a parson. How closely it follows the original can be illustrated from the opening lines. The references don't matter here. In each case the version by Pope comes first and then that of 'Burnet'; note that words taken from the original appear in italics in the imitation:

EXHIBIT 13.12

P. There are (I scarce can think it, but am told)
There are to whom my Satire seems too bold:
Scarce to wise *Peter* complaisant enough,
And something said of *Chartres* much too rough.

P. There are (whate'er you think Sir) *I am told*,
Wretches as bad as me, and full as *bold*,
Who libel all Mankind with *Satire rough*,
And never think they're dissolute *enough*.[24]

Some of the transpositions are exceedingly clever, as when the lines Pope gives to Fortescue, 'Better be *Cibber*, I'll maintain it still, / Than ridicule all *Taste*, blaspheme *Quadrille*', are converted in the chaplain's comments to bring in a recollection of the first Psalm once more: '*Better be* BLACKMORE, *I'll maintain it still*, / Than blaspheme David, or adore Quadrille.' The switch to a clerical, rather than legal, interlocutor allows a different emphasis: thus, 'I love to pour out all myself, as plain / As downright *Shippen* or as old *Montagne*' becomes 'I love to pour out all myself, PROFANE, / And *mock* the SCRIPTURES in *Heroick Strain*.'[25]

A more particular slant is given to one section. Again, Pope is cited first:

EXHIBIT 13.13

Who-e'er offends, at some unlucky Time
Slides into Verse, and hitches in a Rhyme,
Sacred to Ridicule! his whole life long,
And the sad Burthen of some merry Song.

I rave, I foam, my utmost Venom hurl,
And in the *Grubstreet-Journal* libel *Curll*.

By *Popiads*, *Keys*, *Court-Poems*, I'm become
Of Ridicule, his universal Drum;
And shall continue thus my *whole Life long*,
The grievous Burthen of his *merry Song*.[26]

The two lines just quoted about Lady Deloraine and Justice Page are thrown back at Pope: '*Slander or Poison*'s dreaded *from* my *Rage*, / And hanged I shall be, if my Judge be ----.' Instead of Pope's retreat, which 'the best Companions grace, / Chiefs, out of War, and Statesmen, out of Place', his '*Twick'nam* Cott' according to Burnet offers him 'Attainted Peers, Commanders *out of Place*, / And un-hanged *Savage*, with his rueful Face'. The conclusion once more switches from Fortescue's legal jargon ('In such a Cause the Plaintiff will be hiss'd, / My Lords the Judges laugh, and you're dismissed') to the language of the church: 'And your *first* Psalm I fear, will be your *last*. / Be comforted my Son, I'll stand your Friend, / *John Applebee* and I will both attend.'[27] Applebee was a newspaper proprietor and the main outlet through which the dying speeches of criminals, from the scaffold at Tyburn, were released to the public.

The poem has not generally been attributed to Curll, perhaps because it is signed 'Bolt-Court Fleet-street. Feb. 26, 1732–3', an address that never belonged to him, although it did rather later to Samuel Johnson. However, I think he is much the likeliest suspect. The name after this dateline is 'Guthry', that is James Guthrie, chaplain at Newgate gaol since 1725, for whom Bolt Court would have been a convenient residence. The pamphlet is advertised in *Arches-Court Law* (1735), which is certainly a Curllian compilation. As we have repeatedly observed, the bookseller was a specialist in keys, such as the first part of Burnet's work purports to supply. No one else on the scene boasted about *Court Poems* or *The Popiad* in the way the writer does here. Few mentioned the first Psalm so insistently, or drew attention to such allusions in a footnote, as happens here. Few harp on about the villa and grotto at Twickenham in the same fashion. Most strikingly, Curll was the most assiduously close reader of Pope's texts, as we have seen in his commentaries on *The Dunciad*. None of the poet's enemies was capable of burlesquing his very words as neatly as 'Burnet' can: 'Sworn Foe to VIRTUE, and to all her FRIENDS'.

The clincher comes in the fact that Curll included this imitation in the second volume of *Mr. Pope's Literary Correspondence* in 1735, where he appended a note, 'It is hoped the Reader will compare this *Parodie* with Mr. *Pope*'s Imitation of the same *Satire*. E. CURLL.'[28] Virtually all the editorial contents of the *Correspondence* emanated from the bookseller himself. On top of that, Pope's letter to Fortescue on 8 March 1733 leaves no doubt that he believed it to have come from Curll's hand: 'There has been another thing, wherein Pigott is abused as my Learned Council, written by some Irish attorney [Concanen]; & Curll has printed a Parody on my own words which he is proud of as his own production, saying, he will pay no more of his Authors but can write better himself.'[29] Who are we to disagree with Pope, on a matter so close to his regular concerns?

Confident that he had the public ear, Curll now began to advertise in earnest a project that he had long turned over in his mind. At the end of a notice that appeared in the *Daily Journal* on 13 March, listing a long series of lives and last wills, came a new addition:

EXHIBIT 13.14

Now in the Press

20. The Life of Mr. Pope. Containing a faithful Account of him and his Writings. (Founded upon a Plan deliver'd by himself to Mr. Jacob, with two Guineas, to insert it in his Lives of the Poets). Embellish'd with Dissertations, Digressions, Notes, and all Kinds of poetical Machinery, in order to render the Work compleat. Nothing shall be wanting but his (universally desired) Death. Any Memoirs, &c. worthy his Deserts, if sent to Mr. Curll, will be faithfully inserted.

Curll did get some response to this request, because at the end of the same month he acknowledged receipt of materials, containing 'Proof of that natural Spleen which constitutes Mr. Pope's temperament'.[30] The book was said to be 'actually in the Press'; but this momentous work, which Curll long promised, never saw the light of day. Despite that, simply for him to include his nemesis in a list of the eminent dead looked like a sinister warning.

THE COURT OF APOLLO

In May of the same year another sharp riposte came from Giles Jacob, one of the writers most offended by what Pope had done to him in *The Dunciad*. This was a transcript of the supposed 'legal Tryal and Conviction' of the poet. It appeared as an appendix to a miscellaneous volume, which was issued by Roberts under the title *The Mirrour* and had no direct connection with Curll. However, its contents bear centrally on the quarrel. We learn that the plaintiff is John (really James) Ralph of the City of London, Gentleman, and the defendant '*Alexander Pope* of *Twickenham*, in the County of *Middlesex*, Esq; now in the Custody of the Marshal of our Sovereign Lord *Apollo*'. It is a nice touch to have the accused already in custody in a manner long familiar to Curll and some of his writers.

The complaint is one of dullness and scandal, committed by the defendant:

EXHIBIT 13.15

Whereas the said *Alexander* did about the Month of *April* in the Year 1728, Compose, Print and Publish a certain infamous Libel, entitled the *Dunciad*, a Satyr; wherein he the said *Alexander* has abused, vilified and scandalized, not only the said *John Ralphe* in the most notorious Manner, but hath also endeavoured to make Asses, Owls, Fools, Blockheads, Blunderers, Coxcombs, Rogues, Rascals and Scoundrels of many Gentlemen of superior Rank and Figure, eminent for their Learning and universal Accomplishments, as well as their high Stations, hereby maliciously attempting to level the Best and Greatest of Men with the Worst and Weakest, in Expectation that his own Character would stand and remain the Brighter by such a Procedure; and having frequently defamed his Adversaries for no other Reason but because they had better Faces and handsomer Bodies than him self, being thoroughly sensible of his own Defects of Body and Mind; and particularly having called the said *John* a stupid Ass and Owl, whereas he the said *John* has neither the long Ears of that foolish Animal, nor the least Resemblance of any Species of Owls, but being credited by many ignorant Persons, the Fame and Reputation of the said *John* hath greatly suffer'd with his Booksellers, Printers and Hawkers, by the false and malicious Aspersion aforesaid; whereupon he the said *John* says he is the worse, and hath Damage to the Value of 500 *l.* and therefore brings his Suit.[31]

The form of the complaint precisely mimics the one found in the legal actions Curll had faced on several occasions. It's significant that Ralph's grievance concerns the fact that he has been ostracized by the book trade. The court of Apollo has become a sort of employment tribunal.

The feeble 'reply' comes from Savage, acting as Pope's barrister:

EXHIBIT 13.16

For that the Persons he, the said *Alexander* satirized, and with great Decency called Asses, Owls, Fools, Blockheads, Blunderers, Coxcombs, Rogues, Rascals and Scoundrels, deserve his just and extraordinary Names and Characters, because they have more Sense, Learning, Judgment, Sincerity, Modesty and Virtue than the said *Alexander*; and therefore the said *Alexander* was for beating down these Men, especially the said *John Ralph*, as he is advis'd he might lawfully do.[32]

Once more, the imaginary transcript reproduces some of the claims defendants made in sedition trials that authors and publishers underwent in this era.

A jury of critics is summoned to hear the case in the High Court of Parnassus. This 'impartial' body determines 'on the strictest Examination of the Premisses, that the said *John* is a Man of Sense, and that he the said *Alexander* is guilty of the greatest Dulness and Scandal, throughout his nonsensical and filthy *Dunciad*'. The verdict of the judges will surprise nobody: 'the said *John* shall Recover against the said *Alexander* his Damages of Five Hundred Pounds aforesaid; and that the said *Alexander* shall be cast headlong from the Mount of *Parnassus*.' This sentence is greeted with acclamations by the people, who cry 'down with this *Pope* and Pretender to Poetry.'[33] It is no accident that the papacy and the Jacobite claimant both surface as this attack on the poet comes to an end. Curll and his henchmen had not been able to rustle up new accusations to load on him.

For the moment Pope lay low. But he had something in store for his enemy, as the next year would reveal.

14

The Letters of MR POPE:

STAGE ONE, 1735

Now the long-running feud took its strangest turn yet. The tempo of events moved to *prestissimo* over the course of 1735, and over the next three years exchanges multiplied as never before. A huge array of books and pamphlets appeared, as well as articles in newspapers and journals, while the press shot out an almost daily fire of tit-for-tat advertisements. Nowadays, the incitement for this war of words doesn't look especially controversial: it was the first publication of Pope's collected letters in different guises. But, as he had exclaimed at the start of *The Rape of the Lock*, 'What mighty Contents rise from trivial Things.'[1] Parts of this contest did hinge on trivialities, such as minor aspects of wording, nomenclature or dating. However, the respective aims of Pope and Curll ensured that some issues arose that would prove to be of mighty significance in the history of the book.

The tale has been told many times, although usually without much by way of context within the larger quarrel. Right in the heart of the episode, Pope issued his own narrative of the course of events so far, and within five weeks Curll had reprinted this together with detailed objections. Gradually more facts would come out, and in the Victorian era critics placed the most unfavourable construction on Pope's behaviour. This marks one of the phases in his career that did most to damage his reputation with posterity, and it took all of a century for more sympathetic students of the poet to carry out the basic repair work. Yet mysteries remain even today. This chapter and the next will present a number of documents that have never been reprinted, and several others that survive only in remote sources. Even so, many details have had to be left out in the interest of space; it would need a large volume to cover every single intervention by the participants in this frenzied debate. On Pope's side there is deliberate mystification; on Curll's, deliberate provocation.

Before we get into these complex manoeuvres, it should be noted that Pope entered 1735 with a flourish. His immortal apologia in justification of his life as a writer, the *Epistle to Arbuthnot*, came out on the second day of the year. It was also a tender farewell to a dear friend who had prepared himself for death, which occurred at the end of the same month. A little while earlier, the doctor had told him, 'The kindest wish of my friends is euthanasia' (meaning a gentle death, not one brought about on purpose).[2] In other respects the *Epistle* couldn't be called a tender poem, since it includes bitter attacks on Joseph Addison and Lord Hervey, as well as comic grousing directed at would-be writers who besiege Pope's haven at Twickenham (as 'All *Bedlam*, or *Parnassus*, is let out' – the poetasters need to be released from penal confinement, if they are not actually locked up in a madhouse). Their number includes 'A maudlin Poetess, a rhyming Peer' and 'a Clerk . . . who pens a stanza when he should engross', that is, copy out a legal document. Not that the old suspects remain untouched. The text harks back to Grub Streeters such as Leonard Welsted (whom, ominously, '*Curl* invites to dine'), Charles Gildon, John Dennis, Lewis Theobald, Eustace Budgell and James Moore Smythe. As for Curll, the worst thing said about him occurs in a note, stating that in some of his pamphlets, the poet's father was alleged to be a mechanic (manual labourer), a hatter, a farmer and a bankrupt.[3] All these claims were made as part of the onslaughts on Pope, but not always in items from Curll's shop. Incidentally, this was Pope's last sustained treatment of the hacks until they were gathered together again in the *New Dunciad* of 1742.

In April Lawton Gilliver issued the *Works of Mr. Alexander Pope*, volume II, a sequel to the renowned collection from 1717. It contained most of the major works of the 1730s: that is, the *Essay on Man*, the *Moral Essays* and the earliest among the *Imitations of Horace* (I use the labels familiar to us today, which were not those employed at the time). The publication is important to bibliographers and editors, but it contains nothing new about Curll.

E.C. MAKES WAR

The saga of the letters goes back to October 1733, when Pope began to masquerade as 'P.T.', the first of various fake IDs that he would use to perpetrate his deception.[4] In this guise he sent Curll details of his ancestry and youth in response to the bookseller's advertisements. A little later he wrote again, promising to send a large collection of the poet's letters, but leaving his motive vague. With this, Pope embarked on his plan to inveigle Curll into producing a 'spurious' edition of the correspondence, which would allow him to publish an 'authentic' edition, which was the desired aim all along. He needed to do this because it would have appeared unseemly, not to mention narcissistic, for a living writer to compile his own collection. Once he had this strategy at work, Pope could appeal to recipients of his letters to ask for their return, so that they would not fall into the hands of Curll, now that he was shown to be a disreputable scavenger who had acquired this material through underhand means. Such recovered items would then go into the official text. Of course, the poet knew just how anxious the bookseller had always been to get hold of new Popiana, as in the case of the Cromwell letters. He had every reason to believe that Curll would take the bait.

Fast-forward two years, when Curll would find the letter from P.T. and send it to Pope, seeking an accommodation – or so he claims. Instead, the poet inserted a sharp reproof in the form of a notice in the *Grub Street Journal* on 3 April 1735:

EXHIBIT 14.1

Whereas *A.P.* hath received a Letter from *E.C.* Bookseller, pretending that a Person, the Initials of whose Name are *P.T.* hath offered the said *E.C.* to print a large Collection of Mr. *P*'s Letters, to which *E.C.* requires an Answer, *A.P.* having never had, nor intending to have, any private Correspondence with the said *E.C.* gives it him in this Manner. That he knows no such Person as *P.T.* he believes he hath no such Collection, and that he thinks the whole a Forgery, and shall not trouble himself at all about it.

One part of this is true, at least – Pope didn't know anyone called P.T., because there was no such person. In reply, the phantom correspondent accused Curll of having betrayed him 'to Squire *Pope*', and renewed his offer to the bookseller, stating his terms as regards the cost of paper and printing. Curll may have been genuinely upset by the advertisement, and inserted his own:

EXHIBIT 14.2

Whereas *A.P.* Poet, has certified in the *Daily Post-Boy*, that he shall not trouble himself at all about the Publication of a large Collection of the said Mr. *Pope*'s Letters which *P.T.* hath offered *E.C.* to print. This is to certify, that Mr. c. never had, nor intended ever to have, any private Correspondence with *A.P.* but was directed to give him Notice of these Letters. Now to put all *Forgeries*, even *Popish ones*, to flight; this is to give Notice, that any Person, (or, *A.P.* himself) may see the ORIGINALS, in Mr. *P---*'s own Hand, when printed. *Initials* are a Joke; Names at length are *real*.

> *No longer now like Suppliants we come,*
> E.C. *makes War, and* A.P. *is the Drum.*

Even by his usual standards, this was a show of extreme defiance on Curll's part. In his *Narrative* of the affair, Pope suggests that the bookseller had now developed an overweening self-confidence. He goes on to introduce the second mysterious actor who played a role in his charade:

EXHIBIT 14.3

In a few Days more he publish'd the *Advertisement of the Book* as above, with this Addition, '*E.C.* as before in the like Case, will be faithful.' He now talk'd of it every where, said 'That *P. T.* was a LORD, or a PERSON OF CONSEQUENCE, who printed the Book at a *great Expence*, and sought no Profit in it, but *Revenge* on Mr. *Pope, who had offended him:*' particularly, 'That some of the Letters would be such as both *Church* and *State would take Notice of*; but that *P. T.* would by no means be known in it, that he never would once be *seen* by him, but treated in a very *secret Manner*.' He told some Persons that sifted him in this Affair, 'that he had convers'd only with his Agent, a Clergyman of the Name of *Smith*, who came, as he said, from *Southwark*.' With this Person it was that *Curl* transacted the Affair, who before all the Letters of the Book were delivered to *Curl*, insisted on the Letters of P.T. being return'd him, to secure him from all possibility of a Discovery.

'Sifted' here refers to close questioning.

The exchanges were punctuated by more tangled negotiations, as P.T. began to play hard to get. He had asked Curll to announce in the press that he would come to view the printed sheets on 22 April at the Rose Tavern, which stood immediately adjacent to the Drury Lane theatre, and the merest stone's throw from Curll's recent premises in Bow Street. We can recognize its interior because William Hogarth chose it for the scene of the second instalment of *The Rake's Progress* (1733), where the ne'er-do-well Tom Rakewell carouses among women of the town as he waits for a stripper to begin her performance. The bookseller duly did as requested in the *Daily Post Boy* of 17 April. However, in his usual temporizing

THE POET AND THE PUBLISHER

fashion, P.T. deferred the meeting for a week, according to Curll because he was 'in a terrible Panic lest Mr. *Pope* should send some of his *Twickenham-Bravoes* to assault us; but how Mr. *Pope* was to know of this Meeting is the Cream of the Jest'. The bookseller reassured him that for his part he did not 'dread any *Assassination* whatever from Mr. *Pope*, even tho' it were a Poetical One'. Curll grew increasingly annoyed by the delays and the need to operate in the dark. In addition, he considered the price P.T. was seeking, £75 deposit on 650 copies at £3 each, a steep one.

A NIGHT VISITOR

The rapid succession of events that now occurred has been summarized with admirable economy by the editor of Pope's prose, Rosemary Cowler:

> Curll was obviously suspicious by this point, but after further negotiations with P.T. there materialized a new figure of mystery, R.S. – 'a short, squat Man . . . He had on a Clergyman's Gown, and his neck was surrounded with a large, Lawn Barrister's Band' – who brought to Curll, on the night of 7 May, a 'Book in sheets, almost finished,' and some dozen original letters. Matters then began to move swiftly, although there were still numerous communications between Curll and P.T. and R.S. – now further revealed in these notes as R. Smythe – about money and about the earlier correspondence between them, which P.T. wished returned. Both he and R.S. exhorted Curll to advertise the forthcoming publication; but until he had books in hand, Curll was cautious. By 12 May he had received fifty copies – lacking title pages and prefaces – which he soon sold, and at one-thirty that afternoon five bundles, amounting to 190 more books, were delivered to his house. The venture must have seemed a success: the

advertisement had appeared that morning, and the *Letters* were finally on the market.[5]

So the momentous day had arrived when Curll was able to proclaim his great coup in the *Daily Post Boy* of 12 May:

EXHIBIT 14.4

This Day are published, and most beautifully printed, Price 5s., Mr. *Pope*'s *Literary Correspondence* for Thirty Years; from 1704 to 1734, being a Collection of Letters, regularly digested, written by him to the Right Honourable the late Earl of *Halifax*, Earl of *Burlington*, Secretary *Craggs*, Sir *William Trumbull*, Honourable *J[ohn] C[aryll]*, General ****, Honourable *Robert Digby*, Esquire, Honourable *Edward Blount*, Esq, Mr. *Addison*, Mr. *Congreve*, Mr. *Wycherley*, Mr. *Walsh*, Mr. *Steele*, Mr. *Gay*, Mr. *Jarvas*, Dr. *Arbuthnot*, Dean *Berkeley*, Dean *Parnelle*, &c. Also Letters from Mr. *Pope* to Mrs. *Arabella Fermor*, and many other Ladies. With the respective Answers of each Correspondent. Printed for *E. Curll* in *Rose-street, Covent-Garden*, and sold by all Booksellers. N.B. The Original Manuscripts (of which Affidavit is made) may be seen at Mr. *Curll*'s House by all who desire it.

We have met most of the persons named among Pope's friends and allies, and most of the rest do not really matter here, except for his model for the heroine Belinda in *The Rape of the Lock*, named Arabella Fermor in her everyday incarnation. She was a bright young thing who had grown up among the Thames Valley recusant community familiar to Pope in his early days. She left no mark on history other than as a central figure in the brief scandal in high society that prompted the poet to compose the *Rape*.

It has been suggested that the part of the clergyman in the comic opera scenario was played by James Worsdale, who really was an actor as well as a writer and painter. He had been apprenticed to Sir Godfrey Kneller, until he was ejected after entering into a secret marriage with the artist's niece. (Richard Savage-like, he later made the unfounded claim that he was Kneller's son.) However, no concrete evidence has emerged to confirm Worsdale's involvement. As for Smythe, he now became the frontman of the operation, settling arrangements for publication while P.T. crept back into the shadows. Soon afterwards, Curll was summoned to meet R.S. at a tavern in Leicester Fields, another convenient trysting place since it was less than 300 yards from Rose Street. This time he handed over hard cash. Messages rattled to and fro between R.S. and Curll even after the volume came before the public.

As the missives continued, R.S. warned the bookseller that Pope might be able to obtain an injunction against E. Curll by name in Chancery, even though the title page of the collection had carefully omitted this detail, using instead the piratical formula, 'Printed and sold by the Booksellers of London and Westminster'. Again the need for strict secrecy was emphasized.

Back Before the Lords

The next phase of hostilities, involving Curll's appearance before the House of Lords, deserves careful attention. For as long as the feud lasted, it was the single incident to which the triumphant bookseller returned whenever he could. Here was the revenge he had been seeking for twenty years, all the sweeter because it was delivered at such a place as the Lords. He felt himself vindicated by the highest tribunal in the land, in the face of some who numbered among Pope's greatest friends (greatest in two senses). Equally, the publisher could view the outcome as a direct riposte to the poet's attempt to have him suffer another public humiliation. It's important therefore to see exactly what went on during Curll's appearance in the chamber at Westminster.

Perhaps Curll had believed when the edition appeared, seemingly against Pope's wishes, that he now held the whip hand. 'But

A View of the House of Peers, including King George II,
engraved by John Pine, 1749.

the Tables now began to turn,' said Pope. On the very day of publication, a complaint was lodged in the Lords by a manager of
Scottish affairs for Walpole, Lord Islay. The task perhaps came to
him because he possessed strong ministerial connections, unlike
other allies of Pope such as Bathurst, Strafford or Oxford, who
were all unregenerate Tories. Islay's seat also happened to be at
Whitton, near Twickenham, and, like his neighbour, he was a keen
gardener. In any case, Pope would not have wanted a close ally
to make the complaint, since people might suspect some form of
prior contrivance. Islay read out the suspect advertisement in the
chamber, observing that 'as it pretended to publish several Letters
to *Lords* . . . it was a *Breach of Privilege*, and contrary to a standing
Order of the House.' We recall that, more than a decade earlier,
it had been Curll's edition of Buckingham's *Works* that had led to
the creation of this standing order.

343

Nothing of moment was expected when the Lords assembled on 12 May. Just over fifty members, including ten bishops, were present, out of around two hundred who were eligible. This was a normal turnout. On the woolsack sat Lord Chancellor Talbot, a former MP and a loyal supporter of Walpole. The benches were stacked with Whig nominees, many of whom had no cause to love Pope. However, friends such as Islay, Bathurst and Oxford were thinly scattered around the small medieval chamber, originally known as the Queen's Chamber. One item of anticipated business that day was a discussion of the Booksellers' Bill, a measure updating the 1710 Copyright Act, with the aim of increasing the protections afforded to both authors and publishers. Among others, Pope wished to put in place stronger barriers against piracy, and it may be that his manoeuvres over the letters were designed to expose the illicit practices going on in defiance of copyright legislation. As James McLaverty puts it, 'Pope wanted Curll to publish the edition of letters and to be caught doing it.'[6] The bill did not proceed, and an amended version in 1737 was also rejected, partly because of disagreements among its sponsors.

These staid proceedings were interrupted by a more urgent item of business. What ensued over the next four days is concisely revealed in the official transcripts of the House:[7]

EXHIBIT 14.5

12 May 1735

Notice was taken to the House, of an Advertisement printed in the News Paper, intituled, '*The* Daily-Post-Boy, Monday, May 12, 1735,' in these Words; (*videlicet,*)

[Full advertisement reproduced, as above.]

And the said Advertisement being read, by the Clerk:

Ordered, That the Gentleman Usher of the Black Rod attending this House do forthwith seize, or cause to be seized, the Impression of the said Book; and that the said *E. Curll*, together with

J. Wilford, at *The Three Flower de Luces*, behind *The Chapter House*, near *St Paul's*, for whom the said News Paper is said to be printed, do attend this House To-morrow.

The prim language disguises a potentially explosive issue.

EXHIBIT 14.6

13 May 1735

The Order made Yesterday, upon the Complaint of a printed Advertisement, in the News Paper, intituled, The 'Daily-Post-Boy,' giving Notice, 'That there was that Day published, Mr. *Pope*'s Literary Correspondence for Thirty Years,' being read:

Mr. *Wilford*, for whom the said News Paper is mentioned to be printed, attending (according to Order), was called in, and examined as to his being the Printer or Publisher thereof.

Also a Servant of Mr. *Redmaine*, the Printer of the said News Paper, was examined, in relation to the said Advertisement.

Then Mr. *Curll* was called in; and likewise examined touching the same Advertisement, as also the Contents of the Book advertised; and concerning a Note in the said Book, mentioning something of Letters that would be inserted in a Second Volume.

And then he was directed to withdraw.

After which; The Gentleman Usher of the Black Rod, being called upon, gave the House an Account, 'That, in Pursuance of their Lordships Order, he had caused all the Books found at Mr. *Curll*'s to be seized; and believed there might be near Five Hundred.'

Ordered, That the Matter of the said Complaint be referred to the Consideration of the Lords following; (*videlicet*,)

[The names of almost fifty peers listed here.]

Their Lordships, or any Five of them; to meet To-morrow, at the usual Time and Place; and to adjourn as they please: And that *E. Curll*, for whom the said Literary Correspondence is mentioned to be printed, do attend the said Committee; and that the Gentleman

Usher of the Black Rod do produce before their Lordships some of the printed Copies of that Book.

Two days later the committee made its report:

EXHIBIT 14.7

15 May 1735

The Lord *Delawarr* reported from the Lords Committees appointed to consider the Matter of the Complaint made of an Advertisement printed in the News Paper, intituled, '*The* Daily-Post-Boy, *Monday, May* 12, 1735;' giving Notice, 'That, on that Day was published, Mr. *Pope*'s Literary Correspondence for Thirty Years, from 1704 to 1734, printed for *E. Curll*, in *Rose Street, Covent Garden*:' 'That the Committee have looked into the Book produced before them by the Gentleman Usher of the Black Rod, pursuant to the Order of the House; and, having examined the same, do not find that there is any Letter of any Lord printed therein; and therefore conceive, that the Printing of the said Book is not contrary to the Standing Order of the House, of the 31st of *January*, 1721; and the Committee are of Opinion, that the Books seized by the said Gentleman Usher should be delivered back to the said *E. Curll*.'

In his own eyes, this marked Curll's most complete victory in all the long years of the quarrel. We must obviously go behind the dry words of the Lords' journal to see exactly why.

FINISHING POPE

Once the complaint was made on 12 May, the House examined the publisher and printer briefly, and ordered them to appear next day, while Black Rod was instructed to seize copies of the volume. In the afternoon of the same day, within an hour of delivery, a large consignment was impounded. Black Rod's claim that he had seized almost five hundred copies must be a considerable exaggeration if other testimony is to be trusted. Pope affected an air of being offended in a letter to John Caryll: 'But what makes me sick of writing is the shameless industry of such fellows as Curle, and the idle ostentation, or weak partiality of many of my correspondents, who have shewn about my letters . . . to such a degree that a volume of 200, or more are printed by that rascal.'[8] That, of course, was just what he had intended.

Next day, the full examinations began. Fortunately, we have a more detailed record of the committee's proceedings, although these have been largely neglected by students of the quarrel since they were published in 1860.[9] The first to be questioned were Wilford and his assistant, but only in a cursory manner. Then it was Curll's turn. The chairman he faced was John West, Baron De La Warr, a rough-and-ready soldier with an impeccable record as a follower of the ministry. He had a reputation for being an honourable man, and doubtless followed the evidence wherever it lay. Islay testified that he had looked at one of the seized copies, and had noted an 'abuse' of Lord Burlington in a letter from Pope to Charles Jervas. This would seem to indict the author rather than the publisher, but the law of libel was not construed in that fashion, and besides a charge might lie for *scandalum magnatum*, or slander on the holder of a high position. Since the books that had been seized were all in unbound sheets, Curll was called in to fold a set into a volume; but the Lords were still unable to find the letter in question, since it was among a segment of the series that had been omitted from the published book. The bookseller Benjamin Motte told Jonathan Swift that when he appeared, 'Curll was ruffled for them [the missing letters?] in a manner, as to a man of less impudence than his own, would have been very uneasy.'[10]

In the course of his examination, Curll said that he had merely copied out the suspect advertisement after it was sent to him – hardly a strong defence. Against advice he had received from R.S., he told the Lords that he had tried to alert Pope to P.T.'s offer, but the only outcome was the poet's contemptuous advertisement of 3 April. Curll asserted that he had not even looked at the second instalment of books, those seized on 12 May. But when he inspected them in front of the committee, he realized for the first time that they contained prefaces and title pages, missing from the original batch of fifty. (Hmm.) Further questioning concerned his affidavit about the 'originals' that could be seen at his shop; the claim to have letters *from* lords as well as to them, about which he pleaded ignorance; and the promise of a letter from the Duke of Chandos to Pope that would be included in the next volume. On this last he conceded the point. Finally, he stated that he had been hoping to retrieve more original letters from P.T., but so far had not seen them. The committee report shows that he stood up remarkably well to the grilling, albeit employing the very prevarication that he had laid at Pope's door.

Strictly, of course, Curll was not on trial, but his appearance in the chamber produced some authentic courtroom drama:

EXHIBIT 14.8

Notice taken to him that the advertisement mentions that the original letters, of which affidavit is made, may be seen at his house; and he is asked whether he has the originals of all the letters contained in the book, and how he came by them. Says he has not the originals of all the letters. He has the original letters of the correspondence with H.C. He had them from Mrs Thomas, for which he paid her a sum of money; and, being asked what sum, he says ten guineas, and says he is willing 'to produce these letters if their lordships please'.

Asked who made the affidavit. Says he made it, and that the purport of it was, that he believed 'the said letters to be original letters, he knowing Mr. Pope's handwriting, and several of them having the post-mark upon them'.

He is again showed the book, and asked whether he takes upon him to say that this is the book, and the only book, which he published and sold in pursuance of the advertisement. He says, yes, it is the only book, excepting the title and preface.

Asked how he came to advertise with the respective answers of such correspondents, if there is no letter of any lord printed in the book. Says that it was his ignorance; he only meant, by correspondents, such persons as had answered the letters; and says there is not any letter of any lord printed in the book. He read every line of the book before he published it.

Notice taken to him of a note in the book which mentions that a letter from the Duke of Chandos to Mr. P. may be printed in the second volume. Says he knows nothing at present of a second volume; but, if ever he should publish a second volume, he will not print any letter of the Duke of Chandos or of any other lord without their leave.

Asked whether he has any other original letters besides the correspondence with H.C., which he had from Mrs Thomas. Says he has not, but he believes he shall have others; he has been promised them. Asked who promised them him. Says the promise was made him by a penny-post letter; he does not know from whom it came. When he has them, he shall be very willing to produce them.

Asked whether he ever saw P.T. Says he never did.

Asked whether he has any other copy of this book. Says he has not; delivered them all to the officers of the House. Asked whether any other edition was published by anybody else. Says he knows of no other edition. Asked whether he did not sell some of the books before the lords' order came to him. Says he sold about: fifty.

This gets us closer to the nitty-gritty of Grub Street publishing than we are usually able to reach, with the penny-post letter, the post-mark, the admission of ten guineas in payment, the (unexamined) affidavit, the mysterious agent whom the publisher has never met, and so on. Of course, Curll knew Pope's handwriting well enough – he had enjoyed plenty of chances to familiarize himself with it. One blatant lie concerns the second volume, which would appear within a matter of weeks, and must have been already in preparation.

At the end of this battery of questions the committee dismissed the witness, unbowed as he had been when he stepped off the pillory seven years earlier. Lord De La Warr could not find anything offensive in the book, but the matter was adjourned to the next day to see if further copies would show anything damaging. Curll was ordered to appear again, with such 'original letters' as he had in his possession.

The agents supposedly on Curll's side now scented their moment of triumph. P.T. immediately wrote to the bookseller, congratulating him on his 'victory over the Lords, the Pope, and the Devil; for we have sure information that the books will be restored to you either this day or to-morrow' – Pope had evidently been told of the likely outcome. 'The lords cannot touch a hair of your head,' was the verdict. Curll evidently felt the same, since his reply began, 'I am just again going to the Lords to finish *Pope*.' He added, 'My Defence is right, I only told the Lords, I did not know from whence the Books came, and that my Wife received them.' That bit is true, although it offers some insight into what his professional methods had been for all those years past. According to a story passed on much later by Samuel Johnson, Curll took a saucy tone with the Lords on the subject of Pope, daring to tell them, 'He has . . . a knack of versifying, but in prose I think myself a match for him.'[11] This may or may not be true, but it certainly does sound like him. In further exchanges with P.T. he kept up the same confident note: 'LORD --- I attend this Day. LORD DELAWAR I SUP WITH TO NIGHT. Where *Pope* has one lord, I have twenty.'[12]

CURLL TRIUMPHANT

At this point Pope decided it was time to express his outrage at the way his letters had been 'pirated' by Curll. He inserted an advertisement in the press on 20 May:

EXHIBIT 14.9

Whereas a Person who signs himself P.T. and another who writes himself *R. Smith*, and passes for a Clergyman, have transacted for some time past with *Edm. Curll*, and have in Combination printed the *Private Letters* of Mr. *Pope* and his Correspondents (some of which could only be procured from his own Library, or that of a Noble Lord, and which have given a Pretence to the publishing others as his which are not so, as well as Interpolating those which are.) This is to advertise, that if either of the said Persons will apply to Mr. *Pope*, and discover the Whole of this Affair, he shall receive a Reward of *Twenty* Guineas; or if he can prove he hath acted by *Direction of any other*, and of *what Person*, he shall receive a Reward double that Sum.

Of course, the 'reward' was never paid – how could it be? Nothing daunted, Curll came straight back. He placed yet one more newspaper ad, introducing another conspirator, 'E.P.':

EXHIBIT 14.10

This is to give Notice, that another Person who writes himself *E. P.* was likewise concerned with *Edm. Curll* in the said Important Confederacy, who have all jointly and severally agreed to oblige Mr. *Pope*, if he will make it better worth their while, and let *E. Curll* print his Works for the future; who hereby promises, in Justice to all the Purchasers of the said Mr. *Pope*'s Letters bought of him, to deliver this Week *gratis*, the Letters to Mr. *Jarvas*, Mr. *Digby*, Mr. *Blount*, and Dr. *Arbuthnot*, which were wanting in all the Copies seized. And in a Month will be also published, Letters Political and Familiar, by Mr. *Prior*, Mr. *Addison*, Mr. *Pope*, Sir *Richard Steele*, &c. being the Second Volume of Literary Correspondence, &c.– Printed for *E. Curll*.

It is amusing to see the use of legalese terms such as 'jointly and severally'. Curll knew perfectly well that Pope would undoubtedly refuse this offer, but he was getting bolder almost by the minute.

Within a day or two Curll had two manifestos ready to make public. The first is addressed to none other than the peers of Great Britain. He begins it by thanking the justice and honour that the Lords have done him in his hour of greatest jeopardy. He goes on to quote Pope on the need at times for prevarication, describing this as 'an excellent proof of the modesty of Alexander Pope, of Twickenham, Esq.' Then to his plans:

EXHIBIT 14.II

Now, my Lords, to matter of fact. I shall this week publish a new edition of Mr. Pope's Literary Correspondence, &c., wherein the letters to Mr. Jervas, Mr. Digby, Mr. Blount, and Dr. Arbuthnot, which were wanting in all the copies seized by your lordships' order, shall be by me delivered *gratis*. And as I am resolved to detect, if possible, the contrivers of this gross imposition upon your lordships, I will, by way of Supplement, print all the letters I have received from E.P., P.T., and R.S., with some other correspondences, which, as Mr Bayes says, shall both elevate and surprise the public.

I have engraven a new plate of Mr Pope's head from Mr Jervas's painting; and likewise intend to hang him up in effigy, for a sign to all spectators of his falsehood and my own veracity, which I will always maintain under the Scots' motto: *Nemo me immune lacessit*.

The reference to 'Mr. Bayes' here concerns an exchange in the first scene of *The Rehearsal* (1671), a celebrated satire on John Dryden.

As we have seen, Curll did indeed adopt a version of the portrait by Jervas (1714) on the title page of the fourth volume of Pope's letters, but generally his new logo was based on one by Kneller (1716). The idea of hanging up Pope's head, even if only an effigy on a signboard, carries ominous threats. As for the Scottish motto, Curll had quoted it in an advertisement as far back as 1720, while Pope had used it in a headpiece for the *Dunciad Variorum*.

The second manifesto is addressed 'To the Booksellers'. It gives us some idea of the way in which Curll regarded fellow members of the trade:

EXHIBIT 14.12

ROSE-STREET, *May* 22, 1735.

GENTLEMEN, – Being informed that there are clandestinely sent to Messrs Innys and Manby some copies of Mr. Pope's letters, this is to give both them and you notice, that if they, or any person whatsoever, sell one copy of the said letters, but what comes from me, I will take reprisals on their copies. Farther, my new edition will have considerable additions never before printed, with cuts of the most eminent persons, which I will sell you cheaper; therefore use me as you would be used yourselves. The person who complains of me shall be by me used as he deserves.

John and William Innys were prominent members of the fraternity who operated in the booksellers' historic quarter near St Paul's, where Curll had worked briefly in 1720. At this date Richard Manby was a young recruit who eventually rose to become Master of the Stationers' Company in 1765.

So matters stood when Curll readied himself for further provocative acts. As Pope must have realized, he had it in mind to exploit his new mastery of the situation.

15

The Letters of MR POPE:
STAGE TWO, 1735–6

Here was the chance for Curll, flushed with success, to bring out his own edition. About 23 May came the first volume of *Mr. Pope's Literary Correspondence*, now issued under that title and under his own name. This was the opening salvo in a series of five (or six, if we include the later addition of Jonathan Swift's letters). It is not just a reprint of the work that had been fed to him and appeared on 12 May – there had been different morning and afternoon editions of that one, but the bibliographical niceties needn't concern us. The text of this new volume was reset throughout. What Curll seems to have done is tear up a copy of the earlier printing and distribute portions between several printers in order to get the job completed in the shortest possible time.

To make this chapter easier to follow, it will help to set out the full sequence of volumes in the series. Any second or subsequent editions always showed a number of changes in the contents, with items added or deleted. These alterations seem to have been dictated by no rhyme or reason; their presence or absence seems to be down to whether enough copies had been printed of a given section of the book. But that had long been Curll's practice with many of the works he reissued.

> Volume I. 1st edition. Octavo. May 1735. [No 2nd edition known.]
> Volume I. 3rd edition. Duodecimo. June 1735.
> Volume II. 1st edition. Octavo. July 1735.

Volume II. 2nd edition. Duodecimo. September 1735.

Volume III. 1st edition. Octavo. September 1735.

Volume III. 2nd edition. Duodecimo. After September 1735.

Volume IV. 1st edition. Octavo. May 1736.

Volume IV. 2nd edition. Duodecimo. July 1736.

New Letters of Mr. Alexander Pope (version of Volume v).
November 1736. Octavo. (The only edition of this item.)

Volume v. 1st edition in this form. Octavo. July 1737.

Dean Swift's Literary Correspondence. Octavo. May 1741.

A number of piratical versions appeared under imprints such as 'Printed and sold by the Booksellers of London and Westminster', always a reliable sign of illicit publication. As for alternative versions, they begin in August 1735 with *Letters of Mr. Pope, and Several Eminent Persons*, a duodecimo from the shop of Thomas Cooper, a 'trade bookseller' like James Roberts. He was no doubt encouraged by Pope to insert this advertisement repeatedly in the *Daily Journal* and other organs from 29 May:

EXHIBIT 15.1

We hope it is sufficient to prefer this Edition, to say it is NOT printed for *Edmund Curll*, and it is entirely free from his Notes and Impertinencies; it contains, First, The *Preface*, which *Curll*, with good Reason suppressed, as shewing by what Conduct, both to Mr. Pope, and Mr. Cromwell, he obtained these Letters. Secondly, It hath all *those Letters*, which were also omitted in the Books he first published, and shew'd to the Lords; it is in every respect more perfect than any other Edition can be, unless the Author himself be pleased to give us one: As for Mr. *Curll*, every Bookseller may be assured, that he has not the *least Title* to the Copy, nor could have any from his *Anonymous Confederates*, who must have got the Papers out of Mr. Pope's, or a Noble Lord's Library.

In essence, the substance of this edition was the collection Curll had brought out, slightly augmented. Pope admitted to William Fortescue that he 'connived' in the Cooper volume, presumably because it gave him an opportunity to show Curll in a bad light. He had the bookseller deposit copies of the work with the Stationers' Company, the standard way for members of the trade to establish title, but he retained the rights to himself. However, it was not until May 1737 that the first authorized edition came out in folio and quarto.

Meanwhile, the feud proceeded with the same giddy abandon visible throughout 1735. When the Cooper version was advertised in the *Daily Journal* with the insulting comment, 'N.B. This Edition consists of the Letters simply, wholly free from the *Follies* and Impertinence of *Edmund Curll*'s Edition,' it did not take long for the wily bookseller to frame a rejoinder: '*Edmund Curll*'s Follies and Impertinence / Will prove a Match for *Pope*'s Satiric Sense.'[1] Along with this, P.T. and R.S. fulminated in the press against their supposed colleague: 'To manifest to the World the insolence of *E. Curl*, hereby declare that neither *P.T.* much less *R.S.* his Agent, ever did give, or could pretend to give any Title whatever in Mr. *Pope*'s letters to the said *E. Curl*, and he is hereby challeng'd to produce any Pretence to the Copy whatsoever.' The mysterious duo intended to publish the letters they had received from the bookseller, something Pope had no doubt planned to do all along, because this 'will open a Scene of Baseness and Foul Dealing that will sufficiently show to Mankind his Character and Conduct'. As must have been anticipated, this drew an angry retort from Curll, in the longest note that he appended to Pope's *Narrative*, where he went over the arrangements for obtaining and publishing the letters, accusing his partners of cheating him: 'Mr. *Curll* having had in all but 240 Books, tho' a Receipt given for 300, and the last 190 all delivered imperfect'. He ended his declaration, 'I shall say no more till I publish the whole of their Transactions upon Oath.'

It was Cooper's turn to reply. He repaid the bookseller in his own coin by offering to show Curll's autograph letters at his own shop. In his next advertisement, repeated several times, he promised to give Curll £10, 'as much as he gave his Confederates for 200 Books', for every letter to or from Pope 'for which a true provenance can be produced'. He added, 'In the mean Time he hopes every fair Trader will give the Preference to this Edition enter'd in the [Stationers'] Hall Book according to the Act of Q. Anne, which is not (as some imagine) expired, but remains unrepeal'd, and in full Force, upon which Edmund Curll shall be prosecuted, or any other Pyrates of this Book.'[2] There may have been confusion on this point, owing to the fact that the protection granted by the 1710 Act to books already in print, lasting twenty-one years, had now expired. Curll replied simply that he had holograph letters from Francis Atterbury, and some of Pope's own, which he would be printing in the second volume of the *Literary Correspondence* – now an acknowledged publication on the horizon.[3] He always insisted that Cooper's was the pirated edition, 'which all honest Booksellers, and the public, have agreed to discourage'.

SHAMELESS INDUSTRY

Things were getting nastier. Not that Pope's next contribution, on 10 June, was calculated to spread sweetness and light. This was *A Narrative of the Method by which the Private Letters of Mr. Pope have been Procur'd and Publish'd by Edmund Curll, Bookseller*. And, to make the point: *NB. The Original Papers, in Curl's own Hand, may be seen at T. Cooper's*. It was far from a common undertaking, almost unparalleled in the age. Pope gives a blow-by-blow account of the proceedings that led up to the publication of the letters. The very opening words indicate that a matter of wide public concern is at stake:

EXHIBIT 15.2

It has been judg'd, that to clear an Affair which seem'd at first sight a little mysterious, and which, tho' it concern'd only one Gentleman, is of such a Consequence, as justly to alarm every Person in the Nation, would not only be acceptable as a *Curiosity*, but useful as a *Warning*, and perhaps flagrant enough as an *Example*, to induce the LEGISLATURE to prevent for the future, an Enormity so prejudicial to every private Subject, and so destructive of Society it self.

When he came to reply, Curll naturally did not miss the implication. He wrote a snappy retort, which we have previously encountered: 'Mr. *Pope* is the Son of a Trader, and so is Mr. *Curll – par nobile*' (missing out the next word in the quotation from Horace, which translates as 'a noble pair of brothers'), thus emphasizing once more that the two men shared in an indissoluble fraternity.

The main story begins with the publication of the Cromwell letters in 1727. Pope cites Elizabeth Thomas's letter to Henry Cromwell to show that neither he nor Pope had given permission to print them. He goes on to deplore the 'Practice frequent with Booksellers, to swell an Author's Works, in which they have some Property, with any Trash that can be got from any Hand; or where they have no such Works, to procure them'. Pope adds that Curll had previously done the same thing with the correspondence of Matthew Prior and Joseph Addison. This was a practice 'highly deserving some Check from the Legislature', since it was an invitation to every scoundrel to get a penny by producing a scrap of writing. Most readers would not understand that Pope himself had been the one to leak the most recent batch of letters; but as Curll perused the *Narrative*, it must have dawned on him – if it had not earlier – what the real provenance of the material was. As the pamphlet proceeds, it comes to seem more and more evident, first that the author had access not just to messages from P.T. and R.S. that Curll had quoted in his edition and in advertisements, and second that this privileged individual could hardly be anyone but Pope.

There is no need to go through all the letters and advertisements that Pope cites, since we have already touched on the most significant among them. A resonant passage concludes the exercise:

EXHIBIT 15.3

The Effect of this Quarrel has been the putting into our Hands all the Correspondence above; which having given the Reader, to make what Reflections he pleases on, we have nothing to add but our hearty Wishes, (in which we doubt not every honest Man will concur,) that the next *Sessions*, when the BOOKSELLERS BILL shall be again brought in, the Legislature will be pleas'd not to *extend* the *Privileges*, without at the same Time *restraining the Licence, of Booksellers*. Since in a Case so *notorious* as the printing a Gentleman's PRIVATE LETTERS, most Eminent, both *Printers* and *Booksellers*, conspired to assist the Pyracy both in printing and in vending the same.

P.S.

We are Inform'd, that notwithstanding the Pretences of *Edmund Curl*, the Original Letters of Mr. *Pope* with the Post-Marks upon them, remain still in the Books from whence they were copy'd, and that so many Omissions and Interpolations have been made in this Publication as to render it Impossible for Mr. *P.* to own them in the Condition they appear.

Here, then, are the grounds to justify an 'authentic' version, for which Pope had been angling from the start. 'Print' in this passage includes the agency of publishing (finding the material and preparing it for the press), prior to a third stage of selling the finished product to the public. To widen the circulation of the *Narrative*, it was reprinted in Cooper's volumes – but, more to our purpose, the text figures in the next assault by Pope's foe. It appears in the new volume of letters that Curll was preparing, accompanied by detailed refutations and slick comments by the bookseller, embedded *in situ*.

An Excellent Machine

The increasing boldness of his adversary now had Pope seriously worried. His private correspondence is littered with warnings to friends. We have already seen his remarks to John Caryll on 12 May about Curll's 'shameless industry'. It is hard to think that these complaints were wholly sincere, since Pope needed to have his letters leaked to Curll for the fulfilment of his plan. Again, he asks Lord Oxford on 17 June to return some materials relating to Francis Atterbury and William Wycherley, with the obvious intention of using these in his authorized edition. He adds,

> Since I saw you, I have learn'd of an Excellent Machine of Curl's (or rather, his Director's) to ingraft a Lye upon, to make me seem more concern'd than I was in the affair of the Letters: It is so artfull an one, that I longd to tell it you: Not that I will enter into any Controversy with such a Dog, or make myself a publick antagonist to a Tom Turdman.[4]

The director is clearly none other than Pope himself.

The whole affair was getting even more tangled. George Sherburn comments on the 'excellent machine':

> [Curll] also advertised (*St James's Evening Post*, 3 June) 'the receipt of a packet of Bishop Atterbury's letters from Paris, to Mr. Pope', and in the *Post-Boy* (16 June) announced: 'Bishop Atterbury's Letters to Mr. Pope I am ready to shew any Gentleman, and the Original Letters under Mr. Pope's own Hand, which are to be in this Second Volume' [of the *Literary Correspondence*]. Pope probably well knew that much of this

was false: Curll had received no packet of letters to or by Pope and as the event proved had no unpublished originals that concerned Pope . . . Perhaps the 'machine' was the project of an 'authentic' edition, which Pope soon announced.[5]

The poet's unease must have grown when he saw this advertisement in the *St James's Evening Post* on 12 July:

EXHIBIT 15.4

To Mr. POPE,

Sir, We were very lately of one Mind; and, as you say, *Never had, nor ever intended to have any* private *Correspondence with each other.* But, as I assur'd you, I really was, *directed to write to you.* What has been the Consequence, the Town is now well acquainted with. A PUBLICK Correspondence, in Justice to myself, I will hold with you, to convince Mankind that you are not like *Achilles,* invulnerable.

Next *Monday,* the 14th Instant, I shall publish the SECOND VOLUME of your *Literary Correspondence*; and am ready to produce the Originals (under your own Hand and Seal) therein contained.

Bishop Atterbury's Letters to you are, you well know, Genuine; and some other Pieces of that great Man, which I had of his Son, &c. together with his last Will, which fully proves he did not die a Papist.

The *State-Letters* of Mr. Prior, Mr. Addison, and Mr. Harley, open *some Scenes,* which, I dare say, *some People* had much rather should have remain'd closed up, and been eternally forgotten – But as your Christian Prelate says,

– *Reminiscitur Argos* . . .

I have made you my Patron, in sheltering the Contents, above recited, under your Name, and as you are well acquainted with the true Intent of these Kind of Compliments, I hope, Sir, you will not send me *empty away.*

I am, Sir, yours till the next Opportunity, E. Curll.

Rose street July 12, 1735.

P.S. Your House, Sir, in a Curious Print I shall publish next Month; and your Picture from *Richardson* I intend for the Frontispiece of the Third Volume of your *Literary Correspondence*, which is now actually in the Press. E. Curll.[6]

It was a good thing for the bookseller that celebrities were unable to copyright their image, as can happen today. The contents of the volume don't warrant a detailed gloss here, but the quotation from the 'Christian prelate' makes a shrewd thrust; its author is Virgil, and it comes from the tenth book of the *Aeneid*: 'as he dies, he remembers his dear Argos' (the home of his youth). The phrase towards the end alludes to the Magnificat, derived from Luke 1:53: 'He hath filled the hungry with good things; and the rich he hath sent empty away.' Curll always enjoyed showing off his knowledge of the classics and the Bible, in order to match Pope's regular use of these sources.

The poet had further cause for concern. He was now in almost constant touch with his lawyer William Fortescue, seeking a legal remedy for the various incursions on his private property. 'Since I left you,' he wrote, 'I am informed Curl has servd a Process upon Cooper, (the Publisher of the Letters which I told you I connived at, who Enterd them in the Hall-book) for what I know not? only I am told he put an advertisement into a news paper against Curll – I bid him send you the Process, that you may judge what is to be done in it; If any thing be necessary, pray acquaint me.'[7] A more urgent and even desperate note surfaces in a letter around 13 July. Pope wants to know from Fortescue exactly where he stands in terms of getting an injunction while the courts are on vacation:

EXHIBIT 15.5

Curl has reprinted my Letters with the addition of a great deal of Scandal of his own putting upon me, which he advertizes to be published to morrow. I apprehend as it is just after the Term, an

Injunction can't be got out against him. But this you know best, & pray tell me – Nevertheless as I understand, his pyrated book may be *seized* and *damaskd & made waste paper of*, by my authority, or by his who has Enterd them in the Hall book as his property, according to the Act of Queen Anne yet subsisting. If so, I would by all means have T. Cooper & Gilliver who enterd it, search in the Printing houses, & at Curl's own Shop to morrow & destroy all they can. If, to this end, there be any Writing or Powers necessary from me to them, pray let it be sent to me by an Express Messenger to Twitnam, & I'll sign & return it with all speed. Or perhaps They alone who *Enter'd*, may be inabled to do it . . .

Curl certainly publishes to morrow, or I would not have troubled you so suddenly: I knew not of it till yesterday.[8]

To 'damask' was 'to deface or destroy, by stamping or marking with lines and figures' (*OED*). Pope was right that this measure was allowed under the Copyright Act. It is to be hoped that Fortescue was on a good retainer, with all the demands the poet made of him.

This new sense of acute pressure on the poet marks a shift in the balance of power, and it throws into stronger relief the insouciant air that Curll was affecting.

STOLEN AND SURREPTITIOUS COPIES

Things were escalating in a manner that Pope had neither anticipated nor wanted. He found himself like the sorcerer's apprentice, unable to stem the growing flood that his 'machine' had magically set in motion. One extra-legal mechanism of which he could avail himself was an advertisement placed in the official *London Gazette* on 15 July:

EXHIBIT 15.6

Whereas several Booksellers have printed several surreptitious and incorrect Editions of *Letters* as mine, some of them which are not so, and others interpolated; and whereas there are Daily Advertisements of *Second* and *Third Volumes* of more such *Letters*, particularly my Correspondence with the *late Bishop of Rochester*; I think myself under a Necessity to publish such of the said Letters as are genuine, with the Addition of some others of a Nature less insignificant; especially those which pass'd between the said *Bishop* and myself, or were any way relating to him: Which shall be printed with all convenient Speed.

A. Pope. July 14, 1735.

With tension steadily mounting, the poet contacted Fortescue again on 2 August, this time in connection with a different threat, posed by an illicit edition of items from the second volume of his collected *Works*. He needed a new solicitor to explore the chances of a successful lawsuit:

EXHIBIT 15.7

We cannot find out who is the pirater of my works, therefore cannot move for an injunction, (though they are sold over all the town;) that injury I must sit down with, though the impression cost me above £200, as the case yet stands, there being above half the impression unsold. Curl is certainly in it, but we can get no proof. He has done me another injury, in propagating lies in Fog's Journal of Saturday last, which I desire you to see, and consider if not matter for an information.[9]

'Information' is an obsolete term for an official complaint against someone, lodged with a court or magistrate. By this time Pope was inclined to blame everything on Curll, who had proved so skilful in evading legal sanctions. In fact, this time the culprit is more likely to have been Thomas Johnson, a pirate with an ostensible base in The Hague.

But Pope was right about the latest provocation from his arch-enemy, who had been emboldened by his victory in the House of Lords, and became ever more sure of himself. The new challenge appeared on 26 July in *Fog's Weekly Journal*, a continuation of Nathaniel Mist's paper after the proprietor had been obliged to flee to Boulogne, where he took part in the Pretender's information network. The notice is presented as an open letter to the public. Curll gives an account of the main events to this point, and, more importantly, announces his ongoing plans:

EXHIBIT 15.8

From Pope's Head, in Rose-street, Covent-Garden, July 26. Mr. Pope having put me under a Necessity of using him as he deserves, I hereby declare, That the *First Volume* of his LETTERS which I publish'd on the 12th of May last, was sent me ready printed, by himself; and for *Six hundred* of which I contracted with his Agent *R. Smythe* who came to me in the Habit of a Clergyman. I paid the said *R. Smythe* half the Sum contracted for, and have his Receipt in full for *Three hundred Books*, tho' it has since, by him, been honestly own'd that he delivered me but *Two hundred and Forty Books*, and those all imperfect. For this Treatment I shall have Recourse to a Legal Remedy. Mr. Pope in the Grub street Journal (a Libel wherein he has been concerned from its Original) the Daily Journal, and the Daily Post Boy, declared these Letters to be *Forgeries*, and complained of them to the House of Lords; which Falshood was detected before that most August Assembly; and upon my Acquittal, he publishes a very idle Narrative of a Robbery committed upon two Manuscripts, one in his Own, and the other in the Earl of *Oxford*'s Library. This Fallacy being likewise expos'd, he now Advertises *he shall with all convenient Speed* publish *some Letters* himself, particularly relating to his Correspondence with the Bishop of Rochester. But the Publick may be assur'd, that, if any Letters Mr. Pope himself, or any of his Tools, shall think fit to publish, are the same, or any Way interfere, with those I have publish'd, that the same shall be instantly reprinted by me.

The *Second Volume of Mr. Pope's Literary Correspondence*, contains the Remainder of his Own Letters to *Henry Cromwell* Esq; Bishop Atterbury's Letters to Mr. Pope, and some other curious Pieces which I had of his Son . . .

The *Third Volume of Mr. Pope's Literary Correspondence*, I shall publish next Month, ORIGINALS being every Day sent me, some of them to a certain DUTCHESS, which I am ready to produce under *his own Hand*.

I know not what Honours Mr. Pope would have confer'd on him. 1st. I have hung up his *Head*, for my *Sign*. And 2dly. I have engraved a fine View of his House, Gardens, &c. from Mr. Rijsbrack's Painting, which will shortly be publish'd. But if he aims at any farther Artifices, he never found himself more mistaken than he will, in trifling with me. E. CURLL.[10]

Repercussions followed immediately. According to his later account, Curll was surprised to find in the next week's paper an apology by the printer for inserting this notice. When he went round to enquire as to the reason, he was told by the printer, 'who is a very honest man', that he had made the retraction to oblige Mr. Pope. Allegedly the poet, 'with some of his pettifoggers, threatened to bring an information against the paper, which was the only motive for this ridiculous recantation'.[11] Meanwhile, on 7 August the *Grub Street Journal*, a reliable volunteer as ever on the side of Pope, had some good counsel to give to his enemy: 'Curll, let me advise you whatever betides, / To let this third Volume alone; / The Second's sufficient for *all* our Backsides, / So pray keep the Third for your *own*.'

Pope would have to admit that this was not the first nor the last occasion on which the bookseller got under his skin. A few days later he wrote with some trepidation to Lord Bathurst, 'Pray can you find any thing about the Duchess of Buckinghams Letters, or does she know what they are, which that Rascal Curl has advertised? I cannot conceive the least of 'em.' In fact, Curll had dug up only one letter, from around the date of the duke's death in 1721, and it has nothing very compromising in it. Over in Ireland, meanwhile, Swift had got news of his friend's reverse at Westminster: 'I am ashamed of your House of Lords, who could not, or perhaps would not, punish such a profligate villain as Curl, who hath murdred so many poets for thirty years past.' And again in his next letter to Pope: 'You merited a better treatment from the House of Lords, than that they should let so infamous and so abandoned a Rogue triumph over you in so publick a manner.'[12]

Was it possible that Curll would be able to find more ways of annoying Pope at this juncture? He could and he did. On 26 June he sent out into the world a pamphlet called *The Poet Finish'd in Prose*, and bearing the subtitle *Being a Dialogue concerning Mr. Pope and his Writings*. The ostensible target is the recent series of *Moral Essays* and Horatian imitations, especially their pendant, the *Epistle to Arbuthnot*. However, greater emphasis is placed on the poet's life history. One passage suggests that his horse Pegasus once took a false step (presumably meaning *The Dunciad*) and threw his rider to the ground, landing in a dunghill. This caused Pope to break into a delirious fever, with frequent relapses: 'It is no surprise that his Imagination is, during these Paroxysms, a little dirty.'[13] Further, he developed a sexual phobia, deriving from his relations with 'Sappho' (code for Lady Mary Wortley Montagu, in the *Epistle*). His fear of being raped by the lady has led him to avoid the company of women, and to practise self-abuse instead.

The pamphlet ignores the current battle over Pope's letters. It has a single germane section, in which a participant in the dialogue recommends taunting the poet in a form of bear-baiting: 'Talk of a *Monkey*, and he kicks; mention *Tonson, Shakespear*, or Subscriptions, and he roars; but name *Curl*, or the *House of Lords*, and he runs full butt at you as far as his Rope will give him Leave.' Towards the end, one of the interlocutors states that he has assembled a file on Pope's detractors:

> I have . . . got already a *Catalogue* of more than *five Millions*, who accuse Mr. *Pope* of *Vanity, Insolence, Arrogance, Impiety, Knavery, Ingratitude*, and many other Crimes of the like Kind. As this *List* will probably increase to a large *Bulk*, I intend about ten Days hence to load a *Waggon* with it, and send it off to *Twickenham*, that Mr. *Pope* may, like Lord *Jefferies*, entertain himself with hanging 'em by Thousands, whenever he has an Inclination.[14]

The comparison aligns Pope with the notorious judge George Jeffreys, who in the reign of the Catholic monarch James II had sent some two hundred Protestants to the gallows and many more to transportation, following the Monmouth Rebellion. Whigs liked to remind Tories of this piece of recent history.

IN THE HORTULAN DIALECT

While all this was going on, Curll surpassed himself in sheer intrepidity. What he did was all the more astounding at this vulnerable moment because it breached all norms of polite behaviour. He was, after all, facing injunctions and risking some form of retaliation, not just from Pope but also from established members of the book trade. There were still peers such as Oxford and Bathurst who felt aggrieved by his seeming ability to get away without condign punishment when hauled before the Lords. A good lawyer specializing in damage limitation would surely counsel more discretion and less valour. Despite that, his latest move was to commission a leading topographic artist to make a detailed illustration of the poet's house and garden, to which he added a prose commentary clearly implying that an uninvited guest, openly identified as Curll himself, had conducted a close survey of the property. As Maynard Mack states, it looks very much as if 'he has penetrated the actual garden.'[15] Such an invasion of privacy was an act unthinkable in this age for anyone who aspired to genteel status. It rivalled the most intrusive behaviour by paparazzi in our own day.

News of his adventure soon reached the press, as the *Daily Post Boy* reported, 'On Thursday Mr. Curll, with a very eminent painter, went to Twickenham, to survey the house, gardens, statues and grotto, with inscriptions thereon, &c. and has ordered draughts thereof to be taken which will be engraven by the best masters, and published next month without fail.' The *Grub Street Journal* could come up with only a weak retort, that this story of the survey was 'impracticable'.[16] Curll must have been the source of the leak.

He was proud of what he had done. This is how he described the escapade at the start of *Literary Correspondence*, Volume II:

EXHIBIT 15.9

Mr. CURLL is the sole Editor of this Volume, and it *Is*, what the former *WAS*, a *Collection* of what has been printed, and a *Compilation* from *Original Manuscripts*; but not stolen, either from *Twickenham*, *Wimpole*, or *Dover-street*; but at the last Place, while Mr. *Pope* was dangling, and making *Gilliver* and *Cooper* his Cabinet-Counsel, away goes Mr. *CURLL*, on the 12th Day of *June*, in the Year of our Lord God 1735, and by the Assistance of that Celebrated Artist Mr. *Rijsbrack*, takes a full View of our Bard's Grotto, Subterraneous Way, Gardens, Statues, Inscriptions, and his Dog *BOUNCE*. An Account of some of them are hereunto subjoined. And a *Prospect* of Mr. Pope's *House*, from the *Surrey Side*, is now exhibited, in a curious Print, engraven by the best Hands.

The note was signed Philalethes, which we know to be Curll's favourite nom de plume, with the vainglorious motto 'Veni Vidi Vici.'[17] As for the references, Wimpole in Cambridgeshire was Lord Oxford's country seat, and Dover Street his town house, where Pope was currently lodging on trips to London. The Flemish artist Pieter Andreas Rysbrack had moved to London in about 1720 with his more famous brother, the sculptor John Michael.

Copies of the print survive. They display an uninterrupted view of the house, as well as the lawn leading down to the river, with men, women and children alighting from a small boat moored at the bank. This means that the main garden, which was at the rear of the house, was not shown, despite what Philalethes may suggest. The poet's Great Dane, Bounce, is visible, standing near the villa's undercroft, which afforded access to the famous grotto, and which seems to usher us towards its subterranean secrets. Swans drift calmly by on the river. It is an image of tranquillity and social relaxation, undisturbed by the suspicion of any gatecrasher. At the foot of the print are engraved lines from Pope's imitations of Horace, beginning with the verses, 'Know all the distant din the world can keep / Rolls o'er my grotto, and but soothes my sleep.' The distant din was getting closer.

Towards the end of the volume, Curll gave the account he had promised. It supplies a short description of the property:

EXHIBIT 15.10

It must be allow'd, by all who have seen this Place, that the Owner's Description of it is very just; and every Spectator must bear Testimony how little it owes to Art, either the Place itself, or the Image he has given of it.* But, since that Time, he has been annually improving the Gardens, to the Amount of above Five Thousand Pounds, as Mr. *Serle* his Gardener assured us. He has lived with Mr. *Pope* above Eleven Years, and in the Hortulan Dialect told us, that, *there were not Ten Sticks in the Ground when his Master took the House;*

so that all the Embellishments to this natural Situation have been at the sole Expence of Mr. *Pope*. There is now in the Ground a fine Statue of the *Grecian Venus* Dancing (but it is in the leaden Taste); at the End of one Walk, is a *Busto* of Sir *Isaac Newton*. And in a little Summer-House, another of Mr. *Dryden*.

*See his Letter to Mrs *Blount*, Vol. 1 dated *June* 2, 1725.[18]

It is also noted that 'as a very commendable Act of Filial Respect', the owner has erected an obelisk in memory of his mother. Finally, the author supplies Latin inscriptions, one on the obelisk and one at the entrance to the grotto, with English translations. 'Hortulan' is the sort of fancy expression that Curll loved to throw out, although the word was already on its way to extinction. The tone of almost exaggerated respect contrasts with Curll's usual brutally direct manner. Evidently, he had inveigled himself into the premises with the knowledge of John Searle (d. 1746), a local man who had taken charge of practical gardening activities at Twickenham for a decade. Soon afterwards, an item entitled *The Honour of Parnassus* came on to the market; it presumably contained both print and description together, and it is regularly found in catalogues and advertisements of Popiana from then onwards. Most characteristic of all is the footnote, enabling a puff for the earlier volume of *Literary Correspondence*.

From Curll's point of view, this was a major coup. He had broken through his adversary's carefully managed defences and exposed his private retreat to public view. He had revealed the considerable expense to which Pope had gone in improving the garden – all from the ill-gotten gains of the Homer project, we are meant to think. The reader is invited to become a 'Spectator' gloating over an intimate glimpse of the great poet in his domestic surroundings, with a vicarious insight into his familial concerns. Celebrity culture of the sort we know all too well hardly existed before the modern print media got going. Curll was one of the pioneers in this area, and he promoted his Pope brand to the hilt.

Catching a Tartar

Whatever its merits, the first volume of *Literary Correspondence* was largely made up of letters that had actually passed between Pope and his friends, as the advertisement promised. Things were different with the second volume. It contains an array of varied stuff that Curll had assembled over time, including letters by Addison, John Dryden, Atterbury, Robert Harley in his role as Secretary of State, odd bits of Swiftiana previously collected, and much else irrelevant to the quarrel or to the present issue. What there isn't, apart from Cromwell letters, is any correspondence of Alexander Pope, in flagrant breach of the matter promised in the title. How could Curll get away with such a naked fraud?

The answer is simple. He stuffed the volume with an unprecedented range of varied Popiana, displaying his habitual aggression with a vein of mocking triumphalism. The contents of the first edition (there are changes in the second) are topped and tailed by material relating to the poet. Anyone who wants to see in a single place what Curll did to Pope would do well to start searching here.

First comes quite a good engraving of a Godfrey Kneller portrait, a gesture reflecting the appropriation of the poet's identity carried out by the bookseller. The brief preface, 'To the Reader', opens in defiant mood: 'We presume we stand not in need of any more Apology to the *Reader for THIS Publication*, then we did for the Last; for we hereby declare, that Mr. *POPE*, *E.P.*, *P.T.* and *R.S.* are *ALL out of the Question*.' The writer, 'Philalethes', then gives his account of Curll's expedition to Twickenham, described above. He concludes that nothing further need be added, since Curll has 'fully made good his Promise, to the Lords, of being a Match for Mr. *Pope* in Prose'. He can reply to all the attacks by 'this petulant little Gentleman, especially the last, *VENI VIDI VICI*.'

This is followed by a section headed 'To Mr. Pope', which sets out Curll's take on the quarrel to date. Seldom did Pope and John

Arbuthnot receive a stronger tongue-lashing in all the years that they endured harsh words from the bookseller: 'Remember only, that now is my turn to Punish, and if I have not the Spleen of a warpt Poet, or a *Scots* Medicaster, I will find some other Prescription that shall, once more, as *Shakespeare* says, *harrow up your soul.*' Curll pretends that 'a State Decipherer' has been able to decode the initials P.T. and R.S. – an unwelcome reminder of the government spies who had trapped Atterbury, earning a scornful reference in *Gulliver's Travels* to the sneaky methods the ministry used to track down its opponents.

Perhaps the most striking feature of this part lies in a series of distichs: 'Therefore, confess you have a *Tartar* caught, / Be, once, sincere, and frankly own your fault.' Some are travesties of lines by Pope: 'Thus if with small, great Things may be compar'd, / Kind Fate, at length, may wait on Thief and Bard' (the first verse echoes one from *Windsor Forest*). Again: 'Refrain the Path that leads to Evil, / Tell the plain Truth, and shame the Devil.' A characteristic dig occurs at the number of portraits Pope had commissioned: 'Let various Painters draw your outward Part, / But Human Pencils cannot shew the Heart.' Finally, the repeated motif of symbiosis between the two antagonists: 'A fitter Couple, sure, were never Hatch'd, / Some Marry'd are, indeed, but we are Match'd.'[19] After this comes a deliciously impudent scoresheet in pounds, shillings and pence:

EXHIBIT 15.11

Mr. Alexander Pope, *Debtor to Mr.* Edmund Curll
To an *Advertisement* in the *Post-Man*, 1717, promising
Three Guineas to discover the Publisher of his Version
of the *First Psalm* 3 3 0
To a Promise of Ten Pounds, on producing one
of Bishop *Atterbury's* Letters 10 0 0
To discover the *Publishers* of Mr. *Pope's Letters* 42 0 0
    Total .... 52 3 0.

The next item is a reprint of Pope's *Narrative*, with Curll's sniping commentary in footnotes. On the subject of Cromwell's letters, Curll points out that he purchased them from Elizabeth Thomas, 'as justly as Mr. *Lintot* did the Copy of Mr. *Pope*'s *Homer*, &c.' He detects falsehoods on almost every page, and sets out a record of the affair very different from that of the *Narrative*. In response to Pope's comments about the letters of a private gentleman, he asserts baldly, 'Mr. *Pope* is no more a Gentleman than Mr. *Curll*, nor more eminent as a Poet, than he is as a Bookseller.'[20] That just about sums up the gravamen of Curll's defence throughout the quarrel.

Much the same techniques are used in the epigraphs to the next section, entitled 'The Initial Correspondence: or, Anecdotes of the Life and Family of Mr. Pope', where verses from the *Epistle to Arbuthnot* and the *Essay on Criticism* are turned against their author. The opening passages here go over the biography with which Pope is supposed to have furnished Giles Jacob for the *Poetical Register* in 1719, which we have already come across. Then we find a rehash of the affair involving P.T. and R.S., printing for the first item some letters that have been used in the previous chapter.

There is more to come, starting with an adroit imitation of one of Horace's lesser poems, transposing numerous passages of Pope's verse to reflect badly on him. The anonymous author claims to be one of the poet's victims, and pretends to offer a palinode or apology. Last among the preliminary sections we have four quatrains in Curll's most blustering style on the battle in the House of Lords. The title does not aim at any show of modesty: 'Curll Triumphant; and Pope Out-Witted'.

EXHIBIT 15.12

Pope, meditating to disgrace
Those, whom his *Satire* jeers,
Not long since to a wildgoose chace
Entic'd *Great-Britain*'s Peers.

He led 'em to pursue a Wight
 Egregious – *Curll* his name,
Who not surpriz'd, and in no Fright,
 By this pursuit reap'd Fame.

He undeceiv'd the *Nobles* all,
 More cou'd he wish or hope?
While *Pope* had thus contriv'd his Fall,
 He triumph'd over *Pope*.

The *Vomit* foul, the *Dunciad* keen,
 Vex'd *Curll* – *but* all admit,
Tho' *Pope* twice *shew'd he had most Spleen*,
 Curll once *has shewn most wit*.[21]

On the whole, the verse displays more panache than verbal skill, although the antithesis in the final couplet is deft enough. Here Curll openly admits his desire for fame, perhaps for the first time.

The volume was not done, as far as the quarrel goes. In the text we have items such as a letter from Thomas to Curll, dated 16 June 1726, offering the Cromwell materials for publication. Later on, in a section of miscellaneous poems, a few of the old favourites are reprinted, most conspicuously the version of the first Psalm and the one on Moore's worms. The end of the volume is filled with 'Castrations made by the Editor of Mr. Pope's Letters to Henry Cromwell', 'A Key to the First Volume of Mr. Pope's Literary Correspondence' (explaining allusions), the description of his home at Twickenham already cited, and a reprint of the dialogue between Pope and the chaplain of Newgate. No one could say that Curll lacked the salesman's ability to repackage stale goods.

Prudential Methods

In general, the later volumes of *Literary Correspondence* contain a lesser number of items that have a direct bearing on the feud, and Curll was able to score fewer hits. The third volume came out on 20 September, with a second edition shortly afterwards. Proceedings open with a letter 'To the Subscribers', in which the bookseller congratulated himself on the progress of his undertaking:

EXHIBIT 15.13

Mr. *Pope*'s Project to usher his Letters into the World by my Means, was the Foundation of this Scheme of *A Literary Correspondence*; which has been so well received, that it shall be continued while People of Taste approve of it: And that will be as long as People of Taste, who have valuable Performances in this Kind in their Power, contribute their Stores to the Emolument of Mankind. Not but that I am always ready and willing to purchase any Genuine Pieces from such Possessors as expect a *Premium*.

The second Volume of this Work promised (besides Mr. *Pope*'s) to contain Letters to and from Lord *Somers*, &c. notwithstanding which, Mr. *Pope*, in his Spleen, has employed his Sifters to talk his Sense of the Matter to me; particularly 'Squire *Brocade*, whose Objections, intermixed with my Answers, make a very notable Scene.

An interlocutor proves a feeble defendant for Pope, but he does ask one pertinent question at the start: 'Mr. *Curll*, how comes it that you call this Second Volume *Mr.* Pope's *Correspondence*, when there is so much more of other Peoples: This is a mere Imposition upon the Town.' Curll's answer is mostly bluster, but he regains the initiative a little later: 'Some of my Customers, whose Judgment is much esteemed among their Acquaintance, have said that Mr. *Pope*'s Share in this Second Volume is the very worst Part of the Book.'[22] The exchange concludes when Curll issues a pre-announcement of the fourth volume in his series. This desultory section is followed by a letter of endorsement (Curll never tired of inserting these), with an offer of some new Atterbury correspondence.

The most pertinent element here is a message dated 15 September, headed 'E. Curll ad A. Pope'. It begins with the shamelessly inflated statement, 'That our Name and Fame may be equally transmitted to Posterity, in this our *Literary Correspondence*, most earnestly desiring; A faithful Register of Matters of Fact, will be the best Method for obtaining these desirable Ends,' and goes on to contest Pope's claims with regard to the way in which the letters have been assembled. Curll announces that he has exhibited a bill in Chancery against R. Smythe, 'to hold him to his Contract of delivering to me six hundred printed Copies of the *First Volume* of your Letters'. It is no surprise that no record survives of this action, since the defendant was a straw man. There was room for yet another of Curll's deathless rhymes: 'Flatt'ry in ev'ry Shape I hold a Shame, / And think a Lye in Verse or Prose the same. / Bravo [bully] to God, and Coward unto Man, / The Lyar is; deny this Truth who can?'[23] Again, the second line is lifted from the *Epistle to Arbuthnot*.

Not much in the remainder of the volume need concern us, although it reveals something of the bookseller's methods. Even the odd genuine bit from Pope's hand, such as a poem called 'The Challenge', turns out to be the *Court Ballad* of 1717, which Curll had used at least five times previously. The most intriguing item, so far unexplored, is 'A Letter to Mr. P***', concerning asses, and signed Philo-A---. Its battery of allusions, drawn from the Bible as well as a host of classical authors, together with its references to music and the sneer at Bishop Burnet (a particular bête noire), suggest that the likeliest author is the recently deceased Arbuthnot.

Pope maintained his vigilance in the face of such provocation. He complained in an almost resigned fashion to Bathurst, 'Curl has printed Letters of Mr Pope to Miss Blount, not one of which either

I ever writ, or she ever receivd.' On the same date, 8 October, he wrote to a newer friend, Lord Orrery,

> You speak of my defending the Bishop [Atterbury]'s charac-
> ter against Curl, I can hardly defend my own . . . The most
> necessary Prudential Methods against the vilest of Slanderers,
> are complaind of & set forth by them, as Fraud & Injustice;
> To stop their practises is thought an Invasion of their Right,
> when they have so long exercisd them unpunishd by our
> Law, as if it really favourd only Rascals.[24]

He was continuing to watch Curll's legal manoeuvres, and kept in touch with Fortescue in case they should end in a court case. By now Swift too was apprised of events, and he seems to have had a shrewd idea of the nature of Pope's own machinations. In answer to a request to send back the letters he had received from his friend, Swift said with a calculated blandness on 3 September, 'This is an answer to yours of two months ago, which complains of that profligate fellow Curl . . . You need not fear any consequence in the commerce that hath so long passed between us; although I never destroyed one of your letters.' He gave the same reassurance on 21 October: 'You need not apprehend any Curll's meddling with your letters to me; I will not destroy them, but have ordered my Executors to do that office.'[25] That is not what Pope wanted to hear.

As the year drew to an end, an apparently unconnected publication by Curll made clear just how obsessed he was with his opponent. This was *Post-Office Intelligence*, published on 9 December, a collection of love letters supposedly returned undelivered to the general post office. The only fresh item relevant to the quarrel is 'Rational Remarks upon Mr. Pope's Letters', announced on the title page but not always present in surviving copies. The charges are familiar: the poet is an inveterate libeller, his crooked body reflects a crooked mind, and his letters display the taste for blasphemy and indecency seen in his poetry. He has 'libelled fifty Times as many People as poor *Dryden* ever did'. But one sharp new observation emerges: 'Tho' he quotes the *Rhemish* Bible to *Papists*, yet it is plain he has read our English Translation often; for he has it at his Finger's Ends to Profane it, by applying it on trivial and ludicrous Occasions.'[26] This is one of the more perceptive comments made by any of the adversaries: it is exactly true. Although brought up on the Rheims-Douai version, first published in 1582, Pope evidently knew the King James Bible with an intimacy that few Protestants could match.

The Law of Retaliation

The pace slackened for a brief phase early in 1736. Naturally some odd skirmishes went on, since the dunces had no intention of forgiving Pope. One of those still harbouring the strongest resentment was Giles Jacob, who had incurred Pope's scorn partly because of *The Poetical Register*. On 24 January Curll advertised *Liberty and Property: Or, a New Year's Gift for Mr. Pope*, a legal treatise that Jacob addressed to Pope's friend Bathurst. Nothing much in what Jacob wrote bears on the quarrel, but Curll makes sure that we do not forget it in a rollicking dedication to Pope, which he signed and dated on 15 January. In it he replies to an attack by 'Bavius' (the traditional name for an inept writer, borrowed from a poem by Virgil), which had come out in the *Grub Street Journal* a few days earlier. Lines from *The Dunciad* are switched by Curll so as to apply to Richard Russel and his *Journal*. The address to Pope goes over the contents of the first three volumes of *Literary Correspondence*, and previews those of the fourth. Furthermore, he attacks Lawton Gilliver's conduct, unexpectedly defends the Jacobite antiquarian Thomas Hearne, and sneers at those who take Pope's side:

EXHIBIT 15.14

Sir, You very well know, that if the Letters in the said *First* Volume had not been Genuine, You would not have had any Grounds of Complaint, nor would You; I dare say, have implored the Assistance of the Legislature; for You may find in this Book, that *A* cannot bring an Indictment against the Highwayman who robbed *B*, but *B* himself may. This, Sir, is as plain as *Shakespear*'s Crowner's Quest-law; yet so hard bound are the *Brains* of this poor Scribler, and so *shallow* his *Reading* and *Understanding*, that he cannot distinguish between Your OWNING the *Letters* and DISOWNING them; as if a Gentleman who knows the Use o*er Folks* Riches, as well as his *own*, would pay Eleven Shillings for an *Advertisement* in the *Gazette* to be misunderstood!

The joke in the last sentence picks up on Pope's title for one of his *Moral Essays*, addressed to Bathurst, *On the Use of Riches*. As for the line from Shakespeare, it may be recalled as part of the gravediggers' conversation in the last act of *Hamlet*. As often, the dedication ends with black humour, in a politely expressed desire for Pope's death: 'I heartily wish You a better State of Health, than you at present enjoy, or a happy Departure out of this *Vale of Human Misery*.' The familiar couplet rounds things off, as at the end of a scene in Shakespeare: 'Thus the Attacks upon our Fame I've shown, / And turn'd the whole Illusion on the Town.'[27]

Then it was back to the *Literary Correspondence*. On 25 March came the much-heralded 'Volume the Fourth' in the series. This included a section of 'Muscovian Letters', available separately, and letters between Henry VIII and Anne Boleyn. These names appear on the title page along with those of four bishops and sundry worthies, but nothing can dislodge Pope from his role as presiding spirit, even though he makes only intermittent appearances. The first is in the preface, 'To the Sifters', where a malicious little postscript refers to Pope's supposed relations with a woman of the town called Lucretia (pure fantasy):

EXHIBIT 15.15

Pray, with my *Respects* to Mr. POPE, tell him I am sorry that *Ill Health, Ill Humour, Ill Weather, and the Want of a Coach*, should all conspire to prevent his paying that Visit to LUCRETIA,* which she lately expected from Him; and, tho' she will not by any Means admit of the Term *Affectionate*, he may subscribe Himself her *humble Servant*. The Lady is eloped from her last Lodging, but *He* may hear of his *Deary* at the *Old Place*. She hopes the Picture will please, now the Painter has re-touched it.

*A noted Cast-off-Punk, of his pious *Saint-John*. Mrs *Griffith*, alias *Lucretia Lindo*, who has several Letters of Mr. *Pope's*, not worth printing.[28]

Towards the end of the volume, Curll reprints *Court Poems* for the umpteenth time, complete with the original preface, in defiance of all that had come to light in the intervening years. With accustomed boldness, he collects from notes to *The Dunciad* something he calls 'A Character of Mr. Edmund Curll, Bookseller. By Mr. Pope'. To it he adds his own refutations, aptly in his own series of footnotes. The section is bookended by verses. At the start comes a parody of Curll's entrance as the stationers assemble for their games, quoted in Chapter Twelve. The effect is to transpose a contemptuous description, as supplied by Pope, into a heroic stance, in Curll's version:

> *Before the Lords*, Alone, untaught to fear,
> Stood dauntless CURLL (*and spoke to ev'ry Peer.*)
> He triumph'd, Victor of the high wrought Day!

At the conclusion comes a reinforcement of the point:

Court Poems to this Work are join'd,
That All the World may see;
Pope's Falshoods manifested here,
Hinc illae Lacrymae.[29]

It's easy to see the relish with which Curll turns against his opponent a proverbial Latin phrase employed by none other than Horace
in his *Epistles* – some of which Pope was even now using as the
basis of his poetry.

However, the most notable feature of the book is found in the
middle. This section contains a full reprint of *Sober Advice from
Horace*, Pope's imitation of a satire by Horace and his most openly
obscene work. The Latin text is given at the foot of each page, below
the English verses. The *Advice*, which appeared anonymously at
the end of 1734, was something of a gift to Curll. The publisher was
a certain Thomas Boreman, and that fact does not go unnoticed
when the bookseller augments the original title page:

EXHIBIT 15.16

SOBER ADVICE FROM HORACE, TO THE Young GENTLEMEN about Town.
As delivered in his SECOND SERMON.
IMITATED in the Manner of Mr. POPE.
Together with the *Original Text*, as restored by the Reverend RICH-
ARD BENTLEY, Doctor of Divinity. And some Remarks on the *Version*.
Printed for *T. Boreman*, at the *Cock* on *Ludgate-Hill*, 1735; who
having taken the Liberty, lately, to Print some Poems which are my
Property, I here return him the Compliment, in Part, as I always
will, whoever attacks me, by way of *Lex Talionis*, i.e. the just *Law*
of *Retaliation*.
E.C.

The dedication to Pope is supposedly written by the poet in praise
of himself: a form of gentle self-mockery, until it was appropriated

by his enemy. Throughout the poem, Curll adds his own comments, fully entering into its bawdy spirit. He misses no opportunity
to carry the quarrel into his scholia; when there is a reference to
Mother Needham, a notorious brothel-keeper of the age, he does
not hang back: 'A Quondam *Bawd of high Renown*, / In whose
Apartments P— has oft been seen, / Patting Fore-Buttocks, to
divert the Spleen.'[30]

Some copies have bound in at the end of the volume a catalogue
of twenty-five 'New Books'. As has been pointed out, this list 'is
itself a document in the war [Curll] was waging with Pope'.[31] By this
date he was advertising *Seven Select Pieces* by Pope, including some
items whose rights he assuredly did not own; they belonged either
to Bernard Lintot or to the author. At the same time he was marketing *A Collection of the Several Critiques which have been Written
upon Mr. Pope's Works*. Two volumes of this stuff would cost you
ten shillings, but you could get individual items singly at one shilling. Most of these date either from the *Dunciad* era or from the last
few months, but Charles Gildon's old warhorse *The New Rehearsal*
was still plodding along after twenty years. The same advertisement offers the set of *Literary Correspondence*, Pope's select poems,
the *Essay on Man* (another piracy), the print and description of his
house and garden, and four prints of the poet 'in different Attitudes'.

On the day after Curll's fourth volume was published, Pope gave
Fortescue his reaction, with a further statement of intent concerning
plans for an authentic edition:

EXHIBIT 15.17

Your too partial mention of the book of Letters, with all its faults and
follies, which Curl printed and spared not, (nor yet will spare, for he
has published a fourth sham volume yesterday,) makes one think it
may not be amiss to send you, what I know you will be much more
pleased with than I can be, a proposal for a correct edition of them;
which at last I find must be *offered*, since people have misunderstood

Studious he sate, with all his books around, Plung'd for his sense, but found no bottom there; Sinking from thought to thought, a vast profund: Then writ, and flounder'd on, in mere despair.

DUNCIAD. Book I. line III.

William Hogarth, *The Distrest Poet*, 1736, engraving. In the picture on the wall at the top right, Pope is seen beating Curll for his publication of the *Literary Correspondence*.

an advertisement I printed some time ago, merely to put some stop to that rascal's books, as a promise that I would publish such a book.[32]

He was now getting closer to the goal he had originally set himself.

From Curll's point of view, however, things continued to look rosy. He still had to face some effective sniping from the *Grub Street Journal* (see Exhibit 13.10), but he was used to that. In July 1736 he posed a fresh challenge to the poet when he published *An Essay on Human Life by the Author of the Essay on Man*. He knew perfectly well that Pope was not the author of this piece, a piratical version of an undistinguished work by Thomas Catesby Paget.

On the title page he hid behind the name 'J. Witford', a deliberately false imprint suggesting his current partner in crime, John Wilford, but he regularly included the item in his advertisements and catalogues. Overall, during the past twelve months he had set the agenda, and in his own eyes he now held the mastery. He had gained ground on his opponent through much of 1735 and 1736. In an effort to solidify his position, he began to project the fifth and, as it proved, final volume of the *Literary Correspondence*. A truncated version was announced in November: 'This Day is published (from the Original Manuscripts, transmitted from Ireland) with a curious Print of Lord Bolingbroke, *Letters written by Mr. Pope and Lord Bolingbroke, to Dean Swift, in the Year 1723*.'[33] The title page of this preliminary text bore the name *New Letters of Alexander Pope, and Several of his Friends*, but it was superseded the following July by Volume v in its entirety.

But that was after a lapse of time, which had given Pope the chance to assemble his own materials. The dynamics of the feud would now shift once more.

16

FINAL Exchanges, 1737–47

It was time for Pope to get back into the harness. Since the publication of the *Epistle to Arbuthnot* and the last of his four *Moral Essays* at the start of 1735, he had produced no major work. Other issues had occupied his mind, not just battles over the *Literary Correspondence*, but also the publication of the second volume of his *Works* later in 1735. He still held a position of influence among the Opposition circle, although his closest ally among its leaders, Bolingbroke, had gone back to France, disillusioned by the failure to dislodge Robert Walpole. It was not until the spring of 1737 that Pope resumed a full combat role with two new imitations, notably the brilliant *Epistle to Augustus*, one of the most powerful assaults ever mounted against George II and his prime minister. There would be two more in 1738, not counting an epilogue to the series in two parts, where Pope sets out the justification for his satiric aims and methods. They are works of a remarkably savage eloquence, much more abrasive and direct in style than most of his earlier writing. However, they surprisingly forbear to offer any comment on the dunces, except for scattered thrusts at Colley Cibber. It is as though politics has finally driven out mundane literary matters from his concerns; nobody yet knew that he had a revised and much augmented *Dunciad* in store for its victims.

This is a misleading picture in one important respect. In May, Pope brought out the long-awaited edition of his *Letters* in the form he had always desired, which allowed him to edit them however he chose. Here was a justification for his involvement in the bitter feud that had consumed so much of his time. Although Curll made unblushing use of this material in the last volume of the *Literary Correspondence*, the main thing was that Pope had now placed before the public the version of his output, and of himself, that he wanted people to see. In the preface, after expressing regret at the way in which the Cromwell and Wycherley letters had been published, he inveighs against the treatment he had received from the trade:

EXHIBIT 16.1

It is notorious, how many volumes have been publish'd under the title of his Correspondence, with promises still of more, and open and repeated offers of encouragement to all persons who should send any letters of his for the press. It is as notorious what methods were taken to procure them, even from the Publisher's own accounts in his prefaces, viz. by transacting with people in necessities, or of abandon'd characters, or such as dealt without names in the dark. Upon a quarrel with one of these last, he betray'd himself so far as to appeal to the publick in Narratives and Advertisements: like that Irish Highway-man a few years before, who preferr'd a Bill against his Companion, for not sharing equally in the mony, rings and watches, they had traded for in Partnership upon *Hounslow-heath*.[1]

Hounslow Heath was perhaps the most feared haunt of the notorious gentlemen of the road. Covering an area of 25 square miles, its scrubby landscape was crossed by the Bath road. Between the villages of Hounslow and Staines stood gibbets where the bodies of highwaymen hung in chains, sometimes for decades.

The preface moves on to an impassioned attack on the methods used by booksellers to attain their ends. They do not need to be named:

EXHIBIT 16.2

To state the case fairly in the present situation. A Bookseller advertises his intention to publish your Letters: He openly promises encouragement, or even pecuniary rewards, to those who will help him to any; and ingages to insert whatever they shall send: Any scandal is sure of a reception, and any enemy who sends it skreen'd from a discovery. Any domestick or servant, who can snatch a letter from your pocket or cabinet, is encouraged to that vile practise. If the quantity falls short of a volume, any thing else shall be join'd with it (more especially scandal) which the collector can think for his interest, all recommended under your Name: You have not only Theft to fear, but Forgery. Any Bookseller, tho' conscious in what manner they were obtain'd, not caring what may be the consequences to your Fame or Quiet, will sell and disperse them in town and country. The better your Reputation is, the more your Name will cause them to be demanded, and consequently the more you will be injur'd. The injury is of such a nature, as the Law (which does not punish for *Intentions*) cannot prevent; and when done, may punish, but not redress. You are therefore reduc'd, either to enter into a personal treaty with such a man, (which tho' the readiest, is the meanest of all methods) or to take such other measures to suppress them, as are contrary to your Inclination, or to publish them, as are contrary to your Modesty. Otherwise your Fame and your Property suffer alike; you are at once expos'd and plunder'd.[2]

This impressive statement concerns what was often a genuine grievance for established writers. We are bound to read it a little differently, knowing the way in which Pope had set up Curll in the present case. Likewise with Pope's argument that an individual so placed suffers as an author, as a man and as a member of society. Opening private letters, the preface concludes, is a breach of honour: 'What then can be thought of the procuring them merely by Fraud, and the printing them merely for Lucre?'[3] It is a fair argument against Curll's habitual methods, but not one that really applies to the *Literary Correspondence*. Whatever the merits of this case, however, the volume helped to return the initiative to Pope. For the first time in a long while, the bookseller needed to catch up with the poet.

Luckily, Curll was out of the firing line most of the time. Even the appearance of the fifth volume of the *Literary Correspondence* in the summer of 1737 prompted no immediate response from his adversary. The book indeed contained less provocative material than before. To be sure, there were plenty of items of Pope's correspondence with Jonathan Swift, John Arbuthnot, John Gay, Francis Atterbury and others, but these were selected from the authorized edition of *Letters* that the poet had recently issued. Moreover, Curll managed also to restrain himself as regards the facetious notes he generally supplied. Only two items serve as a reminder of the bookseller's most insolent way of taunting his foe. One is the short opening address, 'To my Subscribers *encore*':

EXHIBIT 16.3

GENTLEMEN,

Having, as you All know, honestly Purchased the *First* Volume of Mr. POPE's *Literary Correspondence* of his Agent the Reverend Mr. *Smith*; Published and paid my Respects to my BENEFACTOR in the *Second*; Dispatched BROCADE and TIM LANCET in the *Third*; and, Got rid of the SHIFTERS [*sic*] in the *Fourth*; I now come to give you a just Account of the Contents of this *Fifth* Volume.

Beside, what is here presented to You, I have Several other very valuable Originals in my Custody, which, with these, were Transmitted to me from *Ireland*. And this Volume will be closed with whatever *additional Letters* Mr. POPE shall think fit to insert in his WORKS in PROSE, now printing in *Quarto*, Price a Guinea; but the Controversy between ME and Mr. POPE will never be ended till the

Eyes of one of Us are *closed* (I mean by *Death*, not by Dr *Taylor*) if *Mine* are open longest, to the last Volume of *Literary Correspondence* shall be prefixed A faithful Account of Mr. POPE's Life and Writings, with a true Copy of his Last Will and Testament, if he makes one.

I am, Gentlemen, Your obliged Humble Servant, E. CURLL.

5 Nov. 1736.[+]

John 'Chevalier' Taylor was a well-known oculist, of whom it was said that he 'possessed much skill as an operator, but advertised like a charlatan'.

The other part of the volume that possesses a little of the old shock value is Curll's final set of verses against his antagonist, once more taking off from a Horatian imitation by Pope and twisting the words to his advantage. He alludes to their quarrel over the letters, and then gets in some jibes at fellow members of the trade, whom Pope had recently employed as his agents. The most notable of these is Robert Dodsley, a former servant who had begun an illustrious career as a bookseller and had also written a farce, *The Toy-Shop* (1735):

EXHIBIT 16.4

The Town still judge you in a proper light,
Whether Lampoons or Letters you indite;
Sober Advice from *Horace* you have giv'n,
Yet disavow it in the face of Heav'n,
To this and other Points you're quite excentric,
Till you put in your Claim, that All's Authentic . . .
But what have *Tonson*, *Lintot*, *Lawton*, done,
That you to *Brindley*, *Corbet*, *Dodsley* run?
'Tis kind indeed a Liv'ry Muse to aid,
Who scribbles Farces to augment his Trade.

The parodist moves on to Pope's claims with regard to the persecution Catholics had undergone, and concludes with an almost fond farewell:

EXHIBIT 16.5

It was for *Lintot*'s Gold that you begun
To rime from *Greek* the wrath of *Peleus*' Son,
Rest to your Father's Soul: who from a Lad,
Taught you the Art to know the Good from Bad.
All Laws by Those who smart are thought unjust,
Thieves only swing poor Souls for Breach of Trust.
The Pious hopes of Papists still will fail,
Whilst *Brunswick* Rules and *Hardwick* holds the Scale . . .
    Thus, for your Sake Sir, I have play'd the Fool,
As Boys make random Verses when at School,
And when you offer any thing that's New
Wagging must be my Quill, and so Adieu.
E. Curll.[5]

Of course, he had no means of knowing that one of Lord Chancellor Hardwicke's acts when he held the scales of justice under 'Brunswick' (George II) would be to rule in favour of the plaintiff in the case of *Pope* v. *Curll*.

A BOOKSELLER FOR BREAD

With the *Literary Correspondence* now complete, its publisher grew less zealous in pursuit of his quarry. He kept on advertising his large arsenal of Popiana in catalogues, but his attacks became more sporadic. His decision to publish the translation of a critical commentary on the *Essay on Man* by the Swiss theologian Jean-Pierre de Crousaz must have been meant to elicit a response from the poet, but none came.

It was the same when the two parts of Pope's trenchant *Epilogue to the Satires* appeared under the title *One Thousand Seven Hundred and Thirty Eight*. More than twelve months passed before a riposte emerged with *One Thousand Seven Hundred Thirty Nine. A Rhapsody. By way of Sequel to Seventeen Hundred Thirty Eight* [*sic*], *by Mr. Pope*. The imprint reads, 'printed for J. Cooper, in Fleet-Street . . . Where may be had All Mr. Pope's Works'. There never was such an individual as J. Cooper (as opposed to the very real publishing couple Thomas and Mary Cooper); he had been recently invented by Curll as a convenient way to mislead people. It is quite a short poem, sneering at the supposed qualities – actually defects – of leading Opposition figures, including Bolingbroke, William Pulteney, Lyttelton and William Wyndham, who were all friends of Pope. This form of satiric inversion had been used against Walpole's adherents in the *Epilogue*, where one of those ironically celebrated was Lord De La Warr. This must have served as Pope's payback for the verdict of the Lords in 1735. But the new offering, *One Thousand Seven Hundred Thirty Nine*, soon loses interest in its ostensible target. All we get about Pope is a passage looking forward to a time when he will show 'no Malice or no Envy'.

EXHIBIT 16.6

Whose peevish Pride, without Distinction, flings
His Dirt, on Players, Poets, Peers, and Kings:
Or if he praises, modestly replies,
'Praise undeserv'd, is Satire in Disguise.'
With Names at length behold his Poems swell;
Scandal and Slander make a Poem sell:
Italics, CAPITALS, each Page supply,
Like *Cibber's* Play-Bills, set to catch the Eye,
And raise Curiosity in Passers-by:
This Peerless Poet we as justly name,
A Bookseller for Bread, as Bard for Fame.[6]

In earlier exchanges, Curll and his authors had packed more of a punch, especially when they advanced the charge that Pope had become a commercial vendor of his writings as much as a poet seeking renown for work of high literary qualities.

Equally, the main thrust of another pamphlet is directed against a different enemy of the bookseller, and here Curll's motives pose a puzzle. This was *The Tryal of Colley Cibber, Comedian, &c. for Writing a Book Intitled An Apology for his Life, &c. Being a Thorough Examination thereof; wherein he is Proved Guilty of High-Crimes and Misdemeanors against the English Language, and in Characterising many Persons of Distinction*, published in July 1740. The dedication is signed 'T. Johnson', perhaps a sly nod in the direction of a notorious pirate in the publishing world. It consists of an unauthorized reprint of some essays by Henry Fielding, in his paper *The Champion*, with added comments. The pamphlet contains a section described as 'An Indictment Exhibited against Alexander Pope of Twickenham, Esq; for not exerting his Talents at this Juncture'. This is based on an issue of *Champion* from 17 May 1740. The accusation brought before Captain Hercules Vinegar (Fielding's persona) is that Pope failed to deter 'one *Forage*, alias *Guts*, alias *Brass*' from committing and perpetrating 'all Sorts of Roguery'.[7] 'Brass' was one of the most common nicknames for Walpole, sometimes in the form 'Sir Robert Brass' or 'Brazen Face'. 'Guts' would be an apt name for the portly prime minister, too. 'Forage' clearly points to the charge by the Opposition that Walpole had enriched himself from the spoils of public office – it was true, of course, but no more than was the case with other leading politicians. But there is a more specific allusion. In 1712 Walpole had been accused of corruption during his tenure as Secretary at War, involving two army contracts for forage (military food and provisions). He was actually impeached by the House of Commons for 'a high breach of trust' – just as Pope is here, in effect.

The difficulty is that Pope had been one of the most open and daring critics of Walpole's government, and this renders absurd

the putative defence offered by his counsel – that it was dangerous to speak or write against Guts because by 'the Statute of *Noli
me tangere*' anyone caught in the act would be 'ruined and starved'
along with his children.[8] It is hard to see how Curll thought this
would damage Pope. It may be that he was by now more intent on
his vendetta against Cibber.

One unidentified, but quite talented, poet had fun with both
literary luminaries. This came in the shape of a dialogue called
Sawney and Colley, issued by James Roberts in August 1742. It makes
much of the story concerning Pope's misadventures at a Haymarket
brothel, which we heard about early on. But it also touches on the
great fracas over the letters. Colley addresses Sawney: 'But with
the *Wizard*, CURLL, to *juggle*, / And, *Hocus Pocus*, help him smuggle
/ Thy Correspondence with thy Betters, / Theirs extemp're, thine
studied LETTERS.' The passage continues:

EXHIBIT 16.7

> Nay, more to rivet the Deceit,
> Thy *Lord* must consecrate the Cheat,
> An Insult on the House of *Peers*.
> For which you ought to have *lost your Ears*,
> Then thou and CURLL, akin by Trade,
> Had been *par nobile Fratrum* made.

Sawney retorts angrily at being coupled with Curll, and Colley
offers a mock apology, remembering that the bookseller claimed
he had never lost an ear (which was true, of course): 'And, tho' oft
pillory'd, have still,/ Both your *Auriculars* at will.'[9] Although he
doesn't seem to have published this item, did Curll write it himself?
It's certainly possible.

SWIFTIANA

Once more, there was no public response to the two latest pamphlets from Curll. Privately, his activities continued to irritate the Popians, as their correspondence shows. At the very end of 1736 Pope had sent a warning to Swift, 'this last month Curl has obtain'd from Ireland two letters, (one of Lord Bolingbroke and one of mine, to you) which we wrote in the year 1723, and he has printed them, to the best of my memory, rightly, except one passage.' Very likely the poet had himself fed these letters to the publisher, in a renewed effort to alarm Swift so much that he would send back those that he had from Pope. Further efforts involved the agency of Lord Orrery, a mutual friend of the two satirists who would later write a controversial biography of Swift, the first of many. On 4 March 1737 Pope asked Orrery to intercede to help 'secure [him] against at that Rascal Printer', mentioning his fears that the Dean was now unduly influenced by the people around him in Dublin, and giving dark hints that his friend might be losing his memory – the first intimation here of the dementia that was to cloud Swift's final years. Two weeks later Orrery passed on Pope's letter to Swift. He also referred to 'part of a fifth Volume of Curl's Thefts, in which you'l find two Letters to You (One from Mr. Pope the Other from Lord Bolingbroke) just publish'd with an impudent Preface by Curl. You see, Curl like his Freind the Devil glides thro' all Key holes, and thrusts himself into the most private Cabinets.'[10]

As Swift's mental abilities declined further, there was a new obstacle to Pope's ambitions in the shape of Martha Whiteway, a first cousin once removed of the Dean, now acting through a kind of unofficial power-of-attorney arrangement. The ups and downs of this struggle do not relate to the feud, and we need not follow them in any detail. The upshot was that Pope managed to convince the leading Dublin publisher, George Faulkner, to release a volume of letters to and from Swift that he had been given by the Dean. With a show of knowing it was the right thing to do, Faulkner told Orrery that he could have published the letters without Pope's knowledge. However, since the poet had been

> ill-used by Curll and other booksellers, I was willing to convince him there was a bookseller in Ireland who had honour enough to forego his own advantage rather than offend or injure him, although at the hazard of losing the friendship of the dean, who has ever been my great friend and benefactor.[11]

After this Pope was able to engineer the publication of the letters, first in a surreptitious edition and then in his own works (1740), while taking good care to distance himself from the process.

If Curll had managed to trace the entire course of this skulduggery, he would certainly have exploited it to the full. Before he could do so, there was another public scourging to endure. It occurred with the belated appearance of one of Swift's greatest poems, 'Verses on the Death of Dr Swift', some years after its composition; Pope had some hand in its publication. No doubt Curll would have liked to obtain an advance copy, but he cannot have been surprised when he read the cutting lines:

EXHIBIT 16.8

Now *Curl* his Shop from Rubbish drains;
Three genuine Tomes of *Swift*'s Remains.
And then to make them pass the glibber,
Revis'd by *Tibbalds, Moore and Cibber.*
He'll treat me as he does my Betters.
Publish my Will, my Life, my Letters.
Revive the Libels born to dye;
Which POPE must bear, as well as I.

In reality, Swift didn't have any quarrel with Lewis Theobald, James Moore Smythe or Cibber – they figure in Pope's battles. But, as we have seen, he had his own long-standing issues with Curll, who is not spared in the notes: '*Curl* hath been the most infamous Bookseller of any Age or Country: His Character in Part may be found in Mr. POPE's Dunciad. He published three Volumes all charged on the Dean, who never writ three Pages of them: He hath used many of the Dean's Friends in almost as vile a Manner.' Another note reads, '*Curl* is notoriously infamous for publishing the Lives, Letters, and last Wills and Testaments of the Nobility and Ministers of State, as well as of all the Rogues, who are hanged at *Tyburn*.' This last bit is wrong: actually, the bookseller took little interest in hangings. He preferred to dig up scandals affecting those still living. After this, the annotator moves on to cite Curll's criminal record in excruciating detail: 'He hath been in Custody of the House of Lords for publishing or forging the Letters of many Peers; which made the Lords enter a Resolution in their Journal Book, that no Life or Writings of any Lord should be published without the Consent of the next Heir at Law, or Licence from their House.'[12] Pope and his friends never tired of reminding the public about the judicial humiliations their enemy had suffered.

Eventually Curll found a way to take advantage of the new series of letters published by Pope. What emerged on 30 May 1741 was a volume entitled *Dean Swift's Literary Correspondence, for Twenty-four Years, from 1714 to 1738*. Subsequently Curll claimed that he had followed Faulkner's Dublin edition, a ruse to evade copyright restrictions. The truth was that he took his text from *The Works of Mr. Alexander Pope, In Prose. Vol. II*. In the preliminaries he reiterates his belief that the Dublin printing constitutes 'Lawful Prize here'. As we shall see in a moment, this would be invalidated in the upcoming Chancery suit. He promises that many false insinuations by Pope will be refuted in his notes, and in the fashion of former years asserts that he has provided a '*Clavis* [key] to the whole'.

The preface continues:

EXHIBIT 16.9

Mr. *Pope*'s mean Artifice of tacking eight OLD Pieces and ONE New one, for the Sake of a *Guinea*, or even *Half-a-one*, is scandalously mean, and may be thus justly reprehended:

PoPE will at length, we hope, his Errors own,

'Tis CURLL *diverts*, but PoPE *defrauds* the Town.

The *false Charge*, relating to the Publication of Mr. PoPE's LETTERS by Mr. CURLL, are herein fully refuted, and the Calumny is despised.[13]

When he comes to annotate the correspondence, he lambasts Pope's text, especially when his own name turns up. The method might be regarded as carpet bombing, but it does produce a few hits:

> *N.B. Four Letters* . . . being printed in Mr. PoPE's *Literary Correspondence*, Volume the *Fifth*, we have omitted them here, that the *Purchaser* might not buy them twice: according to Mr. *Pope*'s Practice of re-printing a Heap of *Old Pamphlets* and *News Papers*, joined to these Letters.

> The *Irish* Editor owns, That Mr. CURLL first obliged the Public with Dr SWIFT's and Lord BOLINGBROKE's *Letters* abovementioned, but with an equal *Impudence* and *Ignorance* calls them *Stolen Copies*. This is so far from *True*, that we know they were given to Mr. CURLL by a Peer of the *first Rank*.[14]

For once, though, Curll really had gone too far. He had given Pope the long-awaited opportunity.

A Verdict in Chancery

This chance came with the celebrated trial from which the subtitle of this book has been borrowed. The Chancery case of *Pope* v. *Curll* was heard in the summer of 1741: Pope's complaint was lodged on 4 June, and Curll's reply sworn on 13 June. The poet had obtained a temporary injunction on 14 May. This remained for more than two centuries a leading case in English law regarding copyright in personal letters, as the first serious test of the 1710 Copyright Act.[15] This was the first time we know of that Pope launched such a suit against Curll, although he had taken legal action against other booksellers previously. It should go without saying that many of the issues at stake bear directly on the whole history of the feud, even though the specific complaint deals only with rights in letters and not with published works of literature.

It is tempting to imagine a big courtroom scene. In our mind's eye, we might portray the solemn surroundings of Westminster Hall, and dramatic clashes between the black-gowned lawyers as they fought to gain the ear of the Lord Chancellor and his learned assistants, such as the Master of the Rolls. In fact, proceedings were far more humdrum, with no cross-questioning or sudden interventions by a Perry Mason-like advocate. The written pleadings were submitted, and the presiding officer announced his judgment. Nor were the surroundings as impressive as we would suppose. Until 1739, Chancery proceedings went on in an enclosure at the south end of the Hall, separated from the other courts by a low barrier of wooden boards. The appearance of the chamber was described as 'slovenly', and matters only got worse in the devastating cold of the winter of 1739/40, when the Great Frost spread across Europe. Tarpaulins had to be laid to stop rain soaking Chancery and the King's Bench court, while the roof timbers were found to be rotting. At that date a new Gothic screen was erected to the design of Pope's friend William Kent. A contemporary depiction shows the Chancellor presiding while sundry passers-by, accompanied by their dogs (loose), chat over the low fence with their buddies.

Lord Hardwicke was to play a big part in resolving matters. Philip Yorke (1690–1764) had enjoyed a meteoric rise in the law and politics. He was a former Whig MP, a former Lord Chief Justice, and Lord Chancellor since 1737. As a member of Walpole's inner cabinet, he did not have close relations with Pope. He had helped to draft the Black Act of 1723, a savagely comprehensive measure directed initially against deer-stealers in Windsor Forest, among whom were the husband and son of the poet's half-sister Magdalen Rackett. To historians such as E. P. Thompson, Hardwicke stands as the embodiment of the Bloody Code that disfigured the legal system for more than a century.[16] Despite these strong Hanoverian links, Curll may have felt some apprehension as he faced the Chancellor, since he was among those whom Yorke had prosecuted when Attorney-General in the 1720s. Today Hardwicke is remembered chiefly as the promoter of the Marriage Act of 1753, strengthening the law on such matters as banns and licences in an effort to curb irregular weddings.

Pope's complaint, based on his interpretation of the Act, was drafted by his barrister William Murray, later the celebrated jurist Lord Mansfield.[17] The document is too long and intricate to reproduce in full, but a flavour of its contents will be enough to illustrate its quality. It is made on behalf of 'Alexander Pope of Twickenham in the County of Middlesex, Esquire', and names 'Edmund Curl of the Parish of Saint Paul, Covent Garden, in the County of Middlesex, Bookseller', as the person responsible for infringing on his rights under the Act. Pope specifies about thirty letters of his own to Swift and the same number in return, each of them used by Curll in the volume under review. One key passage runs in this way:

Benjamin Ferrers, *The Court of Chancery during the Reign of George I*, *c.* 1725, engraving. This strangely unsecluded court was one of three at work in Westminster Hall.

EXHIBIT 16.10

Your Orator Charges that the said Edmund Curll and the rest of the
Confederates have and hath sold and disposed of a Great Number and
Quantity of the said Surreptitious and Pyrated edition of the said Letters, and threaten that they will Continue to Sell and Dispose of the
same, in Open Defiance of the Law and of your Orator's Just Title to
the said Letters; in Tender Consideration whereof, and for that your
Orator is without Remedy by the Common Law and cannot Obtain a
discovery of the Numbers which have been Printed and Sold of such
Surreptitious and Pyrated Editions, nor get an Account of the Money
which the said Confederates have received for what they have respectively Sold, nor Restrain the said Confederates from Selling such
Writings so illegally Printed, but by the Aid of a Court of Equity:
To the End therefore that the said Edmund Curl, and the rest of the
Confederates when discovered, may upon their respective Corporal
Oaths true and perfect Answer make to all and singular the Premisses
. . . (your Orator hereby leaving and disclaiming all Penaltys and
Forfeitures whatsoever given or allowed by the said Act).

It is doubtful whether Curll really had any confederates, other than
the printer and, much less vulnerable under the Act, members of
the trade who happened to sell the book. The Irish printing is not
mentioned at all by the plaintiff.

Curll's reply must have been drafted by his counsel, probably
John Browning of Lincoln's Inn. Despite that, some of his habitual
bluster and injured innocence show through the stylized wording. Much of the time he simply pleads ignorance: he is not aware
whether Pope has sold his copyright to anyone, and so on. He argues
that the letters sent to Pope were 'not to be Considered' as the recipient's property – a central issue at stake in the case. Going further,
he contends that such letters were not 'a work of that Nature' for
which protection had been afforded by the Act. He admits that at

no time did he have any express licence to print the letters in dispute, but he is advised that it was legal for him to do so, because they had been first printed in Dublin by Faulkner. Further, he points out that one-third of the book consists of material written by others (Atterbury, Arbuthnot et al.), the rights to which he had obtained through gift or purchase. This does not seem to affect the material issue in the suit. He denies unlawful confederacy, as charged by Pope, and refuses to supply details of publishing arrangements or profits. He reveals only that he had five hundred copies printed, and no more than sixteen had been sold at 4*s* or at 3*s* 6*d.* to booksellers. Finally, he asks to have the suit dismissed and to be allowed to continue the sale of the book.

Perhaps Curll's best, though trickiest, argument concerns the right of Pope to be deemed the 'proprietor' of the letters he had sent or received. Somehow the redundant capitals of legalese language seem to fit the publisher's hectoring manner:

EXHIBIT 16.11

And this Defendant Saith he doth not know, nor can set forth otherwise than as hereinafter is mentioned, whether the Complainant has ever disposed of his Right therein to any Person or Persons, or whether the Complainant hath the sole and Absolute Right of Printing and Reprinting, Vending, or Selling such letters: But this Defendant saith that all the letters mentioned in the Complainant's said Bill of Complaint were, as this defendant verily believes, Actually sent and delivered by and to the several Persons by whom and to whom they severally purport to have been written and Addressed; and therefore this Defendant is Advised and Humbly Insists that the Complainant is not to be Considered as the Author and Proprietor of all or any of the said letters.

So it goes on, with Curll denying that he made any arrangements with other persons about the printing (most likely here, editing) or profits of the edition, 'except the Agreement made by this Defendant with the Person who printed the same'. He prays that the charge against him should be dismissed.

The plea failed. At long last Pope had been able to nail his opponent in a significant legal context. In his judgment, the Lord Chancellor rejected one ground of Curll's defence totally, and he declined to accept another, although with some qualification. He remarked that it would be mischievous if letters passing between the learned should have no protection whatsoever from an Act specific-ally designed 'for the encouragement of learning' (as the measure of 1710 was headed), and instanced sermons as an analogous case. On the question as to whether a letter should be regarded as a gift to the receiver, he concluded that sending it conferred partial owner-ship at most. Perhaps the law might consider the actual paper on which the missive was written as an outright gift, but this did not carry with it freedom to publish the letter. Then the Chancellor reviewed Curll's assertion that it was lawful to reprint material that had appeared in Ireland. He decided against this, too, on the grounds that an unscrupulous pirate could simply arrange to pub-lish material in Ireland, and would then be free to bring it out in England, with no redress possible. The relations between London and Dublin publishers remained vexatious for the remainder of the eighteenth century.

Lastly, Hardwicke met the third strand of Curll's rejoinder. He gave one crumb of comfort to the defendant at the end of his judgment, however:

EXHIBIT 16.12

It has been insisted on by the defendant's counsel, that this is a sort of work which does not come within the meaning of the act of Parliament, because it contains only letters on familiar subjects, and inquiries after the health of friends, and cannot properly be called a learned work.

It is certain that no works have done more service to mankind, than those which have appeared in this shape, upon familiar subjects, and which perhaps were never intended to be published; and it is this makes them so valuable; for I must confess for my own part, that letters which are very elaborately written, and originally intended for the press, are generally the most insignificant, and very little worth any person's reading.

The injunction was continued by *Lord Chancellor* only as to those letters, which are under Mr. *Pope*'s name in the book, and which are written *by him*, and not as to those which are written *to him*.

Pope had certainly got most of what he wanted. The court made no order for the physical destruction of the book, as he may have wished. But Curll was forced to stop advertising the volume; whether he ceased to sell it is quite another matter. He had fallen foul of an essentially new doctrine in law, enunciated in the judgment. As the historian of copyright Mark Rose expresses it, 'In Hardwicke's decision, the author's words have in effect flown free from the page on which they are written. Not ink and paper but pure signs, separated from any material support, have become the protected property.'[18] Or, to put it differently, Swift might own the physical manuscript of a letter sent to him, but the rights of publication remained with the writer, Pope.

One further effort by Curll to cast aspersions on his enemies came with a typically shambolic biography that he issued a few weeks after the Chancery hearing: *An Impartial History of the Life, Character, Amours, Travels, and Transactions of Mr. John Barber, City-Printer, Common-Councilman, Alderman and Lord Mayor of London. Written by Several Hands.* Impartial it certainly wasn't, since it contains many spiteful comments on relevant matters – the aggressive behaviour the alderman displayed, his ungrateful treatment of his mistress Delarivier Manley, his voyage to Rome to seek a meeting with the Pretender, and his rapacious business methods.

Curll wastes most of his preface sparring with the author of a rival life (written probably by Benjamin Norton Defoe, son of Daniel) and reprinting letters to him from the contributors who had answered his requests for material in the *Daily Advertiser*. Swift and Pope don't figure centrally, although the legacies left to them are cited in the printer's will. By now the old man was getting desperate to drum up the adverse publicity he had once regularly fomented to keep the flames of the quarrel burning.

INSEPARABLE COMPANIONS

We now approach the conclusion of our quarrel. Pope had only one major work in the offing, his revised *Dunciad*, issued in four books in 1743. It is a remarkable achievement on its own terms, although more dispersed in its targets than the earlier versions. One shift mentioned earlier is that the headquarters of Dulness have been moved from a site near the Tower of London to the vicinity of Bedlam hospital in Moorfields. There, figures representing mania and depression carved by Caius Gabriel Cibber were set above the gateway. The most significant change is the replacement of Theobald as leader of the dunces in favour of the sculptor's son Colley Cibber. This intensifies the political animus of the poem, since it implicates the court more directly in view of Cibber's function as Poet Laureate to celebrate the royal dynasty. However, it detracts a little from the assault on Grub Street that was so central to the work in its former incarnation. In the revised text, there is nothing much new about Curll. He retains his previous role, but for those familiar with the action it is a little like witnessing an aged pop singer as he revisits the hits of his youth.

In 1742 Walpole finally lost power, after what remains the longest stint as prime minister in British history. That meant, among other things, that a main theme of Pope's poetry for a decade no longer held any currency, even though little would change in the

John Maurer, *The Hospital of Bethlehem* (Bedlam), mid-18th century, engraving.
Regarded by Pope as closely allied to its near neighbour, Grub Street.

governing elite. Cibber, who had supplanted Curll as the main
thorn in Pope's flesh, had turned into an irrelevancy. But now
the poet's fragile health worsened, partly as a result of his lifelong
physical problems. In 1740 he had undergone a painful operation
to deal with a strangulation of the urethra. Realizing his days were
now short, he began to consolidate his legacy. Together with the
ever industrious churchman William Warburton, who had edged
out the poet's other friends to become his literary executor, he
began to assemble what is generally called the 'deathbed edition'
of his works. Only a few poems had been made ready when, a few
weeks before his death, he saw the earliest segment in proof. Drily
he remarked to the Boswellian chronicler of his life and opinions,
Joseph Spence, 'Here am I, like Socrates, distributing my morality
among my friends, just as I am dying.'[19]

The poet died on 30 May 1744, after receiving the last rites from
a Benedictine priest. He was fifty-six. A simple burial service took
place at Twickenham church a week later. It cost just one pound,
and his body was carried to the grave by six poor parishioners.

To the memorial slab that he had set up for his parents inside the church, only his name was added. That was much too plain for Warburton's taste, and he later commissioned a hefty pyramid in honour of his friend, with a bust incised in bas-relief and some lines inscribed with the heading 'Poeta Loquitur' (the poet speaks). Not what the deceased had ordered.

Back to Curll finally. He may or may not have been behind a bulky work rejoicing in the title *Memoirs of the Life and Writings of Alexander Pope, Esq; Faithfully Collected from Authentic Authors, Original Manuscripts, and the Testimonies of many Persons of Credit and Honour: with Critical Observations. Adorned with the Heads of divers Illustrious Persons, Treated of in these Memoirs, Curiously Engrav'd by the best Hands. In two volumes. By William Ayre, Esq;.* This leaves many questions open. We do not know who William Ayre was, if he existed. We aren't sure whether the imprint covers the involvement of Curll; it reads, 'Printed by his Majesty's Authority, for the Author, and sold by the Booksellers of London and Westminster.' Above all, we have no real idea if Curll compiled the book.

Some features undoubtedly point in his direction, such as the impressive royal patent at the start; the slipshod arrangement of the work, with lengthy digressions throughout the text; and the intimate knowledge of Pope's life and works. On the other hand, the treatment of the poet is laudatory for the most part, and we find large chunks of hostile comments on '*E. Curl*, a Bookseller', reproduced without any attempt to refute them.[20] One reader certainly had no doubts about Ayre's true identity. This was 'J.H.', author of a pamphlet issued by Mary Cooper that appeared in response to the *Memoirs*. Its title has an almost equally portentous ring: *Remarks on 'Squire Ayre's Memoirs of the Life and Writings of Mr. Pope. In a Letter to Mr. Edmund Curl, Bookseller. With Authentic Memoirs of the Life and Writings of the said E- C-l.* The writer addresses 'Friend Edmund' with easy familiarity. The supposed 'memoirs' of Curll

Louis-Philippe Boitard, *The Covent Garden Morning Frolick*, 9 October 1747, engraving. Published two months before Curll's own frolic ended, when he was buried at St Paul's church (in the background, centre). The woman in the sedan chair may be Betsy Careless, described as 'the most Charming of all the Courtezans around Covent Garden', with her link-boy 'Little Cazey' lighting the way ahead.

that he promises lack any substance, being composed from the same materials of gossip, legend and fantasy that were shown in the bookseller's own accounts of Pope. J.H. regrets the fact that, bearing in mind his long association with the poet, Ayre did not tell us more of the bookseller, 'your dear Friend and . . . inseparable Companion, Mr. *Edmund Curl*':

EXHIBIT 16.13

Mr. *Pope* himself, you know, had laugh'd away many Pages about him, and his Story, as told by that Gentleman and his Friend, has been a delightful History to ten thousand Readers; he is a Man so nearly concern'd with Mr. *Pope*, was also . . . a necessary Person to be nam'd a good deal at large with him: With all these Recommendations then, and with the Advantage of having had so many and so merry Things said of him, as might have filled up almost a third Part of your Volumes, and that to the Satisfaction of your Readers, how comes it that you repeat so little of all that has been said of him, and scarce allow him half a Page in your Memoirs? How comes it that you, who have so industriously transcrib'd all the other Memoirs of the Friends and Enemies of Mr. *Pope*, should omit just those, and only those that mention Mr. *Curl*?[21]

J.H. regrets 'this Omission of doing proper Honour to so fam'd a Hero'. His book may not tell us much that we did not already know about the bookseller or the poet, but it seems apt that our last exhibit should draw attention to their improbable relationship.

Curll gradually faded from the scene.[22] He had secured a nest egg with a series of works offering undemanding pornography, set in the erotic world of Merryland. It is possible that he was blind when he died at the age of 64 on 11 December 1747, to be buried at the parish church of St Paul's two days later. So the two great combatants lie for eternity, each close to the spot he haunted during life, one at Twickenham, one at Covent Garden. But there will be no repose. It will take eternity for them to settle their differences.

Closing ARGUMENTS

It's time to summarize the arguments on either side of the case. We shall hear first from advocates on behalf of Curll, since they have been more vocal in recent years. But even at the height of his fame and influence, Pope always had to endure strong criticism. We have seen that Curll was by no means alone during the poet's lifetime in pouring scorn on his work. Hostile critics let off an endless series of fusillades against his scholarship, his deficiencies as translator and editor, his political alliances, his religious faith, his mercenary motives, his duplicity, his treachery to the literary profession and much else – not forgetting, of course, his physical appearance. Curll was simply bolder, more persistent and smarter than anybody else in concocting amusing one-liners and dreaming up catchy couplets.

For a generation after his death, Pope did manage to retain almost intact his stock as one of the great English writers, at any rate in serious literary analysis. The earliest important challenge to this estimate was mounted in 1756 and augmented in 1782 by Joseph Warton, who denied him the title of a true poet: 'What is there very sublime or pathetic in Pope?' A quarter of a century later Samuel Johnson issued a judicial review of this verdict in his *Lives of the Poets*, in which he expressed reservations about the private man, but concluded his assessment of the major works with a resounding answer to Warton: 'If Pope be not a poet, where is poetry to be found?'[1] With the notable exception of Lord Byron, the Romantics felt only lukewarm admiration, and this extended into the

Victorian age.[2] William Makepeace Thackeray, who didn't greatly care for the Scriblerians, asserted that 'Pope was more savage to Grub-street, than Grub-street was to Pope' (true or false? we must decide). He even claimed that Pope 'contributed, more than any man who ever lived, to depreciate the literary calling . . . The condition of authorship began to fall from the days of the "Dunciad".'[3] However, some new advocates emerged on the other side of the question, notably John Ruskin, who ranked Pope with Virgil as one of the 'great masters of the absolute art of language'.[4]

After this, in the mid-nineteenth century, two things happened that were most inconvenient from the poet's point of view. The first concerned a writer named Charles Wentworth Dilke. He was editor of the influential *Athenaeum* magazine, as well as a friend of John Keats, Percy Bysshe Shelley and Charles Dickens. Late in life, Dilke (father of a radical politician) developed an interest in the way Pope had engineered the publication of his letters. His studies revealed the extent to which the author doctored the text of his letters. Around the same time more attention began to be given to the machinations surrounding the appearance of *Mr. Pope's Literary Correspondence*. It was known all along that Pope had tricked Curll into issuing the first 'spurious edition'. However, the full extent of his involvement had been only surmised before new enquiries were launched in the 1850s. Now biographers gave greater emphasis to the story, and the result was a more general sense of Pope as a double dealer. By implication Curll could be seen as a harmless dupe.

The second event had to do with the long-planned edition of Pope's entire works, or at least all that the age thought were fit for publication. The first two volumes were edited in the early 1870s by an Anglican clergyman named Whitwell Elwin. In the words of the Oxford scholar Mark Pattison (best remembered as a model for the impotent old man with whom Dorothea Brooke is saddled in George Eliot's *Middlemarch*), Elwin's aim seems to have been to depict Pope as 'a liar, a cheat, and a scoundrel', while 'his so-called poetry is ungrammatical, ill-rhymed, unmeaning trash.' This is no exaggeration: Elwin described *An Essay on Criticism* using such epithets as mean, slovenly, ungrammatical, feeble, inharmonious and imperfect – and that's all from a single sentence.[5] The naked prejudice displayed by the editor on literary and religious subjects caused him to be summarily replaced by a more moderate student of the works, William John Courthope. However, the Elwin and Courthope edition, as it became, remained the standard one for the greater part of a century, and the damage was done in the early volumes. Curll's general reputation underwent no big change, but quite often he would be let off the hook for his actions over the *Correspondence*, simply because of the games Pope had played with him.

This growing sympathy for the bookseller can be detected throughout the vivacious pages of Ralph Straus's biography (1927). Curll has become what is now called a 'loveable rogue', cocking a snook at respectable society in a manner that Bloomsbury would have approved of. Edith Sitwell was obviously strongly influenced by Straus in her entertaining if not very scholarly life of Pope (1930). She portrays Curll as the hapless victim of successive insults and injuries. The pamphlets satirizing him are 'so disgusting as to be unreadable, and there is no trace of wit to be found in them'. Yet, for all that, 'Nothing seemed to improve his character, nor daunt his courage – neither being imprisoned, nor pumped upon, nor pilloried, nor tossed in a blanket.' Curll 'took every revenge in his power', and in return 'Pope has transfixed this ugly, purblind, and blundering moth, for all eternity.'[6] Some would think this is to make Curll out to be more gullible and defenceless than he really was.

Lately, we have seen some strong defences lodged as part of an academic and pedagogic claim for equal treatment of the participants. The advocates for this view will now provide a concluding statement to the court of literary and publishing history.

THE CASE FOR CURLL

Some recent scholarship has sought to portray the combatants as morally equivalent, claiming that Pope employed the same Grub Street mechanisms as did his opponent, and that Curll has been denigrated unjustly by posterity. Indeed, the formerly reviled bookseller has begun to prosper mightily in some circles. Websites solemnly debate whether he should be placed among the heroes or villains of Grub Street. A forum on this very topic was held in the National Library of the Netherlands in 2006. A highly respected scholar of book history suggested that the trade was less polarized than was generally thought between the low-level operators who published cheap, nasty, dirty books and the upper tier who disseminated handsome classical volumes. Grub Street and Pall Mall lay closer than we realized. Meanwhile, the 'worst of publishers' has become, in the view of some, a standard-bearer for the freedom of the press. He can be given the honorific status of a rebel confronting an entrenched and backward-looking establishment.

One reason for this surge in popularity lies in the quarrel with Pope. The poet has long excited hostile reactions, and today critics are often inclined to see him as a traitor to the literary brotherhood, who fouled his own nest by savaging writers and publishers in *The Dunciad*. For some modern commentators, the eminent author carried out his operations very close to Grub Street. 'Pope himself was not above using deception, trickery, and chemistry to get the better of Curll,' in the view of John O'Brien. 'It's easy for us to see that Curll was acting without authority by printing poems, letters, and other material for which he had neither paid nor received permission. But, as Curll himself asked Pope, "Who gave *you* the authority of punishing *me*?"' O'Brien got his students to take part in a mock trial setting poet against bookseller, yet one more incarnation of *Pope* v. *Curll*. The jury returned what he thought was 'a particularly splendid and appropriate verdict, finding both men capable [culpable?] of wrongdoing, and sentencing them to be placed in the stocks within spitting distance of each other'. The students were able 'to articulate the issues in great detail and complexity' and 'to cross-examine each other shrewdly'.[7] A spitting contest was one thing that Pope neglected to put in *The Dunciad*.

Another teacher, Bradford K. Mudge, enlisted graduate students in a class on research methods to assist him in a project involving eighteenth-century libertine literature. He reports that members of the class 'eagerly transcribed *Venus in the Cloister* as a way to sharpen their knowledge of textual criticism', perhaps the first time such a motive has led anyone to peruse this childish bit of porn. After this, the students, 'enthusiastic about justifying the ways of Edmund Curll to man, planned an edition that would appeal to the modern reader'.[8] You can see why they enjoyed that prospect.

For that matter, we did not have to wait until the twenty-first century to recognize that Curll and Pope were locked to some degree in a symbiotic dance. His colleague Thomas Payne brought out a piracy of Pope's *Epistle to Burlington* in 1731, and as we have seen he too bedecked a newspaper advertisement with a slick couplet: 'It is impossible they e'er should part, / *POPE* has the Publick Ear, and *CURLL* their Heart.' Most probably Curll wrote these lines himself. Modern commentators who declare that the antagonists were as bad as one another have an ancient precedent: the claim goes right back to the man himself. When Curll was in legal trouble, he liked to accuse Pope of being equally guilty of similar offences. Thus, he justified printing new versions of stories by Chaucer on the grounds that the same had been done by the great and the good – 'this *lewd Prologue* [to the Wife of Bath's tale] has been modernized by Mr *POPE*, and likewise published by Mr *Tonson*.' In fact, Curll can be called as a witness on his own behalf.

The most sustained and closely argued support Curll has received comes from Bradford K. Mudge, in a book entitled *The Whore's Story* (2000). Like many good trial attorneys, the author saw that the best form of defence is attack. In addition, he adopted a familiar defence strategy by admitting Curll's misdemeanours at the outset, conceding that 'his purpose was profit and books were the means.'[9] Mudge lists many of the literary offences that his virtual 'client' had committed, along with bibliographical frauds and authorial forgeries. He makes no bones about the man's character: 'In short Edmund Curll was an unscrupulous profiteer, a master of masquerade who employed every deception possible to sell books . . . He believed in only two things: his own bottom line and the warning "buyer beware".' With friends like this, who needs enemies?

A different slant is apparent as soon as Mudge embarks on the story of the quarrel, beginning with the emetic episode and moving through *The Dunciad* to the saga of the letters. He proposes 'a reading of the enmity between Pope and Curll [that] moves beyond the personal conflict to show some of the larger issues facing the literary marketplace'. Initially he offers what may appear a surprising comparison: 'Pope would seem to represent the voice of an emerging literary institution that was trying to protect itself – its authors and its books – from commercial defilement. Curll, on the other hand, would represent a kind of predatory capitalism, what might happen today if you crossed Ayn Rand with Larry Flynt.'

Warming to his task, the advocate starts to implicate his opponent in the wrongdoing. He points out that things were different three centuries ago:

> Thus allegorized . . . the contest would still appear to favor the poet. After all, we have adopted more exacting laws about intellectual property that now protect authors from Curllian abuse. And we have cleaned up our bookshops in such a way that the sensitive among us are not offended by the unexpected appearance of dirty books. Thanks to the careful segregation of the pornographic from the literary, those seeking the prurient and not the profound have their shops.

The danger is that we shall miss a strong element of convergence between the principals in the quarrel:

> Although Pope unquestionably championed both authorial rights and literary standards, as demonstrated most clearly in *The Dunciad* (1728–35), his motivations, his manipulations, and his malice tie him all the more closely to the very world he was trying to leave behind. He poisoned Curll in part because the latter had identified the former as the author of poems that took satiric pot shots at the Court.

Actually, as we have seen, the poisoning was triggered by Curll's *misidentification* of Pope as one of the authors of *Court Poems*. At that date, the publisher had not outed any satire that the poet had levelled at the court. We may imagine counsel turning to the jury as he rams home his point: Pope, like Curll, lived by his wits, and the poet no doubt worried that a damaged reputation could jeopardize sales. Self-righteousness and self-interest were not mutually exclusive, and Pope quickly figured out that in this case morality might mean money. The anonymous pamphlet celebrating the poisoned sack, for example, out-Curlls Curll at the very moment it purports to strike a blow against the bookseller's money-grubbing ways.

Mudge goes on to re-emphasize his main contention: 'Pope and Curll want the same thing – money – they employ the same means – masquerade – and they are equally unscrupulous in the deployment of their deceptions.' He refers to Pope's 'downfall', meaning perhaps in the House of Lords, but also in the court of public opinion. By contrast, Curll was 'dressed up as a businessman' and had no need to make any apologies because he was 'just trying to make a shilling or two'. The defendant's lawyer might object here that it would be hard to find respectable members of the business community who looked at Curll's practices in that way.

The moment has come for the peroration. Mudge does not hold back:

> The fact that Pope and Curll were at each other's throats, were deeply entangled in a web of deception, and were trying desperately to outmaneuver the other on the way to financial recompense had to confirm similarity rather than difference. Considered from the position of inherited wealth and privilege, both were whores, and it mattered little that Pope considered himself the Homer of his age. Like the seasoned streetwalker he was, Curll never pretended to be anything else. Right from the beginning he had been honest about his dishonesty: Deception was a part of business. Pope, on the other hand, was passing himself upwards; he wanted to be known as an 'author,' not a businessman. Literature, he would maintain, is a thing of words, not money. If Curll was the streetwalker, brazen and unabashed, then Pope was the expensive call girl who pretended to be a lady of fortune.

At this point the advocate might have rested his case, but there is a further section in which the critic discusses Curll's prosecution for the translation of *Venus in the Cloister*, 'easily the most notorious early eighteenth-century piece of proto-pornography'. We end with a glimpse of Curll on the pillory, where he has 'masterminded a solution' to his apparent disgrace. 'Arguably one of history's greatest spin doctors', he distributes to the watching crowd a broadside that claims that his offence was 'hardly criminal'. Curll steps down from the rostrum, to be hoisted off on the shoulders of his supporters 'to a nearby pub for few pints. Punishment indeed.' Most of the defence has resided in the claim that Curll may have been a villain, but no more so than Pope. But when this closing argument reaches its climax, there is no longer any doubt. The government, like Pope, should have left well alone. Curll is the hero of the hour.

THE CASE FOR POPE

Those who wish to take Pope's side are bound to respond with an attack on Curll. No one can sensibly deny that they have plenty of ammunition to use against him in the supposed court case. Even proponents of the bookseller will accept that he was hardly a model citizen in the world of books. If the trial were held in America, it might be possible to reach an accommodation by what is called in U.S. law a 'stipulation'. This refers to a procedure by which, 'during the course of a civil lawsuit . . . or any other type of litigation, the opposing attorneys may come to an agreement about certain facts and issues.'[10] But anyone seeking to rebut the charges levied against Pope, as they have been outlined by Mudge, must obviously mention Curll's misconduct as well as seek to disprove what has been said about his opponent. In the absence of any full public rejoinder to Mudge or other modern apologists for Curll, we shall have to construct a line of reasoning that advocates for Pope might adopt to oppose their argument.

One area where the poet's defenders would hope to find a vulnerable spot concerns the tendency that has grown up to regard Curll as a sort of primitive rebel. Sceptics will wonder if this might have been a factor in the verdict of the student jury. True, the publisher often found himself cast as a naysayer in an oppositional stance, but generally because he had failed in his efforts to win the support of powerful interest groups. More than once, when authorities turned the heat on him Curll shopped his colleagues, even informing against so inoffensive a figure in the trade as the printer-novelist Samuel Richardson. He was no saint, but it could be pointed out that Richardson did not obfuscate the publishing history of his books by altering titles or dates, or issue spurious 'editions' of a work by inserting a cancel title page. Nor did he invent bogus authors with names resembling the great – or engage in twenty duplicitous practices that we have encountered in the course of Curll's career.

It took a different sort of man from the fussy, shy, easily cowed Richardson to do these things.

Once Curll was carted off to gaol, his first instinct was always to drop into trouble as many printers and booksellers as he could, with the aim of negotiating his own release. Often he went to the very top and sent Robert Walpole news of impending publications. Thus, in 1724 he told the prime minister that Delarivier Manley had a new instalment ready of her notorious bestseller *The New Atalantis*.[11] Spite may have entered into his motive for impugning what he called a 'libel', since he had never managed to get a share in this lucrative work – although he did pass off a number of books, completely unrelated to the original, with titles such as *The Northern Atalantis* or *The German Atalantis*. When Manley died later that year, Curll rehashed a volume from a decade before, her ghosted semi-autobiographical *Adventures of Rivella*, misleadingly titled *Mrs. Manley's History of her own Life and Times*. His critics will point to this as typical behaviour. There was little he wouldn't stoop to.

So keen did the publisher become on the machinery of informing that he actually proposed to Walpole some form of reward for himself. He had been told that he might 'depend on having some provision' made for him in return for his 'unwearied diligence to serve the government', and that he could expect to be given 'something in the Post-Office'.[12] Curll didn't have in mind a job as a counter clerk. He meant that he would manage the oversight of the press, and winnow out seditious publications. When forced into a tight corner, he would always proclaim his affection for the government, and deny knowledge of suspect material – 'neither was there one [copy] seen or sold in my shop,' he used to assert. A decade later he tried again, and sent the Treasury, still headed by Walpole, a proposal to appoint an inspector to supervise the stamp duty levied on the press, and bring the government an additional £10,000 that was currently evaded by those producing ballads, music and pictures.[13] Hardly the record of a man who would die in the last ditch for freedom of speech, with the words of *Areopagitica* on his lips.

The story told here has provided abundant evidence of the bookseller's considerable gift for comedy. Indeed, much of his career played itself out first as pathos and then as farce. The biography by Ralph Straus confirmed this impression of a genial master of ceremonies, exposing the solemnities of a rigid age. In fact, many of Curll's letters to the authorities, when he found himself in trouble, veer between accents of Pecksniffian smugness and a deep vein of self-pity. Nor did the hacks he employed always find him funny when he doled out four or five guineas for their labours – the rate at which Robert Samber worked for translating such marketable items as *Eunuchism Display'd* or *The Praise of Drunkenness*. We have no idea how much money Curll made from these productions – it was possibly less than Mudge supposes – but we have records of his pay scale, and it wasn't one that added to the dignity of authorship.

Paradoxically, another factor may have come to Curll's aid in the rehab programme he has undergone. His heavy involvement in soft pornography has become a positive asset, and his willingness to take on the authorities is now seen as another blow for the freedom of the press. Some might think it a pity that he did not challenge the limits of the law with something more substantial than *Venus* or his tracts on impotence, flagellation and sodomy, mostly inferior translations of flimsy items written decades earlier. But his detractors will admit that he did at least take on the might of the establishment, and drew out the full retinue of the government's legal officers.

In any case, now that both erotic texts and popular culture have come to seem more worthy of study in many quarters than distinguished literature, Curll's stock could hardly fail to rise. A few of his smutty books have been reprinted with the full scholarly apparatus in Pickering & Chatto's series of Eighteenth-century British

Erotica (2002), suggesting that he may be in line for a posthumous pardon from the Royal Society of Literature. Readers could be excused for thinking that Curll played the part of a Maurice Girodias in pushing back the boundaries of artistic expression, but sadly he produced nothing comparable to *The Ginger Man*, *The Naked Lunch* or *Lolita*. Instead, his legacy was to make the world free for Roger Pheuquewell's *New Description of Merryland* (a work describing the geography of the female body as a landscape that men explore and plough), and a tract called *De secretis mulierum* – texts equally bereft of literary merit and of medical value. True, Pope used obscenity in *The Dunciad* and elsewhere, but arguably in the service of a much more sophisticated literary enterprise.

What of the charges against Pope that his opponents have brought forward? The poet's team would quickly leap to his defence. Is Mudge right, they would ask, when he claims that 'Pope's friendships with titled nobility, his estate at Twickenham, and his social pretensions generally all failed to hide the fact that he worked for his money'?[14] He certainly had patrons among the aristocracy and higher gentry, but he also numbered many commoners in the group of distinguished authors whom he championed – Jonathan Swift, John Gay, John Arbuthnot, Nicholas Rowe, Samuel Garth, William Wycherley and others – not a title among them, and even Garth's Whig-bestowed knighthood had as much to do with his medical activity as with his poetry. It was to William Congreve that Pope dedicated his *Iliad*, an unusual gesture for the time, and one that has always been viewed as marking an important advance in the status of authors. He also had numerous contacts in the professions (lawyers such as William Fortescue, clergymen such as the Anglican bishop Francis Atterbury, and physicians and surgeons such as William Cheselden), as well as merchants and City men such as Slingsby Bethel.

Regardless of any fantasies he may have had, Pope would never have pretended to reach a status above that of a private gentleman.

His 'estate' at Twickenham consisted originally of two small cottages that he extended into a villa of moderate size; later he rented a small portion of adjoining land towards the river. The entire property was leased, and late in life he rejected an offer to buy the freehold. His references to the place are always comically belittling, as in his claim that he was content to 'piddle' there 'in five acres now of rented land'.[15] This was a deliberately miniaturized version of the great estates he visited, where the earls of creation had lived for generations in stately mansions amid their vast parks and fancy ornamental gardens.

Mudge's description could also be contested in that it distorts the source of Pope's income. Some came from investments made out of his father's bequest, but more from the Homer translations. A great deal of his best work brought him little revenue, or, in the case of pieces that Curll purloined, nothing at all. It was clearly his aim to take advantage of the Copyright Act to earn what he thought was his due, and he made no attempt to hide this intention. But most writers ever since have done the same. It does not mean that those who made a tough bargain with publishers (think of Graham Greene's deal with Heinemann to subsidize his novels with 'entertainments') had therefore become 'a businessman', as Mudge puts it. It seems a crudely reductive account of Pope's career to look on it simply as a quest for money. He aspired to create great works, to enhance the standing of English literature, to affect the political climate, to uphold his faith, to pay tribute to his family and friends, to honour the place where he had grown up, to pour scorn on those he despised (be they wealthy politicians or penurious authors), and much else. The notion that he was a 'whore' serving the wealthy and privileged classes rings false to many students of the poet. They would argue that his rich patrons regarded him in quite a different light. Outside subscription volumes where they paid their whack, there is little or no evidence that Burlington, Bathurst, Oxford, Peterborough and others offered Pope more than hospitality, moral support and friendship.

As for the imputation that 'Pope considered himself the Homer of his age,' this again will bear some easy rejoinders. First, he loved Homer from very early in life, once he had come across John Ogilby's translation at the age of eight. Second, he devoted many of the best years of his life to the translations of the *Iliad* and, admittedly with some help, the *Odyssey*. Third, his versions would prove among the most widely read throughout the English-speaking world from that day forward, and they continue to attract scholarly attention. Fourth, his overall achievement in a range of genres, particularly these rooted in classical forms, established him while still young as the leading English poet of his time. None of this quite renders him the equal of Homer, but it shows that contemporaries would have found him by far the closest contender. Fifth, he never called himself the Homer of the age. It would be fairer to see him as modelling his career on that of Virgil.

Other supporters would bring up different issues in an attempt to clear Pope's name and dissociate him from the idea that he was a kissing cousin of Edmund Curll. One argument would stand out above all others, and it relates to the permanent achievement of the two men. Curll, it would be said, was a crook who stained the reputation of the book trade, even if he was a bold entrepreneur and a resourceful combatant in print. Pope was indeed a slippery customer who too often dealt in 'genteel equivocation' to disguise falsehoods. On the other hand, he created some of the finest satires in the language, which earned him not just the admiration but also the love of many devoted readers. *The Dunciad* may or may not be as filthy in content as *Venus in the Cloister*, but in comparison with that infantile production, its extraordinary qualities emerge all the more clearly. They derive from its complex mock-heroic design and fund of allusion to classical writers; its inwardness with the course of earlier English literature; its breadth of reference, from journalism to opera; its range of humour, from outright farce to sly verbal hints; its brilliant exploitation of London customs, rituals and topography; and its vivid shifts in style, from the high diction of epic to the pseudo-lyricism of pastoral. Too bad, the argument would conclude, that Curll had to be skewered in the process, but he deserved no more.

PICKING A WINNER

In his biography, Straus declared the result and raised the hand of Curll: 'There is no doubt at all as to whom the honours must be given. For although in a sense Pope may be said to have succeeded in his general design, it was Curll who stepped out of the ring with the insolence of victory.'[16] He was referring to the outcome of the third 'round', fought over the letters, when Curll resisted an attempt to have his publications declared unlawful by the House of Lords. An advocate for Pope could point out that seven years later the poet gained a much more significant victory, which impaired the efforts of booksellers such as Curll to evade copyright restrictions in one particular area – and did so almost in perpetuity. But a good trial lawyer might lead the jury to forget the sequel by emphasizing, as Curll himself did, the triumphant outcome of his subpoena in the Lords. The contest goes on.

EPILOGUE

The court of history never gives a final verdict. That would be a good thing for the spirits of people from the past if they were able to lodge a virtual appeal against their posthumous reputation, to have the decisions of former generations overturned. This reversal happened first with Pope, who by the end of the Victorian age had lost much of the huge international reputation he had once enjoyed, and got back his high standing in the great tradition of English poets only by dint of a protracted recovery exercise mounted in the twentieth century. A little later Curll came into his own, as we have just seen. A whole new group of admirers pulled him out of the waste bin into which he had been thrown by earlier writers. They viewed his supposed insolence as pluck, his contumely as chutzpah, his presumptuous attitude as determination to stand up for his rights.

As with other disputes great and small, it is now open for us to attribute praise and blame where we will. Learned counsel on either side can pose the playground question, 'Well, who started it, then?' Perhaps reparations are due to Curll. Public recognition might require a monument to be erected in St Paul's, Covent Garden, where he was buried close to the site of his last bookshop. This would not have to be very showy to outdo the plain memorial that Pope designed for his parents and himself in Twickenham parish church. He was not admitted to the great and the good in Poets' Corner until 1994, when a lozenge-shaped pane was placed in a new stained-glass window. If the Abbey had a Publishers' Corner, Curll would still not have made it.

This book cannot settle the dispute for good and all. But the evidence assembled here may be useful to those who wish to dispense retrospective justice, or to right what they see as the wrongs meted out to people worthy of greater respect. Adherents in both parties will claim that their man has been maligned, and decry the efforts of their antagonist.

It is easy to understand why the quarrel has continued to echo down the ages. Three hundred years ago the modern tools of publicity were either non-existent or in their infancy. Part of the skill that both Curll and Pope had at their command was a flair for turning literature into news. Both used the burgeoning newspaper and periodical press to their advantage, enlisting the opportunities the medium afforded for advertising and for editorial commentary. Both made their books a weapon in their war of words. Curll did this chiefly through barbed references in paratextual spaces such as prefaces, footnotes, booklists and indexes, along with his favourite ploy of epigrammatic couplets. Pope sometimes replied in kind, for example in the preliminaries to the *Miscellanies* in 1732; more often he inserted devastating portrayals of his enemy into major poems and prose works. The situation is very different from that of previous centuries. Shakespeare may or may not have engaged in protracted feuds with other writers, and for all we know with fellow actors or piratical booksellers. There is no tranche of reliable information for us to consult. On the other hand, as this book has shown, the evidence regarding Pope and Curll lies thickly documented in the archives.

The quarrel could hardly have broken out at any other time. As explained at the start of this book, the old regulatory mechanisms that served to stifle the press had fallen into abeyance. A result was that new avenues for publicity opened, a process fostering the creation of what the sociologist Jürgen Habermas called 'the public sphere'.[1] This term refers to a national sounding board for information, discussion and education. It was this enlarged audience that enabled the grand quarrel to flourish as it did. Curll routinely stoked demand for a forthcoming work in advance by alluding to events surrounding its publication: a good example is the brouhaha involving Dr Arbuthnot before the appearance of the memoirs of William Congreve. Around this same period, the first rush of joint stock companies lured investors into the market, a development that was to have disastrous consequences for many when the South Sea Bubble broke in 1720; on the plus side, they could keep track of share prices in the newspaper. Even more important in the long run was the growth of advertising. The two groups quickest to recognize the possibilities here were the promoters of patent medicines and publishers – and it is not wholly a coincidence that the same people tended to be involved in pushing pharmaceutical products and selling books.

Curll was not the only huckster in these areas, but he was one of the best. Early in his career he spent what must have been a considerable advertising budget for the time in plugging a book called *The Charitable Surgeon*. This offered a sovereign remedy for venereal disease, 'whereby all persons, even the meanest capacities, may, for an inconsiderable charge, without confinement or knowledge of the nearest relation, cure themselves easily, speedily and safely, by the methods prescrib'd, without the help of any physician, surgeon or apothecary, or being expos'd to the hazardous attempts of quacks and pretenders.'[2] Among a bloodcurdling list of items available for purchase are the purging electuary, the diuretic powder, the anodyne fotus (a boiled concoction of poppies and elderflowers, according to the pharmacopoeias), the emetic bolus, the specific electuary, the suppurating plaster, the cooling gargle, the sudorific potion and the detersive injection – not to mention syringes aimed at the nose, throat, yard (penis) and womb. Curll was appointed sole agent at his shop near Temple Bar. Not surprisingly, a favourite target of Scriblerian satire was found in quacks such as Dr Robert Norris or the tub-thumper of anti-worm powders, John Moore. The physician John Arbuthnot seldom tired of berating the more egregious fringe practitioners, and he once mentions the man behind Curll's remedy for venereal disease. The gargle might work, but it seems almost better to live with the disease than undergo the cure. Other products Curll advertised were one for jaundice, 'Pulvis Anti-Icterius'; one for gout, 'Dr Radcliffe's Draught'; one for corns, the 'Specific Indian Balsam'; and another for sexually transmitted disease, 'Guttae Cupidiniae'.

Did Pope notice these things? Of course. He devised his plan for revenge on his adversary with an emetic as apposite punishment for the culprit who tried to persuade sufferers to indulge in the emetic bolus. Then, as we saw in *The Dunciad*, there came a malicious suggestion that Curll himself was a martyr to the clap. It may very well be an unsubstantiated calumny on the man, although other writers accused him of dissolute behaviour. The entire passage is designed to associate the dunces with low life, squalor and insalubrious habits. An underlying suggestion is that individuals dwelling in such circumstances had no business selling drugs to gullible people with distressing ailments – mainly, it need hardly be said, the poor.

This book has explored various factors that contributed to the progress of the quarrel. They included political, religious, social and cultural issues, some of which drew a fault line between the antagonists. Dear juror, it is time for you to make up your own mind.

REFERENCES

ABBREVIATIONS

Corr　　George Sherburn, ed., *The Correspondence of Alexander Pope*, 5 vols (Oxford, 1956)

ECB　　Paul Baines and Pat Rogers, *Edmund Curll, Bookseller* (Oxford, 2007)

JSCorr　David Woolley, ed., *The Correspondence of Jonathan Swift, D.D.*, 5 vols (Frankfurt am Main, 1999–2014)

Lit Corr　[Edmund Curll, ed.,] *Mr. Pope's Literary Correspondence*, 5 vols (London, 1735–7)

NA　　National Archives, London

PA　　J. V. Guerinot, *Pamphlet Attacks on Alexander Pope, 1711–1744* (London, 1969)

PW 1　Norman Ault, ed., *The Prose Works of Alexander Pope*, vol. I: *1711–1720* (Oxford, 1936)

PW 2　Rosemary Cowler, ed., *The Prose Works of Alexander Pope*, vol. II: *1725–1744* (Oxford, 1986)

Sherburn　George Sherburn, *The Early Career of Alexander Pope* (Oxford, 1934)

Straus　Ralph Straus, *The Unspeakable Curll* (London, 1927)

TE　　John Butt and Maynard Mack, ed., *The Twickenham Edition of the Poems of Alexander Pope*, 11 vols (London, 1938–68)

NEWSPAPERS

AWJ　*Applebee's Weekly Journal*

BJ　*British Journal*

CJ　*Country Journal, or The Craftsman*

DC　*Daily Courant*

DJ　*Daily Journal*

DP　*Daily Post*

DPB　*Daily Post Boy*

EP　*Evening Post*

FP　*Flying Post*

FWJ　*Fog's Weekly Journal*

GSJ　*Grub Street Journal*

LEP	*London Evening Post*
LG	*London Gazette*
LJ	*London Journal*
MWJ	*Mist's Weekly Journal*
PB	*Post Boy*
PM	*Post Man*
RWJ	*Read's Weekly Journal*
SJEP	*St James's Evening Post*

PREFACE

1 Adrian Johns, *Piracy: The Intellectual Property Wars from Gutenberg to Gates* (Chicago, IL, 2009). On Curll, see pp. 46–8. There is some question about whether Curll should be regarded as an orthodox 'pirate'; on some of the topics involved, see Stephen Karian, *Jonathan Swift in Print and Manuscript* (Cambridge, 2010), and Pat Rogers, 'The Uses of the Miscellany: Swift, Curll and Piracy', in *Jonathan Swift and the Eighteenth-century Book*, ed. Paddy Bullard and James McLaverty (Cambridge, 2013), pp. 87–100.
2 Isaac D'Israeli, *The Calamities and Quarrels of Authors: Including Some Inquiries Respecting their Moral and Literary Characters* (London, 1859), pp. 278–335.
3 See Thomas Keymer, *Poetics of the Pillory: English Literature and Seditious Libel, 1660–1820* (Oxford, 2019).

INTRODUCTION

1 *JSCorr*, vol. II, p. 277.
2 *ECB*, pp. 140, 210–11. For later cases involving literary property of Pope and Arbuthnot, see pp. 289–90.
3 See *Corr*, vol. III, p. 343.
4 John H. Langbein, *The Origins of Adversary Criminal Trial* (Oxford, 2003), p. 7.
5 Dorothy L. Sayers with Robert Eustace, *The Documents in the Case* (New York, 1987), pp. 1–2.
6 Straus, pp. 49–64, 122–38, 154–87.
7 The bare-knuckle quality of the dispute was aided by the fact that most of the exchanges took place under anonymity, the prevailing condition in which satire was conducted (see Pat Rogers, 'Nameless Names: Pope, Curll, and the Uses of Anonymity', *New Literary History*, 33 (2002), pp. 233–45).

I THE TIME *and* THE PLACE

1 From the representation to the queen in March 1712, cited by Swift in his *History of the Four Last Years of the Queen*. He is believed to have been the co-author himself.

2 For a convenient summary of the issues at stake, see Geoffrey Holmes and W. A. Speck, *The Divided Society: Party Conflict in England, 1694–1716* (London, 1967), pp. 1–7.

3 See Thomas Keymer, *Poetics of the Pillory: English Literature and Seditious Libel, 1660–1820* (Oxford, 2019), especially pp. 96–100.

4 Alain Corbin, *The Foul and the Fragrant: Odour and the Social Imagination*, trans. Miriam L. Kochan (London, 1996), p. 29.

5 See *Corr*, vol. III, p. 469. Pope uses the expression elsewhere, e.g. in *Peri Bathous*, but here he is obviously thinking of Curll's mishap in *The Dunciad*.

6 Sophie Gee, *Making Waste: Leftovers and the Eighteenth-century Imagination* (New Haven and London, 2010), p. 73. See more generally pp. 67–90.

7 Emily Cockayne, *Hubbub: Filth, Noise and Stench in England, 1600–1770* (New Haven and London, 2007), especially pp. 106–30.

8 Jenny Uglow, *Hogarth: A Life and a World* (London, 1997), p. 300.

9 Hogarth's friend Henry Fielding said that the print 'was enough to make a man deaf' to look at it: *The Journal of a Voyage to Lisbon, by the late Henry Fielding, Esq.* (London, 1755), p. 45.

10 James Raven, *The Business of Books: Booksellers and the English Book Trade 1450–1850* (New Haven, CT, 2007), p. 156. For more detailed plotting of localities, see Raven's *Bookscape: Geographies of Printing and Publishing in London before 1800* (London, 2014).

11 *TE*, vol. V, p. 99.

12 Ibid., vol. VI, p. 39.

13 John Gay, *Trivia: or, The Art of Walking the Streets of London* (London, 1716), pp. 31, 70.

14 *RWJ*, 6 May 1727.

15 *TE*, vol. V, p. 91.

16 [George Duckett?], *Pope Alexander's Supremacy and Infallibility Examin'd* (London, 1729), p. 16.

17 Colley Cibber, *A Letter from Mr Cibber, to Mr Pope, Inquiring into the Motives that might Induce him in his Satyrical Works, to be so Frequently Fond of Mr Cibber's Name* (London, 1742), pp. 47–9.

18 An informative article is Jonathan Pritchard, 'Social Topography in *The Dunciad, Variorum*', *Huntington Library Quarterly*, 75 (2012), pp. 527–60.

19 Charles Kerby-Miller, ed., *The Memoirs of the Extraordinary Life, Works, and Discoveries of Martinus Scriblerus* (New York, 1985), pp. 95–6.

20 *Corr*, vol. I, p. 187.

21 See Maynard Mack, *The Last and Greatest Art: Some Unpublished Poetical Manuscripts of Alexander Pope* (Newark, DE, 1984), p. 101.

22 [Edmund Curll], *The Curliad. A Hypercritic upon the Dunciad Variorum. With a Farther Key to the New Characters* (London, 1729), p. 38.

2 *The* ANTAGONISTS

1 *JSCorr*, vol. III, p. 578.

2 *The Memoirs of Mrs Lætitia Pilkington* (Dublin, 1748), vol. II, p. 152. On this author, well known to Swift, see Norma Clarke, *Queen of the Wits: A Life of Letitia Pilkington* (London, 2008).

3 Thomas Amory, *The Life of John Buncle, Esq.* (London, 1756–66), vol. II, p. 382.

4 *The Poetical Works of Elijah Fenton* (Edinburgh, 1779), pp. 51–2.

5 James Prior's *Life of Malone*, quoted in W. K. Wimsatt, *The Portraits of Alexander Pope* (New Haven, CT, 1965), p. xxv.

6 For the little that is known, see *ECB*, pp. 10–13.

7 *Corr*, vol. II, p. 138. For an excellent account of the influence of Pope's handicaps on his life and work, see Maynard Mack, '"The Least Thing like a Man in England": Some Effects of Pope's Physical Disability on his Life and Literary Career', in *Collected in Himself: Essays Critical, Biographical, and Bibliographical on Pope and Some of his Contemporaries* (Newark, DE, 1982), pp. 372–92.

8 The Popes' home, known as Whitehill House, has been greatly altered and expanded in recent years as Pope's Manor. It has served as the office buildings of a number of companies, most recently a firm that supplies luxury cars for hire.

9 For his entry into the livery and the use he made of it, see Pat Rogers and Paul Baines, 'Edmund Curll, Citizen and Liveryman: Politics and the Book Trade', *Publishing History*, 62 (2008), pp. 1–35.

10 For a survey of Curll's business practices, see my essay 'Edmund Curll and the Book Trade', in *Producing the Eighteenth-century Book: Writers and Publishers in Britain, 1650–1800*, ed. Laura Runge and Pat Rogers (Newark, DE, 2009), pp. 215–34.

11 Jonathan Swift, *Journal to Stella*, ed. Abigail Williams (Cambridge, 2013), p. 91.

12 *The Velvet Coffee-woman: or, the Life, Gallantries and Amours of the late Famous Mrs Anne Rochford* (Westminster, 1729), p. 36.

13 *MWJ*, 5 April 1718.

14 See *The Proceedings at the Sessions of the Peace, and Oyer and Terminer, for the City of London, and County of Middlesex on Thursday the 25th, Friday the 26th, Saturday the 27th, and Monday the 29th of May 1732, in the Fifth Year of His Majesty's Reign* (London, 1732), p. 144.

15 *PA*, p. 4. See also Guerinot's comments, pp. xx–xxi.

16 R. A. Brower, *Alexander Pope: The Poetry of Allusion* (Oxford, 1959), p. 2.

17 *TE*, vol. V, p. 104.

18 The major proponent of this view is Isaac Kramnick: see *Bolingbroke and his Circle: The Politics of Nostalgia in the Age of Walpole* (Cambridge, MA, 1968; repr. Ithaca, NY, 1992), pp. 4–5, 205.

19 Cambridge University Library, MS C(H) Corr 1839. For the fuller context, see *ECB*, p. 224.

20 [John Oldmixon], *The Catholick Poet* (London, 1716), pp. 2, 5. See *PA*, passim, for many such attacks.

21 [John Dennis], *A True Character of Mr Pope* (London, 1716), p. 5.
22 Jeremy Black, *Italy and the Grand Tour* (New Haven, CT, and London, 2003), p. 166.
23 Garry Stuart De Krey, *A Fractured Society: The Politics of London in the First Age of Party, 1688–1713* (Oxford, 1985), p. 59.
24 Swift, *Journal to Stella*, pp. 326–7.
25 Ibid.

3 TRUE *and* FALSE REPORTS, 1714–15

1 *JSCorr*, vol. I, p. 611.
2 Ibid., vol. II, p. 47.
3 Jonathan Swift, *Journal to Stella*, ed. Abigail Williams (Cambridge, 2013), p. 207.
4 A provisional list will be found in Pat Rogers, 'The Pamphleteers on Swift, 1710–1716', *Analytic and Enumerative Bibliography*, VII (1983), pp. 16–30.
5 The issues raised by this agreement are explored by James McLaverty, 'The Contract for Pope's Translation of Homer's *Iliad*: An Introduction and Transcription', *The Library*, 6th series (1993), pp. 206–25.
6 For the (very) full title, see *PA*, p. 11.
7 For the Wycherley volume, see Chapter Eight. For Pope's complaint, see *TE*, vol. V, p. 92.
8 *PW 1*, p. 263.
9 [Charles Gildon], *A New Rehearsal, or Bays the Younger* (London, 1714), pp. 8, 41.
10 [John Oldmixon, ed.], *Poems and Translations. By Several Hands* (London, 1714), pp. iii, 211.
11 Ibid., p. 245.
12 *PW 1*, p. 263.
13 *TE*, vol. VI, p. 99.
14 *Corr*, vol. I, p. 214.
15 Advertisement in *PB*, 8 April 1714.
16 *Corr*, vol. I, p. 308. In the same letter Pope adds a much more serious tribute to Lord Oxford's behaviour under the impeachment proceedings: 'The utmost Weight of Affliction from Princely Power and Popular Hatred, were almost worth bearing for the Glory of such a dauntless Conduct as he has shown under it.'
17 *TE*, vol. VI, p. 129.
18 *The Poems of Jonathan Swift*, ed. Harold Williams, 2nd edn (Oxford, 1958), vol. I, p. 138.
19 *Corr*, vol. I, p. 254.
20 See *EP*, 5 November 1715.
21 *The Earl of Mar Marr'd, with the Humours of Jockey, the Highlander: A Tragi-comical Farce* (London, 1715), p. 31.
22 See also letters from Bath on 26 September and 8 October 1715, quoted in *The Political State of Great Britain*, 10 (1716), pp. 333, 348.
23 See *Corr*, vol. I, p. 229.

24 Ibid., p. 305.

25 *PW 1*, pp. 183, 199.

26 *Corr*, vol. I, p. 306.

27 Cited in Sherburn, p. 166, as from the *Weekly Packet*; I have not found it there.

28 John Dennis, *Reflections Critical and Satyrical, upon a Late Rhapsody, Call'd, An Essay upon Criticism* (London, 1711), p. 26.

29 *PW 1*, pp. 7, 16–17.

4 *Poisonous* RELATIONS, 1716

1 *London Post*, 14 January 1716.

2 *Corr*, vol. I, p. 326.

3 Philip Horneck, *The High-German Doctor*, 23 April 1715. Horneck was a prolific journalist and on the government payroll as Solicitor to the Treasury from 1716. His aggressive brand of Whiggery earned him a place in *The Dunciad* and in the *Memoirs of Scriblerus*, where he is called 'a scurrilous Scribler'.

4 Christopher Sinclair-Stevenson, *Inglorious Rebellion: The Jacobite Risings of 1708, 1715 and 1719* (St Albans, 1973), p. 195.

5 Cited ibid., p. 188.

6 *Court Poems* (London, 1716), p. iii.

7 [Edmund Curll], *The Curliad. A Hypercritic upon the Dunciad Variorum. With a Farther Key to the New Characters* (London, 1729), p. 20. See also *Lit Corr*, vol. II, pp. vii–viii.

8 J. P. Malcolm, *Anecdotes of the Manners and Customs of London during the Eighteenth Century* (London, 1808), p. 227.

9 For a reproduction and transcript of Pope's manuscript version, see Robert Halsband, ed., *Court Eclogs Written in the Year 1716* (New York, 1977).

10 *PW 1*, pp. 259–60.

11 Ibid., pp. 262–3.

12 A fuller account of this episode will be found in Pat Rogers, 'The Conduct of the Earl of Nottingham: Curll, Oldmixon and the Finch Family', *Review of English Studies*, 21 (1970), pp. 175–81.

13 *PW 1*, p. 263.

14 *TE*, vol. VI, p. 37.

15 For the details of this tiff, see *ECB*, p. 121.

16 *PW 1*, p. 263.

17 Ibid., p. 264.

18 *TE*, vol. IV, p. 75.

19 *PW 1*, p. 265.

20 Ibid., pp. 265–6.

21 Daniel Defoe, *A Tour thro' the Whole Island of Great Britain* (London, 1724–6), vol. II, p. 136.

22 *FP*, 3 April 1716.

23 Ibid., 7 April 1716.

24 See Sherburn, p. 174.

25 *Corr*, vol. I, p. 339.

26 *TE*, vol. VI, p. 161.

27 Ibid., p. 162.

28 *PM*, 5 May 1716.

29 Paul Baines, *The Complete Critical Guide to Alexander Pope* (London, 2000), p. 20.

30 *Moore' Worms for the Learned Mr Curll, Bookseller* (London, 1716), pp. 1–2.

5 HORRID Wars, 1716

1 For a fuller account, see *ECB*, pp. 76–9. The pamphlet and key documents are found in the House of Lords Record Office, HL/PO/JO/10/6/261/3967.

2 Hertfordshire Record Office, Panshanger MSS, D/EP FSS.

3 John Oldmixon, *The History of England, during the Reigns of King William and Queen Mary, Queen Anne, King George I* (London, 1735), p. [627].

4 For the following paragraphs, see Pat Rogers, *The Letters, Life, and Works of John Oldmixon: Politics and Professional Authorship in Early Hanoverian England* (Lewiston, NY, 2003), and sources cited there.

5 The attacks quoted in this paragraph are among those analysed in Pat Rogers, 'The Dunce Answers Back: John Oldmixon on Swift and Defoe', *Texas Studies in Literature and Language*, 14 (1972), pp. 33–43.

6 *TE*, vol. V, pp. 28–9.

7 [John Oldmixon], *The Catholick Poet* (London, 1716), pp. 1–2. The fullest discussion is Pat Rogers, '*The Catholick Poet* (1716)', *Bodleian Library Record*, 8 (1971), pp. 277–84.

8 See *Corr*, vol. I, pp. 371–5. The bookseller is made to say of translators, 'By G—d I can never be sure in these fellows, for I neither understand *Greek, Latin, French,* nor *Italian* my self.'

9 *TE*, vol. VI, p. 83.

10 Oldmixon, *Catholick Poet*, p. 3.

11 Ibid., p. 5.

12 Ibid., p. 6.

13 *TE*, vol. V, p. 125.

14 John Dennis, *A True Character of Mr. Pope, and his Writings* (London, 1716), p. 10.

15 Ibid., pp. 16–17.

16 Ibid., pp. 4–6.

17 Ibid., pp. 9–11.

18 Sherburn, p. 179.

19 Dennis, *True Character*, pp. 4–5.

20 *FP*, 30 June 1716.

21 *TE*, vol. VI, pp. 164–5.

22 *FP*, 14 July 1716.

23 *Corr*, vol. I, p. 350.

24 See Norman Ault, *New Light on Pope* (London, 1949), pp. 156–62 (quotation from p. 160).

25 *Corr*, vol. I, p. 342.
26 Ibid., pp. 358–9.

6 The LOSS *of* EDEN, 1716

1 By the provisions of this single statute, 2 Wm II, c. 4, many onerous restrictions were placed on the Catholic community.
2 For this threat, see the sensitive account by Paul Gabriner, 'The Papist's House, the Papist's Horse: Alexander Pope and the Removal from Binfield', in *Centennial Hauntings: Pope, Byron and Eliot in the Year 88*, ed. C. C. Barfoot and Theo D'Haen (Amsterdam, 1990), pp. 13–63.
3 *Corr*, vol. I, p. 339.
4 C. J. Rawson, 'Some Unpublished Letters of Pope and Gay', *Review of English Studies*, 10 (1959), p. 377.
5 *Corr*, vol. I, pp. 336–7.
6 [Samuel Wesley], *Neck or Nothing: A Consolatory Letter from Mr D-nt-n to Mr C--rll upon his being Tost in a Blanket, &c.* (London, 1716), pp. 11, 13, 15–16. I think the refrain may be meant to echo the old ballads in which a pilgrim asks the way to Walsingham, the medieval shrine in Norfolk.
7 *Corr*, vol. I, p. 350.
8 *PW 1*, p. 277.
9 A more detailed exploration of the issues will be found in Pat Rogers, 'Looking for Mr Curll's Authors: Pope's *Further Account*', in *Documenting Eighteenth Century Satire: Pope, Swift, Gay, and Arbuthnot in Historical Context* (Newcastle upon Tyne, 2012), pp. 101–22.
10 *PW 1*, pp. 278–9.
11 Ibid., pp. 280–81.
12 Susanna Centlivre, *A Bold Stroke for a Wife* (London, 1718), p. 60.
13 *PW 1*, pp. 281–2.
14 Ibid., pp. 284–5.
15 See *MWJ*, 26 July 1718.
16 *TE*, vol. V, p. 125.
17 *SJEP*, 10 December 1716, cited in *PW 1*, pp. civ–cv.
18 *AWJ*, 9 November 1717.
19 The pamphlet provoked two replies: one, a verse epistle plausibly attributed to Arbuthnot; the other called *A Letter from Sir J[ames] B[aker]*. Ault thinks the latter may have come from Curll, but I believe this is unlikely.

7 The SECOND Aesop, 1717

1 *PM*, 10 January 1717.
2 John Gay, *Dramatic Works*, ed. John Fuller (Oxford, 1983), vol. I, p. 210.
3 'E. Parker', *A Complete Key to the New Farce, Call'd Three Hours after Marriage. With an Account of the Authors* (London, 1717), pp. 4–5, 13.
4 [John Durant Breval], *The Confederates* (London, 1717), pp. 2, 5.
5 Ibid., pp. 32–4.
6 Ibid., p. 39.

7 *DC*, 25 and 28 February 1717.

8 John Dennis, *Remarks upon Mr. Pope's Translation of Homer. With Two Letters concerning Windsor Forest, and The Temple of Fame* (London, 1717), sigs. A1v, A2r, B2r.

9 Ibid., pp. 26–8.

10 Ibid., pp. [39], 91–2.

11 Leonard Welsted, *The Works, in Verse and Prose*, ed. John Nichols (London, 1787), pp. 37–9. For the context, see *ECB*, pp. 101–3.

12 For a more complete analysis, see Pat Rogers, 'Wit, Love, and Sin: Pope's *Court Ballad* Reconsidered', in *Eighteenth-century Encounters: Studies in Literature and Society in the Age of Walpole* (Brighton, 1985), pp. 56–74.

13 *Corr*, vol. I, p. 407.

14 *The Court Ballad: By Mr Pope* (London, 1717), p. 1.

15 Colley Cibber, *Love Makes a Man: or, The Fop's Fortune* (London, 1701), p. 44.

16 [Giles Jacob], *The Rape of the Smock. An Heroi-comical Poem* (London, 1717), sig. A4r.

17 *The Iliad of Homer, translated by Mr Pope* (London, 1715–20), vol. I, sigs. F3r–F4r.

8 An *Abominable* CATALOGUE, 1718–19

1 *Corr*, vol. I, pp. 447–50.

2 Colley Cibber, *The Non-Juror: A Comedy* (London, 1718), p. ii.

3 Colley Cibber, *An Apology for the Life of Mr Colley Cibber, Comedian, and Late Patentee of the Theatre-Royal. With an Historical View of the Stage during his own Time. Written by Himself* (London, 1740), p. 302.

4 *A Clue to the Comedy of the Non-Juror* (London, 1718), pp. 6, 8.

5 *EP*, 18 February 1718.

6 *The Plot Discover'd: or, a Clue to the Comedy of the Non-Juror. With some Hints of Consequence Relating to that Play. In a Letter to N. Rowe, Esq; Poet Laureat to His Majesty* (London, 1718), verso of title page. Also used in Curll's advertisement, *PB*, 20 March 1718.

7 [Charles Gildon], *Memoirs of the Life of William Wycherley, Esq; With a Character of his Writings* (London, 1718), pp. 15–16.

8 John Durant Breval, *Play Is the Plot* (London, 1718), p. 21.

9 The overwhelming probability is that Arbuthnot was the true author. See 'Satire as Mock-science: The Scriblerians and the Search for the Longitude', in Pat Rogers, *Documenting Eighteenth Century Satire: Pope, Swift, Gay, and Arbuthnot in Historical Context* (Newcastle upon Tyne, 2012), pp. 45–62.

10 [Daniel Defoe?], *The Secret History of the White Staff, Purse and Mitre* (London, 1715), p. 23.

11 *Onanism Display'd*, 2nd edn (London, 1719), p. vi. The only recorded copy of this work is a microfilm at the National Library of Medicine, Washington, DC. For background, see Francis Doherty, *A Study*

in Eighteenth-century Advertising Methods: *The Anodyne Necklace* (Lampeter, 1992), pp. 151–6.

12 *MWJ*, 5 and 12 April 1718. The first article is almost certainly by Defoe; the second may or may not be. We saw in Chapter One that Pope used the same expression, 'Tom Turdman', for those responsible for indecent publications.

13 [Edmund Curll], *The Curliad. A Hypercritic upon the Dunciad Variorum. With a Farther Key to the New Characters* (London, 1729), p. 14. Curll refers to this incident while making the same argument in *The Humble Representation of Edmund Curll, Bookseller and Citizen of London, Concerning Five Books, Complained of to the Secretary of State* [London, 1725], p. 5.

14 [Edmund Curll], *Curlicism Display'd* (London, 1718), pp. 2, 24.

15 Ibid., pp. 26–7.

16 G. H. Healey, ed., *The Letters of Daniel Defoe* (Oxford, 1955), p. 459.

17 *MWJ*, 30 August 1718.

18 *Corr*, vol. II, p. 328.

19 Maynard Mack, *The Garden and the City* (Toronto, 1969), p. 25. Mack is the best guide to the importance of the garden as a clue to Pope's essential values. On the move to Twickenham, see also Pat Rogers, 'Pope's Homes: London, Windsor Forest, and Twickenham', in *Home and Nation in British Literature from the English to the French Revolutions*, ed. A. D. Cousins and Geoffrey Payne (Cambridge, 2015), pp. 127–40.

20 *EP*, 7 March 1719.

21 [Giles Jacob], *The Poetical Register: or, the Lives and Characters of the English Dramatick Poets. With an Account of their Writings* (London, 1719), pp. 284, 289.

22 [Curll], *The Curliad*, p. 4; John Dennis, *Remarks upon Several Passages in the Preliminaries to the Dunciad* (London, 1729), p. 46.

23 J. McLaverty, 'Pope and Giles Jacob's *Lives of the Poets*', *Modern Philology*, 83 (1985), pp. 2–32, is an important assessment of how Pope used Curllian materials for his own purposes.

24 *Corr*, vol. II, p. 31.

9 CRIMES *and* PUNISHMENTS, 1720–24

1 For a discussion of investments in South Sea by Pope and his friends, see Colin Nicholson, *Writing and the Rise of Finance: Capital Satires of the Early Eighteenth Century* (Cambridge, 1994), pp. 51–90.

2 [William Bond?], *An Epistle to His Royal Highness the Prince of Wales* (London, 1720), p. 6.

3. *DP*, 2 November 1720.

4 'Mr Arundell', *The Directors, a Poem: Addressed to Mr Stanhope* (London, 1720), p. 32.

5 *PB*, 22 March 1720.

6 *DP*, 12 April 1720.

7 See *Miscellanies: The Third Volume* (London, 1732), pp. 27–35. For a review of the issues here, see Pat Rogers, 'Pope's *Strange but True*

Relation of Edmund Curll: Blasphemy, Anti-Semitism, and the City of London', *Modern Philology*, 117 (2019), pp. 127–48.

8 *Miscellanies*, pp. 31–2, 33–4.

9 *An Answer to Duke upon Duke &c.* (London, 1720), pp. 1–2. Pope's ballad and the reply are discussed in '*Duke upon Duke*: Satiric Context, Aims and Means', in Pat Rogers, *Documenting Eighteenth Century Satire: Pope, Swift, Gay, and Arbuthnot in Historical Context* (Newcastle upon Tyne, 2012), pp. 161–80.

10 *DC*, 17 February 1720.

11 William Clark, *Party Revenge* (London, 1720), p. [40].

12 Joseph Spence, *Observations, Anecdotes, and Characters of Books and Men*, ed. James M. Osborn, 2 vols (Oxford, 1966), vol. I, pp. 202–3.

13 NA, SP 44/81/389. For Curll's work as a government informer, see *ECB*, pp. 150, 223–4.

14 *PW 2*, p. 24.

15 *PW 1*, p. 326.

16 *JSCorr*, vol. II, p. 327.

17 *TE*, vol. V, pp. 132–3.

18 *DP*, 10 March 1721.

19 John Gay, *Poetry and Prose*, ed. V. A. Dearing and C. E. Beckwith (Oxford, 1974), vol. V, p. 217.

20 First published from the Longleat manuscripts in A. R. Waller, ed., *The Writings of Matthew Prior* (Cambridge, 1907), vol. II, p. 335.

21 *Journal of the House of Lords* (London, 1767–1803), vol. XXI, pp. 659–61.

22 Ibid., p. 667.

23 *The Works of the Most Noble John Sheffield, late Duke of Buckingham* (London, 1721 for 1722), sig. [a]4v.

24 *Pasquin*, 13 and 20 February 1723. The best analysis of the episode remains Sherburn, pp. 219–27; see also *ECB*, pp. 146–8. The words of Pope Gregory's thirteenth-century decree were regularly cited by Protestant controversialists.

25 *Corr*, vol. II, p. 159.

26 *Pasquin*, 20 May 1723.

27 Sherburn, p. 223.

28 *Journal of the House of Lords*, vol. XXI, pp. 660–61.

29 J. Markland et al., *Cythereia: or, New Poems upon Love and Intrigue* (London, 1723), pp. 90–92. For other versions, see *TE*, vol. VI, pp. 144–5.

10 PRISON, 1724–7

1 *Heydegger's Letter to the Bishop of London* (London, 1724), pp. 3, 5.

2 *DC*, 15 April 1724.

3 A fuller account, based on NA, SP 35/49/50 and SP 44/80/175–6, will be found in *ECB*, pp. 156–7.

4 The quotation comes from an important discussion in *FP* on obscene writing, with relation to Prior, Mist and others (reprinted in the *Political State*, 28 [1724], pp. 203–8).

5 *CJ*, 15 July 1727.

6 This section is based on a number of sources in NA, especially SP 44/81/394, 399–400; SP 35/55/102; and SP 35/58/99, 101. A fuller account will be found in *ECB*, pp. 157–8.

7 NA, SP 35/58/75, 101, Curll to Charles Delafaye, 27 October 1725. Again, there is a more detailed discussion of these matters in *ECB*, p. 158.

8 Bodleian Library, Rawlinson MSS, C195. Richard Rawlinson collected and possibly supplied Curll manuscripts.

9 Edmund Curll, *The Humble Representation of Edmund Curll; Bookseller and Citizen of London, Concerning Five Books Complained of to the Secretary of State* (London, [1725] pp. 5–6, 11.

10 See *MWJ*, 4 December 1725; *RWJ*, 7 December 1725 and 1 July 1726; and other sources cited in *ECB*, p. 159.

11 Cited in Straus, p. 106. I have not found the newspaper in question.

12 *Hereditary Right Exemplified: or, a Letter of Condolance for Mr Ed---d C--l to his Son H---y, upon his late Discipline at Westminster* (London, 1728), pp. 19–21.

13 *DJ*, 11 February 1726.

14 For Curll's difficulties with Staunton's books, see NA, SP 35/61/9 and 9(i), and other sources cited in *ECB*, pp. 160–61.

15 NA, SP 35/61/14, 30.

16 John Strype, *A Survey of the Cities of London and Westminster: Containing the Original, Antiquity, Increase, Modern Estate and Government of those Cities* (London, 1720), vol. II, p. 30.

17 Here I follow earlier sources, including Straus, p. 113, on the date of this letter, although I suspect it was written three years earlier.

18 *LJ*, 12 November 1726.

19 *DJ*, 16 November 1726.

20 *EP*, 5 July 1726, cited in Straus, p. 114.

21 *DJ*, 23 January 1727.

22 For her remarkable and little-known career, see *ECB*, pp. 233–4.

23 The key series of documents are found in NA, SP 35/64, 20–30. Fuller citations appear in *ECB*, pp. 165–6.

24 NA, SP 35/64/33. Further legal orders and correspondence between Curll and the authorities are found in SP 35/64 and SP 44/80, cited in *ECB*, pp. 165–6.

25 *The Poetical Works of Mr William Pattison, Late of Sidney College Cambridge* (London, 1728 for 1727), pp. 44, 46.

26 [Richard Savage?], *An Author to be Lett* (London, 1729), p. 3. For more on this, see Chapter Twelve.

27 [Edmund Curll, ed.], *Miscellanea. In Two Volumes. Never before Published* (London, 1727 for 1726), vol. II, pp. 145–6.

28 *PW 2*, p. 198.

11 PILLORY, 1725–8

1 *TE*, vol. V, p. 91; *The Repository of Arts, Literature, Commerce, Manufactures, Fashions and Politics*, 11 (February 1814), p. 63.

2 Robert D. Hume, 'Before the Bard: "Shakespeare" in Early Eighteenth-century London', *ELH*, 64 (1997), pp. 41–75 (quotation from p. 43).

3 Sherburn, pp. 240–44.

4 Wikipedia, 'Double Falsehood', www.wikipedia.com, accessed 14 November 2019.

5 *AWJ*, 31 July 1725, quoted in William Lee, *Daniel Defoe: His Life, and Recently Discovered Writings* (London, 1869), vol. III, pp. 409–10.

6 *Corr*, vol. II, p. 164.

7 [Pope et al.], *The Odyssey of Homer. Translated from the Greek* (London, 1725), vol. V, p. 226.

8 Ibid., vol. I, verso of title page.

9 *LJ*, 17 July 1725.

10 The proposals for the *Iliad* were reprinted on the closing leaf of *The Rape of the Lock. An Heroi-comical Poem. In Five Canto's*, 3rd edn (London, 1714), p. [54].

11 [Jonathan Smedley, ed.], *Gulliveriana* (London, 1728), p. 317.

12 [Spring Macky], *The Adventures of Pomponius* (London, 1726), vol. II, p. 28.

13 [Edmund Curll], *A Compleat Key to The Dunciad* (London, 1728), pp. 9–10.

14 *TE*, vol. V, p. 106.

15 *Corr*, vol. III, p. 449; vol. II, p. 14. For Cromwell's not very persuasive explanation of how the letters came into the hands of Thomas, see vol. II, pp. 439–40.

16 Ibid., vol. III, p. 80.

17 [Edmund Curll], *The Curliad. A Hypercritic upon the Dunciad Variorum. With a Farther Key to the New Characters* (London, 1729), p. 22.

18 *Corr*, vol. II, p. 419.

19 Ibid., pp. 438–9.

20 *PW 2*, p. 89.

21 Ibid., pp. 91–2.

22 Irvin Ehrenpreis, *Swift: The Man, His Works, and the Age*, vol. III: *Dean Swift* (Cambridge, MA, 1983), p. 493.

23 *Corr*, vol. II, pp. 477–8.

24 From an article in *BJ*, 25 November 1727, probably by Matthew Concanen, reprinted in *A Compleat Collection of all the Verses, Essays, Letters and Advertisements, which have been Occasioned by the Publication of Three Volumes of Miscellanies, by Pope and Company. To which is Added an Exact List of the Lords, Ladies, Gentlemen and Others, who have been Abused in those Volumes. With a large Dedication to the Author of the Dunciad, Containing some Animadversions upon that Extraordinary Performance* (London, 1728), pp. 2–3. The work was issued by the phantom publisher 'A. Moore'.

25 *NA*, 11/944/3430, and other documents cited in *ECB*, pp. 166–7; Sir John Strange, *Reports of Adjudged Cases in the Courts of Chancery, King's Bench, Common Pleas, and Exchequer* (London, 1755), vol. II, pp. 791–2.

26 For a full transcription of the report, see *State Trials*, vol. I: *Treason and Libel*, ed. Donald Thomas (London, 1972), pp. 135–43. For Fortescue's

dissenting view, see John Fortescue Aland, *Reports of Select Cases in all the Courts of Westminster-Hall* (London, 1748), p. 100.

27 *JSCorr*, vol. III, p. 144.

28 Most of the papers cover Curll's conviction, some with evident relish, starting in *DJ*, 13 February 1728.

29 See Thomas Keymer, *Poetics of the Pillory: English Literature and Seditious Libel, 1660–1820* (Oxford, 2019), most relevantly here pp. 166–7.

30 J. M. Beattie, *Crime and the Courts in England, 1660–1800* (Princeton, NJ, 1986), p. 464.

31 Keymer, *Poetics of the Pillory*, p. 96.

32 Robert B. Shoemaker, *The London Mob: Violence and Disorder in Eighteenth-century England* (London, 2004), pp. 94–5.

33 *MWJ*, 27 July 1723. See also NA, SP 43/66.

34 V.A.C. Gatrell, *The Hanging Tree: Execution and the English People, 1770–1868* (Oxford, 1994), p. 70.

35 James Sutherland, *Defoe* (Philadelphia, PA, 1938), p. 95.

36 See Keymer, *Poetics of the Pillory*, pp. 142–4.

37 T. B. Howell, *A Complete Collection of State Trials and Proceedings for High Treason and Other Crimes and Misdemeanors from the Earliest Period to the Year 1783, with Notes and Other Illustrations* (London, 1816), vol. XVII, p. 160.

38 An apparently unique copy of the broadside that Curll handed out at Charing Cross is preserved in the John Johnson collection at the Bodleian Library. See further *ECB*, pp. 168–9.

39 Henry Fielding, *The Covent-Garden Journal*, 27 June 1752, quoted in Keymer, *Poetics of the Pillory*, p. 159.

40 Percy A. Scholes, *The Oxford Companion to Music* (Oxford, 1938), quoted in Rex Harris, *Jazz* (Harmondsworth, 1952), p. 214.

41 ['Caleb D'Anvers'], *The Twickenham Hotch-potch* (London, 1728), pp. vi–vii.

12 *A Confederacy of* DUNCES, 1728–9

1 [Richard Savage, ed.], *A Collection of Pieces in Verse and Prose, which have been Publish'd on Occasion of the Dunciad* (London, 1732), p. vi.

2 The most broadly informative reading is still Aubrey Williams, *Pope's Dunciad: A Study of Its Meaning* (London, 1955). For a good short introduction, see Howard Erskine-Hill, *Pope: The Dunciad* (London, 1972). A host of specialized works illuminate different facets of the poem.

3 *TE*, vol. V, pp. 98, 103–5.

4 The relevance of this circumstance was first pointed out by Valerie Rumbold in *The Dunciad in Four Books* (Harlow, 1999), p. 157.

5 *TE*, vol. V, pp. 105–7.

6 Maynard Mack, *The Last and Greatest Art: Some Unpublished Poetical Manuscripts of Alexander Pope* (Newark, DE, 1984), p. 106.

7 *TE*, vol. V, pp. 108–9.

8 Ibid., pp. 112, 117–18.

9 Ibid., pp. 118–19.

10 Ibid., pp. 119–23.

11 See Virgil, *Georgics*, IV, 371–3. Pope had recollected this passage in *Windsor Forest*, when he attributes golden horns to another river god, Father Thames.

12 [Edmund Curll], *A Compleat Key to The Dunciad* (London, 1728), p. 12.

13 Ibid., p. 13.

14 *TE*, vol. V, pp. 104–5.

15 Ibid., pp. 64, 97.

16 A device close to what the rhetoricians Pope had studied would call 'apophasis', that is, saying something by asserting that you are not going to mention it.

17 *TE*, vol. V, p. 123.

18 [Richard Savage?], *An Author to be Lett* (London, 1729), p. 11.

19 *Corr*, vol. II, p. 508.

20 [William Bond et al.?], *The Progress of Dulness* (London, 1728), pp. 33–4.

21 *Puddles and Mire: The Female Dunciad* (London, 1728), pp. vii, 15, 43.

22 *PA*, p. 154.

23 *Codrus: or, The Dunciad Dissected. Being the Finishing-stroke* (London, 1728), pp. 18, 21.

24 [Jonathan Smedley], *Gulliveriana: or, a Fourth Volume of Miscellanies. Being a Sequel of the Three Volumes, Published by Pope and Swift. To which is Added, Alexanderiana; or, A Comparison between the Ecclesiastical and Poetical Pope. And many Things, in Verse and Prose, Relating to the Latter. With an Ample Preface; and a Critique on the Third Volume of Miscellanies Lately Publish'd by those two Facetious Writers* (London, 1728), p. 332.

25 [Jonathan Smedley], *The Metamorphosis: a Poem. Shewing the Change of Scriblerus into Snarlerus: or, The Canine Appetite: Demonstrated in the Persons of P-pe and Sw--t* (London, 1728), p. 6.

26 [Curll], *Compleat Key*, pp. iii–v.

27 *PA*, p. 112.

28 *TE*, vol. V, p. 9.

29 *DJ*, 17 July 1728.

30 *The Popiad* (London, 1728), pp. 6–7.

31 Ibid., p. [8]; *DP*, 14 June 1728.

32 *The Popiad*, p. 32.

33 *DJ*, 27 April 1729.

34 Ibid., 9 May 1729.

35 [Samuel Johnson], *An Account of the Life of Mr Richard Savage* (London, 1744), p. 44.

36 [Edmund Curll], *The Curliad. A Hypercritic upon the Dunciad Variorum. With a Farther Key to the New Characters* (London, 1729), pp. 18–19.

37 Ibid., p. 3.

38 Ibid., p. 38.

39 'Charles Wilson', *Memoirs of the Life, Writings, and Amours of William Congreve, Esq; Interspersed with Miscellaneous Essays, Letters, and Characters, Written by him* (London, 1730 for 1729), pp. x, ²15.

13 The PUBLIC Ear, 1730–34

1 For a thorough study, see Miriam Leranbaum, *Alexander Pope's 'Opus Magnum', 1729–1744* (Oxford, 1977).

2 *TE*, vol. IV, p. 325.

3 See Christine Gerrard, *The Patriot Opposition to Walpole: Poetry, Politics, and National Myth, 1725–1742* (Oxford, 1994).

4 *TE*, vol. IV, p. 125.

5 [Henry Fielding], *The Author's Farce; and The Pleasures of the Town. As Acted at the Theatre in the Hay-Market. Written by Scriblerus Secundus* (London, 1730), p. 11.

6 Ibid., p. 20.

7 Ibid., p. 35.

8 *DJ*, 20 January 1732; *GSJ*, 27 January 1732.

9 *DJ*, 31 December 1731.

10 *A Miscellany on Taste. By Mr Pope, &c.* (London, 1732), p. [25].

11 *GSJ*, 29 January 1730.

12 Ibid., 16 April 1730.

13 [Leonard Welsted?], *One Epistle to Mr A. Pope, Occasion'd by Two Epistles lately Published* (London, 1730), pp. 16–17.

14 In May another bookseller had indeed advertised *Complete Antiquities* in ten volumes. This turns out to be Curll's own long-running series, which he had jealously guarded until now.

15 *GSJ*, 16 April 1730.

16 Ibid., 26 October 1732.

17 Ibid., 31 July 1735.

18 Ibid., 15 January 1736.

19 James Bramston, *The Man of Taste* (London, 1733), p. 8.

20 *TE*, vol. IV, p. 13. From the point of view of the quarrel, it is significant that libel should be at the centre of the poem.

21 Ibid.

22 Richard Blackmore, *A True and Impartial History of the Conspiracy against the Person and Government of King William III of Glorious Memory, in the Year 1695* (London, 1723), p. 4.

23 'Atex. Burnet', *Achilles Dissected: Being a Compleat Key of the Political Characters in that New Ballad Opera, Written by the Late Mr Gay. An Account of the Plan upon which it is Founded. With Remarks upon the Whole* (London, 1733), p. 20.

24 *TE*, vol. IV, p. 5; *Achilles Dissected*, p. 21.

25 *TE*, vol. IV, pp. 7, 9; *Achilles Dissected*, pp. 23–4.

26 *TE*, vol. IV, p. 13; *Achilles Dissected*, pp. 25–6.

27 *TE*, vol. IV, p. 17; *Achilles Dissected*, pp. 28, 30.

28 *Lit Corr*, vol. II, p. 82.

29 *Corr*, vol. III, p. 355.

30 *DJ*, 30 March 1733, a comment recycled in *Lit Corr*, vol. II, 2nd edn, p. xix.

31 [Giles Jacob], *The Mirrour: or, Letters Satyrical, Panegyrical, Serious and Humorous, on the Present Times . . . To which is added a Legal Conviction of*

Mr Alexander Pope of Dulness and Scandal, in the High Court of Parnassus (London, 1733), pp. 77–8.

32 Ibid., p. 78.
33 Ibid., pp. 79–80.

14 *The Letters of* MR POPE: Stage One, 1735

1 *TE*, vol. II, p. 144.
2 *Corr*, vol. III, p. 417.
3 *TE*, vol. IV, pp. 96–7, 100, 125.
4 The primary source for the account here is Pope's *Narrative of the Method by which Mr Pope's Private Letters were Procured and Published by Edmund Curll, Bookseller* (1735), reprinted with helpful notes by Rosemary Cowler in *PW 2*, pp. 319–56. Curll's scathing comments on this *Narrative* will be found in *Lit Corr*, vol. II, pp. i–xvi, and his own report of the affair, 'The Initial Correspondence', follows on pp. 1–48. References supplied here are confined to citations outside these sources.
5 *PW 2*, p. 321.
6 J. McLaverty, 'The First Printing and Publication of Pope's Letters', *The Library*, 6th series, 2 (1980), pp. 264–80.
7 The documents that follow are taken from *Journal of the House of Lords* (1767–1830), vol. XXIV, pp. 550–56.
8 *Corr*, vol. III, p. 455.
9 The proceedings of the committee on 14 May, with De La Warr's report to the House the next day, are reproduced in Whitwell Elwin and W. J. Courthope, ed., *The Works of Alexander Pope* (London, 1871–89), vol. VI, pp. 432–5.
10 *JSCorr*, vol. IV, p. 153.
11 Samuel Johnson, *The Lives of the Poets*, ed. John H. Middendorf (New Haven and London, 2010), vol. III, p. 1118.
12 *Lit Corr*, vol. II, p. xiv.

15 *The Letters of* MR POPE: Stage Two, 1735–6

1 *DJ*, 24 May 1735; *DPB*, 27 May 1735.
2 *GSJ*, 12 June 1735; *DJ*, 16 June 1735.
3 *PB*, 16 June 1735.
4 *Corr*, vol. III, pp. 468–9.
5 Ibid., p. 468n.
6 *SJEP*, 12 July 1735.
7 *Corr*, vol. III, p. 469.
8 Ibid., pp. 472–3.
9 Ibid., p. 477.
10 *FWJ*, 26 July 1735, quoted in *Notes & Queries*, 2nd series, vol. X (1860), p. 204.
11 *Lit Corr*, vol. II, 2nd edn, pp. xxv–xxvi.

12 *Corr*, vol. II, p. 481; *JSCorr*, vol. IV, pp. 118, 171, 174.

13 *The Poet Finish'd in Prose. Being a Dialogue concerning Mr Pope and his Writings* (London, 1735), p. 13.

14 Ibid., pp. 39, 75.

15 Maynard Mack, *The Garden and the City* (Toronto, 1969), p. 307.

16 *GSJ*, 19 June 1735.

17 *Lit Corr*, vol. II, pp. iv–v.

18 Ibid., pp. ⁴79–81. This section shows that Curll knew, better than most, what was important to Pope.

19 Ibid., pp. x–xvi.

20 Ibid., p. ²i.

21 Ibid., p. 48.

22 Ibid., vol. III, pp. v–vi.

23 Ibid., pp. ²x27–xii.

24 *Corr*, vol. III, pp. 501–2.

25 *JSCorr*, vol. IV, pp. 171, 204.

26 *Post-Office Intelligence* (London, 1736 for 1735), pp. v–vi.

27 [Giles Jacob], *Liberty and Property: Or a New Year's Gift for Mr. Pope* (London, 1736), pp. v, xii.

28 *Lit Corr*, vol. IV, pp. vi–vii.

29 Ibid., pp. 148–52.

30 Ibid., p. 59.

31 R. H. Griffith, *Alexander Pope: A Bibliography* (Austin, TX, 1922–7), vol. II, p. 334.

32 *Corr*, vol. IV, p. 7.

33 *LEP*, 11 November 1736.

16 FINAL Exchanges, 1737–47

1 *PW 2*, p. 369.

2 Ibid., p. 371.

3 Ibid., p. 372.

4 *Lit Corr*, vol. V, p. ii. This was an augmented version of the volume of *New Letters*, published in November 1736.

5 *Lit Corr*, vol. V, pp. 241–2.

6 *One Thousand Seven Hundred Thirty Nine. A Rhapsody. By Way of Sequel to Seventeen Hundred Thirty Eight, by Mr Pope* (London, 1740), pp. [5]–6.

7 *The Tryal of Colley Cibber, Comedian, &c. for Writing a Book Intitled An Apology for his Life, &c. Being a Thorough Examination thereof; wherein he is Proved Guilty of High-Crimes and Misdemeanors against the English Language, and in Characterising many Persons of Distinction. Together with an Indictment Exhibited* (London, 1740), p. 28.

8 Ibid., p. 29.

9 *Sawney and Colley: A Poetical Dialogue* (London, 1742), pp. 17–18. On the title page, the quotation from Horace, *Par nobile fratrum*, is used again (see Chapter Fifteen, p. 362).

10 *Corr*, vol. IV, pp. 50, 60; *JSCorr*, vol. IV, p. 398.

11 *Corr*, vol. IV, p. 271.

12 *The Poems of Jonathan Swift*, ed. Harold Williams, 2nd edn (Oxford, 1958), vol. II, pp. 560–61.

13 *Dean Swift's Literary Correspondence, for Twenty-four Years, from 1714 to 1738* (London, 1741), sig. π2ʳ.

14 Ibid., p. 26.

15 The case has naturally been extensively discussed, most thoroughly by Mark Rose, *Authors and Owners: The Invention of Copyright* (Cambridge, MA, 1993), pp. 59–66. For its relation to the feud, see also Pat Rogers, 'The Case of Pope v. Curll', in *Essays on Pope* (Cambridge, 1993), pp. 184–9.

16 See for example the passages of savage irony in E. P. Thompson, *Whigs and Hunters: The Origin of the Black Act* (Harmondsworth, 1977), pp. 208–11, 217, 250–51, 257.

17 The original documents are found in NA, C11/1569/29. Rose, *Authors and Owners*, pp. 145–53, prints a modernized transcript. My reading differs only in small particulars and typographic accidentals.

18 Rose, *Authors and Owners*, p. 65.

19 Joseph Spence, *Anecdotes, Observations, and Characters of Books and Men*, ed. J. M. Osborn (Oxford, 1966), vol. I, p. 261.

20 'William Ayre', *Memoirs of the Life and Writings of Alexander Pope, Esq* (London, 1745), vol. I, pp. 288–301.

21 'JH', *Remarks on 'Squire Ayre's Memoirs* (London, 1745), p. 41.

22 For Curll's last days and his posthumous reputation, see *ECB*, pp. 309–13.

Closing ARGUMENTS

1 The key passages from Warton and Johnson are assembled side by side in John Barnard, ed., *Pope: The Critical Heritage* (London, 1973), quotations respectively from pp. 381, 521, 507.

2 For Byron's enthusiastic response to Pope, see Nicholas Gayle, *Byron and the Best of Poets* (Newcastle upon Tyne, 2016).

3 W. M. Thackeray, *The English Humorist of the Eighteenth Century*, ed. Edgar F. Harden (Ann Arbor, MI, 2007), pp. 71–2.

4 John Ruskin, *Lectures on Art* (New York, 1870), p. 73.

5 Mark Pattison, 'Pope and his Editors', *British Quarterly Review*, 56 (1872), p. 231; Whitwell Elwin in Whitwell Elwin and W. J. Courthope, ed., *The Works of Alexander Pope* (London, 1871–89), vol. II, p. 24.

6 Edith Sitwell, *Alexander Pope* (New York, 1962), pp. 188–9.

7 John O'Brien, 'Grub Street: The Literary and the Literatory in Eighteenth-century Britain', in *Teaching Literature: A Companion*, ed. Tanya Agathocleous and Ann C. Dean (Basingstoke, 2003), p. 46.

8 Bradford K. Mudge, ed., *When Flesh Becomes Word: An Anthology of Early Eighteenth-century Libertine Literature* (Oxford, 2004), p. 9.

9 Bradford K. Mudge, *The Whore's Story: Women, Pornography, and the British Novel, 1684–1830* (Oxford, 2000), p. 158. The following paragraphs are based on pp. 158–72.

10 Law Library, 'Stipulation', https://law.jrank.org, accessed 9 September 2019.

11 Straus, pp. 94–6. See Chapter Nine, with further examples cited in *ECB*, pp. 150, 157–8.

12 Quoted in Straus, p. 95.

13 Cambridge University Library, MS C(H) Corr 2086, printed in full in *ECB*, pp. 235–6.

14 Mudge, *Whore's Story*, p. 164.

15 *TE*, vol. IV, p. 65.

16 Straus, p. 155.

EPILOGUE

1 See Jürgen Habermas, *The Structural Transformation of the Public Sphere: An Inquiry into a Category of Bourgeois Society*, trans. Thomas Burger (Cambridge, MA, 1992).

2 *The Charitable Surgeon: or, The Best Remedies for the Worst Maladies, Reveal'd*, 2nd edn (London, 1709), title page.

Select Bibliography

This list indicates some books that have been particularly useful in the compilation of this volume, and provides suggestions for further reading. It does not attempt to set out an exhaustive catalogue of the vast secondary literature on Pope, Curll and their associates.

TEXTS

The satirical works directed against Curll can be found in *The Prose Works of Alexander Pope*, vol. I: *1711–1720*, ed. Norman Ault (Oxford, 1936), and vol. II: *1725–1744*, ed. Rosemary Cowler (Oxford, 1986). An indispensable primary source is *The Correspondence of Alexander Pope*, ed. George Sherburn, 5 vols (Oxford, 1956). Some useful volumes have already appeared in the Longman Annotated English Poets series, while a new Oxford edition of the works is in progress. However, for the present the standard edition remains *The Twickenham Edition of the Poems of Alexander Pope*, ed. John Butt and Maynard Mack, 11 vols (London, 1938–68). There is a good version of *The Dunciad in Four Books* by Valerie Rumbold (Harlow, 1999).

Some of Curll's pamphlets have been reprinted in various volumes of *Popiana* included in *The Life and Times of Seven Major British Writers* (New York, 1974–5).

BIOGRAPHICAL STUDIES

The most complete and searching biography is Maynard Mack, *Alexander Pope: A Life* (New Haven, CT, 1985). Still useful on the beginnings of the quarrel is George Sherburn, *The Early Career of Alexander Pope* (Oxford, 1934), Chapter Six. Shorter but incisive is Felicity Rosslyn, *Alexander Pope: A Literary Life* (Basingstoke, 1990). A more limited approach is Pat Rogers, *A Political Biography of Alexander Pope* (London, 2010).

There are two full-length biographies of Curll. Ralph Straus, *The Unspeakable Curll* (London, 1927), is entertaining and chatty. Paul Baines and Pat Rogers, *Edmund Curll, Bookseller* (Oxford, 2007), is more staid, as well as naturally more up to date.

The most accessible works on writers in and around Pope's circle are Leo Damrosch, *Jonathan Swift: His Life and his World* (New Haven and London,

2013); Isobel Grundy, *Lady Mary Wortley Montagu* (Oxford, 1999); and David Nokes, *John Gay: A Profession of Friendship* (Oxford, 1995). A full analysis of the similarities and dissimilarities between two great satirists is Dustin Griffin, *Swift and Pope: Satirists in Dialogue* (Cambridge, 2010). The best all-round description of the Scriblerian group and its activities will be found in *The Memoirs of Martinus Scriblerus*, ed. Charles Kerby-Miller (New Haven, CT, 1950; reprinted New York, 1985).

POPE AND GRUB STREET

A valuable catalogue raisonné is J. V. Guerinot, *Pamphlet Attacks on Alexander Pope, 1711–1744* (London, 1969). A few snippets from these items are contained in *Penguin Critical Anthologies: Alexander Pope*, ed. F. W. Bateson and N. A. Joukovsky (Harmondsworth, 1971). A survey of Pope and Swift in relation to the Dunces will be found in Pat Rogers, *Grub Street: Studies in a Subculture* (1972; reprinted London, 2014).

An outstandingly informative website, created by Allison Muri, contains a range of digital aids including maps, prints and tables, and can be found at www.grubstreetproject.net.

Not much has emerged in recent years about individuals who figure in the story, often in their capacity as writers for Curll, but it is worth digging out older studies of Lewis Theobald, Ned Ward, Colley Cibber, Susanna Centlivre, John 'Orator' Henley, Richard Blackmore and Leonard Welsted, among others. For a colourful account of some of Curll's contemporaries among publishers and authors, see Philip Pinkus, *Grub St Stripped Bare: The Scandalous Lives and Pornographic Works of the Original Grub St Writers* (London, 1968).

SPECIAL TOPICS

A number of specialized works illuminate relevant aspects of Pope's career. They include the following: on his publishing history, David Foxon, *Pope and the Early Eighteenth-century Book Trade* (Oxford, 1991), which can be supplemented by James McLaverty, *Pope, Print and Meaning* (Oxford, 2001). On his political ideals as embodied in his retreat at Twickenham, Maynard Mack, *The Garden and the City* (Toronto, 1969). On the ideology of the opposition, Christine Gerrard, *The Patriot Opposition to Walpole: Poetry, Politics, and National Myth, 1725–1742* (Oxford, 1994), and more speculatively Isaac Kramnick, *Bolingbroke and his Circle: The Politics of Nostalgia in the Age of Walpole* (Ithaca, NY, 1992). On his attitude towards the financial revolution, Howard Erskine-Hill, *The Social Milieu of Alexander Pope* (New Haven, CT, 1975), and Colin Nicholson, *Writing and the Rise of Finance: Capital Satires of the Early Eighteenth Century* (Cambridge, 1994). On the events that affected the life of Pope and many others, John Carswell, *The South Sea Bubble*, revd edn (Stroud, 2001); and on the commodification of literature, Catherine Ingrassia, *Authorship, Commerce, and Gender in Early Eighteenth-century England* (Cambridge, 1998). On contact with Joseph Addison and other writers, Norman Ault, *New Light on Pope* (London, 1949); and on the split between Scriblerians and Buttonians, Bertrand A. Goldgar, *The Curse of Party: Swift's Relations with Addison and*

Steele (Lincoln, NE, 1961). On the world of coffee houses, Markman Ellis, *The Coffee House: A Cultural History* (London, 2004), especially Chapter Nine, and Brian Cowan, *The Social Life of Coffee: The Emergence of the British Coffeehouse* (New Haven and London, 2005); and on *Court Poems*, the edition by Robert Halsband (New York, 1977). For a good anthology, covering several matters relevant to the quarrel, see *Eighteenth-century Popular Culture: A Selection*, ed. John Mullan and Christopher Reid (Oxford, 2000). A particularly vivid evocation of the environment in which Pope and Curll lived is Emily Cockayne, *Hubbub: Filth, Noise and Stench in England, 1600–1770* (New Haven and London, 2007); see also Sophie Gee, *Making Waste: Leftovers and the Eighteenth-century Imagination* (New Haven, CT, 2010), especially Chapter Three.

On the background of graphic caricature, see Ronald Paulson, *Hogarth*, 3 vols (New Brunswick, NJ, 1991); and Vincent Carretta, *The Snarling Muse: Verbal and Visual Political Satire from Pope to Churchill* (Philadelphia, PA, 1983); together with a lively biography, Jenny Uglow, *Hogarth: A Life and a World* (London, 1997); and a judicious introduction, Derek Jarrett, *The Ingenious Mr Hogarth* (London, 1976). On Pope's medical history, Marjorie Hope Nicolson and G. S. Rousseau, *'This Long Disease, My Life': Alexander Pope and the Sciences* (Princeton, NJ, 1968). On his posthumous reputation, *Pope: The Critical Heritage*, ed. John Barnard (London, 1973); and on patronage, James Lees-Milne, *Earls of Creation: Five Great Patrons of Eighteenth-century Art* (London, 1962). On drama and playhouses, *The London Theatre World, 1660–1800*, ed. Robert D. Hume (Carbondale, IL, 1980); and Malcolm Goldstein, *Pope and the Augustan Stage* (Stanford, CA, 1958). There is no adequate full-length study of Pope's religion, but a start will be found in A. R. Humphreys, 'Pope, God, and Man', in *Writers and their Background: Alexander Pope*, ed. Peter Dixon (London, 1972), pp. 60–100; and Brian Young, 'Pope and Ideology', in *The Cambridge Companion to Alexander Pope*, ed. Pat Rogers (Cambridge, 2007), pp. 118–33. See also John Bossy, *The English Catholic Community, 1570–1850* (New York, 1975). For the wider satiric picture, see Ashley Marshall, *The Practice of Satire in England, 1658–1770* (Baltimore, MD, 2013). The cultural controversy over Ancients and Moderns that underlies many of the satires in the period is reviewed by Joseph M. Levine, *The Battle of the Books: History and Literature in the Augustan Age* (Ithaca, NY, 1991).

LEGAL MATTERS

The most important study of the background to Curll's prosecutions and Pope's treatment of the law is now Thomas Keymer, *Poetics of the Pillory: English Literature and Seditious Libel, 1660–1820* (Oxford, 2019). For *The Dunciad* as a virtual pillory, see Paul Baines, 'Crime and Punishment', in *The Cambridge Companion to Alexander Pope*, ed. Pat Rogers (Cambridge, 2007), pp. 150–60. There is no fully satisfactory history of the laws governing obscene literature in England. A brief but informative review of the context in which Curll operated can be found in David Foxon, *Libertine Literature in England, 1660–1745* (New Hyde Park, NY, 1965). For a view of the quarrel emphasizing with some sympathy Curll's work as a pornographer and his court battles, see Bradford K. Mudge, *The Whore's Story: Women, Pornography, and the British Novel,*

1684–1830 (Oxford, 2000), Chapter Five. A classic work on censorship that retains a great deal of value is Laurence Hanson, *Government and the Press, 1695–1763* (Oxford, 1936). On the legal background to issues of literary property, see Mark Rose, *Authors and Owners: The Invention of Copyright* (Cambridge, MA, 1993). A good analysis of the issues involved in the Chancery suit will be found in Rose's subsequent book, *Authors in Court: Scenes from the Theater of Copyright* (Cambridge, MA, 2016), Chapter Two.

THE BOOK TRADE

As well as Foxon, *Pope and the Early Eighteenth-century Book Trade*, listed above, see John Feather, *A History of British Publishing*, 2nd edn (Abingdon, 2006); James Raven, *The Business of Books: Booksellers and the English Book Trade, 1450–1850* (New Haven and London, 2007), especially Chapter Six on locations; and *The History of the Book in the West: 1700–1800*, ed. Eleanor F. Shevlin (Abingdon, 2010). Also by James Raven, *Bookscape: Geographies of Printing and Publishing in London before 1800* (London, 2014), is highly informative on the physical milieu in which Curll worked, and where Pope set much of *The Dunciad*. The most satisfactory life of a major figure is Kathleen M. Lynch, *Jacob Tonson: Kit-Cat Publisher* (Knoxville, TN, 1971). One branch of the contemporary trade is discussed in Adrian Johns, *Piracy: The Intellectual Property Wars from Gutenberg to Gates* (Chicago, IL, 2009). A brief introduction to Pope's relations with Curll, Bernard Lintot and other publishers is James McLaverty, 'Pope and the Book Trade', in *The Cambridge Companion to Alexander Pope*, ed. Pat Rogers (Cambridge, 2007), pp. 186–97. See also Joanna Maciulewicz, *Representations of Book Culture in Eighteenth-century English Imaginative Writing* (Cham, Switzerland, 2018). For a good study of the social context of authorship, see Brean S. Hammond, *Professional Imaginative Writing in England 1670–1740: 'Hackney for Bread'* (Oxford, 1997). See also a key work by J. A. Downie, *Robert Harley and the Press: Propaganda and Public Opinion in the Age of Swift and Defoe* (Cambridge, 1979), one of a number of contributions of this author on the growth of political journalism.

POLITICS

Much of the huge and increasingly specialized literature devoted to early eighteenth-century politics does not bear very directly on the issues considered here. However, a painless introduction to the period can be found in W. A. Speck, *Stability and Strife: England, 1714–1760* (London, 1977). A clear picture of the discord that racked the age emerges from the materials presented in Geoffrey Holmes and W. A. Speck, *The Divided Society: Party Conflict in England, 1694–1716* (London, 1967). The bitter arguments over war and peace are dramatically reconstructed as a struggle between two remarkable figures, Jonathan Swift and the Duke of Marlborough, in Michael Foot, *The Pen and the Sword* (London, 1957). Also relevant is J. A. Downie, *Jonathan Swift: Political Writer* (London, 1984). Readable biographies of figures pertinent to the quarrel are Elizabeth Hamilton, *The Backstairs Dragon: A Life of Robert Harley, Earl of Oxford* (London, 1969); and H. T. Dickinson, *Bolingbroke* (London,

1970). Background to the quarrel can be found in Rachel Carnell, *A Political Biography of Delarivier Manley* (London, 2008). An excellent brief life is Tim Blanning, *George I: The Lucky King* (London, 2017). For a concise study of the 'Robinocracy', see Jeremy Black, *Walpole in Power* (Stroud, 2001).

JACOBITISM

The best short introduction in this heavily populated area of historical enquiry is Murray Pittock, *Jacobitism* (Basingstoke, 1998). On the Rising, see Daniel Szechi, *1715: The Great Jacobite Rebellion* (New Haven and London, 2005). The mindset of Stuart adherents is explored thoroughly in Paul Kléber Monod, *Jacobitism and the English People, 1688–1788* (Cambridge, 1989). G. V. Bennett, *The Tory Crisis in Church and State, 1688–1730* (Oxford, 1974), is key for the Atterbury Plot.

LONDON

There are several good histories of the capital, but the most illuminating all-round study of this period is Jerry White, *A Great and Monstrous Thing: London in the Eighteenth Century* (London, 2012). Peter Earle, *A City Full of People: Men and Women of London, 1650–1750* (London, 1994), is especially strong on the world of tradespeople from which Pope and Curll both originally sprang. Robert O. Bucholz and Joseph P. Ward, *London: A Social and Cultural History, 1550–1750* (Cambridge, 2012), also helps to fill in the world inhabited by the poet and the publisher. A good evocation of daily living is Maureen Waller, *1700: Scenes from London Life* (London, 2000). On the area around Covent Garden and Drury Lane, E. J. Burford, *Wits, Wenchers and Wantons – London's Low Life: Covent Garden in the Eighteenth Century* (London, 1986), is funny, lively and astonishingly inaccurate, with a Curllian disdain for the correct facts. For its literary treatment at the hands of the Scriblerian group, see Christine Rees, 'Gay, Swift, and the Nymphs of Drury Lane', *Essays in Criticism*, 23 (1973), pp. 1–21. On the poet's Thames-side retreat, see Anthony Beckles Willson, *Mr Pope and Others at Cross Deep Twickenham in the 18th Century* (Twickenham, 1996). Twickenham, Richmond, Chiswick, Marble Hill and Windsor Forest are all well described in Mavis Batey, *Alexander Pope: The Poet and the Landscape* (London, 1999), a beautifully illustrated book.

Acknowledgements

Some sections of 'Closing Arguments' appeared in a slightly different form in an article, 'Speaking of the Unspeakable: The Rehabilitation of Edmund Curll', *Book Collector*, 63 (2014), pp. 243–50. Permission to reprint this material is gratefully acknowledged.

Numerous people have aided my work on this subject over several decades. Here I can list only the most immediate acknowledgements, relating to this book. First comes Paul Baines, with whom I published a bio-bibliographical study of Curll in 2007, and who has generously shared his immense knowledge and understanding of the subject. The present work inevitably covers some of the same ground as its predecessor; but, since it concentrates on just one aspect of the bookseller's career, I have been able to go into more detail and visit unexplored areas. I am greatly indebted to David Watkins of Reaktion Books for commissioning the project, and for his continuing support. My largest personal debt is naturally to Adrienne Condon, who puts up with more than she should as a result of the excessive hours that have gone into my pursuit of Pope and Curll. I have shamelessly exploited her considerable skill in spotting my more culpable errors. Thanks are also due to Rosanna Fairhead for her vigilant copy-editing. The dedication reflects a friendship that was forged fifty years ago between two junior colleagues in the excellent English department at King's College, London. Thanks, Christine, for showing me the ropes.

Dade City, Florida   P.R.
Shepton Mallet, Somerset   May 2020

Photo Acknowledgements

The author and publishers wish to express their thanks to the below sources of illustrative material and/or permission to reproduce it:

Beinecke Rare Books & Manuscript Library, Yale University, New Haven, CT: p. 33; The Metropolitan Museum of Art, New York: p. 384; © National Portrait Gallery, London: pp. 47, 401; photo courtesy Sotheby's: p. 12; photo © Tate: p. 31; courtesy Thomas Fisher Rare Book Library, University of Toronto: p. 139; © The Trustees of the British Museum: pp. 153, 311; from William Warburton, ed., *The works of Alexander Pope Esq., Volume v, Containing the Dunciad in Four Books* (London, 1752), courtesy The New York Public Library: p. 283; Wellcome Collection (CC BY 4.0): pp. 286, 407; Yale Center for British Art, Paul Mellon Collection, New Haven, CT: pp. 41, 343, 409.

Photo Acknowledgements

INDEX

Page numbers in italics refer to illustrations. Main references are shown in bold type. AP = Alexander Pope: EC = Edmund Curll.